War in the Boats

Potomac's
MEMORIES OF WAR
Series

Outstanding memoirs that illustrate the personal realities of war as experienced by combatants and civilians alike, in recent conflicts as well as those of the distant past. Other titles in the series:

War in the Boats

My World War II Submarine Battles

Capt. William J. Ruhe, USN (RET.)

Foreword by Tom Clancy

POTOMAC BOOKS, INC.
Washington, D.C.

First Memories of War edition published in 2005

Copyright © 1994 by Brassey's, Inc.
Foreword copyright © 1994 by Tom Clancy

First Brassey's Five-Star Paperback edition 1996

Library of Congress Cataloging-in-Publication Data

Rhue, William J.
War in the Boats:my World War II submarine battles/William J. Rhue.
     p.   cm.
   Includes index
   ISBN 1-57488-028-4
     1. Rhue, William J.   2. World War 1939–1945—Naval Operations—
Submarine.   3. World War, 1939–1945—Naval Operations, American   4. World
War, 1939–1945—Personal narratives, American.   5. World War, 1939–1945—
Campaigns—Pacific Ocean.   6. United States. Navy—Biography   7. Seaman—
United States—Biography.   I. Title.
D783.R84   1994
940.54'26—dc20   93-25372
[B]   CIP

ISBN 1-57488-734-3 (paper)

Designed by Lisa Chovnick

10 9 8 7 6 5 4 3 2 1

Printed in Canada

Contents

Illustrations

Foreword

It seems so long ago now, and so much has changed. World War II was probably the last of the "normal" wars, by which I mean that war was itself considered a normal, if unpleasant, form of human activity, the *ultima lex regls*, the final law of the king. That is no longer the case, and even in the 1940s, questions were being asked. Already World War I had been called "the war to end all war," and while that noble idea had proven false—and while that war had actually been merely the first act of the overthrow of an entire world order, of which World War II was the crashing finale—the seeds of its truth had been planted in fertile soil. It became the job of the post-war generation to bring those seeds to fruition, to make real the dreams of our parents and grandparents; something not yet done, but tantalizingly close.

It will not be long before children look to their parents and ask what the "war thing" was all about. Nor will it be long before parents have trouble answering the question. And yet the reason this is true is to be found in people like Bill Ruhe, for World War II *was* the last real war, and it was their actions which made it so. But what was it like?

The problem with histories is that they leave so much out. Partly that is a matter of focus. A war is by its nature a vast event, and covering all of it is simply not possible. There is also the problem of perception and memory. People generally remember things more favorable to themselves than might really have been the case, for the mind edits the information it records, and what it remembers in the first place is governed by perception, not what the observer actually saw. The antidote for this problem is the combination of a good observer and written contemporary records.

What Bill Ruhe saw as a junior officer in a submarine was most often circumscribed to the volume of a modest closet, yet there is information here that most histories leave out, for historians generally err to the large rather than the small, forgetting that in the latter we find much of the former.

What was it like? Not what was done, how and when and where and by whom but . . .

What was it like to live in part of a war? This is something which will probably fascinate and befuddle for centuries to come. As medical science advances we forget that human longevity is almost as recent a development as global peace will soon be, and attitudes about life were markedly different only a century before our time. The perceived meaning of courage, the general absence of understanding about prolonged exposure to stress, the rules of manhood, the value of life itself—all of these things were different in 1943, albeit only in degree, but degrees quite large enough to dislocate our ability to understand the men our fathers and grandfathers were. Which is the value of books like this one. I've known Bill Ruhe for about seven years. This book merely describes the start of a distinguished career, but its eloquence explains his later accomplishments. A skilled observer for whom every day was something new, Bill tells us what it was like from the smallest details (how toilet bowls failed to survive destroyer attack) to the really important ones (did we really use our submarines effectively?). I often tell would-be writers that there is no such thing as an unimportant fact. Bill knows that truth as well. Historical truth is a mosaic, a vast interactive picture of a moment in time which has been formed by a nearly infinite number of factors, and in this account of life in submarines we find a great deal of truth, because we have a lot of facts to absorb. But Bill Ruhe's greatest service is to be found in his deeply engraved image of our fathers as young men, and in understanding who they were and what they did, we can now measure the ways in which they shaped the world which they passed on to our generation.

TOM CLANCY

Preface

In 1942, I was a twenty-six-year-old ensign, just three years out of the Naval Academy. Even then an avid student of the character of wars and the kind of men who fought them, I was eager to see combat for myself and perhaps to record how a war was actually fought. To help me understand my experiences as a submariner in the Pacific during World War II, I regularly kept a journal, on which this book is based. (Fortunately for me, my commanders turned a blind eye to this security infraction.) Its dialogue is therefore in the colorful and concise idiom of the World War II submariner and thus contains pejorative references to the Japanese. They were, after all, trying to kill us at the time. No offense is meant today.

Naturally, most of the perceptions I recorded were those of a single individual—myself. However, my submarine war was fought in the three main types of submarines, or "boats" as submariners called them: the primitive S-boat of World War I vintage, the pre-World War II fleet boat, and the greatly improved fleet boat built during the war. Additionally, my eight patrols ran the gamut of submarine action: they included virtually every mission, happening, and vagary of the Pacific War. It could be said, then, that my experiences comprehensively covered those of most of the U.S. submariners in that theater. I hope that this makes *War in the Boats* one of the more inclusive descriptions of naval warfare.

The reader should understand that my notes were not those of a professional historian. Rather they were a young officer's impressions of a unique and very dangerous kind of warfare on a tightly knit group of men. I meant this book to be less of a history than an informal study of men at war: about submarine warfare and how it affected the men in the boats. My fascination at the time with Stephen Crane's *The Red Badge of Courage*, with its vivid—albeit fictional—descriptions of the nature of the men who fought in the American Civil War, provided guidance to what I wanted to achieve. Like Crane, I felt the combat actions were less interesting than the impact they had on the combatants themselves.

Fifty-two American submarines were sunk in the war. Over 3,500 American submariners lost their lives—nearly twenty-two percent of all who fought. For the most part, these young men were "resolute in their acceptance of death"—a key element in the character of a true warrior, according to Musashi, the sixteenth-century samurai. They were truly a "special breed of cat," fully engaged in a special kind of war. Fifty years ago, submariners thought of themselves as the elite of the U.S. Navy. They still do today.

I would like to thank Rear Adm. Karl G. Hensel, USN (Ret.); Comdr. Robin Garson, RN (Ret.); Col. Giles D. Harlow, USAF (Ret.); Chief Yeoman A. J. Dempster, USN (Ret.); and, for her help in preparing the manuscript, Susan Megee.

1

The Rusty Old
Sewer Pipe

The departure of the S-37 on June 22, 1942, for her fifth war patrol was furtive and embarrassing as she headed silently on her batteries down the Brisbane River. Even her captain, Lt. J. R. Z. Reynolds, seemed ashamed of the very little that his boat—affectionately called "the rusty old sewer pipe" by her crew—might do to prevent the juggernaut of advancing Japanese forces from invading Australia. Yet that seemed to be Rear Adm. Francis Rockwell's questionable excuse for sending this broken down S-boat on patrol up into the Solomon Islands area. Perhaps the admiral had recalled that the S-37 was the first submarine to sink a Japanese destroyer in World War II. She'd done that off Makassar City in February of '42.

The old-crock S-boats of Submarine Division 201 at New Farm Wharf, of which the S-37 was a barely operating member, were viewed by the Australians as their first line of defense against a Japanese invasion. The Aussies had implicit expectations that somehow these boats, which had fled from Manila to Australia in the first year of the war, would terrorize the Japanese Navy into abandoning their plans to land forces in Northern Australia.

The Coral Sea Battle on May 7-8 and the Battle of Midway in early June had eased the Aussies' fears as to the imminence of being invaded. But the big build up of Japanese warships in Kavieng and Rabaul at the northwest end of the Solomon Islands indicated that moving Japanese troops south of New Guinea was contemplated and U.S. submarine action was dictated. Yet for more than two months, the S-37, which had arrived in Brisbane with sixteen burned out main bearings in her two diesel engines, had been under repair.

Each attempt to get her back to sea had uncovered new irregularities that impaired her seaworthiness or simply made her inoperable. Finally, with Lt. Al Puishes, the tall, broad, friendly repair officer of the submarine tender *Griffin* on board, the S-37 was taken to Moreton Bay to verify her readiness to go on patrol. It was hoped that the tests conducted under the supervision of Al Puishes would not uncover critical discrepancies that would force the S-37 to return to port. If Al was satisfied with the S-37's seaworthiness in Moreton Bay he would be put aboard the pilot boat and be returned to the *Griffin* where he'd report that the S-37 was cleared to go on patrol. Then the 37 would proceed out to sea and head north for the Solomons.

But such was not the case.

Initially, the test results proved favorable. The two diesel engines took the 37 to the bay in good style. Then, a cautious trim dive to forty-five feet produced only a few minor leaks. After that, the 37 was gently eased onto the muddy bottom of the bay at 103 feet depth. There, the new plates that had been welded on the 37's hull to cover extensive hull pitting under the main motors were hammered by Al Puishes to ensure that the welds were holding. They were. But going "deep" proved the 37's undoing.

"How deep should we go, Al?" Captain Reynolds cautiously asked.

Al, the authority on *Griffin* repair work, after some deep profound thought, recklessly said, "135 feet."

Deep? 135 feet? That was little more than half the test depth of an S-boat. Yet Al had reckoned that 135 feet was as deep as the S-37 could go safely under her present condition. Moreover, Al's lack of confidence in the integrity of the rusty old sewer pipe was justified. When the 37 moved into deeper water and slowly glided down to 135 feet, lots of water began to flood into her. The drain pump in the pump room below the control room gushed vast amounts of water. It was difficult to tell where so much water was coming from. The forward head was also reported to be overflowing onto the forward torpedo room deck plates. Its leaky outboard valve was badly in need of tender work. But of greatest concern was the shower of water that poured through the packing glands of the two periscopes. The torrent of cascading sea water forced the S-37 to be brought back to periscope depth. There, the captain, properly dressed in a raincoat and wearing a sou'wester rain hat, made some periscope observations. As an added insult, the number one periscope jammed in train. At this, the 37 was surfaced and headed back to New Farm Wharf, while Captain Reynolds kept muttering, "This boat is all fouled up like Hogan's goat." His ironic laughter which followed was his usual reaction to the discovery of each new major discrepancy.

When the 37 tied up alongside the *Griffin* at noon, there was much razzing from the *Griffin*'s off-duty repair people who were lounging on the rails around her topsides. Stung by their lack of sympathy, and even more determined to get the 37 out on patrol by the next day, I collared "Deep Dive" Puishes as he went across the bow and into the side of the *Griffin*. Together we walked a series of repair requests to each appropriate refit gang so as to get the work done before the end of the day. As engineering officer I had to get the repairs quickly completed.

Before beginning the expedition from repair shop to repair shop, I'd started calling Al, "Deep Dive." His ironic, "Let's go deep—about 135 feet" was so ludicrous that Al was instantly and indelibly labeled with the nickname "Deep Dive."

On return to the S-37, it was reported that a twenty-millimeter cartridge was wedged against the barrel of number one scope in the topside periscope well. This seemed typical of the bad luck which the S-37 created for herself.

With the 37's repair work under way, I remembered that I had not seen any books on board that would provide decent reading while on patrol. So I went to the *Griffin*'s library and helped myself to twenty books and had an enlisted man help me carry them over to the 37. One of the books, *Victory Through Air Power* by Alexander de Seversky, looked particularly interesting. The book's dust jacket said that today's wars would be won by bombers rather than by ground forces. Yet the last two years of assaults against England and Russia by Goering's Luftwaffe had not produced decisive results. But did the U.S. use of aircraft in the Battle of Midway and Doolittle's raid on Japanese cities from an aircraft carrier off Tokyo illustrate that the Pacific War would be won by the use of U.S. air power?

On June 23 at 0800, the 37 was "released to go on patrol." She followed the 38-boat down the Brisbane River. Before leaving, I'd bet my classmate "Harry Dog" Forbes that the 37 would beat his 38-boat to ten degrees south latitude. The ten dollar bet certainly looked safe when only two hours later the S-38 headed back to port with a broken circulating water pump. Evidently, other S-boats were as bad off as the 37.

The 37, after a quick dive to get a trim, went down to 150 feet for a deep dive. This produced little flooding so the 37 was surfaced and headed north. Unhappily, the number two scope's hoisting wire ran off its drum when Tex tried to raise it. A tedious wire-splicing job by Gorsky, the auxiliaryman, put number two back in commission. Tex Lander, the executive officer, meanwhile, had used number one to ensure an accurate course between the minefields that were known to be on either side of the swept channel out of the bay.

As the 37 rounded the northern tip of Moreton Island, she moved into heavy head-seas that broke over the bridge each time the 37's bow dipped into a big wave. I had the bridge watch and although I was taking a good soaking from the warm seas, I was elated at finally being on the way "to the war."

I recalled that back at Sub School in the summer of 1941, we students felt that a war with the Japanese was imminent but that it couldn't last more than a few weeks. It was assumed that there would be a major war in the Pacific since the U.S. would have to check the continuing Japanese conquests in East Asia. It also seemed certain that at the start of a conflict with the Japanese, the U.S. fleet would head west, engage the Japanese fleet and wipe it out. That would put a stop to the Japanese plans for invading the islands of the East Indies. U.S. submarines as far-out pickets for the U.S. Pacific Fleet, would get the first crack at the Japanese warships. The subs would sink a few ships and make it easy for U.S. battleships and aircraft carriers to mop-up what was left of the enemy's fleet.

There was no warning from our Sub School instructors that the "little Nips" with their thick-lensed glasses and copy-cat reputation could run a competent navy. Even more difficult to believe was that their submarines might do some damage to U.S. ships. Yet the reason that I was on the S-37 bound for the Solomons was because the submarine SD air-search radars I was supposed to install on the Brisbane-based U.S. submarines were on the bottom somewhere west of Hawaii. A Japanese sub manned by a weak-eyed skipper with supposed trouble seeing through a periscope had torpedoed the U.S. merchant ship carrying my SD radar parts, a week before I arrived in Australia. All of the hurry to get me to Brisbane in a four-plane flight of B-26s flying from Hickam Field proved to be a wasted effort.

After Submarine School in 1941, I had gone to Radar School at Bowdoin College in Maine to learn the theory of the new invention, radar. And that's where I was when the Japanese attacked Pearl Harbor on December 7th, 1941. The attack instantly changed my leisurely routine of physics classes and ice skating on a nearby pond, to a quick wrap-up of the schooling and then a transfer to Bell Labs in Whippany, New Jersey. In the next few weeks there, I was able to comprehend the new radar technology being applied to all sorts of ships. This was followed by a month at the Naval Electronics Laboratory in Washington where I specifically zeroed-in on the SD radar to be used in U.S. submarines. It was a simple device for detecting aircraft. All it produced was an echo-spike on a viewing screen, with the range to the plane read from a line along the bottom of the screen. There were no means to get a bearing on the detected aircraft. But the SD would markedly change the nature of submarining as learned at Sub School. Fleet exercises off the Hawaiian Islands had shown that a submarine at periscope depth was clearly visible to overhead aircraft. In the clear, brightly lit waters of the Pacific, it was believed that it was too dangerous to be at periscope depth if there was any chance of being overflown by an antisubmarine plane. Hence, attacks on enemy warships were felt to be practical only at depths where the submarine became invisible from the air. Eighty feet or deeper. But with the SD radar, a sub could stay at periscope depth and go deep only when the range to an aircraft was less than about two miles. This was the range that an aircraft might spot a shallow running submarine.

Unfortunately, the S-boats of the Asiatic Fleet that had fought their way to Australia, a step ahead of the steadily advancing Japanese invasion forces, would not get an SD radar until a second shipment from the U.S. arrived at Brisbane.

Meanwhile, I was on the submarine tender *Griffin* in the job of radar repair officer with nothing to do but decode messages. So it was a happy moment that started me whistling a Mills Brothers tune when a message said that the shipment of SD radars would be delayed several months. Without hesitation I bearded the *Griffin*'s skipper, "Red Hot" Smith, in his stateroom and told him I wanted to go to sea in a boat, until there were some radars on hand to install.

"Red Hot," reputed to be a fire-and-brimstone skipper, was both amused and sympathetic to my gung-ho request. "I can't blame you, young man, for wanting to see some action," he said enviously. "So, if there's a boat alongside which has a vacancy, you've got my permission to transfer to her. But why join a broken-down S-boat since you can probably get on a big fleet boat when they arrive here in a couple of months?" He confidentially added, "Several have been ordered to Brisbane for refits after their next patrols."

The fleet boats were relatively new and were much larger than the nine hundred ton S-boats that were built just after World War I—and were of about the same size as the devastating German Type VII U-boats used in the Atlantic. The U.S. fleet boats were 308 feet long compared to the S-boat's length of 225 feet. The big subs could do a sixty-day patrol. They carried twenty-four torpedoes and had a crew of seventy-two men. In fact, all three capabilities were about double those of the S-boats. But, probably the most important difference, was that the fleet boats had air conditioning and the S-boats did not. This was a critical difference when conducting a patrol close to the equator.

Knowing all this, I still went aboard each of the five "rusty, old sewer pipes" alongside the *Griffin* to locate a vacant officer-billet. Luckily, the S-37 had one. And the S-37 was repairable, needed an engineering officer, and was scheduled to go on patrol on April 20. This would get me up into the Solomons to see some early battle action. So I eagerly accepted Captain Reynold's invitation to bring my gear aboard his boat and fill his vacancy.

But the S-37 took a month longer than planned to make her sufficiently seaworthy enough to be risked on a patrol. Meanwhile, the other four boats of Division 201 had gone north for their patrols, had returned, and two had already departed on their next patrol before the 37 cleared Moreton Bay and set course for Rabaul. Still I was delighted to be on the 37's bridge as the officer of the watch, contemplating the many torpedo targets that lay ahead.

The lookouts were warned that several Japanese submarines had been sighted recently just to the north of Moreton Island. "No sluffing off" was the attitude demanded for the men topside. Concern for being shot at, however, was divided, as the 37's engineering plant developed trouble after trouble.

Then at 1400, a spray valve broke up in the port engine, putting it out of commission for the afternoon. This was followed by lube oil suction being lost for a moment. The 37 was thus forced to temporarily run on battery power. Suction was regained, but without finding out why it was lost. Hearing about this, the captain growled one of his dictums, "It ain't right, but there's nothing wrong."

When I went off watch I tried to get some sleep. But the 37 was rolling so heavily—as much as thirty-nine degrees on a side—that I couldn't stay in my bunk. Yet I didn't feel like tying myself down.

Shortly into the twenty-fourth, Chief Grady reported that the boat had used 230 gallons of lube oil on the first day at sea. At that rate, the patrol could last only eleven days. Fortunately, Grady reappeared later and said he'd found a big hole in a lube oil line and that he had repaired it.

On my 0900 to 1200 bridge watch, everyone was stripped to shorts and leather sandals. They were enjoying the first hot sunshine in several months. The air temperature was up to seventy-nine degrees. Standing a one-in-three watch of only three hours was Tex Lander's idea and should keep the top watch-standers more alert when on watch. But it was hard for Bobby Byrnes, Billy Gibson, and me to get much sleep in our six hours off watch.

In the afternoon, the 37 was submerged and the crew was taken through a series of submerged drills. The new men caused many foul-ups as each phase of the Watch, Quarter and Station Bill was tested. There was much joking about "the greenhorns, who didn't know their ass from a hole in the ground." But the crew began to get deadly serious about getting ready to fight. They rushed to their stations, carefully checked the gear they would have to use, and actually sounded like good sailors as they gave their reports over the sound-powered telephones.

After the captain had surfaced the boat at the end of the drills, the electric stills were started to make freshwater. Chief Albert, the engine room's lead man, and a grizzled remnant of "the old navy" reported that the stills "worked like a charm." This was apparently something new for the S-37 which could never make enough water for more than just watering the batteries.

On my 1800 to 2100 watch, the captain brought a chart with him to the bridge to show the route he'd plotted through the straits between New Ireland and New Britain to the 37's patrol area off Rabaul. With reports of greatly increased naval activity out of Rabaul it looked as though the 37 was in for a rough time. Yet the captain showed no sign of nervousness as he discussed the antisubmarine defenses likely to be encountered in getting to the 37's final station.

By Thursday the twenty-fifth, the seas had calmed sufficiently to exercise the gun crews at "Battle Stations, Gun Action." Many of the men had donned old, bedraggled khaki coats and long, torn khaki shorts which extended below their bony knees. The costumes—and that's what they looked like—were discarded Australian Army outfits that had been found in several bags of rags, drawn from the supply depot in Brisbane. The men resembled either poverty stricken duck hunters or what I imagined the "Tobruk rats" (the Aussies fighting at Tobruk, Libya) looked like. Some of the men were giggling about their Halloween-like, silly costumes as they assembled in the control room for the battle-surface drill.

As diving officer for this exercise, my job was to surface the boat rapidly without an angle and high enough out of the water to get the upper hatch open, allowing the gun crews to pour out quickly and man their guns. With the captain on the periscope ensuring that the seas were vacant around the 37, I ordered flank speed. Eight knots. Then with the planesmen holding the 37 down with a flat aspect I had the main ballast tanks blown. At the moment when the increased buoyancy of the 37 started her to rise, "Planes on zero" was ordered.

Stationed at the top of the trunk leading to the bridge, the quartermaster was ready to hammer the dogs loose on the upper hatch. Just below him on the ladder leading to the hatch was Bobby Byrnes, the darkly handsome, heavy-set gunnery officer. He was watching through the glass eye-port in the front of the tiny conning tower for the main deck to break clear of the water. When the dull-black main deck was seen to be awash he loudly ordered, "Open the upper hatch." Then he clumsily scrambled to the bridge followed by his three gun crews that had been stacked on the ladder rungs below him. I looked up the ladder from the control room to watch the men scurry to their gun stations. Though they banged the upper hatch with the tools and bands of .50-caliber ammo that they carried topside, there was only subdued, quiet cursing.

The four-inch gun crew had been directed to fire three rounds from the deck gun out into the empty seas. Meanwhile, the two .50-caliber machine gun crews, set up their guns on the cigarette deck aft of the bridge and fired twenty rounds of .50-caliber ammo. Then at the captain's command to "Clear the topsides," the gun crews came scurrying back down the ladder with much pushing and shoving. In fact, some of the men tumbled down to the control room deck as the men above tried to get below with too much unbridled eagerness.

It was surprising how men who had seemed so lackadaisical about readying the 37 for a patrol could suddenly be so intensely serious about being ready to shoot it out with an antisubmarine warship that might force the 37 to the surface.

During the four-inch gun drill the gun crews were reminded that all the empty shell cases had to be saved and returned to the tender. This seemed certain proof that the U.S. was in for a long war!

The attitude of the crew in the battle drills was a welcome change from the crew's griping and reluctant approach to the long hours of work that had been necessary to get the 37 back into operation. The crew had been like a bunch of union workers who were not going to do a single stitch of work beyond their eight-hour, five-days-a-week contract. The engine room gang had reacted to their tedious job of renewing the bearing surfaces on the burned-out bearing surfaces by demanding that they be given higher ratings, full weekend liberty and also occasional sleep-ins. One of my machinists in particular, who was dogging his work, had highly resented a threat to bring him to mast for shirking his duties. At this, he had whiningly protested, "You've never been bombed, depth charged or gone without food, Mr. Ruhe." Then he snidely suggested that I wasn't going to be "brave" when the depth charges started exploding real close to the S-37. It made me wonder how I'd react to a depth charge attack. But my mind was made up. I'd show no signs of fear even if I could scarcely breathe or my legs felt like jelly.

There had been considerable dissension amongst my workers and it didn't help to have Chief Albert put me down. When I asked him why the men used such a painstakingly slow way to do a job, he would curtly say, "Because that's the way it was done on the O-boats fifteen years ago and that's the way we do it today." When I suggested I could show him a better and faster way to produce smooth, rounded bearing surfaces, he snorted and spat on the deck to show his disgust. Addressing everyone topside, he loudly declared, "These young squirts," meaning me, "will always have a better way of doing things which they know nothing about."

We'd been told at the Naval Academy that it was the chiefs "who actually ran the Navy." But Chief Albert's reaction to my suggested changes made me wonder if that's the way the Navy should be run. And could that kind of Navy be successful in a modern war?

After dark, Tex, who had taken the 1800 to 2100 bridge watch, as he occasionally did, spotted a suddenly exposed light about a thousand yards off. Then there was a momentary white flare that burned out. Tex seemed to think it came from a U.S. sub. Not taking any chances, he had the 37 turn tail and open out at full speed. Then he had Billy Gibson, the communications officer, come to the bridge to ascertain if there was any classified explanation for a sub's use of flares in Billy's safe. Billy assured Tex that there was nothing. In his taciturn, smilingly self-assured manner, Billy was hard to disbelieve.

Upon reflection, it was evident that Tex was justified in his concern as to whether Billy, a newcomer to the Navy, had grasped the importance of his communications duties. His handling of an ALNAV dispatch dealing with promotions of the officers was a case in point. Billy had collected a pile of general messages from the tender just before the S-37 departed on patrol. Then, feeling that no one had the time to look at them until the 37 was well at sea, he didn't put the file board with the messages clamped on it on the wardroom table until the middle of the night after he'd come off watch. For the most part, the radio traffic consisted of unclassified Class E messages telling of some problem back in the States with some man's children, finances, sickness or whatever. But the ALNAV promulgated from the Secretary of the Navy's Office hit the jackpot. When Tex read it, he immediately called me on the bridge to tell me that I had just been promoted to lieutenant and that if the captain was there with me to tell him that he'd made lieutenant commander in the same ALNAV. Captain Reynolds was beside me and the news made him chuckle with great satisfaction.

It was nice to think about the extra money I would now be getting—over two thousand more dollars a year than an ensign's pay. As an ensign I had gotten $125 a month base pay, plus fifty percent of base pay for hazardous duty in submarines, plus $18.75 for a ration allowance and $40 more for quarters since I was married. But that wasn't enough to support my wife back in the States. She was forced to live at her mother's home on the scant $3,000 a year I earned as an ensign.

When I went off watch and had a chance to study the ALNAV, it showed that Bobby Byrnes also made lieutenant and Billy Gibson

had made lieutenant, junior grade. There was cause for much celebration.

When had I made Lt. (jg) without knowing it? A mystery.

When back on the bridge on the mid-watch, the brilliant full
moon caused me to remember that the Japanese always started their
invasions a few days after the full moon. Thus, action up in the
Solomon Islands area seemed highly likely. Then there'd be plenty of
opportunities to see how brave I was.

All day of the twenty-seventh, I worked on getting the engineering
record books up to date. When I'd taken over my engineering job
two months ago, it was discovered that for the most part records
didn't exist on the S-37. Evidently, those responsible for keeping up
the records felt that the 37 wasn't going to last very long in the war.
So why bother with records for a boat that was going to be sunk?

After nightfall, I went to "breakfast" in the wardroom. The eating schedule had been changed so that dinner was at midnight and
supper was just after dawn. This was to conform to an all-day submerged routine that was starting next day. "Then we start taking
off poundage" I prophetically wrote in my journal. It made good
sense to have the crew up all night and sleeping in the daytime
when in enemy waters. When submerged there was far less chance
of being surprised by enemy warships or aircraft and there was
plenty of time to galvanize the crew into action, if threatened. On
the surface at night, however, surprise by the enemy was far more
likely and split-second actions were sometimes required to ensure
survival.

Only the captain and I sat down to eat breakfast. He told me of
how he planned to operate close to Rabaul and still remain undis-
closed until a good firing opportunity was presented. He also philos-
ophized about the terrible loneliness in having to think through his
problems alone, and then the uncertainty that he was necessarily
right. Hence he felt it was a good idea to share some of his thoughts
with me and get my reaction.

I was much flattered to be asked to play this role.

During the night, Grady reported to me that he had cleaned a
plugged-up sump drain and that on breaking down the drain line
he'd found an electric light bulb and numerous large bolts clogging
the drain. Also, he sadly noted that a fuel transfer-line that had
split—dumping fuel oil into the bilges—had shown definite hacksaw
marks. "That's some sort of sabotage," he angrily observed.

After surfacing at dark on the night of the twenty-eighth, additional lookouts were used on the bridge because the S-37 was passing
close to Rossel Island where, it was claimed, there were enemy lookouts to spot transiting U.S. submarines.

That wasn't enough to worry about, however. An electrician reported that there were heavy grounds on the starboard main motor and the batteries couldn't be charged until he had cleared the grounds.

On hearing the electrician's report, Captain Reynolds muttered, "Going to sea in this boat is fighting two wars—one against the Japs and another to keep this old-age tub running."

To understand the routine of operations of an S-boat on war patrol, I kept a detailed account of the next twenty-four hours' activities in my journal.

With the changed night-to-day routine in effect, I came off the midwatch and unthinkingly climbed into an empty bunk and went to sleep. Exhaustion had gotten the better of my sound judgement. One wasn't supposed to sleep before the boat was dived for all-day submerged operations.

The bunkroom for the five S-37 officers was in the forward part of the after battery compartment. It held only four make-shift beds of canvas, lashed with rope to the rectangular pipe frames of an upright double-deck iron structure. One of the beds was exclusively for the captain's use. The other three beds were shared by the remaining four officers.

Thus, when an officer vacated a bunk to go on watch, the officer coming off watch would have a hot, smelly sweated-on piece of canvas on which to sleep. "Hot bunking it" was aptly applied to this way of sleeping on an S-boat in tropical waters. If the previous sleeper had sweated profusely, the officer taking over the just vacated bunk would unlash the canvas from its iron frame, turn it over to dump out the puddle of sweat and then relash the canvas to the iron frame with the dry side up. It was not very satisfactory, yet it was more bearable.

Blankets were rarely used and sheets, never. Pillows were formed from folded dungarees.

It wasn't the business of sleeping in a pool of sweat that best showed the true vindictiveness of a "pigboat" towards its occupants. It was what happened when the diving alarm sounded for a dive at dawn, commencing an all-day submerged patrol. It was the first important lesson of S-boat life. One just had to learn to live with it, accepting gracefully and without complaint the hardships of an antique boat on war patrol.

The honking of the diving alarm was followed by the main induction air valve banging shut—blocking the flow of air to the diesel engines and sealing off the boat. With the opening of the inboard exhaust valve, which was positioned directly over the officers' bunks, the engine exhaust and battery gases were vented into the compartment and poured down over my prone body. The stinking, hot fumes brought me dazedly awake—with much choking and gagging. It gave one the feeling that the 37-boat keenly disliked her officers.

The 37 was now on an all-day submerged routine, starting before daylight and ending after darkness had set in. The temperature in the boat during the day climbed to almost one hundred degrees and hung there. The humidity also climbed to close to one hundred percent. This caused moisture to condense on the cool inner side of the hull and drip onto the decks. At the same time, the pressure inside the boat built up to as high as fourteen inches of pressure. This was about seven pounds per square inch above atmospheric pressure. The build-up of pressure was mainly due to leakage of air through the leathers of the air-activated electrical controllers for propulsion.

My morning watch was stood in the control room. An all-around look through the periscope at forty-five foot depth was required, followed by a return to eighty feet for twenty minutes of "listening" on the sound gear.

At eighty feet, a submarine that was painted black with lampblack added to dull the paint's finish was supposed to be invisible from the air. The dulled paint should not reflect sun-glint, it was felt, from even the most brilliant beams of a tropical sun.

The watch was casual with most of my time being spent in a camp chair, immobile to reduce the sweating. I sipped chilled lemonade and ate a cold can of pears. Hot coffee to keep one alert was out of the question and cigarettes were too soggy to be smoked.

The men on watch with me in the control room—the planesmen, helmsman, the man on the diving manifold, the man on the high pressure air manifold and the quartermaster keeping the ship's log—relieved the great boredom of the watch by telling stories about past S-37 happenings.

Penhollow, a brash talkative signalman and presently on the helm, told about how he'd gotten aboard the S-37 after the Java Sea Battle. "I was the American signalman on the Dutch cruiser *DeRuyter* interpreting U.S. flags and signals for the Dutchmen. Then, when she was sunk by Japanese gunfire, I got into a lifeboat which drifted around until the S-37 surfaced close by and came alongside our boat. Then, Captain Reynolds shouted over to us, 'Are there any Americans in the boat?' I quickly called back, 'I am' and without waiting for permission, scrambled from the lifeboat to the 37's main deck. From there I climbed to the bridge and proceeded below without anyone topside stopping me."

A planesman told about the 37's Filipino messman, Maderos, who, on hearing a string of exploding depth charges and thinking they were torpedo hits, exclaimed with great glee, "Boy, we're sure giving the Japs hell."

But mostly the enlisted men's talk was about who they got into or didn't get into when they were ashore in Brisbane. This sort of talk turned me off as it did for all officers.

Periodically, I would take two salt pills to maintain my vitality and avoid heat prostration. I also cautioned the men in all compartments to reduce their movements about the boat. Too many going in the same direction, as when a gang of men headed from the crew's mess to the forward room to get some exercise, would badly disturb the trim of the boat. Pumping water to regain a trim made a considerable amount of noise and could disclose the 37 to a searching anti-submarine ship.

The periscope kept fogging, requiring a drying out process after the 37 was surfaced. Gorsky, the auxiliaryman, would then put a moisture absorbent into the barrel of the scope.

I was back on watch at 1800 with surfacing at 1905 contemplated. Shortly, all white lights in the control room were doused and the illumination was changed to a dim red. Men going topside thus had their eyes night adapted, allowing them to see far better in the darkness.

At twilight, the captain and Tex, the exec, came to the control room without being called. The captain took over the scope and Tex moved to the diving station while I was directed to be the surfacing OOD. Now that we were clearly in enemy waters the captain had designated me to be the first person on the bridge after the 37 rose clear of the water. Earlier I had told Captain Reynolds that before the war I had been the destroyer *Roe*'s OOD whenever she operated in total darkness. My carrot-nourished eyes were felt to give me such superior night vision that I had to stand the *Roe*'s bridge watch for ten straight hours on the night of the new moon during fleet exercises. Hence, Captain Reynolds hoped that with me being the first topside I'd spot any nearby vessel and get the 37 back under before she was discovered.

Before climbing the ladder to position myself under the hatch to the bridge, I checked to see that all people involved in surfacing the boat were on hand. In the dim red haze of the control room, the green indicator lights on the diving panel cast a greenish-red glow on the lookouts who were close beside me. They looked like strange people from outer space. Beyond them, wearing only shorts, was Tex with his shadowed, inscrutable, squinty eyes and Mexican features. In the low light he looked like a Chinese coolie in an opium den. And at the periscope was the captain. He was wearing a sou'wester rain hat to keep the water that flowed through the packing gland in the top of the scope from blanketing his eyes as he peered for surface ships close at hand.

The captain's first futile look into the fogged periscope and out into impenetrable darkness made him shake his head dolefully as he lowered the periscope. "Surface" he muttered disgustedly.

When the 37 was blown clear of the seas, I went topside through the opened hatch and confirmed that the main deck was well out of the water. On this night-surfacing evolution devised by the captain, I then quickly studied the inky blackness, and spotting nothing I yelled "all clear" down to the control room. On hearing this, the lookouts and the quartermaster arrived on the bridge to take their watch stations. Thick steam from inside the boat was issuing from the upper hatch, and billowing around the bridge watch.

I thought I was to be the OOD for only the moonless surfacings. But Tex later said, "The night-surfacing procedure went so well that the captain has a good secure feeling about it. Coming up blindly with badly fogged scopes shouldn't get us into very much trouble."

The captain, when he came to the bridge, guessed that the Japs might have radars on their ships, so we had to spot them in the dark before they shone a searchlight on a suspicious radar contact. The 37? He sounded needlessly worried about Japanese radars, for which there was still no evidence.

On the early morning of July 2nd, the S-37 was at the bottom of St. George's Channel. The boat's garbage, in bags heavily weighted with big pieces of iron diesel engine parts, had been dropped overboard, leaving no trace of the 37 being in the vicinity. Then she was dived at first light.

At dawn, the soundman got a contact making 240 rpm and announced to Bobby Byrnes who was on watch that "It sounds like a submarine making high speed." It couldn't be one of ours, so Bobby passed the word "Battle Stations, Battle Stations."

First blood? The crew moved eagerly and nimbly through the bulkhead doors to their stations. There were no pileups as they sped past each other. I brought the 37 up to forty-five feet to give the captain a quick look through the "search scope," on the bearing indicated by the soundman. Not having donned his rain hat in his hurry to take a look, he soon looked pathetic, as though he'd been caught in a summer downpour. "There's nothing on that bearing," he stuttered as he lowered the scope. The shake in his voice sounded like he was scared—like seeing a poisonous snake within a few feet. A submarine, with its low silhouette was difficult to see even when close at hand and was dangerous if it let go a torpedo in the direction of the 37's periscope.

The contact faded out quickly as the 37 headed up the channel. The mountains of New Britain on the port side rose to over seven thousand feet and were discernible through the scope. When Tex took a navigational fix on some of the mountain peaks he determined that the S-37 was being pushed along by over three knots of current. And later in the day the towering volcano close to Rabaul came into view. It was active with thin wisps of smoke moving skyward.

After surfacing at dark, Billy Gibson, using a strip cipher, decoded a secret message addressed to the S-37. It told of a sighting by a U.S. aircraft of several Jap merchant ships plus four warships in the harbor of Rabaul. Included was a seaplane tender, an XAV that had been converted from the seven thousand ton, 480 foot long merchantman, the *Kiokawa Maru*. Tex looked up this ship in the Japanese Merchant Ships manual and then declared to those of us in the wardroom that "This is the baby we're going to sink." Pleased at this, the captain with a chuckling laugh, said, "Tell the crew, Tex, that whoever sights her first gets a quart of liquor." I wondered if that meant a bottle of our good medicinal brandy.

Seaplanes were essential to the Japanese reconnaissance effort down through the Solomons and it was in that area that the Japanese were expected to make their next island landings. Sinking the *Kiokawa Maru* would not only delay their island-taking plans, but should also affect Japanese plans for invading Australia.

The 37 was only a day away from Rabaul so Tex hauled out the detailed charts of Rabaul harbor and the offshore areas close by. There was no chance the captain would take the 37 inside the harbor. The reported antisubmarine defenses made that impossible. Yet, operating close to the mouth of the harbor might make sense. But not much, because the Dutch charts, dated 1905, had soundings that were both irregular and sparse and showed no sunken ships in the treacherous waters at the base of the volcano. In fact, all of the charts of the sea areas around New Britain and New Ireland were turn-of-the-century British or Dutch charts. Apparently no one in the United States had guessed that there would be a war in the Solomon Islands area. Thus, when the S-40 had to drop an Australian coast watcher on New Ireland, there was no chart for figuring where the man could be safely landed.

Again, I decided to expand my notes for the next day, to show what it was like in a pigboat on war patrol and within four degrees of the equator.

Submarines back in the thirties, those old boats before the advent of the fleet boats, were fondly and appropriately called pigboats. Without air conditioning, with cockroaches everywhere, with cranky machinery and suffering in general from the infirmities of old age, these pigboats were nevertheless endured with good spirit by the young submariners who manned them. Men in their 20s readily adapted to a life like that lived in the S-37. There was little griping about living conditions. The few "old timers" on board, however, were less tolerant of the demands put on one's body by the environment in the pigboats and were continually putting in for transfer to a new fleet boat.

In sharp contrast, griping about the lack of enemy ship contacts was now the pastime. It was an occupation of frustration, even making one forget about the miserable life led by an S-boat sailor.

That's the way it was on July 3, 1942, when I began my midnight to 0300 watch on the bridge. The 37 was on the surface gliding quietly across the waveless waters at the top of St. George's Channel near Rabaul. The cool, gentle breeze wafted the perfumes from the tropical vegetation on the island of New Britain in an exhilarating contrast to the foul-smelling, hot, humid air issuing from the 37.

There was no moon and hence only impenetrable darkness surrounded the 37. Without radar, and that was the case for both sides, the 37 moved cautiously back and forth at four knots waiting and waiting for something to break the monotony.

The lookouts and bridge watch peered into the blackness to detect an enemy threat before the 37 was detected. It was very peaceful, yet I could hear a lookout muttering in a low tone, "Anything is better than this freaking, boring lack of something to shoot at."

The other lookout agreed. "I could be doing the same thing I'm doing here, if I was back in my mother's house."

The quartermaster, close beside me, asked, "When are we going to see anything, Mr. Ruhe?"

I grunted, "Never, I guess. At this rate, we might as well head home to Brisbane."

"We can't do that until the tenth," the quartermaster reminded me. "That's what our orders say."

When Billy Gibson relieved me at 0300, he mentioned that it wasn't too bad below. "I tried sleeping a little and the air being pulled through the boat by the diesels was fairly cool, so I wasn't sweating at all." I had noted that the air topside was seventy-four degrees. Very comfortable.

Billy had just left a dry bunk, a bed that was inviting me to catch a few hours of sleep before the boat heated up after submerging for an all-day patrol. Passing up supper at 0600, I climbed into an officer's bunk, the one that was vacant. But before doing that I carefully stowed my sandals inside a magazine. It was too sickening to see one's sandals covered with a horde of little brown bodies ravenously licking the salty sweat deposited by one's smelly feet.

For a long time I drifted through a peaceful sleep—dreaming of willows, green meadows, cool streams and slim blonde girls in organdie dresses gracefully walking through this pleasant scene. Then the diving alarm honked. The 37 was being submerged for the all-day submerged patrol. The main induction valve for the air to the diesels banged shut. At this, the battery gases circulated inboard flowed over the officers lying in their bunks. A hot, choking, stifling, acrid blanket of chlorine-tainted air swirled around me, changing my dreams to one of volcanoes, fiery pits of brimstone, frying bacon and scorched meat. But I seemed to doze on, only choking a bit and hazily recalling later on when I woke up, that I wished I could remember the nasty swear words I had used in my final dream. One of the dreams showed me being caught in a sewer pipe too small to inch through. I was trapped and sweating, and shaking uncontrollably. Then I was in a room whose walls closed in on me until they were tight against my body. I seemed to realize that I had to wake up to be free of this torment.

When I did force myself awake, I had the feeling that I had experienced a claustrophobic dream brought on by the heavy cloud of stifling air dumped on my slumbering body. Even though I was thinking foggily, I realized that at all other times I felt snug and secure inside the submarine—like a child in a mother's womb that is safely protected from the outside world. Moreover, I wasn't alone with this sense of well-being about living inside a submarine. The men I talked to about this agreed that they felt more comfortable and free of concerns while in a sub than when on a surface ship. In fact, if a man did react to the closeness of a submarine he was transferred out of submarines in short order. How a man could like being in subs was a mystery to most civilians. But liking it was taken for granted by all submariners.

At 0900 I was back on watch, but in the control room, taking a periscope look every fifteen minutes. After a quick look, the 37 was taken back down to eighty feet to avoid a sighting by enemy antisubmarine aircraft. Clad only in khaki shorts and leather sandals, I sat for most of the watch in a camp chair. The deck in the control room was littered with towels for sponging up the water dripping off the inside of the submarine and off the men who were carrying out all submarine control functions by means of hand operations. The S-37 was "running quiet" because the soundman had detected the pinging of a searching destroyer somewhere in the vicinity. The helm and the bow and stern planes were in hand operation to reduce the noise. That meant exhausting work for the men who had to turn the heavy control wheels for maintaining the sub at an ordered depth and on an even keel. A fresh pair of men, fortified with salt pills, would slide onto the benches at the bow and stern plane control stations while fagged-out planesmen who had just finished fifteen minutes of strenuous work went to their bunks to recuperate.

Silent running was so demanding of strength and endurance that a strength club had been formed in the forward room with at least thirty members of the crew taking part in the lifting of weights and strenuously exercising with barbells. This group of men provided the staying power to keep the 37 mobile and silent as a ghost. It was also this group of strongmen who supplied a man for each compartment which had a main ballast tank vent. Opening and closing these stiff, balky vent mechanisms put a premium on heavy biceps and thick shoulders.

The periscope watch was a duplication of the mid-watch I'd stood earlier. No contacts; only an empty sea around the 37. To relieve the boredom I occasionally climbed into the conning tower when the sub was at eighty feet. There, I'd peer out of the two glass ports set in the bulkhead. The brilliant sunlight lit the seas around the S-37 so clear that fish drifting past the slowly moving sub were as easily viewed as in an aquarium. But of primary interest was the spotting of where small globules of rainbow-colored oil detached themselves from the hull and drifted upward. A few bubbles of oil were no worry. But a stream of them could leave an easily identified trail on the surface. On one observation of the waters aft of the conning tower I noticed that the occasional small spheres of oil moving towards the surface had more than doubled in frequency so I called Gorsky, the auxiliaryman, to the conning tower to identify where the oil was coming from and help guide him to the spot that needed fixing.

When Billy Gibson came to relieve me of the watch he said that Bobby Byrnes, the first lieutenant, while tapping a spot on the main drain in the forward engine room, had his sharp pointed hammer go right through the drain. He had let the hammer remain stuck in the hole and had firmly shored it up so it would stay there until the end of the patrol. This was a normal response to an injury to the S-37: "Don't fix it, just do what's necessary to live with it."

The temperature in the control room had moved up to ninety-seven degrees when I headed aft to try to get a little sleep. But when I studied the bunk that Billy had just vacated I decided not to go through the routine of unlashing the canvas from its iron frame and turning it over to dump out the half-inch of sweat that was puddled there. So I went forward to the wardroom to play cards with the captain.

Captain "Dome" was sitting there disconsolately playing solitaire and wearing only his baggy, below-the-knees khaki shorts. His sweat-gleaming, flabby upper body was white from lack of sun and his prominent dome-like forehead was only a slight pink from the rare moments he'd been on the bridge in the daytime at the start of the patrol.

I suggested we play some cribbage, so he shoved some sweat-stained cards together and then reached behind him for the cribbage board that sat on the sideboard. It looked damaged, as though it had been thrown to the deck many times in the past by close-aboard exploding depth charges.

The tiny, wood-paneled officers' wardroom hugged the port side of the forward battery compartment. It was in behind many triple-tiered enlisted men's bunks and offered no privacy for serious discussions between the officers. Still, Captain Reynolds, before dealing me a hand, decided to tell me of his plans for the next few days.

"Tonight, after we've completed the battery charge, we'll go up along the New Ireland coast, past Duke of York Island, and then patrol close to the entrance to Rabaul. It's going to be pitch dark so we should get there without being detected. There are only a few patrol days left so we have to take the 37 where we're bound to see any ship entering or leaving Rabaul."

The captain was throwing his previous caution to the winds. Going back empty-handed had become of far greater concern to him than the high risk in this decision. His face had brightened and his low chuckling laughter had returned as he conspiratorially mapped out additional details on how the 37 was going to bag a ship or more and then go back happy to Brisbane. He concluded with, "After we've gotten some Jap ships we'll have to go north and up around New Ireland before we head home." He added, "We'd never make it, going back past Duke of York and down the channel, after the fuss we'll create."

Although I didn't exactly share the captain's optimism, I was so elated that the S-37 was now certain to see some war action that I wasn't about to throw a wet blanket on his plans. I sensed that the captain was telling me about his strategy to get my reaction and approval and he must have realized how I felt when I muttered the Australian expression, "Good-o."

I also recognized that this was the big opportunity to see some war action and find out whether I could stand up well under actual danger. It was why I had worked hard to get on a boat going on patrol instead of staying on the *Griffin* to repair and install submarine radars.

We started our game of cribbage with our elbows on the table near the edge, holding the cards with our arms at a slight angle so the sweat streaming down our bare arms would drip off our elbows to the deck without soaking the pile of cards in the center of the table. Overhead was a fine net of gauze for catching wayward cockroaches which prowled across the cork insulation on the hull above the wardroom table. Occasionally one would lose its grip and fall straight downward, and like an acrobat who had missed his catch on a trapeze, it would fall into the netting. Then with little bouncy motions the cockroach would make its way to the edge of the gauze and fall clear of our bodies as it dropped to the wardroom deck—out of our way and out of the play of the cards.

At mealtime the obvious utility of this covering of mosquito netting was proved a thousand times as our soup stayed clear and untroubled by falling insect bodies. We had learned how to live with that specific problem very well.

The captain, about to play a card and having edged it to the tip of his fingers to reduce the amount of sweat accompanying the placement of the card on the table, suddenly froze. I followed the riveted stare of his eyes. They were focused on the barely visible feet of a torpedoman in a bunk nearby. The feet seemed to be relaxing and edging dangerously close to a heavy, steel fan suspended at the end of the bunk and playing its air on the dozing man's long frame. Closer, closer, the feet moved towards the whirring blades of the fan. Then the toes made contact and there was a dull, sickening thud as the chopper was brought to a sudden stop. A low, groaning moan followed. The feet were withdrawn from view. But shortly the feet reappeared, now stained with flecks of blood. Still, the torpedoman had gone back to sleep and his feet began to relax once more. The toes moved steadily towards the speeded-up blades of the fan. The dozing man had, as the captain noted, "learned to live with it."

We turned back to our card game, aware that this little act was being repeated many more times during the afternoon in other parts of the 37. We were proud of pigboat sailors for the way they'd adapted to living in the S-boat environment.

Because of the steadily increasing pressure within the boat I wasn't thinking clearly and managed to lose steadily to the captain. By 1800, when I had to relieve Bobby Byrnes of the watch in the control room, I was thankful for calling it quits to such a miserable card game. As usual, Bobby reported "all clear" on the seas above and repeated the usual orders to "have a look at forty-five feet and then go back down to eighty feet for fifteen minutes and use only a foot of scope." He added, "It will be dark enough to surface at 1915."

All day, the air leaking out of the air-operated motor control leathers had seeped into the sub until by the time I took over the watch the pressure gauge in the control room showed seven inches of pressure inside the boat. That made surfacing the 37 after dark a tough problem for the OOD, me. I had to go up through the upper hatch in the conning tower when its dogs were hammered open by the quartermaster.

The captain, taking a final look through the periscope just before surfacing, was dressed in oilskins and wearing a sou'wester hat to protect him from the water cascading down through the scope's upper bearings. He had little chance, as he peered through the badly fogged optical tube, of spotting a ship on the darkened ocean. One could find a dog on a foggy, rainy night more easily. So he had to trust me to get up to the bridge fast, for the safety of the 37-boat.

When the hatch was freed, the air in the boat was released to the atmosphere with a great "woooshhh." I went up into the upward-rushing airstream without being blown overboard, then quickly took a look for nearby threats. My "all clear topside," started the lookouts to their posts on the shears. At the same time the order "Open the main induction" released the rest of the boat's air pressure to the atmosphere.

Below in the boat, as the air under pressure was released, a dense, cold impenetrable fog was formed inside the boat. For a short moment the visibility in the 37 was reduced to zero. Then the diesels were started and the chilling fog was dissipated as air was sucked through the boat by the diesel engines. Those below shivered. But they had the glorious feeling of being freed from the oppressive heat for the next few hours.

Within minutes after the S-37 had settled down to her nightly routine of cruising slowly along while the engines were pouring amps back into the battery, Tex arrived on the bridge with a tin bucket and a large cake of sand soap. There was insufficient freshwater for baths since the electric stills, like everything else, were barely making it—"it" in this case being enough water for the batteries. One officer jokingly mentioned that we ought to start saving our spit or we wouldn't be able to dive for the final couple of patrol-days because of lack of battery power.

Tex attached a manila line to the bucket, tossed it over the side, scooped up a bucketful of seawater, then poured the water over his back. For the second bucketful of water which was poured over his front, he loosened his g-string-like vanduci so the water would cleanse that part of him that couldn't stand the raspiness of the salt water soap. Used on the rest of his body, the soap was like sandpaper as it passed across his tender Guam blisters—the tiny, pus-filled eruptions that formed on a man's skin from too much sweating.

I decided only to sponge off with sea water since Tex's routine caused him to curse and mutter "grimmo" in a tortured way.

After I was relieved of my bridge watch, I went below and used the officers' head in the forward room. In normal fashion, I first filled the head bowl with water. Then, after emptying my bowels I dumped the refuse into the trap below the bowl by opening the flapper valve in the bottom of the bowl. The next step in the process of using a pigboat's head was to build up fifteen pounds of pressure in the air-blowing tank. Then with my foot firmly pressed down on the lever for the flapper valve, I tripped the blow-valve shooting the heavy air pressure into the trap and supposedly forcing the refuse out to sea through a one-way sea valve. Nothing happened. The pressure on the gauge attached to the trap remained at fifteen pounds. Since there was bubbling around the flapper valve in the bottom of the head bowl it was obvious that the discharge line to sea was clogged. Should I try it again? With more air pressure? The answer was no. Additional pressure only raised the risk of having the refuse in the trap blow up into one's face. So I decided to let Maderos, the officer's steward, handle the matter. He was an expert!

Maderos had "been in the boats" since they first appeared on the Asiatic station. The wizened little Filipino knew all the tricks for handling this erratic gadget. He was known to use up to fifty pounds of air pressure to free the overboard discharge. He'd do this even though he recognized that such pressure was somewhat greater than the design of the head allowed.

As usual, Maderos first tried fifteen pounds several times. Then he went to twenty-five. He was smart enough to keep his head well clear of the bowl as the additional pressure caused the bubbling through the flapper valve to increase to a fountain-like spray. When I saw Maderos bleeding forty pounds of air into the blowing tank I departed. Cowardice has its fine points.

Moments later Maderos rushed to the wardroom, splattered with flecks of brown glop. He was sobbing. "You can beat me until I'm dead, Mr. Ruhe," he said, with evident anguish, "but I'm not going back there to clean up that mess."

I looked at him with amazement. He was the expert? Hah! My look of contempt for his failure made him truly dejected.

"The flapper valve collapsed," he said defensively, and then turned away.

That concluded my notes for July 3—a day like any other day in the life of a pigboat sailor.

At 0100 with a battery charge completed and the moon on the rise, the 37 was submerged to run undetected through the less than ten-mile separation between Duke of York Island and New Ireland. Making about 4.5 knots eased through the narrow passage, she was kept at forty-five feet. Frequent looks were taken to see if the enemy on the beach was being alerted to the 37's transit.

Many pin-points of light on both shores were blinking on and off as though the Japanese were talking back and forth with blinker guns. Exchanging information on the 37's movement? Bobby Byrnes, the officer of the deck, excitedly insisted he could read actual letters being transmitted. But he couldn't tell what the senders were saying. (Of course he couldn't! The messages would be in Japanese, which Bobby certainly didn't know.) Bobby's imagination was running riot as it frequently did when he saw some strange occurrence while on watch.

When the captain was called to the bridge, he carefully studied the lights on both shores and noted that they might be from native villages that were not very well blacked-out. "Doors are being opened and shut on poorly lit huts" he guessed, nervously. Then he returned to the wardroom and put his red glasses back on.

July 4th should have produced some fireworks. But it didn't. With the 37 north of Rabaul and in a position to intercept merchant ship traffic in and out of the busy port, the captain seemed to be acting a bit braver. But the 37 was still too far from Rabaul to cover several other shipping lanes in use by the Japanese. Too much caution had been the scourge of the Asiatic S-boat skippers. They had sunk only three ships up to the time they arrived in Australia. Now our captain would have to get a bit hungrier for a sinking if he was going to get the 37 into a really good shooting position.

At noon, the captain had the word passed that all hands could get a shot of Bols gin in the messhall to celebrate the national holiday. Six earthenware gallon jugs of Bols had been bought in Soerabaya, Java, by Tex on what he called an inspiration. Then he had donated his store of gin to the crew. In short order the crew polished off all the gin.

I questioned Tex about bringing liquor aboard a U.S. naval ship and then serving it to the crew. He knew that there were strict rules against drinking on board. Yet Tex studied me quizzically, as though I was a naive child. Then he said slyly, "Hell, this is war and today's the Fourth so what's the big deal?"

Tex was as passionate about the Fourth of July as a tomato, and the war seemed to have made little impact on him. He didn't want to leave a bad impression with me, however, so he added, "This is the first time I've ever seen an entire crew drinking on a submarine." But, then, submarines didn't have many guys like Tex who would give up a precious store of liquor just to celebrate a special occasion.

My only excitement on the Fourth came from watching hordes of sharks swim past the scope when it was dipped a foot or two below the surface of the brilliantly lit sea.

Later that night, Billy brought a decoded message to the bridge that told of a Japanese invasion force of troop transports escorted by two carriers, and at least thirteen other major warships being sighted in the vicinity of Tulagi at the lower eastern end of the Solomons. The next message told of landings on Guadalcanal.

On the fifth, the all-day submerged patrol was, on the captain's orders, conducted at periscope depth with the scope up and down every minute. The captain was getting braver. He reminded us that "We've got to leave station on the tenth in accordance with our orders. So we'd better see something in a hurry."

When I went to the bridge to take the 2100 to 2400 watch, my good night vision justified Captain Reynold's reliance on me to be the surfacing OOD on dark nights. Before relieving Bobby Byrnes, I picked out a smudge in the darkness. It seemed to be a small boat about five hundred yards away, and heading for the 37. While I was studying the craft through my binoculars, it suddenly shone a dim light in the direction of the 37. Bobby promptly dove the 37 to sixty feet, passing forty-five feet in just thirty-two seconds. The 37 then cleared the area. Forty-five minutes later she was quietly resurfaced with no further contacts made during the remainder of the night.

Apparently the small craft had heard the noise of the 37's engines on battery charge and had closed to investigate.

The sixth was an exhausting day of waiting. The 37 was submerged through the day staying at forty-five feet, with looks every five minutes.

I played the captain a game of chess after my watch had ended. He quickly resigned, claiming that he couldn't concentrate on the game.

Surfacing after such a day was particularly welcome due to the cool breeze pulled through the boat when the diesels were started.

However, engaging the diesels to the propellers was a difficult procedure. After finally getting the clutch to function, attempts to adjust the clutch linkage revealed that all of its slack had been used up. It could only be hoped that there would be no further slippage before the end of the patrol, or the 37 might never make it back to Brisbane.

On the seventh there was some griping about nothing to shoot at. Yet the morale of the men remained high and their mood expectant, despite there being only three more days left on station. At 1700, the soundman picked up the noise of screws making 150 rpm. There was little excited reaction. When the periscope was put on the bearing of the sound contact, the captain could see the masts and stack of a distant merchant ship.

"Battle stations, torpedo attack" was announced over the loudspeaker system as the general alarm started its "bong, bong."

The 37's crew moved quietly and in an orderly way to their battle stations. And waited.

The 37 was taken to eighty feet and for half an hour her battery was drained by using full speed and a normal approach course to close the track. But heading ninety degrees from the ship's track failed to reduce the range. When the 37 was brought back to forty-five feet, a quick look showed only the tips of the ship's masts. The 37 was evidently farther from the ship's track than when the approach was started. The attack thus had to be aborted as the ship disappeared in the direction of Rabaul.

This made the captain decide to move the 37 so close to Rabaul harbor that no ship could steam by without the 37 getting a torpedo shot at her.

I didn't feel that the captain was playing the role of a reluctant dragon. But he was so ingrained with extreme caution that the crew's pressures for action were only now being felt by him. The captain as a submarine skipper inspired affection rather than admiration.

Before diving on the eighth, it was possible to see signs of activity in the villages along the beach at the mouth of Rabaul harbor. Then after submerging, the 37's patrol path took her so close to Rabaul that a single look at thirty-five-foot depth with twelve feet of periscope exposed showed the tops of several ships anchored inside the harbor.

When a bombing attack was clearly heard in the direction of Rabaul, it seemed apparent that MacArthur's bombers were in action and some Japanese ships would be driven out to sea and over the 37.

Action was at hand. Yet there was no sign of nervousness in the men around me. There was no compulsive talking, a sure sign of tension in the men who had nothing to do but wait. I noted that my own thoughts about what was likely to happen didn't include the possibility of dying or even being injured. I took it for granted that "it can't happen to me." In a sea battle, a submarine was certainly the place to be. And most of the men felt the same way.

At 1355, Tex, who was on the periscope, shouted, "Battle stations, torpedo attack" and rang the general alarm. As the captain entered the control room, Tex, in a matter-of-fact voice said, "Here she comes. It's the *Kiokawa Maru* and she's painted warship gray." Tex then told the captain, "The sea is smooth as glass and the scope is leaving a long white feather across the water." He recommended that the captain use only six inches of exposed scope when the captain ordered "Up periscope."

The captain's quick look indicated that a big ship was about ten thousand yards off and hugging the shoreline. This was based on a stadimeter range of 1-1/4 spaces on the scope's ranging grid that measured the height of the top of the foremast above the water. "Give her a five degree port angle on the bow," the captain ordered. Then, "Down scope." As the scope was being lowered, the captain added, "There's a small patrol boat, probably a subchaser, on the port side of the big ship." An escort.

"Their course is 270° True," Tex noted. The *Kiokawa Maru* was returning to port, not leaving it.

The 37 was put on a normal approach course but remained slow at three knots to conserve the battery. The captain ordered, "Seventy feet." To Tex's query as to whether he'd seen any aircraft on ordering the 37 deep, the captain admitted, "I didn't look for any."

As an afterthought the captain ordered "Make ready three tubes. Set four feet on the torpedoes and we'll use zero gyro angles on all three torpedoes, and fire a longitudinal spread." That meant sending the torpedoes along the same path, letting the forward advance of the target spread the torpedoes down the ship's side.

The trim of the 37 seemed very good in my judgement as diving officer. Her response to the planes was also good as the boat maintained depth easily.

I looked around the control room at all the players. There was plenty of time to think about how this attack was affecting me, but I was more interested in the other officers' reactions. Billy Gibson, the plotting officer, was smiling broadly—which seemed to say "This is really 'it.' It's what I've been waiting for." Billy was the only non-Naval Academy officer, and didn't seem to regard his submarine job as much more than a pastime. He seemed to see his submarine duty as being part of a skilled trade. It was a great experience for the unflappable, elf-like Billy. Bobby Byrnes, tight-lipped and grave, was sitting in the door to the forward battery compartment and was inputting the captain's periscope data onto a "Banjo" that he held on his lap. This was the only fire control device on an S-boat. It was an elliptical metal plate inscribed with angles, bearings, and ranges, and had adjustable metal arms to produce a firing solution for the torpedoes. Tex, with a round white, plastic "Is-Was" hanging around his neck, stood close to the captain in the center of the control room and appeared relatively indifferent to the attack problem developing. His taut deliberateness in playing the assistant approach officer role was reassuring. The captain, on the other hand, showed signs of nervousness, standing on his toes and pumping his heels up and down, while taking deep breaths as though to clear his head.

I wondered if I should feel scared—because I didn't.

Back at forty-five feet, ten minutes after the first look, the captain's quick observation of the target produced an estimated 5,500 yard range and a fifteen degree port angle-on-the-bow. Tex muttered, "The captain's look shows the big ship to be making a speed of about fourteen knots and that doesn't seem right." Tex's guess was, "She's making only about ten knots." Again, the captain failed to look for aircraft. Almost certainly a plane would be escorting the seaplane tender back to port, it must be somewhere around, or so Tex thought. The captain confirmed that the target was the *Kiokawa Maru*. "She's heavily loaded, with many large steel drums on her main deck," he noted. The captain also failed to mark the bearing of the subchaser before the scope was lowered.

"Where's the escort? Where's the escort?" Tex repeated until the captain finally said, "I think he's abeam of the target on our side." But the captain didn't sound convincing. However, he kept the 37 at periscope depth, and took hurried looks at the threatening escort, saying nothing.

The captain's third observation of the big ship produced a range of 3,800 yards. This indicated a lower speed. But it also appeared that the captain's stadimeter readings were suspect. The 270° course of the target looked good.

With so much time in an attack like this to mentally calculate the fire control solution, using only thumb rules, I wondered why Bobby Byrnes was agonizing over his Banjo settings. But I didn't realize how bad the data was that was being juggled by Bobby and Billy. Neither of them had a solution. It wasn't like an attack teacher problem at Sub School. There, the data was reasonably accurate throughout an entire simulated approach.

When the captain raised the scope at 1359 and took a look, he really started jumping up and down. "The escort's so close I can see the rivets on his sides!" His voice had risen an octave above normal. "The men on the forward three-inch gun are pointing straight at me!" Tex begged, "Where's the target? Where's the target?" The captain, acting flustered and perplexed, answered, "I don't know. I can't see her, the subchaser is blanking me out. He's only about fifty yards away . . . There are lots of men at the depth charge racks on his stern."

Then Tex pleaded, "Forget about the escort, Captain. Please give me a bearing on the big ship as soon as the subchaser pulls clear." Was Tex using good manners just to get the captain's attention?

The captain kept the scope raised. Then, after the escort's stern had passed by the scope, the captain yelled "Mark the bearing!"

Tex read the bearing from the top of the scope, looked at his Is-Was, and announced to the captain, "I'm using ten knots for target speed. We'll use thirteen degrees for the lead-angle for our zero-gyro-angle fish." Tex had craftily applied the old thumb rule of "speed plus three" to get a workable lead-angle.

Without assent, Tex then grabbed the handles of the scope away from the captain, swung the scope to the proper bearing. At this, he told the captain, "Start firing the torpedoes when the target's jack-staff is on the cross hair." Tex also directed the man on the firing key to punch-out the torpedoes at eight second intervals when firing was ordered.

"What's the range, Captain? . . . The range?" Tex was getting frantic.

"I can't tell—she's more than filling my scope."

"A range Captain . . . we need a range," Tex persisted.

Then, without a "Stand-by to fire," the captain shakily said, "That's it . . . Commence firing. Commence firing."

With the announcement from the forward room, "One fired," the captain ordered "110 feet—and fast." And, "Put hard dive on the planes and all ahead flank." The controllerman answered, "We're pulling two thousand amps a side, Sir." Maximum battery power!

I noted that the bow had suddenly gotten very light after all the fish had left their tubes with a satisfying jarring of the boat. They were on their way. But their launch tubes, not being properly vented, were full of air. Thus, getting the 37 to nose downward seemed temporarily impossible. So I asked the captain to rush men forward to help get the bow down while I vented the tubes to remove the entrapped air. Evidently, the poppet valves had not functioned properly on firing, preventing the tubes from reflooding after the torpedoes had been air-ejected.

"Every man go forward," the captain shouted. Many men responded, dashing wildly from the after battery and control room to the forward room like a pack of wild horses. Up there they added a considerable amount of weight to the bow and helped the 37 take a down angle. But then the 37, nosing rapidly downward, threatened to go out of control, and sink fast. Flooding of forward trim was immediately stopped, the men were ordered to move aft on the double and the captain directed "Put a bubble in number one main ballast tank." But the vent on the ballast tank had been left open due to the imminence of a depth charge attack. Consequently, a shot of high pressure air went right out through the open vent as a big bubble that rose to the surface—marking the location of the S-37 for the enemy.

As soon as I heard the air shooshing through the open vent, and seeing a red light on the diving board, I had the vent closed so that some of the air was trapped in the ballast tank. This stopped the 37's descent and helped to get her back to 110 feet.

Meanwhile, twenty-five seconds after the first torpedo had left its tube there was a heavy explosion, closely followed by a loud boom that rocked the 37. Then there were two more torpedo explosions close together. The times for the first and second torpedo hits indicated that the range to the ship had been only about 600 yards. Noises of a sinking ship were clearly heard on the sound gear.

I had the momentary thought that we were killing lots of people. But it was only in a detached and impersonal way. It was like dropping bombs on a city. None of the victims could be mentally imaged as flesh and blood individuals.

The soundman kept reporting the bearing of the screws of the escort but he'd lost all sounds from the main target. "The escort's

hooking around to starboard," he reported. The captain was reminded to order "Rig for depth charge."

All of the men around me could hear the escort's screws through
the hull, and were looking upward to gauge when he'd pass overhead and lay a string of depth charges on the 37.

As soon as I announced that the 37 was back in good trim, the
captain ordered "Right full rudder, come to north."

Up to then, there had been no mention of how we were going to
evade the escort's counterattacks. In fact, there had been no plan for
clearing the area of battle. But the "right full rudder" seemed to do
the trick because the two depth charges that exploded near the 37
were well clear astern and did only minor damage: some broken
light bulbs, a bit of a shaking of the 37, and there was a report that
the head-bowl aft had shattered. We still had porcelain bowls that
splintered easily.

Billy Gibson was smiling broadly. For him this was fun. Or was it
just camouflage for fear?

The men stood quietly in place, staring with shadowed eyes at the
officers who were expected to get them out of this trouble. Actually,
I sensed their eyes were mainly on me. They were wondering how
brave the overbearing "greenhorn" would be "when the depth
charges started rattling and smashing the boat." I wasn't going to
show them a single sign of fear. And didn't, even though my stomach
felt queasy, and my legs felt so tired that I leaned on Billy's plotting
table for support. I noticed the captain was showing grave concern,
and was holding tightly to a rung of the ladder leading up to the
bridge. Was this to withstand the shock of the next depth charge or
to steady his shaking legs? Even Tex had a grip on something. Tex's
jaw was clenched and he had a "this is grimmo" look.

There was a continuous reporting of the sound of the escort's
screws, somewhere nearby. Then the turn-count of the screws was
reported to have increased markedly. The subchaser was making
another run at his invisible enemy.

I looked to see the captain's reaction and was certain that a small
amused smile had crept into his face. His eyes even glistened merri-
ly. I had the thought that the enemy's imminent re-attack had caused
the captain to think of the phrase "as rascals are wont to do." This
came from his favorite poem, "The Hermit of Shark Tooth Shoal,"
that was a Robert Service tale about Alaska. The captain was evidently chuckling quietly as he seemingly recited to himself: "Oh, the
north country, is a rough country, that mothers a bloody brood . . . "

Just thinking about something nice and cold, the Arctic, was
pleasant. My hands were clammy cold, yet I seemed to be sweating
far more than normal from the suffocating heat in the control room.

A look around showed all the men's bare torsos glistening with dripping sweat.

What a strange way to fight. No anger being shown. No posturing or barking of commands by the officers. In fact, an outsider would wonder which were the officers and which the enlisted men. There were no insignias worn, no special uniforms, no superior attitudes. We were all "in the same boat." With increased respect for each other at this moment. Even the motor machinist, who was cranking the stern planes and who had resisted my orders when we were repairing the burned-out diesel bearings, was acting like the Rock of Gibraltar.

When two depth charges were heard splashing into the water off the subchaser's stern and which exploded far astern of the 37, there was an easing of tension. The captain guessed, with a relieved smile, that the Japanese warship had attacked the position of the air bubble that had been released by the 37 earlier. That seemed reasonable since there were no further attacks. The subchaser had evidently decided that he'd killed his submarine. Still, he kept milling around for several hours.

By late afternoon all sounds of screws had been lost. It looked like things were over, so I had a chance to reassess my own reactions to the battle. I recognized that I never felt nauseous, couldn't identify any moment of real fear, and decided that I'd been too busy doing things to have time to worry. I asked several of the men around me for their reactions. Theirs were about the same as mine. But I felt that some of the men who had nothing to do probably did suffer from the tension. At any rate, there were no reports of any of the men blacking out, screaming, vomiting or clutching up. If any of the men had shown indications of uncontrolled fear they would have been taken off duty promptly and transferred out of subs on return to port. Proper screening for submarine duty generally keeps this sort of thing from happening.

At 1830 the captain ordered the 37 back to periscope depth. But as the boat came shallow, pinging was clearly heard astern. So the sub was taken back down to ninety feet. At 1915 she was brought back up to periscope depth. The captain took a quick look around, announced "All clear" and then "Stand by to surface."

The 37 was surfaced and the hatch opened—but too quickly. I was blown up and out through the hatch, and was saved from being tossed overboard by holding onto the hatch lanyard. The uprush of released air treated me like a Ping Pong ball being ejected by a jet of air. I was balanced on the out-rushing gale a few feet above the bridge for a few seconds before subsiding back onto the deck, as the pressure of the air venting out of the sub diminished. The binoculars that I had carried around my neck on a thong were gone. They'd been torn free and blown overboard.

A hasty look around the horizon showed nothing. "Start the engines" was ordered, and while charging her batteries the boat began pulling clear of the area.

Each hour it was easier to breathe. The air in the boat, now clean and cool, put the men on a real high. There was a great feeling of euphoria for all hands.

When I went below and looked into the after battery room where many of the men were sitting around the mess tables, I was amazed at the din of chatter. Everybody was talking at once and wild claims flew around the room like a horde of bats. The same was true in the wardroom where Billy, and Bobby, and Tex were all talking with nobody listening. I had left the captain standing on the bridge. He was taking my watch to give me "a little rest." He had been in a gloomy, contemplative mood when I left him. And he told me later that he was worried he'd showed his extreme nervousness to the crew. That was bad. He also felt that perhaps he wasn't fit to be a good submarine skipper. I thought otherwise.

I felt that the battle had gone well. With very little fire-control information and that mostly bad, the captain had still put the S-37 into an almost ideal firing position. Moreover, he had properly deferred to Tex's advice. The captain had operated under extreme pressure and Tex far less so. This made it easy for Tex to do a superb job as assistant approach officer.

There certainly was no knocking success. The captain had sunk an important warship and the battle had been orderly and simple in its execution. And decisive in its results!

Emphatically, the Mk-10 torpedoes with their simple contact exploders had functioned satisfactorily.

When I went back to the bridge to relieve the captain of the deck watch he said that he had decided to hunt for ships up and around the northern tip of New Ireland, then go home down its east side. He thought that trying to ease back down St. George's Channel was too risky in light of the heavy antisubmarine activity generated by the S-37's success. Two more days would be added to the length of the patrol but with an unreliable submarine, the captain felt it was the only way to get home safely.

During the night of the ninth, the sea was so oily smooth that the reflection of the stars could be seen on the sea's surface. For the last three nights the captain had been sleeping on the chart desk just under the upper hatch to the bridge. By curling up tightly with his knees almost on his chest he barely fitted on the top of the three foot by three foot wooden desk. Now, although he slept fitfully, he would from time to time cry out unintelligibly in alarm about something he was dreaming. He seemed, nevertheless, to be getting some useful rest and proved cheerful and alert next day. His chess game was back in order and he was winning a few of the games we played. His theory in sleeping up in the conning tower was that he had to be close at hand to respond to any enemy action that suddenly evolved out of the darkness. It was also a way to get some much needed sleep by avoiding the oppressive heat below.

July 10th was the day the 37 could leave station and head back to Brisbane. The 37 stayed submerged all day while moving out towards a sea lane that had been used in the past by Japanese ships.

Later that night, while I was on the watch with the captain huddled below me on the chart desk, I could hear him periodically mutter in his sleep—something that sounded like pure gibberish. But then he started shouting a series of orders up at me with complete clarity and assurance in his voice, as though he were wide awake. "Man the four-inch gun, he's closing fast" . . . "Clear the bridge!" . . . "Take her deep."

I called down to him, "Are you awake, Captain?"

He shouted back, "Dammit, dive the boat, we're surrounded."

The "we're surrounded" was the giveaway. It was certain that he was having a wild dream because I could see that the sea around the 37 was clear of ships of any type, at least out to a considerable distance.

Down in the control room the men heard the captain's rantings and dashed to their diving stations. Hence, I called down the trunk to the control room to have everyone stand easy, "The captain's having a nightmare."

On July 11, the captain had the word passed "All men must shave their beards before arrival at Brisbane." This was regretfully received. The men had a certain swagger and maturity when they were wearing beards that wasn't the case when they were clean shaven.

By my calculations the 37 had 1,100 miles to go and at 175 miles per day that was at least a six-day trip. I also noted that we were finally in sea areas for which we had charts. Interestingly, my search through the boat for a Bible, feeling the need for a little religious meditation, proved fruitless. Chief Grady said he'd never seen one aboard the 37. Yet it seemed evident that Someone was looking out for this crew and the old 37. That was certain! More and more I felt that there was a small guardian angel perched on my shoulder at all times.

On the thirteenth, Tex relieved me on the mid-watch. He said he'd been acting as the ship's doctor and had dressed a deep cut in Borlick, the auxiliaryman's finger. Tex admitted to having no medical experience. But his compassion was considerable as he told me how difficult it was for him to listen to Borlick's yells as he, Tex, sewed up the cut. "Our sewing needles don't seem very sharply pointed," he said gloomily. When I asked him if he'd given Borlick a shot of brandy to ease the pain, he admitted that he hadn't, but perhaps should have. He didn't like the job of being doctor and suggested that next time I take a crack at the job. He then said I was now custodian of the medical books, the surgical instruments, the first aid kit and the remaining quart of medicinal brandy.

Running submerged on the fourteenth was a trying workout for the planesmen. The waves had increased to where the 37 rolled heavily even when down at seventy feet. Winter had moved into the southern latitudes with a great ferocity, making it difficult to handle the sub while maintaining the routine of regular periscope looks every twenty minutes. When a periscope observation was required, the 37, trimmed heavy over-all, was brought to forty-five foot depth using six knots of speed. Just before the scope broke the surface of the water, speed was cut to two knots to reduce the periscope's feather on the sea's surface. Then as a quick look was taken, the 37 would sink so rapidly that trim was not regained until the 37 had sunk to almost one hundred feet.

After dark, shortly after surfacing, the word was passed, "Dump all garbage overboard." The men who then climbed the ladder to the bridge hauling large cans of garbage with them, cursed good naturedly as they banged their cans up through the trunk. Once on the bridge they carefully timed the toss of their garbage into the ocean's waves so that the stinking refuse wasn't blown back in their faces by the violent wind. But then an unexpected mountainous wave climbed over the 37's bow and poured over the bridge. At that instant, Montero, the stewardsmate, was pulling his way through the upper hatch. The quartermaster on the bridge tried to close the hatch to minimize the flooding down the trunk. But the hatch was jammed on Montero's body and a massive torrent of water cascaded down the trunk to the control room. His garbage pail sailed downward onto the heads of the men pulling their cans up the ladder. Two of the men were washed, along with much garbage, down to the control room. Water two inches deep and a slimy filth soon covered the control room deck.

The captain, who was on the bridge at the time of the big wave, was almost swept overboard. His reaction was to order that all men be tied to their bridge stations with ropes around their waists until the seas abated somewhat.

When I took the topside watch the waves had become even more dangerous. Thus, on each big wave that crashed over the bridge, I'd trip the latch on the hatch with my foot and help to snap it shut. Two large drain holes cut into the bottom of the bridge would then quickly drain the enclosure. Hence, there was only a brief moment when the men on the bridge were completely under water.

But on one wave that smashed over the 37 and filled the bridge to overflowing, the water stayed up around my shoulders. Peering around, I could see only one lookout close to me. The other lookout and the quartermaster had disappeared, apparently washed overboard. It was a frightening moment. However, by probing with my foot, I came in contact with the body of a man trapped in a drainage hole. I pulled him clear, as he sputtered and gasped for air. Then I dragged the other man from the second drainage hole where he was similarly caught. Both men loudly cursed their immersion. They did, however, shorten the span of the ropes that they tied to their stations so they subsequently would not wind up being sucked into the drainage holes and being nearly drowned.

On the following night, the captain, who was curled up and sleeping on the chart desk, was swept off the desk by an unprepared-for big wave that hit before the upper hatch could be closed. A man coming up the ladder saved the captain from tumbling down to the control room. This would have been a real tragedy. As a result it ended the captain's sleeping in the conning tower and the confusion that his nightmare-induced rantings caused.

By late Friday the seventeenth, the cooks were complaining that the 37 was just about out of food. Lots of ham remained, but only a few cans of soup, some beans, and some flour were left. All eggs, powdered milk, cereal, and bacon were gone. Then the possibility of using the "emergency rations" occurred to Bobby Byrnes, the commissary officer. He asked for, and received, the captain's permission to open up the emergency lockers and add the food therein to the crew's menu. The captain felt that in the last few days of this patrol there was little possibility that the 37 would be sunk on a shallow bottom with the crew trapped but still with a chance of being saved. Normally the lockers contained Spam, C-rations, canned fruit and other staples. But when Bobby opened the lockers in the forward and after torpedo rooms he found only a stash of many cans of peculiar-tasting Dutch butter that had been issued in Java and many cans of cranberry sauce. Thus, for breakfast Bobby's cooks served ham and water-made biscuits plus cranberry sauce. For lunch it was the same and for supper, ditto. But there were only three days left, so there was much joking about not having to starve "because we aren't Jewish."

On Saturday there were fewer large waves, the air was colder and it was comfortable sleeping below decks. The electrical department, however, was getting more and more fouled up. The captain, after several of my reports on the great number of electrical breakdowns, said ironically, "Leave for me is just getting away from dumb electrician's mates." Tex felt the same way about sexy enlisted men in general, because he was treating two of the crew for gonorrhea and he didn't like that daily task one bit.

Having a lull in making observations about the 37's operations, I decided to jot down some of the lessons that could be learned from this patrol. After several contemplative watches on the bridge, I decided that first, it seemed evident that keeping the old S-boats operational and using them to make war patrols was very sensible. Having considerable numbers of submarines, regardless of type or age in diverse ocean areas, should spread out the enemy's antisubmarine efforts and provide an expanded threat to the Japanese movement of ships for carrying out invasion plans. In addition, Japanese planners would be likely to overestimate the submarine threat facing them, thus complicating and confusing their plans.

"Even though the S-boats are quite broken down," I noted, "their men aren't in equally poor shape. In fact, they continue to function well. They are stable psychologically, have above average IQs and are competent in fixing things while at sea and are cool in combat. The crew is far more important to a submarine's success than its equipment."

Unfortunately, the S-37, with only a thirty-day endurance, was able to spend only eight days in the patrol area. It would seem that she could have been kept going for a longer time, permitting more time on station. A resupply submarine near the S-37's patrol area might have replenished her for another thirty days of endurance. This would have increased her time on station about four-fold. The Germans did this in World War I, using "milch cows," their replenishment subs, to greatly increase the number of sinkings. But air conditioning would necessarily have to be installed in the 37 if the men were to last for sixty days at sea.

With good submarining, I felt that even an antiquated boat can operate effectively in heavily guarded enemy waters and attack well-protected ships with a high element of surprise.

The great pressures put on a captain during an attack, particularly when using the periscope in a submerged attack, apparently create great pressures on the captain's thought processes. This causes a certain amount of confusion. Might it not be better to have the executive officer man the periscope? This would give the captain far greater freedom to think clearly and absorb the data being generated, so as to make better attack decisions.

United States war planners evidently failed to foresee the possible extent of Japanese invasion plans. The lack of charts for the S-37's patrol area would indicate that invasion of islands below the equator were not included in the war games played by the U.S. Navy before the war.

Sunday the twentieth proved to be the last day before arrival at New Farm Wharf. The captain was so eager to put on a show when the 37 went alongside the tender that his eyes sparkled with anticipation. He kept chuckling to himself. He directed me to paint a large sign that read "Deceased, *Kiokawa Maru.*" I also designed a black death's head pirate flag that the quartermaster sewed together on his sewing machine. While this was going on, a major field day was held both topsides and throughout the boat. Much painting, shining of brass and disposing of trash over the side ensued.

During mid-morning of the twenty-first, arrival day, I was sleeping peacefully when the collision alarm snapped me awake. All the bulkhead doors were slammed shut and tightly dogged before I could get to the control room. Trapped in the after battery, I had to wait and hope there would be no collision that might send the sub to the bottom, like the *Squalus* in 1939. The 37 was moving frantically—backing, stopping, going ahead, then backing full. Finally, at "Secure from collision" the doors were opened and Billy came aft to explain what had happened.

As he related it, "We had started up the swept channel in Moreton Bay without having exchanged any recognition signals with the shore station guarding the entrance to the bay. When the 37 passed over a detection coil in the channel, a controlled mine ahead in the channel was automatically activated to blow up the intruder. The shore station, alerted by a signal from the detection coil, illuminated the 37. Recognition signals were exchanged and the activated mine was turned off. The shore station blinked over to the 37, 'You were lucky this time. There were still five seconds to go before you triggered our mine.'"

For coming alongside the tender *Griffin*, the 37 flew the skull and cross-bones flag that I had designed. There was also a second small Japanese warship flag now painted on the side of the conning tower. And everyone topside was clean-shaven.

After tying up, four oilskin-clad members of the crew emerged from the engine room hatch, dragging a vegetable box with them. It was draped with a Japanese warship flag and carried the sign "Deceased, *Kiokawa Maru.*" Then, to much shouting and cheering from the men who lined the tender *Griffin*'s rails, the box was tossed into the harbor. A string, however, was attached to the box so that shortly it could be retrieved. There were strict orders against dumping things into the harbor while alongside the *Griffin*, and the captain wanted to demonstrate that, as crazy as submariners might seem at times, they were still far from anarchy.

Then there was much visiting, much talk and much confusion. Mail was brought aboard. I quickly scanned the pile of letters from my wife and chose the first and last by date. I swiftly read them to ensure that things were still going fine back home. The rest were stored in my locker to be savored after things quieted down.

Captain Reynolds went to the tender to tell the staff he wanted to be relieved of his command of the S-37. On his return he told us that the staff would assign Lieutenant Tom Baskett, the exec of the 44-boat, to command the 37-boat. Baskett was from the Class of '35 Naval Academy and was a star man, standing 14th in his class. He proved to be only two years older than me.

In the afternoon, Bobby came back to the 37 to pick up his "shaving gear" so he could, in his words, "stay overnight in Brisbane and relax."

But, first things first. Neither Billy, Tex, nor I wanted to spend another day in the company "of millions of cockroaches" that prowled around and over us at all hours. "Millions" seemed a gross exaggeration until we swung into action to wipe out the vast hordes of "curious, busy little brown fellas."

Tex had promised to go to the tender and get a tankful of "gas" to eliminate "the little devils." Billy and I stayed aboard the 37 as part of the in-port watch section, and waited for Tex's return. After supper he showed up and said that no gas to kill the roaches was available on the tender. So he'd gone into Brisbane to a hardware store and "confiscated" a drum of Flit. The store owner had assured him that Flit was ideal for killing insects of all types. ("But were roaches insects? They seemed more like animals.") Tex then delivered a handwritten note to the owner that said, "There is an immediate need for an insecticide for the control of cockroaches on the U.S.S. S-37. I am therefore authorized to officially requisition one container of Flit for the U.S. Navy; signed Lieutenant R. B. Lander, USN."

This seemed a foolish ploy, except that the store owner graciously donated a drum of Flit to Tex and used his truck to have it delivered to the 37's main deck. As Tex noted, "He acted as though I was doing him a big favor by letting him deliver his Flit to a U.S. submarine."

Tex had also brought along two Flit guns. So Billy and I went to work. The after battery room was evacuated. After which, Billy and I wearing oilskins, rubber gloves, and gas masks entered the compartment with our Flit guns. Tightly sealing the crew's messing compartment and where the crew had their food prepared—a rather ideal spot for breeding roaches—we started soaking the cork insulation that lined the inside of the hull. This produced immediate havoc. The little silver-winged fellas popped out of their hiding places as their bodies were seared by the atomized spray of Flit from our guns. In the throes of great agony, they jumped to the deck and scurried around trying to find the lowest point in the compartment. It would have been the drains, but we'd plugged those. So they dove into the rectangular channel that indented the compartment's deck and that was the means for holding the canvas covering over the batteries. More and more roaches piled into the channel fighting their way towards the channel's bottom until it was filled to overflowing with little dead bodies.

At this, Billy and I stopped the spraying and retreated to the wardroom. When Tex was told about the mayhem we'd committed, he seemed doleful about a future without the little wanderers to playfully distract him from the 37's vengeance. Tex then had the thought that we could get a good estimate of how many cockroaches had just been killed. He found a small wooden match box and carefully measured it in order to calculate its cubic-inch volume. Then he sent Billy and me aft, with our gas masks, so Billy could fill the matchbox with little dead bodies while I measured the dimensions of the channel. Deriving statistics and understanding their significance was a major pastime on submarines. Statistics were always of great interest, even for the dumbest subjects: Do submariners produce more girls than boys? What percentage of the crew drink tea? Are athletes the best submarine skippers? What's the average collar size of torpedomen?

When we got back to the wardroom Tex dumped "the little devils" out of the box and carefully counted them. After this, he figured how many dead cockroaches there were to the cubic inch. He took my dimensions for the channel and converted them to the cubic-inch volume of the roaches' resting place. Finally, he announced the number of dead cockroaches in the overflowed channel. "Over four million!"

Most gratifying was the crew's response to a draft for five men to go back to the States for "new construction." This meant a new fleet boat with air conditioning. Of the fifteen men who were offered the chance to go, only two actually said they wanted to leave the 37.

Sometime later, S-37's sinking of a ship off Rabaul was confirmed by Japanese intelligence. However, the gray-painted naval auxiliary sunk was the XAP *Tenzan Maru* and not the *Kiokawa Maru*. Sinking a naval troop transport may have been just as damaging to the Japanese objective of consolidating their hold on Guadalcanal, as would be the loss of a seaplane tender. Furthermore, Tex and the captain's misidentification of the ship that was torpedoed was not surprising since both ships were converted merchant ships.

2

A Mare's Nest

Monday, August 17, saw the start of the S-37's sixth war patrol. Instead of being late getting underway, as could be expected for one of these worn-out old boats, there were no last-minute repairs to be made. Hence, she pulled away from New Farm Wharf at 0755, five minutes ahead of schedule. And I was still aboard the 37, having ascertained that no SD radars would arrive in the next month.

There was much clapping and occasional shouts of encouragement from Aussies who, on their way to work, spotted the S-37 standing away from the nest of submarines alongside the tender *Griffin* and heading out into the stream of the Brisbane River. They hurried to the river's edge to give the men on the 37 their friendly waves.

Up on the tender, leaning over the top-deck rails, a mob of tender sailors yelled down at the captain a lot of well-meant advice. "Go get 'em, skipper!" "Sink the bastards!" "Don't come back empty handed." The latter admonition was a reminder that too many of the S-boats were returning without any newly painted, tiny Japanese ship-flags on their conning towers.

The new captain, Lt. Tom Baskett, appreciatively nodded towards the tender workers. He was smiling broadly at the exhibition of goodwill from all directions. Normally a very reserved person, I suspected that his great good humor stemmed from more than the send-off being accorded him and his boat. My first thought was that he must be getting a very good patrol area—much better than he might have expected as a submarine officer in his first command.

Since much had happened up around Guadalcanal at the eastern end of the Solomon Islands it seemed a good guess that our patrol would be in that area. In the last ten days, the action around Savo

Island certainly indicated that there was a need for a submarine to confuse the issue.

Tex was conning the 37 down the river, so I took the opportunity to move beside the captain on the bridge and softly say to him, "Are we headed for Guadalcanal, Captain?" The smile faded from his face and his jaw tightened. Tight-lipped, he mumbled, "Yes, that's where we're headed." Then he resumed his pleased smile and began waving back at the Aussies who had now regained his attention.

The captain noted my continued quizzical scanning of his pleased face for a clue as to what was going to happen. So he leaned towards my ear and quietly said, "I'll announce the *good* news to the crew after we finish our test dive and head out for our patrol."

Everyone seemed happy to see a submarine headed for patrol. In the past ten days the activity around Guadalcanal had been stepped up. On August 8th, U.S. Marines had been landed on the island and had seized control of Henderson Field from the Japanese troops that had invaded Guadalcanal in early July. The expected Japanese response came on August 9th when a large force of Japanese warships encountered a U.S. force protecting the U.S. foothold being consolidated on the island. Incredibly, the Japanese heavy cruisers in the pitch blackness of a moonless night had opened fire on the force of U.S. heavy cruisers, before the radar-equipped U.S. warships had any indication of the presence of the enemy. Some of the U.S. cruisers were hit fatally by the initial Japanese salvoes of eight-inch shells and were sunk before the U.S. ships were able to get off a single salvo from their own eight-inch guns. The U.S. Navy suffered its worst defeat since Pearl Harbor. The *Quincy*, *Astoria*, and *Vincennes* were sunk outright and the *Chicago* was seriously damaged. In addition, the Australian cruiser *Canberra* also in company with the U.S. heavy cruisers was sunk. How could it happen? U.S. forces had radar and the Japanese ships didn't. Was U.S. intelligence faulty and the Japanese had recently put radars on their ships? The Japanese forces, from all available information, had suffered no losses. But there was one bright moment after this debacle when, on the night of August 10th, the S-44, the boat from which Captain Baskett had just been transferred, intercepted four of the returning victorious Japanese cruisers and sank the heavy cruiser *Kako*. Captain Baskett had been so happy about the S-44's sinking of the *Kako* that he held a party at the quarters he was assigned to in Brisbane and had a few of his new-found friends, mostly women, on hand to toast the S-44's skipper, Dinty Moore, with large glasses of Emu Bitters beer. Then when the beer ran out he apologetically offered his guests some excellent French champagne that had been issued to him, in lieu of more beer. The rationed supplies of Aussie beer were being rapidly exhausted by our submarine sailors who wanted beer, not wine or liquor. And they got what they wanted from the liquor authorities who leaned over backward to give the U.S. submariners everything they desired or needed. The champagne that was served was an elegant brand, but I noted that the Aussie girls sipped it suspiciously, and some, after further toasts were drunk, slipped half-empty glasses onto a sideboard.

Captain Baskett resembled the reigning King George V closely enough for the girls to treat him with a bit of awe and considerable deference. His thin, patrician face, his self-assured bearing, and his urbane manner were attractive to submariners as well as those civilians he mixed with socially. I had learned that he had a great affection for classical poetry and that one of his favorite poems was Milton's "Lycidas," which he could recite verbatim. So after the toasts were finished, I begged him to recite a few lines from "Lycidas" for the girls, who for the most part were products of fashionable finishing schools in Sydney, or back in England. The captain bashfully hesitated, looking for a little coaxing from his audience. This he promptly got. So he began:

"Yet once more, O ye laurels, and once more,
Ye myrtle brown, with ivy never-sear,
I come to pluck your berries harsh and crude,"

At this point, I interrupted him. "Recite it with gestures, Captain," and I added, "It's much more effective that way." He smiled at me appreciatively, since it heightened the effect of his recitation. He resumed, repeating the line "I come to pluck your berries harsh and crude," and illustrated this with outstretched hands as though plucking the myrtle's black berries. Then he continued:

"And with forced fingers rude
Shatter your leaves before the mellowing year,"

and gestured as though he was destroying the myrtle's foliage before it had borne ripe fruit. This produced much musical laughter from the girls. At this, the captain indicated that no further lines from "Lycidas" would be forthcoming. I urged him to at least recite the final lines that seemed to reflect the fate of submariners, but he said, "There's another time for that," and urged his guests to have more champagne.

Now, as the 37 headed down the Brisbane River my thoughts drifted to Captain Baskett's savoir faire in other social situations. But my thoughts were interrupted by a sighting of the British cruiser *Ajax*. She was heading-in to the up-river port of New Farm Wharf. The *Ajax*, of River Plate fame, along with the light cruiser *Achilles*, had fearlessly tackled the heavily gunned German pocket battleship *Graf Spee* in late 1939 and forced her to scuttle off Montevideo in the South Atlantic. She was now crossing Moreton Bay, inbound. Captain Baskett, foreseeing that the 37 would pass close to the *Ajax* as the 37 exited from the foot of the Brisbane River, ordered the quartermaster to "On the double, run up our colors to the top of the shears." It was difficult to imagine that our rusty old sewer pipe had ever rendered honors to another warship. I also momentarily wondered whether there was an American flag stowed somewhere in the boat. Yet the quartermaster hurried below, reemerged shortly with a U.S. flag, and had it tied to the partially raised number one periscope—by the time our bows overlapped. "Have all hands stand at attention to port," the captain quietly told the quartermaster who then loudly ordered "Attention to port." Surprisingly, the crew on the "Hand salute" order snapped to smart salutes, with or without hats on their heads. It was quite a sight, the shabby S-37 with its men in dirty dungarees passing the spotlessly clean and freshly painted heroic British warship with its crew "manning the rails" in gleaming white uniforms. When the hand salutes were finished the S-37 sailors stood silently appraising the British sailors who had broken into loud cheers for the 37's men as though we submariners were the real heroes of the war. It was like a tramp on a sidewalk watching a passing shiny limousine with its occupants waving gaily at the seedy figure on the edge of the pavement.

Shortly after the S-37 entered Moreton Bay, the captain ordered the boat to be dived to test the success of the refit work done by the *Griffin's* repair people. As the 37 dove slowly and carefully to forty-five feet, the captain was under close scrutiny by the men in the control room. It was their first opportunity to gauge whether their new skipper was more concerned with the mechanical problems of the crotchety 37-boat than with the state of readiness of her crew for fighting the Japanese up in the Solomons. They looked closely for signs of nervousness—a twitching of the jaw, a shaky tone in his voice, a wobbling of the legs. But reassuringly, Captain Baskett, with a small, confident smile, called for reports from all compartments on any problems encountered. He had seemingly accepted the adequacy of his crew in getting his boat ready to fight, and he merely grunted a pleasant "well done" when I quickly reported that I had a good trim at forty-five feet.

Captain Baskett's expectations that all was OK with the 37-boat were rapidly confirmed as the reports that flowed into the control room from all the compartments told of only a few small, readily repaired leaks. But, the after scope was sticky in train, and the drain pump was sparking. They could be rapidly repaired. So the captain without a flicker of uncertainty ordered, "150 feet." For Dome Reynolds this would be the moment of crisis. But there was no agonizing about going deep for Captain Baskett. For a moment I reflected on how we now referred to the previous captain as "Dome," rather than Lieutenant Commander Reynolds or "the captain" and how affectionately we all felt about him, despite the fact that he had voluntarily "turned in his chips."

After a few minutes at deep submergence, with no frantic reports of heavy flooding and imminent disaster, The captain brought the 37 back to forty-five feet, had a quick look around and then surfaced the boat. The radioman was ordered to send "Affirm" to the staff back on the *Griffin*. This meant that the S-37 was fully ready to go on patrol and was heading out of the bay to proceed to her assigned patrol area.

When Caloundra Head was passed abeam and the 37 steered north into choppy seas, the captain announced over the 37's loud-speaker system, "This is the captain. We're proceeding to Area Roger north of Savo Island and close to Guadalcanal and have a very important and very tough job to do. The Japanese will be trying to drive our Marines off the island. The S-37 will be positioned to warn our forces in the Guadalcanal area of any threatening Japanese war-ships. We'll also attempt to sink a few enemy ships while we're doing this picket job." The captain's voice was calm and resolute. A good voice. In fact, it was businesslike and without a hint that the 37's mission was extremely dangerous.

Protecting the U.S. Marines' toehold on Guadalcanal was critical to the U.S. strategy of breaching the Japanese outer defense perimeter that was formed to protect their Indochina and East Indies conquests. The Japanese outer defense perimeter ran from New Guinea, down through the Solomons, then up through the Gilbert and Marshall Islands to Wake. So even the war-weary S-37 had a major role to play if the United States was to win its way back across the Pacific, retake the Philippines, and finally defeat the Japanese Empire.

It wasn't a promising situation for the 37 or for her new skipper. It might be more than he could handle with a rusty old sewer pipe to do the job. Yet I did feel that the officers and crew of the S-37 would do the job. There was no sign that any of the men were worried about the outcome of the patrol. But that was normal for the submariners I'd talked with. All seemed resolute in their acceptance of death, showing the traits of the Japanese Samurai. If "it" happened, that was part of the job. But one didn't dwell on the possibility.

When Monk Hendrix, a Naval Academy '39-er, had handed me a letter to his mother "to be sent to her when I don't come back from our next patrol," I was both surprised and amused that there was someone who had a premonition of death and was sufficiently worried about it to write a last letter for his mother. This sort of thing didn't happen often.

My thoughts about Monk and the letter to his mother were interrupted when Captain Baskett addressed the crew over the 37's MC announcing system. "Here's the really good news," he smilingly said. "After this patrol we'll have a short refit back in Brisbane then the 37 will head back for San Diego for an overhaul." He waited for the cheering throughout the boat to die down before he continued. "There'll be leave for everyone so you can get back home for a couple of weeks."

I was elated. In a month or so I'd be seeing my recently born son and be with my wife. What a break. Less than a year of the war and I'd be home again. And me a father!

My first watch on the bridge from 2100 to midnight seemed to stretch on and on endlessly. Just getting used to doing nothing except peer off into moonless darkness took much readjusting from the frantic and hectic pace of "rest" leave when in port. It was relaxing just to be back in the well regulated at-sea routine of three-hour watches with four watch standers. Tex Lander took a regular turn with the rest of the junior officers. The stars seemed particularly bright and friendly and the waves bounced off the bow with a lulling pleasant rhythm. The patrol had started well.

At dawn on August 18, the 37 made a trim dive and was back on the surface within a few minutes. There'd been no report of leaks. The 37 seemed in better shape than at any time during the war as she hurried north at 325 rpm on the screws. She was running faster and smoother than might have been expected. There was, however, a short stoppage of one engine during the watch, when a jelly fish apparently got stuck on the screen across the circulating water intake. It was easily blown clear.

At breakfast the captain noted that the heavy volume of plain-language messages being received indicated that the Japanese were sending their first-string forces into the Solomons to dislodge the U.S. Marines at Henderson Field.

The activity in "The Slot" was heating up. Yet, the captain suggested that he and Tex get started learning how to play bridge. I'd be the teacher. So after breakfast I got Billy Gibson to make a foursome and then started to demonstrate to Tex and the captain the Culbertson point-count system for bidding. But I wasn't very attentive to my bridge teaching job. I was doing too much thinking about being with my Carol, soon. And then, having a game only when Bobby Byrnes was on watch, because he refused to play bridge, wasn't going to provide the captain with much of an opportunity to learn the game.

On the nineteenth a message from headquarters changed the 37's patrol station from north of Savo Island and a line running between Savo and Cape Esperance on the western tip of Guadalcanal to an area south of Savo Island. The S-41 was moving into Area Roger, which the 37 would vacate.

In the wardroom there was a generally relaxed, pleasant atmosphere as the captain displayed a fine, subtle sense of humor that produced many good laughs. His memory of precise details for many subjects and his accuracy concerning historical facts discouraged the usual wild exaggerations in the wardroom conversations.

The weather had changed radically by August 20th. The 37 rolled heavily with cold green seas sloshing over the men on the bridge continuously. In the afternoon there was a short breakdown of one engine but, as reported by Chief Grady, a rapid change of the intake valve on the second-stage of the main compressor put the boat rapidly back on both engines. The engineroom gang had become very competent in making speedy repairs. Thus, Captain Baskett didn't have to worry about keeping his boat operating. A newsflash on the radio told of a second front being opened in Europe with the invasion by the British at Dieppe, France. But a later broadcast labeled the so-called invasion "only a large commando raid." Still, the reports created much good spirit throughout the boat. The talk in the crew's mess was about the trip back to the States. Before Christmas!

Friday the twenty-first was the last day of surface running during daylight. The air topside had gotten much hotter, yet the winds remained high. In fact, the seas had become so heavy that periodically the propellers came out of the water as the 37 pitched wildly. And the after battery compartment was a foul mess of spilt coffee, beans, sugar, canned fruit and broken plates. But there was no slowing down the S-37. The continuing reports of Japanese ships in the Solomons area indicated a massing of shipping in and around Rabaul and imminent movements towards Guadalcanal. There was a great sense of urgency about getting the 37 to her patrol station.

Next day, we remained submerged all day in accordance with orders to stay down in daylight when north of twelve degrees South. The seas were running so high that there was much trouble in taking periscope looks without broaching. A message from ComSubRon 5 said that there were "no friendly ships north of Cape Esperance." But why send this sort of information to the 37? Later a message from the same source ordered the S-37 to move north of Savo Island when Area Roger was vacated by the 41-boat on August 27.

Early on the twenty-third a landfall was made on Guadalcanal. Tex had been worried about the accuracy of his star sights. They were taken the previous evening through a misty cloud hanging over the water. But as usual, my excellent night vision allowed me to be the first to see a dark mass on the horizon and identify it as Cape Esperance.

At first light, the 37 dove for her all-day submerged patrol. She was then kept continuously at periscope depth on the premise that any Japanese plane so close to the U.S.-held Henderson Field would be too busy looking for Marine fighters in the air to do any searching for a submerged submarine. Periscope looks were taken every ten minutes showing no more than a foot of scope above the water. With the seas much calmer close to the islands at the foot of "The Slot," depth control of the 37 was a simple matter. The periscope watch was actually boring.

There was an ominous quietness throughout the day. But that was the way the Japanese played it. Nighttime was when they swung into action.

When back on the surface just after dark, a message was received from ComSubRon 5 telling of an enemy convoy enroute to Tulagi where the Allies had another foothold in the lower Solomons. The S-41 might see some action, but the 37 was stuck in the southern area below Savo Island and couldn't cross over to get at ships that were headed to a spot north of Guadalcanal. It was bad luck.

At midnight when the general alarm started bonging and word was passed to "Man all battle stations" the captain charged from the wardroom to the control room with an eagerness that was great to see. The diving alarm honked and Bobby Byrnes scrambled down the ladder to report not oncoming ships but that he had sighted a submarine at high speed headed directly at the 37. Even before the 37 was leveled at forty-five feet, the captain had raised the night periscope and was asking for a bearing on the submarine from Bobby. But Bobby had forgotten to take a bearing before he left the bridge. So he just pointed off to the port side of the 37 to indicate that it was somewhere in that general direction. The captain frantically swung the scope back and forth on the port side trying to locate the oncoming enemy submarine. Unfortunately, in the dim light of a clouded-over quarter moon he couldn't spot it. "It looked like a hazy gray ghost" Bobby suggested, as the sound-man reported the sound of screws to port. "He's at almost twenty knots" the soundman guessed. Then all of us in the control room heard the sound of high speed screws churn directly over the 37. It was evident that the enemy submarine was oblivious to the 37's presence and that it was too late to get off a torpedo shot, even at her stern.

The whole sequence of events was as unnerving to the captain as it was to me because I'd let Bobby keep the dive while I tried to get a plot started on the submarine. However, all the pencils had disappeared from their storage tray and in the red-lit dimness of the control room I couldn't even locate plotting paper, thumb tacks or rulers in the drawers of the plotting table. What a way to be prepared to take on the expected Japanese submarine that was sent to clear out U.S. submarines acting as pickets in The Slot.

Later, on my midnight to 0300 watch, a message was handed to me that I read using a shielded flashlight. It told of a fleet of warships heading down The Slot toward Guadalcanal.

Before daylight, the 37 was submerged for her all-day patrol and looks were increased to every five minutes to ensure plenty of advance warning of enemy ships. The build-up of tension was noticeable in the crew as the men moved about with unsmiling faces and talk was reduced to curt sentences dealing with the sub's operations.

The enemy submarine encounter and the message on the approaching warships were forewarnings of trouble, probably within hours. There was plenty of time to build up a good case of nerves. My adrenalin had started flowing when I heard the general alarm sounding and my heart speeded up when Bobby reported seeing the enemy submarine. But the entire incident was over before I felt any sense of fear, or the possibility of being torpedoed. It was easy to see why Bobby, on suddenly seeing a submarine speeding towards him, got nervously confused. It was like having a rattlesnake rear up unexpectedly in the grass close to one's feet. Bobby, like a good officer of the deck, should have rehearsed the step-by-step procedures when spotting a threatening submarine. Getting the bearing came first. It was like a centerfielder fielding a ball hit to him with men on base, and being mentally prepared to throw the ball to the correct bag to nab a base-runner.

After surfacing just after dark, twelve lighted planes were sighted overhead winging back towards Henderson Field. They'd apparently been out bombing the approaching force of Japanese warships. Then I noticed a narrow, clearly defined oil slick off the 37's bow. It had a strong smell of diesel oil, indicating that a submarine had pumped her bilges.

At 2204 I was aroused from my "hot bunk" by the cry of "Battle stations . . . Torpedo attack." The diving alarm followed. A Japanese raiding party was coming in from the west. The captain had been on the bridge with Billy when they saw, at about five miles, four destroyers in column, ahead of two trailing heavy cruisers on either flank. All were barreling towards Guadalcanal at very high speed. Since they were making their approach south of Savo Island it was guessed that the S-41 had been spotted above Savo and the Japanese were steering clear of her area. At least Bobby had dived the S-37 before she was discovered by the patrolling enemy submarine that was encountered earlier.

The captain and I had jokingly discussed the possibility of the S-37 doing something truly important at this point in the Pacific campaign. I'd suggested that the captain be ready with some ringing words to fit the circumstances—words like John Paul Jones's "We have just begun to fight," or Admiral Farragut's "Damn the torpedoes, full speed ahead."

Thus, just after the captain had taken a long steady periscope look at the advancing warships, I edged close to him with a notepad in my hand and said: "Now's the time to say something that will go down in history to mark this moment."

Highly amused at the idea and without giving it more than a moment of thought he said, "We have put our foot in a mare's nest. How does that sound?"

It sounded fine to me. So I handed the quartermaster my notepad and said, "Go ahead and put this in the Log and credit the words to the captain."

On towards the 37 the Japanese warships rushed. They were closing on us so rapidly that there was almost no time to get a decent set-up on the lead-destroyer. Consequently, the captain kept the periscope continuously raised in order to get a good picture of the developing situation. However, even though he put the S-37 into a good firing position with a 1,500-yard range and a ninety-degree starboard track on the lead-destroyer, with the firing of four torpedoes, the attack went haywire. Tex, the diving officer had lost depth control. Then I heard the captain quietly curse and turning towards Tex sadly mutter, "You've dunked me, Tex."

There was a six-degree down angle on the 37 and she was sinking slowly. Evidently, too much water was taken aboard up forward with the firing of the four torpedoes. So Tex had to put on speed and start pumping water out of the forward trim tank to regain forty-five feet, despite the noises being created—none of which were torpedo explosions. Either the 37's noise, or the bio-luminescent torpedo wakes, had been spotted by the lead destroyer. Consequently, he had maneuvered to make the torpedoes miss. In tropical waters much light was emitted by torpedo-agitated microorganisms.

Then all hell broke loose. One destroyer after another churned directly across the 37, despite the 37 being in a continual tight turn to port. Each destroyer, on short-scale pinging, exploded two depth charges close to the 37's hull—breaking glass and shaking the boat, but not much more. The "click-WHAMMMMM" of each charge was clearly heard through the hull. It was guessed that the "click" was the detonator being triggered and the "WHAMMMMM" was the main charge going off.

After sixteen depth charges had been dumped on the 37, the two following cruisers thundered on past with the 37's soundman reporting: "The screws of the big ships are passing down our sides, but they're not close." Then a little later: "The screw noises of all the ships have faded out to the east."

Without delay, the captain ordered "Surface." He neglected the usual preliminary order "Stand-by to surface." He then rapidly swung the scope around to make certain that there were no close ships, particularly the enemy submarine, as the 37 was rising to the surface. It was imperative that the Marines on Henderson Field be quickly warned of the imminent shelling of the airfield by the heavy cruisers with their eight-inch guns.

With the 37 on the surface a few minutes before midnight, a radio antenna was rigged from the front of the bridge to a jackstaff placed on the bow, and a "flash" contact message was sent to headquarters in Perth. Tex, Bobby and I were on the bridge in addition to the captain. We scanned the satiny smooth waters around the 37 for any sign of the Japanese sub that we felt was lurking close by. One engine was put on the battery charge while the captain had the 37 zig-zag wildly to spoil the aim of the enemy sub if she decided to let go a fish at the 37.

At around midnight, we began seeing dim flashes of gunfire out on the horizon to the east. The muffled uninterrupted booms from the big guns of the Japanese ships drifted back to the 37. They indicated that the heavy cruisers were not being bothered by U.S. Marine aircraft. The 37's contact message had evidently not been received on Guadalcanal. But at 0231 a secret dispatch from ComSubRon 5 was received that directed the S-37 and the S-41 to close Lunga Roads at maximum speed, "and attack enemy forces shelling the airfield."

Back on the bridge I found that the battery charge had been secured and that both engines were bent on the screws, with the 37 making flank speed to close Lunga Roads. When I told the captain about the inappropriateness of his "mare's nest" quote because the dictionary said "a mare's nest is a situation of confusion and disorder," he laughingly suggested, "Well, then change mare's nest to read 'rat's nest,' and leave it in the Ship's Log."

Although it had taken the Japanese force only a little over an hour to get to Lunga Roads after they passed by the 37, it would take the 37, hurrying at fourteen knots, at least two and a half hours to get there. By then dawn would be breaking and the shelling would have stopped. We'd be lucky to be in a submerged position to intercept the Japanese force as it headed back up The Slot. Still, the captain pushed the 37 on at her maximum speed. To her destiny?

By 0317 we could see dead ahead tracer streaks across the sky along with bright flashes from rapid gun-fire. And it was at that time that I spotted what I thought were the shears of a submarine well astern and on the 37's port quarter.

I'd begun having the shakes from the moment the 37 had been ordered to close Lunga Roads. An irrational and growing sense of fear had begun to invade my body, making me shiver and sweat. Reporting the sighting of the sub to the captain had taken much self-control, along with a tight gripping of the bridge combing to support

my rubbery legs. I couldn't let the captain detect signs of nervousness either in my voice or in my body.

For the first time in the war, I felt really scared. The captain's
bland reaction to my report only heightened my anxiety. Too casually, he said, "That's the S-41. I was wondering when we'd start
seeing her."

The captain swung his binoculars back to the 37's port quarter
but couldn't spot the dark blob, that I could see quite clearly with
my better night vision. Even the lookouts hadn't spotted the dark
anomaly on the ocean's surface.

My estimate of the range to the submarine following the 37 was
five to six thousand yards and no more. Still, I couldn't see her bow
wake through my binoculars. I stared hard for many minutes, feeling that the friendly, or enemy, submarine must be closing the 37 at
a speed a bit higher that the 37's.

If it was the S-41, a less battered boat, she would make a knot or
more than the 37. So I felt that if it was the S-41 following the 37,
the lookouts would soon make her out and set my fears to rest.

But if it was the Japanese sub, the one Bobby had seen a day ago,
she'd be a newer boat and able to make as high as seventeen knots.
Thus she should close the 37 to torpedo-shooting range in less than
an hour.

The thought made me shake even more violently. So much so, in
fact, that I weakly lowered myself down into the conning tower and
crouched in the back of the tiny cubicle in the most shadowed part
so as to be unnoticeable by the quartermaster or anyone climbing
from the control room up to the bridge.

I watched the luminous minute hand on the conning tower clock
moving ahead inexorably slowly, and had decided to go back up to
the bridge after thirty minutes to see if the submarine trailing the 37
had moved dangerously closer.

As the minutes agonizingly passed, there were no reports from the
bridge that a submarine back aft had been sighted. Was the captain
feeling that I was slipping a cog by imagining that there was an actual enemy threat right behind the 37? In times of high tension, a few
false reports could be expected. They were the nature of war itself.
And the fellow making a false report was always a bit suspect.

I climbed back to the bridge a few minutes before thirty minutes
had elapsed and looked for the dark blob on the port quarter. It was
still there and didn't look much closer, except that I was now able to
make out a white sliver of a bow wake in front of the dark blob.
When I told the captain that "the sub is still following us but is now
a little closer," my throat was so dry that I had difficulty mumbling
the words. I added, "She looks close enough now to get off a long-
range torpedo shot, Captain."

In a barely audible murmur the captain merely acknowledged my report with a "Thank you." Thanks, for what?

How else could I alert the captain that we might have an enemy sub within firing position? So I told the captain of my foreboding.

He laughed tolerantly. Again he indifferently swept the seas off the 37's port quarter with his binoculars. He couldn't see the sub but just then a lookout sang out, "I have a submarine in sight to port, about thirty degrees off our stern."

"Does she look like the S-41?" the captain casually asked.

"Perhaps," the lookout guessed.

I wasn't relieved by the lookout's sighting. Nor were my nerves steadied by the captain's lack of concern for what we might be getting into—either from the trailing sub, the warships that were still shelling the airfield, or perhaps even from the Japanese bombers which had begun dropping loud, crashing bombs in great numbers, in the area of Henderson Field.

I couldn't stay on the bridge and let any of the men see my shivering body, so I returned to the back of the conning tower to get a grip on myself. And to think.

How had this feeling of terror overcome me? Was I feeling real fear or was I letting an overanxious imagination get the better of me? Was I physically exhausted or even a little sick? Perhaps I had the flu or some sort of tropical fever that caused me to be irrational and to sweat and shake violently.

I certainly had lots of time to think about how badly my body was reacting to the situation. I had nothing to distract my mind. It was a sure formula for building up a good case of the nerves. "I've got to do something, not just sit here," I thought. But I felt rooted to the spot, unable to move until the radiant hands of the clock had moved ahead another thirty minutes.

After just twenty minutes I could no longer delay going topside.

The sub was still there back on the quarter and a little closer. But it continued to be more of a dark blob than a silhouette of a sub's conning tower and shears.

"It's the 41," the captain reassured me, even before I observed that the sub looked to be a little bit closer.

Then at 0503 the dark blob disappeared from the ocean's surface in a mass of luminescent whitish foam. I stared even harder through my binoculars at the spot where the submarine had submerged, expecting to see the wakes of a couple of torpedoes heading for the 37 from the spot where the sub had gone down. I was convinced that the blob was *not* the 41-boat. But the seas remained dark and menacing.

At about the same time, the booming of shell-fire and the crashing of bombs stopped and deep silence enveloped the 37. The noise of

the two diesels suddenly sounded deafeningly loud. Almost automatically, the captain ordered, "Slow to one-third speed." That was hardly the right command if a torpedo was about to be shot at the 37.

Nothing happened in the next few minutes as the first light of
dawn crept into the eastern sky. There were no returning warships,
no Marine fighters overhead, no sign of an unfriendly submarine,
and the Japanese bombers had left the area. The Jap warships had
apparently retired on a course that took them to the north of Savo
Island.

The 37 coasted ahead before turning back towards Cape Esperance
and she zig-zagged radically to spoil the aim of a lurking submarine.

My heart slowed down. I stopped my infernal sweating and was
suddenly conscious of having steady legs. I also recalled that the
captain had made no attempt to exchange recognition signals by
blinker gun with the unidentified submarine that had followed the S-
37 for several hours.

As the 37 headed back toward her station south of Savo Island, I
still believed that my fears were justified. Perhaps when the S-41 left
station to head home, her patrol summary would tell something
about her response to the Lunga Roads incident.

Even though I experienced this episode of uncontrolled fear, I
was determined to remain on the 37 and see her back to the States
after this patrol.

At dawn the 37 was dived and proceeded submerged at 2.5 knots
back to her patrol station. All day, the seas around the 37 remained
empty. Then at 1741 the soundman reported "submarine screws to
the east." For the next half hour the screw sounds were tracked. They
were moving north of the 37 and on a parallel course well clear.

At darkness it seemed safe to surface. But when the 37 came
up and the lookouts rushed onto the bridge, one of them immediately spotted a submarine surfacing off the 37's bow. Captain
Baskett diligently studied the unidentified submarine to determine
if it was the S-41. He estimated the range to the stranger at
about 1,500 yards and then cautiously observed that, "Her silhouette
is quite different than an S-boat and although she's bigger than
the 37 she doesn't look like one of our fleet boats." It had to be a
Jap sub!

Unhurried and deliberately he ordered the 37 to be dived. As he
headed below he quietly told the quartermaster to pass the word
"Battle stations, torpedo attack" over the sound-powered telephones so the 37's attack would be developed as quietly as possible. The captain also instructed the quartermaster to "Have forward room ready three torpedoes and report back when they are
fully ready to fire."

When down in the control room, Captain Baskett glued his eye to the periscope and painstakingly swung it back and forth across the bearing of the sub where last seen. But his look was hampered by water flowing from the scope's packing gland down over his head and having to contend with considerable periscope vibration. Not surprisingly, he couldn't see the enemy sub. And soon the sub's screws faded out, ending what had seemed a golden opportunity to destroy the 37's deadly opponent.

I turned into my bunk for some much needed sleep but slept only fitfully at best. Every unusual sound snapped me fully awake. I was understandably jumpy.

On the next bridge watch, Billy Gibson dove the boat when he spotted a submarine to the south of the 37. However, when down, the soundman was unable to hear the screws of the submarine, nor could the captain pick up the submarine through the scope. A phantom sub?

Shortly after the 37 was dived at daylight for her all-day submerged patrol, the soundman reported a submerged submarine passing close to the 37. But long looks through the periscope failed to pick up the enemy submarine's exposed scope. Evidently, she was moving about submerged, hunting for the 37, which was operating in a dead-quiet mode. A cat and mouse game was being played and the 37 was "the mouse."

Just after surfacing, the captain saw in the gathering darkness, two bow wakes close together. The wakes looked as though they were being generated by two PT boats within a few feet of each other. The wakes were closing the 37 extremely fast; so down the 37 went. But once under there was nothing heard and nothing seen through the periscope. "The Loch Ness sea monster," the captain whimsically noted. He then decided that what he'd seen was possibly a twin-float seaplane taking off directly at the S-37.

When back on the surface, the duty radioman intercepted a plain-language message that said that four Japanese battleships and two of their aircraft carriers had been damaged in a big fleet battle southeast of the Solomons on the twenty-fifth. This was the Battle of the Eastern Solomons that saw the Japanese lose the carrier *Ryujo*, and the U.S. have her carriers *Enterprise* and *Saratoga* badly damaged. The Japanese retreated toward the atoll of Truk with their cripples, and never gave the 37 a chance to fire a single torpedo at the fleeing ships.

Close to midnight, Tex, with the watch on the bridge, sighted a ship in the same approximate position as the seaplane. After he dove the 37 to start an approach on the target the captain failed to see anything through the periscope, while the soundman thought he might dimly be hearing the ship's screws. The Loch Ness sea monster again?

Although all of the officers seemed a bit edgy, that didn't seem to be an explanation for phantom contacts. The talk in the wardroom was exclusively about being stalked by the Japs and how the situation might be turned around and the 37 become the hunter instead of this being-the-hunted business. Perhaps there was more than one Japanese submarine sent out to get the 37?

In the midst of this tense and anxious discussion, the captain irrelevantly recalled details of the 37's Ship's Party—held a few days before the 37's departure from Brisbane. He recalled that, "The men were very happy, exuberant and gallant. They all had dates and their Australian girls were very attractive. But the drinking was heavy and the dancing wild. Some of the most romantic sailors bent their girls almost to the floor as they demonstrated 'Hollywood' kisses." This he felt was quite amusing. The captain continued, "One pair collapsed to the floor in the middle of a passionate kiss, only to have the sailor roll over on top of his girl and continue the prolonged kiss." Then he added, "Remember how the fight erupted in the head. Its walls bulged and groaned as loud crashes were heard? I asked Bobby to go into the head to pacify the fighters but Bobby came right out, saying, 'Let them work out their problem without me interfering.'" The captain's tolerance and affection for his crew was evident in the restrained grin he showed during his recollection of what happened at the Ship's Party. Then, he had no more to say. What was he trying to tell us?

Taking the captain's silence as a cue, we resumed our talk about the enemy submarine that was out to get the 37.

For the next several days the 37's scenario was unchanging. An enemy sub would be detected and the crew would be called to battle stations fruitlessly. Japanese warships were giving the 37's patrol area a wide berth. So there was nothing to shoot at. The 37's highly restricted coverage close to a line between Cape Esperance and Savo Island had her frequently disclosed and made her fair game for searching Japanese submarines. She was also useless as a sentinel for reporting enemy warships headed for Guadalcanal.

It seemed as though the situation would change when the 37 was ordered to move north of Savo Island taking over the patrol area of the S-41 on the morning of the 28th. The 41-boat had terminated her patrol and was heading back to Brisbane. The new area allowed the 37 to roam far from Savo Island, if that appeared to be tactically sound.

Before changing patrol stations, Billy, at one hour past midnight of the twenty-seventh, spotted in the dim moonlight a sub scuttling across the wake of the 37. But it was so far off that Billy wisely decided not to dive the 37-boat. Rather, he continued charging batteries, expecting trouble shortly.

After I'd taken the subsequent watch and discovered a heavy oil-slick leading towards Cape Esperance, it seemed certain that the enemy sub had kept on going while pumping her bilges as she headed eastward. I followed the slick hoping to finally spot the sub, but the slick was suddenly terminated, indicating that the sub had submerged. An immediate turn-tail maneuver was executed in case the Japanese sub was lining up the 37 for a torpedo shot.

That evening a message told of the U.S. destroyer *Gamble* surprising a surfaced Japanese submarine near the 37's patrol area and blasting it with gunfire. Hopefully, that meant good riddance to the sub that had been bothering the 37 over the past few days. But it meant that the S-37 was operating dangerously close to friendly U.S. forces.

Once north of Savo, it seemed as though patrolling there might be somewhat more peaceful. And it was, for three days. There were no submarine contacts. While each night we safely watched a display of flashing lights from bombs exploding on Guadalcanal and Tulagi. Searchlights played back and forth across the skies searching for Japanese bombers. Frequently, red tracer-streaks shot up into the skies, like skyrockets taking off from the jungles of the beleaguered islands.

A U.S. newscast that I heard over the radio in the conning tower, the first night north of Savo, said that there had been only three U.S. submarines sunk so far in the Pacific war and that "U.S. submarine sailors when interviewed by the press claimed that the Japanese three hundred-pound depth charges were too light to do serious damage to their submarines and were set so shallow that it was easy to avoid their explosive power by going deep." Tokyo Rose followed this up in her nightly broadcast, warning "U.S. submarine sailors" that "our Japanese warships are going to start using far bigger depth charges with settings so deep that there'll be no way to avoid being sunk." This caused our radioman to append a war slogan to the clipboard used for the routing of messages. It read: "Shoot off your mouth and pull a rickshaw."

On the twenty-ninth, a message from ComSubRon 5 said that a raiding force of five Japanese ships was expected that night and that the S-37 should stay clear of the Tulagi area because U.S. motor torpedo boats had commenced operating there.

Each night, lately, lighted planes came from the east, orbited over the 37 and joined into groups of three or four planes. They then doused their lights and headed northwest up The Slot. In a few hours a group of lighted planes would be seen circling close to the 37, then individual planes would peel off and head back towards Tulagi.

On the first of September just after submerging for the day's patrol, the soundman picked up the noise of submarine screws. The enemy sub had probably been conducting an approach on the 37 which luckily had dived a little earlier than usual.

In the afternoon, four heavy underwater explosions were heard, coming from south of Savo Island. It was hoped that the 42-boat, that had moved into the 37's vacated area, was eliminating our submarine threat.

At twilight, as the 37 was surfaced on a calm sea and in low visibility, the first lookout on the bridge, reported that there was an island close at hand on the starboard side. He pointed it out to the captain, who followed him up to the bridge. The captain took one look, estimated it was a submarine at about five hundred yards and without ordering "Clear the bridge," shouted "Dive, dive" and hurried down the ladder to the control room as the S-37 raced downward to eighty feet—expecting a torpedo any second. When the 37 broke the surface of the sea, she must have been seen immediately by the enemy submarine. But we were up and then back down so fast that neither sub had a chance to shoot a torpedo.

As a result of this encounter, the captain decided that when on the surface the 37 would keep two torpedoes ready with the tubes flooded so that a rapid snap-shot would be possible before diving.

I was asleep the early morning of the second when I heard "Stand-by to fire the two ready torpedoes." This was followed by the diving alarm. I was out of my bunk and speeding into the control room as the people from the bridge scrambled down the ladder. "It was a big submarine, cutting across our bow, but he turned sharply away when he saw us," the captain explained to Tex. There was no opportunity to let go the torpedoes usefully. They would have only been thrown away.

When I went forward to check the two torpedoes whose tubes had been flooded, I rapidly determined that the torpedoes when pulled from their drained-down tubes were full of water. They would have performed no better than a pair of dummy fish if fired.

The Mk-10 torpedoes weren't satisfactory for this sort of cat-and-mouse game. And from all indications, the Japanese submarines were competent and their crews were alert and efficient. They were certainly tough and capable opponents, and had good torpedoes!

Shortly before sundown, nine loud explosions were heard in the direction of Savo Island. Through the scope, there were no indications of what was under attack. No warships were being bombed, no debris was flying into the air, and no structures were being blown up on Savo Island. Was the bombing being done by U.S. planes from Henderson Field, or by Japanese bombers flying down from Bougainville?

As a follow-on to the bombing, in inky darkness on the bridge that evening, Billy was startled by a series of blinked bright lights beamed from Savo towards the 37. Billy's first reaction was to yell "Dive, dive." But he waited for a few seconds and the blinking stopped. Were the people on Savo trying to get a message to the 37-boat?

I noted that Tex was looking a little strained from all of these crazy goings-on. In fact, goofy dreams involving submarines had invaded all of our slumbers.

When Billy relieved me for the early morning watch, he told about the dream he had just had. As he related it: "I was at home and telling my high school gang about fighting the war near Guadalcanal and being hunted continually by enemy submarines. I was feeling quite a hero. But then I was rudely interrupted by one of my stay-at-home friends. He claimed that he was a 'real hero of the war' because he worked for pay-and-a-half on Saturdays instead of double pay." Billy then said, "I was so impressed by my friend's great sacrifice for the war that in a following scene in my home-town—but with a different gang—I humbly retold the story of my pay-and-a-half friend as an example of true heroism."

Before midnight, and after I'd turned in for some sleep, there was a cry from the bridge, "Standby one and two." Bobby Byrnes, who had the watch, saw what he thought was a submarine close aboard. He started swinging the 37 to line her up for a zero gyro angle shot.

The captain hurried to the bridge and in the moonless darkness determined that it was not a submarine but something much bigger and farther out. And it was moving slowly, since no bow wake was visible. Ahead of the big ship another somewhat smaller ship came into view. An escort? The captain whispered to Bobby, "The big ship has a long, low silhouette with lots of bulk around its forward mast. She's half again longer than the other ship." A crippled cruiser limping back to Rabaul? The bomb explosions heard at sunset might have been U.S. dive bombers attacking a Japanese raiding force. So the present targets could be stragglers from that force heading back up The Slot. The timing was about right for landing troops on Guadalcanal and then heading home past Savo Island.

Down in the control room I watched the 37's gyro repeater steadying on a ship's course of 347° True. Then I heard a quiet order to "Fire one." Ten seconds later there was another but barely audible command, "Fire two." I felt reassuring jolts to the 37 as both torpedoes were sent on their way.

After a minute there was the command "Dive, dive," and down came four men from the bridge. The quartermaster remained in the conning tower to secure the upper hatch, which really needed securing as a torrent of water was dumped into the control room. Then he yelled that a dog was stuck under the hatch but that he was clearing it. The flowing water that had followed the men who scrambled down the ladder, suddenly subsided.

I glanced at the control room clock. It read 2219.

When I asked the captain the range and speed of the targets he said that he'd estimated the range as about 2,500 yards to the big target and its speed as no more than nine knots. He had used the speed-plus-three thumb rule and corrected the 37's course to lead the target by twelve degrees so as to have straight bow shots for both torpedoes. The targets, he felt, were broadside-to when the torpedoes were fired and that they would produce a spread across the big ship of about fifty yards.

Then Bobby started explaining that the small ship had swung around and was headed towards the 37. At this, he said, "The captain pulled the plug and down we went." There was no explanation as to why the 37 wasn't kept on the surface and two more fish readied to make sure of finishing off such a big ship. Bobby did add: "I saw the wakes of the two torpedoes nicely leading the target before I followed the captain down the ladder."

Neither the captain nor Bobby seemed to be intently listening for the hoped-for torpedo hits. But at just about two minutes after the first torpedo had been fired there was an explosion and then another ten seconds later. The men in the control room said, "Those are both hits." At the same time, the soundman reported, "Two torpedo hits heard on sound."

The 37 was taken to 150 feet as one set of screws was reported to be closing the 37. The other set of screws, according to the sonar operator, "are moving very slowly and slowing down. They have a heavy beat, like a very big ship." Soon after, the soundman said that he was now hearing only one set of screws and that they were fading out towards the northwest.

The entire attack was very unsatisfactory. The 37 should have stayed on the surface and put more torpedoes into the big ship to make sure she sank. Had she only been damaged and was then taken in tow by the smaller ship? We couldn't know the effect of the 37's torpedoes until we resurfaced and examined the area for signs of wreckage that might indicate that the big ship had gone down. But, even if she had, we'd probably not get credit for her sinking because the Navy dive bombers heard earlier would already have claimed her as being hit and sunk.

I recorded in my journal that "I felt practically nerveless through-out the attack. With no sweating." Also, that "I'm getting used to this kind of business."

Then, in the early morning, the 37 approached a large oil slick in the general area where the attack had occurred. The 37 was conned down the slick's path to where it originated. At that spot, bubbles of oil were coming up from below and bursting at the sea's surface. The nasty aroma of oil was so strong that men inside the boat were suddenly aware of a definite smell of oil as the sub was circled around the spot looking for additional evidence of a sinking. There were boards and chunks of wood in the water around the oil slick but no life preservers. Perhaps observers on Savo Island might pro-vide an assessment of the 37's attack success.

Tex relieved me of the watch and an hour later dove the 37. He claimed that a submarine was trying to ram the 37. The submarine's screws were heard by the soundman as the 37 submerged. It was no Loch Ness monster! Tex then eased the boat down to 120 feet as the enemy sub passed overhead, with her screws being heard through the hull. Alarmingly, the 37 started getting heavy from a big leak near the stern.

I ran aft to discover that the engines were flooding because of a blown out plug in the header. An engineman had left the bypass to an engine's muffler open on the dive. By the time I got to the engine-room the bypass had been closed and the flooding was stopped. But things were "grimmo" as the Jap sub hovered somewhere above us. With extra speed, a trim was maintained while the engines were drained and the bilges pumped to sea. It took until 1000 to get the 37 back to forty-eight feet for some cautious looks.

After midnight, a message was received from ComSoWesPacFor advising of friendly ships operating north of Savo Island on September 4. Then at 0622 after diving, a large "Hypo" flag on a bamboo pole that was fixed to a float, was sighted through the periscope. It was supposed to mean something to somebody but there was no Signal Book on board the S-37 and no one could remember how "Hypo" had been used in peacetime.

Within an hour, two U.S. 1,200-ton four-stack destroyers were sight-ed heading for the 37. They were converted troop transports that used two of their firerooms as troop berthing spaces. The pings from their sonars centered on the 37, indicating that they held contact on her. But the destroyers paid no attention to their submarine contact and they never got closer than 2,000 yards. After orbiting off Savo for the next two hours they headed into an inlet of the island. Each destroyer flew a "Sail" flag at its foretruck and carried a flag hoist of "Unit Hypo Victor." This also proved meaningless to everyone on the 37-boat.

After noon, the destroyers came out to sea from the island and then disappeared in the direction of Tulagi. Having friendly ships in the S-37's patrol area meant that from now on every ship had to be identified before a torpedo was fired. And that meant that in the blackness of night we'd have to exchange recognition signals by blinker light. If it happened to be an enemy ship being challenged, the 37 might be blasted with shell-fire before she could be dived. Consequently, the sensible thing to do was to pull well clear of Savo Island until the sixth when the 37's orders called for terminating the patrol and heading home.

Shortly after the two destroyers had departed, Bobby Byrnes, who was on the periscope watch in the control room, reported seeing an enemy periscope. The soundman confirmed that there were "faint propeller beats on the same bearing." It was more of the same.

At breakfast in the wardroom, just after coming up for the night's patrol, we sang "Happy Birthday to You" to the captain, who on September 4th had become twenty-nine years old. Seven years out of the Academy and he had command of a submarine! But he was a lot older than the average U-boat skipper who, at this point in time, was no more than about twenty-four years of age.

I took this opportunity to ask the captain to recite Milton's "Lycidas." All of it, and with gestures. At this he smiled appreciatively, but said he'd only recite the last part:

> ". . . Comes the blind fury with the abhorred shears
> And slits the thin-spun life. But not the praise."
> ....
> "(Lycidas) . . . perhaps under the whelming tide
> Visit's the bottom of the monstrous world.". . .
> ....
> "Fame is the spur that the clear spirit doth raise
> (That last infirmity of a noble mind)
> To scorn delights and live laborious days."

Was "Fame" actually the captain's goal as a commanding officer? He was certainly living a Spartan life to achieve it.

Then the captain recited the final lines:

> "At last he rose and twitched his mantles flew:
> Tomorrow to fresh woods, and pastures new."

He stood up, raised his smiling head, smoothed his shirt and flung his hand outward in a "noble" gesture, that indicated that he would shortly leave the 37 to get command of a big, new fleet boat on which he would gain both "praise" and "fame."

In the middle of the captain's recitation, Tex called from the bridge to report that a bright light had flared up on Savo Island and then had been rapidly extinguished, without anything further happening.

When I took over the watch at 2100, I immediately had to get someone to relieve me so that I could check on a major casualty to the starboard engine. There proved to be a cracked head on number seven cylinder of the starboard engine and there was water in the cylinder. This necessitated seven hours of mule-hauling the five-hundred-pound cylinder head out of the engine and putting in a new one. It also meant that the 37 was forced to lay-to. The other engine had to rapidly pour amps into an almost exhausted battery. It was a highly dangerous situation with a Japanese submarine lurking somewhere close by. And it was a real damper on the captain's birthday celebration.

On the early morning watch, I was handed a message reporting that "At least two enemy destroyers shelled Tulagi at 0100." Expectantly, the men on the bridge peered to the east to spot the two destroyers dashing back up The Slot past the 37. But when four illuminating flares drifted down through the skies south of Savo, and then another four a few minutes later, it seemed evident that the two destroyers had made their escape through the 42's area. Another message told of a Japanese transport with an escort of two destroyers having landed some troops on Malaita Island, only forty miles from Florida Island. It was an amphibious landing on a shoestring. One of desperation.

The captain was so unhappy about operating in an area plagued with the presence of friendly ships and enemy submarines that he decided to start easing the 37 off station before the deadline to depart "at sunset of the fifth."

The 37 ran on the surface during the day of the sixth and made the Rossel Islands before dark. This was important, to ensure that the 37 would not go aground like the S-39 had managed to do. The heat was oppressive and stifling, forcing the crew to exist in the blasts of high-speed fans. Heavy rains topside had made the inside of the sub so humid that sweat dripped all over the strip ciphers and paper on which I was recording decoded messages. Moreover, it was necessary to decode messages for four straight hours. The messages lacked brevity and violated virtually all good rules for communication security. Evidently, U.S. communication staffs were overloaded with inexperienced newcomers who didn't understand the principles of simplicity and speed in communications.

On the seventh, the waves had grown so mountainous that the engines were cut to 2/3 speed and the 37 was forced to run with the upper hatch closed. Since air for the engines had to be drawn into the boat through the main induction, large shots of seawater kept pouring into the engineroom. This forced the bilge pumps to work overtime. Also, the water from the freshwater tanks, with all the rolling and pitching had turned a dark rust-color, and was full of pieces of dirt. Therefore, I had to send Montero, the stewardsmate, back to the evaporators to get a pitcher full of clear water for use in the wardroom.

The next few days were more of the same. Men on the bridge kept coming below with battered heads and cut faces. One lookout, washed from his perch, had gashed his face on an angle iron. A bloody mess, he was led to the wardroom for my medical help. I was now the Ship's Doctor, there being no medical rating on board and Tex was sick and tired of the job. The deep cut running from his forehead to his split jaw needed surgery. So I cleaned the injury of broken bone, cartilage and smashed teeth, poured a lot of hydrogen peroxide into the wound and then sprinkled ground up Sulfa into the gash. My attempts to sew up the man's face with the dull needles available, resulted only in much cursing and agonized screaming. So I closed the wound with adhesive tape and decided to let the tender's doctor complete the job. The man was then given a half glass of Old Overholt brandy to assuage his pain.

By Thursday the tenth the weather had cleared and field day was held. It was amazing to see how dirty the boat had gotten. Trash of all sorts was everywhere.

With little happening in the next few days, I thought a lot about the 37's assignment to the Guadalcanal area.

The 37's sixth war patrol had started with great expectations as to the important role she could play in the Pacific campaign. But there were shortcomings. I underestimated the Japanese response—their having at least two competent, big Jap subs continually harassing the 37's operations and keeping tabs on her proximate position at all times.

In retrospect, the admiral's strategy for employing the 37 was badly flawed. As Captain Baskett wrote in the patrol report he was preparing, "A submarine is better employed in enemy shipping areas than at a point of concentrated enemy attack. Pinned to a narrow station with the enemy aware of the 37's location, she was worse than useless on our station." And when friendly forces began to operate in the 37's patrol area she should have been pulled clear. But wasn't.

Worst of all, the admiral's employment of the 37 had virtually eliminated her capability to attack enemy targets with surprise—the most important element in submarining. In effect, any submarine used in a blockade role tended to be misused. (Tellingly, the frequent use by the Japanese of their submarines in a blockade strategy during the war, not only squandered their threat against U.S. ships in the Pacific, but also resulted in their submarines suffering heavy losses to U.S. forces because their positions were readily established.)

Reflecting on what might have been versus the hard facts of what actually happened made me reappraise my desire and intention to get back as quickly as possible to be with my wife and new son Billy, Jr., I began to realize that fighting the war in a broken-down and relatively ineffective S-boat would not provide much of a legacy for a future naval career. Nor would it provide satisfying memories of my contribution to the war effort. This war was an opportunity not to be missed. It was thus prudent to get off the 37-boat and be assigned to a big fleet boat to make some truly successful patrols, and hopefully to have a crack at sinking a Japanese sub with a better than an even chance of being successful.

S-boats were old (twenty or more years) and the equipment was about worn out. The fleet boats on the other hand were no more than three or four years old and the equipment, except for the Nelseco diesel engines, was proving reliable.

An S-boat's habitability was terrible. The periscopes vibrated too much and the fire control of torpedoes was crude and too much a matter of by-guess-and-by-God. By comparison, the fleet boats had air conditioning, bunks with mattresses for all hands, several heads, and enough water for showers. Also the fleet boat periscopes had only minor problems. They exhibited little vibration. They had barely noticeable leakage of seawater. And they had little fogging, and what they had could be readily eliminated by putting a moisture absorbent inside the periscope barrel. But what I liked most about the fleet boats was that they had an Mk-1 analog fire control computer that promised more than the bow-and-arrow guesstimates of the S-boats. And then the fleet boats had fifty percent more speed on the surface and could therefore become a significant threat in night surface attacks, as was being demonstrated by the German U-boats in the Atlantic.

I would have to do it. Transfer to a big boat and not go home. Or I'd spend the rest of my life regretting it. But how to tell the captain?

By Saturday the twelfth, the weather had cleared. So the captain let the cigarette deck be filled with half-naked crewmen. Field day was held throughout the 37.

By that evening, the seas had picked up and a pelting rain had set in. Tex finally got some star sights and discovered that the 37 was far off course. Consequently, the sub did some brutal ploughing into heavy waves to close Cape Moreton Light off Brisbane by dawn of the thirteenth. As before, we were challenged by the army shore station guarding the bay and as before the army used an incorrect challenging procedure. When a correct recognition signal was sent by the 37, the shore station gave the wrong reply. There was much blinking back and forth to straighten things out, and all the while the 37 was posing as good bait for any Japanese submarine that might be lurking off the entrance to Moreton Bay. Identified or not, the 37 proceeded on in through the swept channel and headed up the Brisbane River, arriving at New Farm Wharf by 0800.

Immediately after we had tied up to the S-41 in a nest alongside the *Griffin*, I dashed across the gangway to the 41-boat to find out from her officers what had happened to the 41 on the night of the twenty-fifth—the night our two boats had been ordered in to Lunga Roads to intercept the Japanese warships that were shelling Henderson Field on Guadalcanal. The 41's Exec said, "We never received any orders to close Lunga Roads because we were held down by a pair of Japanese destroyers who depth charged us until well after midnight." He added that "We were really dumbfounded by a message which we received at about four the next morning which told the 41 to resume station in Area R. We never did find out where the 41 should have been until right now, from you."

The submarine that had followed the 37 to Lunga Roads was unquestionably a Japanese submarine trying to get into a firing position! No wonder I had generated such a level of uncontrolled fear. My extreme concern was more than justified.

As for the cruiser we hit with two torpedoes on the night of September 2, bits of intelligence and rumors indicated that a Jintsu-class cruiser had been lost before her expected arrival at Kavieng "in the first days of September." Admiral Christie's endorsement to the patrol report was reassuring: "The persistence of an oil slick for 3 days, whereas no oil slick was present prior to firing, strongly supports the belief that a destroyer or light cruiser sank from the two torpedo hits." As a result, the admiral classed 37's patrol as "successful."

There were additional clues dealing with the mysteries of this patrol. On the fourth of September, because of rumors that the Japanese had occupied Savo Island, the 1st Raider Battalion of Marines from Tulagi were ferried to Savo in the converted U.S. destroyers *Little* and *Gregory*. Finding no Japanese on Savo the Marines went on to Guadalcanal.

The man whose face had gotten my primitive medical treatment, saw the tender doctor who said, "Your wound has stayed good and fresh and can easily be mended. The 37's doctor has certainly done a fine emergency job on your face." Oh?

At one point, I tried to locate Monk Hendrix and find out about the letter he wrote to his mother. But he'd been transferred to the fleet-boat *Sturgeon* and had gone off on patrol. So I never heard what happened to his letter.

When the S-42 arrived back at Brisbane, her exec said that when the 42 moved into the area south of Savo Island that the 37 had just vacated, two torpedoes were fired at her by a submerged enemy submarine. One of the wakes of the fish passed under the four-inch gun forward of the bridge. But it was an illusion because the wake lagged the deep-set torpedo that had passed just ahead of the bow. The exec noted that on smelling the hot-running torpedo oil coming from the torpedo's wake, he had remarked to the quartermaster: "I've never smelled anything yet that smelled so much like fiery brimstone." A guilty conscience? The exec also said that they were hunted by one or more Jap subs all through their entire patrol.

On arrival at New Farm Wharf I had looked around for the "big boats" that were supposed to be there by the time we arrived back. When there were no fleet boats in port, I was momentarily pleased. I would just have to stay on the 37 and go home. My problem seemed solved.

But then on October 3rd, four of the big boats arrived, two days before the 37 was scheduled to leave for the States. So now I'd have to tell the captain of my decision to stay behind. But not to install radars, because several civilian technicians had arrived to do that job.

I walked irresolutely into Captain Baskett's cabin on the tender *Griffin*. He had moved to the tender in the last few days before the S-37's departure. I felt a certain hesitancy in taking the final step that would cause me to lose the opportunity to be home before Christmas. A little breathless and conscious of my heart, I went straight to the point. "Captain, I want to get off the 37 and get on a fleet boat. I feel I ought to make some more war patrols this year."

The captain was pleased in a fatherly way. "I'm all for that, Bill." He looked ready to pat me on the head. "We can manage with only four officers for the trip to San Diego. But we'll all miss you on the way back." He was thinking about more bridge lessons, and some guitar lessons that I'd just started giving him. Then as an afterthought he asked, "Will you paint me a watercolor of the S-37 in her nest alongside the *Griffin* before we leave?"

I promised to start the painting immediately. And did. But it was not until five minutes before the S-37 backed out into the Brisbane River that I passed the completed picture to the gangway watch for delivery to Captain Baskett.

Then, it was quite a sad affair to wave good-bye to Tex, Billy, Bobby, and Tom Baskett. They, however, exuded such cheerfulness as they waved back that I had a twinge of regret and depression. And I had a foreboding of the trouble a big boat could get me into if she had an aggressive skipper to serve under. I knew I was asking for it.

Much later, I heard that Tom Baskett had finally gotten command of a big boat. The *Tautog*. After three runs with her in 1944, he had sunk eight confirmed ships. Then he transferred to the *Tench* in '45 for two runs and sank four more ships. He finished the war as one of the top U.S. submarine skippers. He achieved "Fame" but wasn't dead "ere his prime . . . under the whelming tide."

3

The Red Dragon

On November 23d, 1942, at 1330, the "Dragon," so named by the crew of the fleet boat *Seadragon*, pulled noiselessly away from New Farm Wharf on battery power and set sail for the Solomon Islands. She was headed out for her fifth war patrol. The day was warm and balmy as the Dragon moved into the Brisbane River. Summer had just started "down under" in Australia, and wildflowers were in great profusion along the river banks. Meadows beside the river were an unusual lush green, unlike the scorched-brown color of the Australian countryside for the past ten arid months of the year.

When well clear of the dock, two diesel engines were started up with a loud roar and propulsion was shifted from the batteries to the main engines. Shortly, water was sprayed into the engine exhausts to muffle their sound. Still there was sufficient noise to alert a large number of Australians to the Dragon's passing. They flocked to the banks of the river to gather there and watch the Dragon's departure. Many of the spectators yelled words of encouragement to the men who were topside.

"Get one for me, cobber" was meant for the captain. He waved toward the voice at the side of the river.

"Good luck, mates," "Happy hunting," "Go get 'em, Yanks" were shouted to include all of us. Words of encouragement were more in evidence than on the S-37's departure. It was like running out on the football field back at the Naval Academy, with the people in the stands up on their feet cheering loudly to get the Academy players hyped up for a big game.

To the Aussies, "the Yanks" were keeping the war away from their shores, so they were very appreciative of the American presence "down under." Their good-humored shouts and hand clapping as the Dragon passed them, reminded me of an old Pathé news scene showing our World War I doughboys marching down New York's

Fifth Avenue towards their transports at the Battery. They were going overseas "to make the world free for democracy." The troops were laughing and marching with springy steps as though delighted to be going to their slaughter in the trenches of France.

The Dragon's crew had much the same carefree optimism about going back into the war. Nobody seemed to be a reluctant dragon. The Dragon was going on patrol, certain of doing a great deal of damage to the Japanese. Then in sixty days she'd return to the United States where the crew would celebrate with their families. It was common knowledge that after this patrol the Dragon would be overhauled at Mare Island, California. And that meant at least a month of leave to go home.

After entering Moreton Bay at the foot of the river, the captain ordered the boat to be dived in order to check her seaworthiness before heading out on patrol. Once submerged, I started overhearing Chief Quartermaster Bueb reporting to the captain the discrepancies within the boat that were being received over the sound-powered telephone: "The battery wells are dry . . ." "Only a few small leaks in the after room . . ." "There's a bit of leakage around the pit-log arm, but we can take up on the packing . . ." "The pumproom bilges are dry . . ." "No sign of water under the motors."

At one point, the excitable, youthful chief blurted to the captain, "Even the negative tank functioned well on the dive, Sir." It seemed an unnecessary report and I wondered why Bueb had made it.

The Dragon was a great improvement on the 37-boat that had so many leaks on her first dive after her refit that she had to return to New Farm Wharf to get them fixed before again trying her deep dive and then proceeding on patrol.

Even though the *Seadragon* was a badly battered and patched up veteran of four successful war patrols, there were no excited reports of things not working. There was nothing to make the Dragon return for more tender refit work.

It was great to be on a boat that was ready to fight. Submerging and then going deep was a routine affair. The Dragon was taken to only two hundred feet but that was much deeper than would have been risked with the S-37. This was still a far cry from the reported nine hundred feet some Nazi skipper had gone to and still brought his U-boat back to the surface to fight more of the war.

When the Dragon was surfaced after only a brief time submerged, she was swung through 360° to record the deviations of her magnetic compass on all headings. The refit had caused some magnetic changes in the boat's configuration that had to be compensated for by adjusting the position of the steel balls that were located alongside the compass. Then the diesel engines were revved up to full speed and the Dragon charged northward like a horse let out of the barn after a long confinement.

Making eighteen knots, the Dragon departed from Moreton Bay and passed Caloundra Head at 1600. She was headed into a flat, calm sea. Two lookouts, standing watch on the cigarette deck were added to the two regular watch standers who were perched on the Dragon's shears. The men topside intently looked for signs of a Japanese submarine lying in wait, hoping to torpedo an exiting U.S. boat.

A Jap sub had been reported several times in the past weeks just outside of Moreton Bay. A swirl in the water had been seen after the sub had dived. His shadow was observed by fishermen out on the horizon at night. Several brief periscope exposures had been spotted.

"The price of safety is eternal vigilance," I kept mumbling to myself as I went on watch with Rollo Miller on the bridge. I was to be the junior officer of the deck under Rollo in a make-you-learn status for at least one week. Then I'd be qualified as a regular officer of the deck of a "fleet boat."

Rollo promptly advised me with a note of humorous, fatherly superiority in his voice that "You S-boat sailors had better pay close attention to the way we do things on these big boats." Then he flippantly counseled, "When you're standing watches with me there'll be no guitar playing or harmonizing with the lookouts." This comment reflected his days with me as a roommate at the Naval Academy. He added, "This is war and we've got to be serious about it." Rollo serious about something?

Rollo was, in fact, responsible for my being aboard the Dragon. After the S-37 had left without me, I had to find myself another submarine to go to sea with. But there were no vacancies on any of the big subs for more than a month. During this time I did personnel work and decoded messages for Red Hot Smith, the tender Griffin's skipper. Then Lt. Cmdr. Pete Ferrall, the skipper of the Seadragon, which was alongside the Griffin, learned that he could get his exec, Bub Ward, a Prospective Commanding Officer cruise on one of the subs leaving shortly on patrol. After that one patrol, Bub would get his own boat. So Bub was transferred off the Dragon and Rollo immediately saw the chance to get me aboard to fill the gap left by Bub's transfer.

Rollo then told Captain Pete that I was available, a topnotch war-experienced officer, and most importantly that I was a very good Hearts player. That put me on the spot from the moment I moved on board. Rollo felt that Captain Pete was doubtful about having me ordered to the Seadragon. So he appealed to the captain's Naval Academy loyalty by emphasizing that we had been roommates there. At this the captain laconically muttered, "Tell him to get his orders from the Flag Secretary." And that was it. The captain, I was to learn, did things intuitively. But he was always quite sound.

"Go get your orders fast," Rollo urged, "Because we're leaving Monday at noon." That was on Friday, the twentieth of November. I rushed to the tender *Fulton*, a newly arrived submarine tender, to get Jack Lewis, the Flag Secretary, to write some orders for transfer from my tender job to the *Seadragon*. Yet it wasn't that easy. Jack Lewis had to initiate a dispatch to Admiral Lockwood, Commander of Submarines Southwest Pacific at Perth, asking his approval for the transfer.

With the weekend intervening, no action was taken. So Monday morning found me without an answer to my request. Still, I carried all my belongings over to the Dragon, hoping that the admiral's reply would arrive before the 1330 sailing time.

Just before noon, a yeoman came over from the tender with a copy of my orders to the *Seadragon*. When I handed them to Smokey Manning, the exec, he gave me the traditional "Welcome aboard," along with a powerful handshake. Certain that I'd join the Dragon before sailing, he relayed to me the captain's wishes and "You'll bunk with the captain in his stateroom." To my surprised, quizzical look, Smokey added, "The captain wants it that way." This was very unusual since all the skippers I had heard about had their own private stateroom. They never suffered the bother of another officer thrashing around in a nearby bunk or having to hear a messenger wake the junior officer to go on watch. Even worse, having to smell the sweaty guy after drills. Smokey relayed more instructions, "The captain will tell you which drawers you can use. And you'll be sleeping in the top bunk, over the captain—who doesn't snore."

More important, I wondered what my job would be. So I asked Smokey casually what was lined up for me.

Smokey's answer sounded mighty indifferent, as though I was considered excess baggage. "I guess you'll fill Bub Ward's spot as assistant approach officer in the conning tower and you'll also learn the boat." That was it. The Dragon had managed with only five officers on previous patrols so only the loss of an executive officer should make a difference. And Smokey clarified this by saying that he would continue to be the diving officer at battle stations and that "Luther Johnson, a Georgia Tech man, was now the engineering officer."

All of this confounded my ideas of how a submarine was organized, at least as I'd learned it at Submarine School. Perhaps for one run it wouldn't make any difference. But once the Dragon was back in the States in overhaul, I felt the captain would change the organization, tighten it up, and give me a good job.

As I stood beside Rollo at the front of the bridge with binoculars glued to my eyes, I wondered whether a card game came first on this boat. My first watch at sea was devoted solely to looking and making sure everyone else topside was concentrating on the waters around us to spot a periscope or incoming torpedoes. Even the men lounging around on the cigarette deck aft of the bridge, while carrying on relaxed conversation, were not watching each other but were focussed on the flat ocean from which might come a sudden, unexpected attack. Moreover, a four-hour watch gives a person a lot of time to think, and I was wondering if the Dragon would do much of a job of sinking ships, considering the laissez-faire attitude that I was encountering.

Rollo, as though guessing my thoughts, quietly reassured me, as he continued to sweep his binoculars across the sea, that the captain was a brave guy who'll sink some ships. "He'll scare the hell out of you when we're in battle and he's already got seven ships under his belt." As for the Hearts business, "it's his only recreation and he needs it to relax. Remember this, he has to be in command of the outcome of the games to reenforce his status as the smartest lion in the jungle." Rollo made it clear that he'd set me up by claiming I was a good card player. "The captain feels he's an expert at Hearts and tries to humiliate any other player who thinks he can play as well. Just take your losses pleasantly, Ruhe, because the captain will really lay it on, if you get mad at his tactics. Bub Ward got mad on one occasion and threw his cards on the table when the captain gave him the Queen of Spades once too often. So the captain threw *his* cards on the table and stomped out of the wardroom."

I was properly forewarned, but found it hard to believe that getting the upper hand in a mere cards game in the middle of a war could be very important. But it was.

The *Seadragon's* sailing orders read: "Conduct unrestricted warfare along the east coast of New Ireland between latitudes four degrees and six degrees South until January 3, 1943, and then proceed to Pearl Harbor." But such orders didn't promise much action since the battle for Guadalcanal seemed to be drawing to a close. Perhaps there'd be another attempt by the Japanese to sail a fleet of warships down The Slot, escorting a group of transports for the relief of the remaining Japanese troops on Guadalcanal. But that didn't seem likely because of the heavy losses they would probably sustain. If the Japanese did start moving in December, the Dragon would see brief action against the big Japanese warships coming out of the fleet anchorage at Kavieng, on the northern tip of New Ireland. And that would be it, since no merchant traffic was using the northeast side of New Ireland as a pathway to the Solomons. A one-attack business. After having the 37 forced deep by columns of Japanese warships on my previous patrol with little opportunity to fire torpedoes, this patrol seemed to be stacking up as a real loser. Still, the Dragon was a far more powerful boat that the 37-boat and might strike a telling blow against the Japanese fleet.

The Dragon had ten torpedo tubes, six forward and four aft and was carrying twenty torpedoes. This meant that initially the torpedomen were sleeping on top of torpedoes rather than in the bunks that were rigged after the torpedoes had been shot. Four more torpedoes might have been carried in topside deck tubes, but they were empty. The existing torpedo shortage caused the Dragon to carry less than a full load of fish.

With air conditioning, the crew was in far better physical shape than the men on the 37-boat. They weren't bothered by the Guam blisters that were endemic to the overheated, 100 percent humidity in the old S-boats. Nor did the crew slide on decks made slippery by the moisture dripping from the inner side of the hull. Additionally, there was no sleeping in pools of sweat, even though a patrol was close to the equator. Most importantly, the Dragon had been fitted with an SD air-search radar that could pick up aircraft out to about twenty miles. But low flyers could get in undetected by flying beneath the upward beamed lobe of radiation.

I liked the idea of being on a submarine with a name instead of a number. A "*Seadragon*" sounded dangerous. But the dictionary disappointingly said that a seadragon was a small, black, spiny fish of the sculpin variety. It had a large head, broad mouth and a little body. In fact, one of the fishermen on board told me that it was "the ugliest looking fish there is. When you catch one on a rod and line you always throw it back in." The dictionary claimed that it was good to eat and was used in bouillabaisse.

With Rollo running the deck watch close beside me on the tiny open bridge there was much time to recall all that I'd heard about his doings since I last saw him, enroute to Submarine School in early 1941.

He was at the bombing of Cavite and took part in the removal of people from Corregidor. He helped in the first appendectomy aboard a submarine, the *Seadragon*, and took MacArthur's belongings from one of Buckley's PT boats along with a ship-load of sick U.S. medical personnel down to Australia. Then he had a torpedoman shoot a torpedo inboard through the forward room that just nicked the chin of a chief who was shaving in front of a mirror on the after bulkhead. But the best story he told was about the Tokyo Rose broadcasts in which she identified "the scourge of the China Seas" as "the red submarine" that was sinking a good many important Japanese troop transports.

"Rollo" was a nickname he had picked up on entering the Naval Academy. His guileless, boyish, smooth-faced demeanor along with his curly blond hair and cynical amused expression had suggested a likeness to a comic-strip character named Rollo who was a momma's boy and always plotting pranks against his comic-strip friends. Rollo was such a tolerant person that he put up with my doings in a gracious manner, only chiding me for my own good, he claimed. His war patrols had left no mark on him. No jitters, no moodiness. He was just a steady, competent, relaxed officer in the middle of a really hot war. It was going to be fun to be with him again.

When I asked him why the *Seadragon* looked so beat-up around her topsides with dents in the shears and welded plates randomly spaced over the outside of the conning tower, he told me of the bombing of the Dragon back in the Philippines. "It was three days after Pearl Harbor. We were tied up alongside the *Sealion* at Cavite when about fifty Jap bombers came over—so high we could scarcely see them from the deck of the Dragon. The Japs dropped bombs all over the place and a lucky Jap bomb hit the *Sealion* alongside with lots of shrapnel piercing the Dragon's conning tower as well as riddling the Dragon's topsides. Smokey Manning and Sam Hunter were in the Dragon's conning tower at the time. Sam was killed outright by a big piece of shrapnel which hit him in the head. Smokey had only a few fragments of metal, like shotgun pellets, pepper his skin."

Smokey, overhearing Rollo's description of the *Seadragon*'s baptism by enemy fire, came forward from the cigarette deck and thrust out a bare arm to show several tiny scars. "I had to dig lots of small pieces of metal out of my skin for the next several days," he explained.

I asked him if he'd gotten a Purple Heart for his injuries.

Smokey merely shrugged, as though such wounds were inconsequential. However, he did note that for some time after the bombing his back had ached continuously and he thought that he'd also felt the effects of a bad whiplash.

"It might be valuable to have a Purple Heart after the war," I suggested. I was taking it for granted that Smokey would last out the war. I remembered: "You might get some extra money for a proven wound. They did after World War I."

"For these nicks?" To Smokey, Purple Hearts were no big thing. That was understandable, as he told of how he and Rollo had dashed ashore after the *Seadragon* was damaged and fought the fires around the dock that were caused by bomb hits on oil tanks and storage sheds. Their first effort, Smokey said, was to get torpedoes out of the buildings alongside the dock so they wouldn't blow up and kill everyone fighting the many fires everywhere. "It was a helluva touch-and-go thing. Rollo and I kept running around, dragging injured guys free of the sheds that were engulfed in flames, throwing burning boxes and trash into the bay and pushing torpedoes on their dollies into the water beside the pier. We were doing this while avoiding rivers of burning oil which flowed across Machina Wharf." Then he recalled that some ship was firing a lot of anti-aircraft shells into the air. But when he glanced up occasionally, he saw no sign of any of the bombers being hit. "Rollo and I kept ordering people around so they wouldn't be acting so futile. There were lots of guys acting like sheep. Later we got Dick Hawes's fleet tug, the *Pigeon*, hooked onto the Dragon, and had Dick haul her away from the blazing inferno of Cavite and over to Corregidor. There she was repaired by the tender *Canopus* in a month."

Smokey was now the executive officer of the Dragon, following Bub Ward's departure. Smokey was a short, solid, smoothly coordinated former halfback on Navy's football team. He'd been mainly a blocking back who brutally mowed down his opponents when he was leading a running play. He was tough and seemingly indifferent to the *Seadragon*'s daring attacks and hairy escapes. But he still looked worn out from it all. Smokey was a man's man, and wasn't about to act like "the second in command," lording it over all of us. His short-cropped, dark brown hair and square face, along with a developing scraggly beard, never showed much emotion. In fact, all of the Dragon's officers, except for Franz Hoskins, were stolid, low-key guys, particularly the captain who was the most phlegmatic and reserved of them all.

The captain, Lt. Comdr. Pete Ferrall, was at least ten years older than the rest of us. He was very paternalistic and gave small bits of advice to us. Yet it was only when he felt some sort of coaching was badly needed. He seemed too little concerned, however, with how the *Seadragon* was being operated. But Rollo assured me that the Dragon would sink ships because the "old man" was unafraid of Japanese ASW forces. "He sleeps very soundly," Rollo observed, "and his hands don't shake."

Although I had to sleep in a bunk over the captain, I had little trouble sleeping, as he was a quiet person, both awake and asleep. When working at his desk he thoughtfully kept the desk light shining downward on his books and letters.

The captain had also sidled up to the front of the bridge from the cigarette deck. He seemed interested in what "the old hands" were telling the "new man on board." Smokey had started telling me about how Tokyo Rose had reported on her radio broadcast that a red submarine was sinking some ships off Camranh Bay, Indochina. "That was the Dragon she was talking about." He was about to explain why Tokyo Rose called the Dragon a red submarine, when the captain interrupted.

"Ruhe, do you actually play Hearts?" he asked.

"Yes sir!" I knew immediately I shouldn't have been so emphatic. Rollo, sensing a bristling reaction from the captain, weakly explained, "He's a Pennsylvania Dutchman like me, and we're all good Hearts players." Rollo was from Williamsport, Pa. I was from Allentown.

"Like you?" the captain said sarcastically.

"Not like me," Rollo defensively noted. "He's really good!" To which the captain said ominously, "We'll see." Then to Smokey,

"Let's get the game started after supper tonight." Smokey's "Aye, aye, Sir" was perfunctory and not troubled.

As the captain disappeared down the hatch headed below, Rollo, in a not too quiet aside said, "And every free hour the captain has from now on we'll be playing Hearts. Like ten hours a day." Then in a consoling way, Rollo added, "Ruhe, you're not going to find much time for your reading."

"How much do you play for?" I was beginning to have some qualms about this Hearts game business.

"It's only a cent a point to keep the game honest and stop us from horsing around," Smokey said. Then, a bit snidely, "The captain likes a good serious game. And don't worry about losing. It's a cheap game."

At supper that evening, I asked Smokey about the "red submarine" that Tokyo Rose had stridently identified as "a U.S. pirate submarine savagely sinking unarmed, innocent Japanese merchant ships, leaving no survivors." Tokyo Rose was understood to be a turncoat Japanese-American girl. She spoke good English in her broadcasts from Japan. "The reason we know that she calls the Dragon a red submarine," Smokey said, "is because all the black paint topside washes off quickly after the Dragon gets to sea and the red lead used for priming the hull is all that's left as a covering. In a couple of days, the Dragon will look like hell." The *Canopus* at Manila had done a hasty and rotten job of repainting the Dragon after all her welding work had been completed. And "The crew loves the special attention being given by Tokyo Rose to the Dragon," Smokey noted. "The radiomen keep her broadcasts tuned in whenever we're on the surface. The captain, moreover, always tells the crew what she has to say about the red submarine. Sometimes the Dragon isn't even at sea, but she'll still give a nasty report about the red submarine's inflammatory actions to spice up her program." Then Smokey remembered how, after the Dragon sank the *Lisbon Maru* on her previous run, "Tokyo Rose viciously chanted, 'all you Australians and GIs listening to this broadcast should know that the red submarine's latest victim was a ship carrying seven hundred Australian and British prisoners of war from Singapore to Japan. None of the survivors from the torpedoed ship were rescued by the red submarine's barbaric crew. They stood on the deck of their submarine and laughed at the drowning men.' But the *Seadragon* had never surfaced and Captain Ferrall never saw any sign of survivors in the water while looking through the periscope at the ship going down."

"What was the point she was trying to make?" I asked.

"I suppose she was trying to show the Australians how cruel American submariners are and to stir up the Aussies against us."

I had the thought that there were similar broadcasts from England about U-boat atrocities against British ships particularly before the U.S. entered the war against Germany in 1941.

Just before supper, I asked Rollo about the rules for the captain's Hearts game. "We always have five players, the sixth officer stands the deck watch. When we play at night the captain and the exec wear red goggles so that they are night-adapted in case they are called to the bridge by the officer of the deck. Hence, the captain has drawn outlines in black on all red numbers and spots on the cards, so they can be used while red glasses are worn."

Rollo had properly forewarned me about the perpetual and time-consuming nature of the wardroom's only form of recreation. When I asked where books of fiction were normally kept, noting that the wardroom library shelves had only a Bowditch and a Dictionary, Rollo gave me a curt, "Who has time to do any reading on this boat?"

As predicted, the Hearts game immediately demonstrated that I was going to be discriminated against by all the players. It was quickly evident that all the officers, particularly the captain, were intent on teaching me a little humility and driving me into the red, real fast. Every time I took a trick, the rest of the players, if they had the opportunity to dump a heart or the Old Lady on me, would deliberately do so. The captain invariably chuckled when he slapped the Queen of Spades on a trick of mine. But more infuriatingly, Franz Hoskins would make a big ceremony out of giving me the Queen. With lots of "heh, heh, hehs" and with a big toothy smile, he'd slowly place the queen on my trick with a dramatic flourish. It was like putting a one hundred dollar bill, with everybody looking, into a hat passed for donations.

At supper, I mentioned my first-day impressions of the *Seadragon* to the captain. I told him that I sensed that the Dragon was destined for something really big in the war. The captain was much amused by this but seemed in agreement. He then told me how the *Seadragon*, on her day of being christened with champagne at Electric Boat Company, had refused to slide down the building ways when the chocks were knocked out from under her keel. "She was only the second warship in U.S. history to fail to be launched on schedule. The first was the *Constitution*. So the Dragon should be very special."

On the twenty-fifth of November a dispatch was received that shifted the Dragon's patrol area to "the east coast of New Britain, from 4°20' to 6° South latitude." This new patrol area made a lot more sense. It put the Dragon in St. George's Channel, between New Britain and New Ireland and close to Rabaul—the Japanese stronghold and staging point for forays down through the Solomons to retake Guadalcanal. The last big fleet action on November 15th had seen a large force of Japanese battleships, cruisers and destroyers sortie from Kavieng. They went down through The Slot and then attacked a large force of U.S. warships that were patrolling close to Guadalcanal. In the resulting action, the U.S. force sank the Japanese battleships *Hiei* and *Kiroshima* as well as several destroyers. The U.S. lost seven destroyers and had the battleship *South Dakota* badly damaged. Yet, "The Battle of Guadalcanal" was considered to be a U.S. victory since it drove the Japanese Fleet back to Kavieng and Rabaul to regroup and lick its wounds.

In the past twenty-four hours, the Dragon had used over four thousand gallons of fuel. But these fleet boats were designed to steam half way around the world if necessary. The Dragon carried over 100,000 gallons of diesel oil and enough food for ninety days at sea. Prophetically, someone with excellent foresight had recognized that U.S. fleet submarines were going to need very "long legs" to fight a war across the vast reaches of the Pacific Ocean. The Dragon could travel fourteen thousand miles at twelve knots.

By the twenty-sixth, Hoskins and I were exercising regularly on the cigarette deck. In between sit-ups, push-ups and stretching exercises, we would try some close harmonies, including the favorite of the Asiatic Squadron, "Meet Me by the Slop-Chute on the Old Wang Poo." Lt. jg Franz Hoskins was lean and energetic. His silver hair and flashing white teeth were charmingly attractive. A Physical Education graduate of the University of Washington in 1938, he had gotten a commission in the Naval Reserve and come on active duty in the spring of 1941. This made him senior to Rollo and me in the Navy hierarchy. But we refused to recognize that he outranked us. And, it wasn't important to Captain Pete, because on the Dragon he treated all of the officers about the same, with nobody rating anything special, even Smokey. And the captain never demanded any special service from the stewards, or attention and respect from any of the crew. He took such things for granted. This was one of the most attractive things about submarine life, the easygoing officers who could get results without being officious and overbearing.

On the afternoon of the twenty-seventh while the *Seadragon* was submerged for drills, Smokey Manning, who was on the periscope, reported seeing a submarine running on the surface at a considerable distance off. My reaction on hearing "submarine" was the same quiver of excitement I'd felt on seeing a rattlesnake. My heart pumped faster, my throat went dry and I felt a cold tingle down my spine. It didn't matter whether the rattler was in striking distance or further away, I still felt the sense of immediate danger. The sub was headed on a northerly course at high speed. The sound operator reported: "The submarine's screws are making 280 rpm." About eighteen knots. Smokey passed the periscope over to the captain who had hurried to the conning tower. "Her silhouette looks like one of our own boats," the captain noted, in a steady voice. "It's probably the *Sailfish*. She was due to leave a few hours after us." The captain then guessed that she had gotten no closer than four thousand yards. So we couldn't have gotten a shot at her anyhow, had she been an enemy submarine.

Dinty Moore's new command, the *Sailfish*, was the former *Squalus* that sank in May 1939 when its main induction valve failed to shut on a dive. The *Squalus* was salvaged, refitted and renamed. Under Dick Voge on her first four war patrols, she had been a successful boat.

Noting what appeared to be furrowed lines on Smokey's face that dragged down the corners of his eyes and mouth, I commented to him that "It's pretty much of a shock to see a strange submarine out in these wilds." He looked at me contemplatively for a few seconds then he slowly muttered, "It isn't that at all. My back just hurts like hell." I should have recognized that a tough guy like Smokey, with his trying war experiences, wouldn't be much affected by suddenly spotting a sub that might have shot a torpedo at the Dragon. But what did a sore back mean? A psychological reaction? The submarine war getting to Smokey? I'd seen this sort of thing in some of the crew on the S-37.

On the twenty-ninth, all-day submerged operations were begun astride the Rabaul-Shortland Islands route into The Slot leading to Guadalcanal. At this point, I was directed to start standing deck watches on my own, without Rollo's questionable guidance. It was also evident that the other officers were going to have beards the rest of the patrol. But my sprouting beard had felt so scruffy and unclean that I shaved it off and remained clean shaven.

The Dragon's first enemy contact came at daylight of the thirtieth. Smoke was detected far to the north in St. George's Channel. Finally, the tops of four vessels became visible and indicated that the ships were crossing from New Ireland to Rabaul. After a brief period of time the ships moved out of sight.

All day while submerged, "pinging" was heard from what seemed to be a shore station at Rabaul and another on the New Ireland side of the Channel. The captain guessed that it was an active sonar barrier to keep American submarines at arm's length from the harbor of Rabaul. The barrier was just south of Duke of York Island and would protect the shipping coming into Rabaul from the north. So for the time being, the captain decided not to risk giving the Dragon's presence away, but to wait for some shipping that would sooner or later head down the channel to resupply Japanese garrisons throughout the Solomons and possibly the eastern part of New Guinea.

Two planes were spotted through the periscope at twilight and shortly before surfacing. With the moon on the ascendancy the surface of the sea was quite bright. Thus, being spotted by an aircraft for the first few hours of nighttime was possible. But fortunately, the Dragon's SD air-search radar should pick up any aircraft well out from the Dragon and well before a plane's pilot could spot a submarine on the surface. Worry about night aircraft patrols would actually start on nights close to the full moon.

The Hearts game was begun a few hours before the midnight dinner. The midnight meal was occasioned by the crew's need to be awake all through the night to ensure rapid response to enemy contacts. When the game was stopped to get the wardroom table set for dinner, I asked the captain when he would qualify me in submarines. I wanted to start wearing dolphins, even though insignias were never worn while on patrol. Even the captain's khaki shirt lacked gold Lt. Comdr. leaves on the tips of the collar. Everyone in the crew was well aware of the rank and precedence of the officers and petty officers without a visible reminder. The Chiefs, however, wore their hats around the boat, probably to remind the crew of their special position in the crew's hierarchy.

The captain told me to show him the rough sketches that I'd been making of the *Seadragon*'s various systems: high pressure air, fuel supply, electrical, trim system, etc. When I showed him my drawings that were still to be finalized for my notebook using colored inks and a ruler, the captain surprised me with a positive but somewhat indifferent, "OK, you're qualified." As an afterthought he suggested that I get the yeoman to write a qualification letter for him to sign.

Rollo and Hoskins had been listening to the discussion about me being qualified. They asked, "How about us?" The captain regarded them thoughtfully for many seconds. Then he quietly and sadly said, "Not yet for you two." There was a dismissing finality to his decision. Why? Why was I given such a break? Was the captain a little fed-up with Rollo and Franz's lackadaisical concern for getting qualified? It did seem that their four war patrols had more than qualified them to be dolphin wearers. What the captain had done showed a side of him that couldn't be guessed at.

December began with what had been predicted would be the pattern of the Dragon's patrol near Rabaul. Lots of destroyers. Destroyers searching for the Dragon. Destroyers escorting ships. Destroyers speeding to Buna, New Guinea, with supplies. Destroyers joining large numbers of warships to fight sea battles around Guadalcanal.

Before dawn, as a battery charge was being completed, four destroyers were sighted far to the north. Their active sonars were yelping. They seemed to be searching for a U.S. submarine close to Rabaul. At daylight, one of the destroyers headed at high speed directly for the Dragon. His maneuver indicated that he'd spotted her. So down she was taken in a "crash dive." Chief Bueb, in the conning tower as the captain climbed down from the bridge, reminded him to tell the diving officer to "use negative," so as to get the Dragon deep, faster. The captain, with a small amused smile, leaned over the hatch to the control room and matter-of-factly ordered, "Two forty feet and use negative." Bueb breathed a long sigh of relief. Once deep, the Dragon silently crept down the channel to ease away from the swirl of water she'd created on submerging.

In about fifteen minutes, the screws of all four destroyers were heard, weaving search patterns across the spot where the Dragon was last seen. For the next two hours they moved back and forth "pinging" but getting no closer to the retreating Dragon. Finally, their screws faded out. Although faint pinging could still be heard. I watched the reaction of the captain to this hunt for the Dragon. There wasn't any.

In the afternoon, many explosions were heard over the sound gear coming from the direction of Rabaul. Then, after surfacing just after darkness had closed in, an intercepted message told of MacArthur's bombers battering the harbor of Rabaul to slow the congregating of ships for the recapture of Guadalcanal. The message gave the essence of the battle fought off Lunga Roads at Guadalcanal. The message also told of a big fleet battle fought off Lunga Roads at Guadalcanal on the thirtieth of November. Eight Japanese destroyers carrying reenforcements had met a large force of U.S. warships. The Japanese had lost one destroyer from gunfire and the U.S. lost the cruiser *Northampton* and several destroyers while also suffering heavy damage to three cruisers. The Japanese destroyers' torpedoes that caused this defeat of U.S. naval forces carried warheads twice as heavy as their U.S. counterparts and had far greater range, which was estimated to be about twenty-three thousand yards from observations made in the Java Sea battle. U.S. torpedoes by comparison were a joke.

Before dark, two Asashio-class destroyers were sighted off in the distance, heading down the channel at high speed. The Asashios were the enemy's biggest destroyers and were distinguishable by a single broad white stripe painted around their gray stacks. The captain guessed that they were carrying supplies to Munda on the Island of New Georgia, just short of Guadalcanal.

December 2nd in the afternoon, four Asashios came barreling up the channel, returning from their battle at Lunga Roads. Although the *Seadragon* was pushed hard on the batteries, the nearest destroyer passed on by at five thousand yards, out of torpedo range. These heavily engined "tin cans" could make speeds well in excess of the fastest U.S. warships. They seemed eager to get home to Rabaul where their crews would celebrate their big victory at Guadalcanal. As for other surviving Japanese destroyers, the captain felt that their battle damage had caused them to lag in returning to their main base.

That night, Pinafore, the Filipino steward, placed a pile of clothing that he'd laundered and ironed on my bunk. When I began stowing the clothing in my tiny locker, I noted that two pair of skivvies were stenciled with Sam Hunter's name. Seeing this gave me a queasy feeling of anxiety. Was it OK to wear a dead man's clothing? I couldn't remember in what classic I'd read that it would be bad luck to do so. But one couldn't pay much attention to superstitions while aboard a submarine and still function satisfactorily. So I added Sam Hunter's underpants to the few pieces of clothing stowed in my locker.

Early the next morning, a small, heavily smoking merchant ship was sighted out to the east and the soundman reported hearing pinging on the same bearing as the smoking ship. The captain reasoned that it was probably a "Q-ship," a disguised antisubmarine vessel trying to entice the Dragon into an attack. Fortunately, it was too far away to shoot at, because Captain Pete would have treated such a disguised and heavily armed ship with disdain. For certain, he would have fired a couple of fish at her, given the opportunity. And probably regretted it. Based upon reports from other submarines that had shot at Q-ships, even if U.S. torpedoes had been set on two feet for depth of run, they still would have probably run under such shallow-draft ships. In fact, when a U.S. submarine had tackled an old, small, heavily smoking merchant ship and fired three torpedoes at her, all torpedoes had harmlessly passed under their target, that then turned to ram the U.S. submarine. The Q-ship displayed far more mobility and speed than any harmless merchant ship could have mustered. Then when the range closed rapidly, the decrepit soot-blackened vessel had uncovered a big gun on her main deck and opened fire. That was enough for the U.S. sub. Her skipper promptly dove his boat away from the action. An act of well-reasoned discretion.

First the Dragon was hunted by destroyers. Then a Q-ship. A Jap submarine next? The captain emphasized, at the Hearts game that night, that all of us be extra alert on watch because we could shortly expect to find that a Japanese sub was hunting for the Dragon. Also, that with the moon cycling towards full, a night submerged attack from down-moon could be easily executed by an enemy submarine. And we'd see his torpedoes only when they were close aboard.

After dinner at midnight, the Hearts game was automatically resumed, but only three officers plus the captain were in their seats and ready for the routine. "Who's missing?" the captain irritably asked. "Lard," Hoskins observed with a sardonic smirk, "Rollo's on watch." For Hoskins, "Lard" was a good nickname for Luther Johnson, the most junior officer. Hoskins, a physical fitness nut, seemed to resent Johnson's lethargic way of life. Johnson's round, Buddha-like face and its stillness of expression showed no discernible emotion. It matched his flabbiness. Also, Johnson's placidity, the opposite to that of Hoskins' showy, flashy self-confidence, just seemed to rub Hoskins wrong.

The captain stared hard and angrily at Hoskins in an uncharacteristic display of irritation. Then he snapped, "I don't want you or anyone else on this submarine making fun of one of my officers." That was final.

Hoskins accepted the captain's reprimand with a cheerful "Aye, aye, Sir." That made the captain even madder. Hoskins' manner then shifted from one of outright friendliness to one of bewilderment and unease. The captain, meanwhile, shoved his chair aside and headed for his stateroom, tossing over his shoulder as he left, "Let me know when Mr. Johnson shows up."

Nobody risked an "Aye, aye, Sir."

When Johnson arrived at the wardroom, the captain quietly returned and started the game without glancing at Hoskins. I expected to see the captain focus his play on Hoskins to show his disfavor, but he continued to place the Queen of Spades on each trick of mine whenever it was possible to do so. As did the rest. Was I still being taught humility?

Just before dawn, with the Hearts game still in progress and just after the Dragon had been dived for her day's submerged operations, a rumbling noise could be heard through the hull. Startlingly, two heavy tremors of several second's duration severely shook the boat. We sat numbly. Our cards dropped onto the table. "We're aground!" the captain growled, while looking at the depth gauge on the wardroom bulkhead. The gauge showed the Dragon to be at one hundred feet, where Rollo was getting a good trim before starting operations at periscope depth. I reminded, "We should be in over a thousand fathoms of water, Captain." But he leapt from his seat and dashed for the control room. When the captain then risked a few pings with the fathometer, there were indications that the depth was about 1,600 fathoms. Obviously, the Dragon had not gone aground. The captain subsequently guessed that the volcano at Rabaul had blown up and its explosions were being felt far down the channel, many miles from Rabaul, and in the form of earthquakes that transmitted their power through the water. This was confirmed by Tokyo Rose on her nightly broadcast. She told of a big earthquake that was felt throughout the Western Pacific. She said it was thought to have been generated in the vicinity of Rabaul on the Island of New Britain.

The hull of the Dragon had undulated over a series of short, powerful high-frequency, deep ocean waves in much the same fashion as she would have bounced across a rocky floor on the ocean's bottom.

On being told by the radioman of Tokyo Rose's broadcast about the earthquake, I remarked, "She could have noted 'that's where the red submarine is now operating and where she'll be eliminated by our grand and powerful antisubmarine forces.'" The last time I'd had a good look at the conning tower and shears of the Dragon in bright moonlight, it was evident that all of her black paint had washed off and hence she actually was a "red submarine." Thus, if the Dragon was seen on the surface in broad daylight by the enemy, Tokyo Rose could alert the Dragon's crew to Japanese intentions to destroy "the scourge of the China Seas now operating in the vicinity of Rabaul."

Just before diving at dawn, a small two thousand ton tanker without an escort was sighted to the north. The Hearts game was adjourned. The Dragon was submerged and we went to battle stations. By 0700, the captain had maneuvered the Dragon into a good shooting position. Two forward tubes were ready and the torpedomen were standing by to punch the firing valves to eject the torpedoes. But the gyro angles in the torpedoes were lagging the generated gyro angles from the Mk 1 Torpedo Data Computer manned by Hoskins in the control room. The gyro setting spindles that projected from the top of the tubes into the torpedoes' gyro pots, were apparently binding and not properly changing the gyro angles.

Hoskins shouted up to the captain in the conning tower, "The gyros aren't matching."

The captain yelled back, "How badly are the gyros off?"

"Too much," shouted Hoskins. "We can't fire."

"How much is too much?" The captain didn't seem to trust Hoskins' judgement.

"We can't fire."

"Go ahead and fire!"

"They're off too much. We'd just be wasting torpedoes," Hoskins pleaded.

Back and forth they argued, until the captain disgustedly said, "Have the torpedomen match the gyros by hand." Hoskins, foreseeing this, had competently directed the forward room to do this. Thus, the torpedomen standing by the ready tubes were watching the gyro indicator panel and were turning the gyro-setting spindles by hand so the gyros in the torpedoes' gyro pots would match the generated gyro angles.

By the time that the torpedomen began reporting "gyros matching in hand" the small tanker had passed on by the Dragon, leaving only an up-the-stern shot at an extreme torpedo range. So the captain, with a scarcely visible sneer, ordered the tubes secured. The Dragon's Mk-10 torpedoes were of World War I vintage. Their mechanisms were well-worn by peacetime tests. So the binding of the spindles was not unexpected.

I had reminded the captain to look for aircraft during one of his periscope observations. He had quickly scanned the skies and reported "nothing there." Hating to see the Japanese ship get away scot-free, I impetuously urged him to "surface and sink the Jap ship with our four-inch gun." It was easy for me to be brave when I had no responsibility for the outcome.

A slight frown creased the captain's forehead. Then with a tolerant fatherly smile, and as though patting me on the head for being an enthusiastic but impractical son, he slyly said, "Not this time, Ruhe, we're too close to Rabaul to get away with it."

I should have bitten my tongue before voicing such a dumb idea. The captain, fortunately, was a seasoned warrior who knew the risks involved, far better than I, who was just beginning to appreciate the problems of command.

At noon, Rollo sighted a large flight of bombers high above the raised periscope. They seemed headed for Rabaul. Ours or theirs? Rollo couldn't tell.

On the sixth, the only things sighted were two planes. And on the seventh, Pearl Harbor day, only a single plane was spotted. Disappointingly, the day came to a close without any fireworks. In fact, the Dragon's patrol was going along far too quietly for my hyped-up expectations.

A message during the night told of a U.S. PT boat torpedoing a Japanese ship down in The Slot. Then the captain allowed the Hearts game to be stopped for a few minutes while Smokey told about the Dragon's secret mission before the fall of Corregidor. "Captain Pete was ordered off patrol to pick up some important people at a pier near Mariveles and transport them to Freemantle, Australia. It was late at night on February 4 when PT 680 came alongside the Dragon and delivered aboard a group of very sick and emaciated officers, most of whom were doctors. They were being evacuated from the Philippines. The PT 680 skipper said he needed two torpedoes so he could get back into action. So Captain Pete gave him two of the Dragon's. Meanwhile, our captain had to argue with a member of MacArthur's staff aboard the PT boat, about the Dragon not being able to take to Australia MacArthur's household furnishings, which were stacked on the PT boat. The staff officer was very officious and threatened that 'the General's furniture had to be carried to Australia.' Captain Pete didn't fall for that rank-has-its-privileges crap and was unmoved. He pleaded that there was no space aboard the Dragon to stow anything extra. The passengers 'could be squeezed into the boat, but nothing else.' Finally, a compromise was reached and two boxes of MacArthur's clothing were taken aboard. By two in the morning, the *Seadragon* left the pier and headed for Australia."

As Smokey was finishing his PT-boat story, a man came forward to report to the captain that one of the men back in the crew's quarters "is in great agony and groaning loudly because of a badly abscessed tooth."

The captain asked, "Is Lipes the pharmacist mate trying to help the man?"

"Yes, sir," the messenger said, "but Lipes says he can't handle the job and is going to need help." This caused the captain to turn to Smokey and request that he go aft and solve the problem.

Lipes unable to handle the job? Lipes, the enlisted man who successfully performed an appendectomy on the Dragon during her previous patrol—now needing help on an abscessed tooth problem? I was tempted to go back with Smokey to see what might happen. But nobody ever abandoned the Hearts game without the captain's express permission, and he seemed to indicate that only Smokey was excused.

A few minutes later, Smokey was back. "The guy was in real agony, so I got agreement from him to have the tooth pulled. Lipes had tried and he wasn't strong enough to yank it out in the regular way." Smokey was preparing us for a horror story. I could see it coming. "So I had the man lie on the deck," Smokey continued. "Then I got his buddies to hold his head in a fixed position and a couple more guys pinned his body to the deck so he couldn't writhe around. After much screaming and cursing by the man, I wrestled the tooth out using a pair of regular pliers from a tool box. But first I dipped the pliers in torpedo alcohol to make it antiseptic."

I shuddered at what had gone on back aft. It was brutal. And, there was Smokey telling about it in a matter-of-fact way with none of the other officers showing the slightest sympathy or emotion. I guess that after the appendicitis operation this sort of thing was merely business-as-usual for Dragon officers.

Smokey's closing comment was, "Well, I guess there won't be anymore men complaining about toothaches on this patrol."

On the eighth, all hell broke loose. And why not? The eighth was the actual date of the Japanese attack on Pearl Harbor a year ago. This was so for those on the western side of the international date line, which was where the Dragon happened to be.

At 0800 three destroyers in column tore past the Dragon doing twenty-six knots. They were headed for Munda in the Solomons. The minimum range to the destroyers proved to be 2,700 yards. It was too far for a decent torpedo shot against such high-speed destroyers.

Twenty-five minutes later, three more destroyers hove into view, going the same direction and even faster. Back the crew went to battle stations. Going after destroyers was like hunting tigers. Always very dangerous. The mere announcement that destroyers were in sight made my heart thump faster and always gave my stomach a momentary twist. Destroyers were designed primarily to destroy submarines, and the Japanese ones seemed built to scare us. Very fast and agile like tigers, when they turned on a submarine it became a matter of getting off a last ditch shot or rapidly going deep to get clear of the destroyer's depth charges. In rare cases some of the skippers were keeping their periscopes up as the destroyer headed for the scope. They hoped to stop the destroyer with a down-the-throat shot that would at least take off the destroyer's bow and stop the DD dead in the water. A very risky business! It was like trying to hit a tiger in the head as he was in a final leap at a hunter.

The three "tin cans" seemed to have spotted the Dragon's periscope as their column did a sudden ninety degree turn to starboard causing the destroyers to pass astern of the Dragon, rather than ahead. What confusion that generated. The captain immediately had the four stern tubes made ready to fire. But the after room reported that the gyros in the torpedoes were not matching the generated gyro angles being sent aft from Hoskins' computer. Again the Dragon failed to shoot even though the closest range was down to two thousand yards.

Fleet-boats just didn't have the submerged speed necessary to get into a good attack position against destroyers making more than twenty-five knots. The Dragon's maximum submerged speed of about eight knots was insufficient. Moreover, at such high destroyer speeds the torpedo gyro angles changed rapidly, requiring smooth gyro setting operations. This was not the case for the Dragon. The Squadron Eight torpedo officer, after getting complaints from other boats about sticky gyro-setting spindles, had recommended that they be exercised daily to free up their movement. But I felt that, whereas it might be practical to do this for the new Mk-14 torpedoes, a daily exercising of the spindles used in the old World War I Mk-10s only caused the old setting-mechanisms to be worn out, causing binding.

A few minutes after the three destroyers had disappeared "over the hill," the captain spotted a single destroyer headed toward the Dragon. The Dragon must have been spotted, I felt. This was evidenced, as reported by the captain, by the many white-clad Japanese sailors lining the destroyers' topsides as the destroyers swept by. But the captain seemed to think that this was a different DD running much slower than the first six. He was also zigzagging radically and was pinging all around. Still, his pings never zeroed in on the Dragon as the captain conned her into a good shooting position. Three torpedoes were ready forward. When the range was 1,450 yards all three torpedoes were fired, with zero gyro angles, at the DD's starboard beam. A longitudinal spread was used, shooting all three torpedoes down the same track. It was a perfect set-up!

Then the captain growled, "The first torpedo is spewing out a large plume of smoke. It clearly marks the torpedo's path toward the destroyer." Then in disgust, he mumbled, "He's spotted the smoke and is turning away." And immediately after, "Oh shit, all three torpedoes are missing down his starboard side." What a tough break. It was guessed that some negligent torpedoman had left the smoke ring out when assembling the torpedo. This allowed the release of a great amount of hot combustion gases into the water.

Back came the destroyer at high speed, so the captain ordered the Dragon taken deep. "And use negative?" Bueb suggested. "Hell, yes" the captain said angrily, "we're in for it." Bueb's concern about getting deep fast caused a few tight grins in the conning tower. The smiles eased the grimness of the situation slightly. Then the Dragon was showered with many depth charges. Fifteen by my guess, with three at a time. Chief Bueb, who was keeping count on the number dropped, suddenly tossed his pencil into the air in utter frustration. It was too much to ask of him to keep that sort of score.

The depth charges were all set shallow, probably on fifty meters. They knocked the corking off the overhead, broke some light bulbs and started some small leaks. Only the first one, that sounded and felt like someone had hit the top of the conning tower with a tremendous sledge hammer, was close enough to make the conning tower shudder. The captain meanwhile kept the DD astern and went slow, swinging off the course to the south when the destroyer speeded up to fifteen knots to drop his charges. Any slower and he might have blown his stern off with his own depth charges.

Later, I heard Rollo innocently asking Hoskins if our depth charging was as bad as the mistaken bombing of the *Sargo* by an Australian Air Force plane in February, when Franz was with her. "No way," Hoskins insisted, "the damage we got then was far worse. Even the *Sargo*'s porcelain toilet bowls were fractured." Ours were not damaged, however. I checked them. At this, Rollo gave me a broad wink.

The destroyer hung around, pinging away. Then five heavy explosions were heard fairly close to the Dragon. They sounded like aerial bombs going off because they had a medium-loud "bong" before each very loud "bang." Perhaps American bombers had come to the rescue. Or perhaps a Jap bomber was bombing the disturbed water caused by the depth charges. At that point the pinging had stopped and the destroyer's screw noises could not be heard. The Dragon's attacker was thus either presumed sunk or driven away.

When the Dragon was brought back to periscope depth, the seas were empty. So the captain decided to surface and get out a message to warn the U.S. area command that at least six fleet destroyers were headed toward The Slot at high speed.

On surfacing, a radio antenna was rigged from the shears to a post set in the main deck aft. Then, an attempt was made to transmit a warning message about the six DDs on 8470 kilocycles to any station receiving on that common, ship-to-shore frequency. After trying futilely for fifteen minutes to raise any station anywhere, the antenna was dismantled and the Dragon was submerged.

During the time on the surface, a radioman had tuned to the frequency used by MacArthur's bombers. He was searching for clues as to the aerial bomb explosions that had been heard. There was nothing on that score but he did hear some American flyers claiming "bomb hits on a force of six destroyers."

When back on the surface after dark, the radioman intercepted a newscast that claimed that MacArthur's bombers had sunk two destroyers and seriously damaged one more near Bougainville at the head of The Slot. That seemed to indicate that the force of six destroyers we'd seen earlier had been reduced to only three still operational. This news caused reserved, cautious cheers from the crew. It meant there'd be three less DDs to worry about when they returned to Rabaul.

Next day on the ninth, while I was on watch manning the periscope in the conning tower, I suddenly spotted many huge geysers of water rising high into the air out beyond the horizon. Many seconds later came the sounds of bursting bombs and gunfire. I brought the Dragon up to fifty-two feet to better see what was happening. Through the spray of straddling bomb bursts, I could then make out the tops of—not the three DDs I expected to see—but at least five on their way home. They were zigzagging wildly at top speed. "Well, at least MacArthur's bombers had sunk one Japanese DD," I concluded, as the five destroyers disappeared from view, heading up the channel.

About ten minutes later there were more bomb explosions out on the same bearing. The topmast of a single destroyer, traveling at reduced speed and smoking heavily from fire damage, hove into view. It was the sixth destroyer! And he kept heading north through straddling bomb bursts until he went out of view.

I had studied the skies above the geysers of water, with the periscope in low power, but couldn't see a single bomber. They were evidently far too high to be seen in the bright sunlight. They were at least seventeen thousand feet up. Bombers trying to hit ships at that altitude had little chance of hitting the slim, high speed, zigzagging DDs. It was like the Army pilot Colin Kelly's claim of dropping a bomb down the stack of the battleship *Haruna* and sinking it at the beginning of the war. Kelly's claim had proved an optimistic delusion since the *Haruna* was spotted by a U.S. submarine a few weeks later.

The tenth was uneventful except for seeing in the late afternoon, a heavily smoking, small ship far out on the horizon. Again, distinctive "pings" were heard on the bearing of the slowly moving ship. It was unquestionably the same Q-ship, trying to entice the Dragon into an attack. The captain didn't bother to waste any amps to close the contact.

After surfacing, the radioman picked up several messages from ComSoWestPac telling of numerous Japanese shipping movements into Rabaul over the next few weeks. The freighters were being routed into Rabaul from the northwest. Then their destroyers and submarines would carry their cargoes south to New Guinea or the Solomons.

On watch, it was a delight to sniff the clean night air with its honey-like jungle perfumes coming from both sides of the channel. With the SD radar continually in operation, the Dragon seemed safe from aircraft attack. Even if Japanese planes were direction-finding the Dragon's SD emanations, they wouldn't see the Dragon in the moonlight until close at hand. Moreover, dives were made when SD contacts had closed to about six miles. The nights, unfortunately, had a light haze over the waveless seas so that sailboats and small patrol boats might get close to the Dragon without being seen. What was needed was a surface-search radar for real safety at night.

On December 11, while close to Cape St. George at the foot of New Ireland, a large freighter was sighted in the morning twilight. It was just after diving. The cargo ship was escorted by a minelayer, a converted destroyer that nervously and protectively patrolled back and forth across the bow of the freighter. The two ships were making ten knots and were headed up to Rabaul. The cargo ship was high in the water. It was empty. At battle stations, Rollo remarked that since it was the "third day" we'd see lots of action. He noted that the "hot" days had been the second, fifth, eighth, and now it was the eleventh. The captain's several looks at the freighter identified her as the *Johore Maru* of 6,100 tons.

By 0700 the Dragon had worked into a good submerged firing position. Two torpedoes were ready up forward with depth settings of six feet. A spread of four degrees between torpedoes was used. Distrusting Hoskins' computer solutions, the captain used Rollo Miller's Mk VIII Banjo solution.

The first torpedo was observed to hit solidly under the ship's mainmast on the starboard side. The explosion wrecked the freighter's engine room, stopped her screws and caused her to list heavily to starboard. The second torpedo, according to the captain, went under the target. Its wake, as observed, went into the side of the freighter forward of the bridge without exploding.

The captain softly cursed the second torpedo for malfunctioning and the first Mk-10 torpedo for having an insufficient 385-pound warhead to sink a simple cargo ship outright.

After the hit was heard in the conning tower, Chief Bueb began gesticulating with his downward-pointing thumb. When Bueb heard the captain order "rig for depth charge" and then immediately thereafter, "go deep, emergency, and use negative," a broad smile spread across the chief's face. The captain had noted, as the periscope was being housed, that the minelayer had hooked around and was headed for the Dragon "with a bone in his teeth."

Within minutes, eight depth charges were showered down on the Dragon. The Dragon had gotten to 250 feet just before the "click" of the detonator in the charge and then the very loud "WHAM" of the exploding warhead were heard. The charges were all close. They shook the boat, made lights flicker, shattered a lot of glass, but did little additional damage.

Shortly, there were three more depth-charge explosions, but sufficiently distant so that the captain ordered "Fifty-eight feet." Then when that depth was reached, he quickly located the damaged freighter at about four miles off. She was dead in the water with the minelayer laying-to just ahead of her and trying to pass a tow rope over to the *Johore Maru*'s bow.

The captain put on speed to close the two ships, while remaining at periscope depth. He was asking for trouble and he got it. On the next look he spotted a plane zooming the Dragon's scope. This was followed by a bomb going off directly overhead. But it was a surface explosion that had little effect on the Dragon.

The captain then took the Dragon to one hundred feet and bent on high submerged speed to close for another attack. After seven minutes the Dragon was slowed and brought to fifty-eight feet—only to catch two more surface-exploding bombs. Down the Dragon was taken for more seven-knot running at one hundred feet. Then, when back at fifty-eight feet it was evident that the freighter was being towed by the minelayer and was moving slowly towards Rabaul. The observed range of 3,500 yards to the freighter was too great to risk a torpedo shot. And it was reported that the battery was getting very low. The captain had paid little attention to the amount of battery power he was expending. To him, getting into a firing position came first. Then he'd worry about having enough battery left to pull off his evasion tactics. It was scary.

Although successive navigational fixes showed the Dragon making little headway against a 3.5 knot current setting south, the captain wouldn't give up. But finally, because of the low battery, he had to give up the fruitless pursuit. Meanwhile, Lipes, the pharmacist mate, reported that a seaman had gone into a catatonic state during the last depth-charging. The captain told me to go below with Lipes and see what could be done about the unconscious enlisted man. Lipes led me to a tall, skinny comatose man who was lying in a lower bunk in the after battery. The man's eyes were rolled up into his head. The skin of his face was bloodless white with a slight greenish tinge. And he was as stiff as a board. His only sign of life was the tip of his tongue flicking out and in and quivering like a snake's tongue. Lipes rubbed the man's wrists and held ammonia close to his nose without results. The unconscious man was the first submariner I'd ever seen who had suffered so much shock from excessive fright that he'd gone into a coma. The fear of where the next depth charge was going to explode had devastated the man—who was on his first war patrol. The men who were standing around watching Lipes's first aid said that the seaman had been taking everything too seriously, that he was a loner and never took a shower until he was "ordered by Mr. Hoskins to take a bath," and that he never talked to his ship-mates. After things quieted down he finally snapped out of it. But from then on he was taken off all duties and transferred from the Dragon when she arrived in port. Oddly, as I thought about this very frightened man, I recognized that I hadn't felt any fear during the depth-chargings probably because I was completely busy helping the skipper in his escape tactics.

At dinner, while we were discussing the day's torpedo attack and the depth-charging, Rollo suddenly patted Hoskins' shoulder solici-tously, and suggested that the Dragon's punishment was a whole lot worse than the bombing suffered by the *Sargo* when Franz was aboard.

"No way," Franz protested, like a broken record, "the *Sargo* had to go back to the States to repair the bomb damage."

Rollo, with a conspiratorial smile, kiddingly reminded, "We're going back to the States soon to repair all *our* damage. So what's the difference?"

Franz changed the subject. He sensed that it was a put on.

Saturday was a blank. However, riding the surface at night while charging the batteries had begun to be a very risky business. The moon was nearing its full phase. This forced the Dragon to stay well offshore and clear of the narrow parts of the channel. Occasional patrol boats were being sighted close to the beach, even against the dark background of the shore. But they were too small to be hit with torpedoes. So we steered clear of such targets. Their pinging could be heard by our soundman as far as ten miles away, making them easy to track.

The Dragon's passive sonar capability for detecting high-speed destroyer screws was only about six thousand yards, while the pro-pellers of merchant ships were heard no farther away than about four thousand yards.

On Sunday the thirteenth, several bombers were sighted, several distant explosions were heard, and the Dragon was hunted by a destroyer. The captain identified it as a Shiratsuke-type and said that there were large numbers of men on the forecastle looking for periscopes. When the destroyer closed to three thousand yards, and with the Dragon's three forward torpedo tube doors open, the DD reversed course, put on speed and left.

Early Monday, just after midnight, two destroyers were seen searching the Dragon's area. One of them forced the Dragon down by its close approach. Despite the bright moonlight on the water, the DD proved to be invisible when the 1.4-inch attack periscope was used. The 4-inch, number-one scope, which was somewhat better for night work, made visible the DD's wake. The destroyer kept changing his course radically to avoid being shot at, but never got real close and finally headed away.

On the fifteenth, while submerged after dawn, a Japanese hospital ship, readily identified as the *Hikawa Maru*, was carefully observed through the periscope. She had all the proper markings, a painted white hull with a green stripe around her middle and large red crosses painted on both sides. But she was zig-zagging and had a small warship as an escort. Both were clear violations of international law. It was thus suspected that the hospital ship was carrying contraband: war supplies, troops, critical materials for the Japanese war-making economy, etc.

That night at about 2100, Hoskins and I had gone up to the cigarette deck to get some fresh air and to harmonize a few songs. The moon was bright in the skies and a dense haze hung over the water. Rollo had the bridge watch. Hoskins and I were paying no attention to anything except our harmonizing, when Rollo rushed back to softly berate us for not seeing some destroyers which had appeared out of the mist astern, at about six thousand yards range. Rollo growled "We're fighting a war, you clowns. Keep your eyes open." Then, as we hurried forward to go through the conning tower hatch, Rollo yelled, "Dive, Dive," skipping the "Clear the bridge" command. The quartermaster, at the helm, rang the diving alarm. The lookouts dropped from the shears and went below, just ahead of Rollo who pulled the hatch shut behind him as he hit the conning tower deck. Then he slid down the ladder to the control room like a fireman going down a greased firehouse pole to get to his fire engine. He snarled, "You jerks," as he passed us on his way down to take over the dive. Immediately, the general alarm started bonging away as Rollo yelled over the loud-speaker system, "Battle stations. Battle stations. Torpedo attack."

When the captain arrived in the conning tower, I told him that there were at least three destroyers headed towards the Dragon at high speed, on a southeasterly course. "They probably didn't see us," I advised, as the captain ran up the forward scope for a look. But, as before, all he could see was the destroyers' wakes, towards which he headed the Dragon. A firing solution was impossible to obtain, as the DDs passed about 2,500 yards ahead. Then the soundman reported that there were more high-speed screws coming up astern. So the captain switched to a stern shot. But the rapid change in bearings of three DDs astern indicated that they would pass close to the Dragon. With gyro-setting problems, the captain decided not to risk a torpedo shot.

Within minutes after the destroyers' screw noises had faded away, the captain had the Dragon back on the surface to transmit a contact report on the six destroyers. This time the message was "Rogered" by a shore station at Pearl.

An hour later, while the Dragon was still on the surface, a destroyer was seen prowling around the spot about five miles away where the message had been broadcast. Down the Dragon was taken to make an approach on the searching DD. But the DD moved out of range and headed back towards Rabaul.

The seventeenth was another one of those "third days." In the morning, an approach was made on a large freighter painted with jagged, light and dark gray camouflage stripes. A small destroyer buzzed around in front of the freighter dropping single depth charges randomly, apparently to scare away lurking submarines. The exploding charges, however, didn't faze the captain. He aggressively pushed the Dragon towards a good firing position. But on each successive look after a few minutes of submerged running, he discovered that the freighter had changed course to some unexpected new direction. Four times the scope was raised with the captain ordering, "Final bearing and shoot." But each time the fire control set-up was all wrong. Twice the captain shifted from a bow to a stern shot and then back again to a bow shot after taking the next look. Confusion! The set-up never looked good enough to risk firing a torpedo because a quick change in gyro angles would be required and the gyro-setting problem took over. So the freighter moved safely on by.

Luther Johnson's plot showed that the freighter had used a brand new zig plan, one never seen before. It looked like a broad and continuous sine curve.

While asleep in the afternoon, I heard the word "submarine" coming from the control room. I was out of my bunk like a shot—rushing barefooted and in my skivvies for my battle station. The captain was close behind.

Hoskins had the periscope watch in the conning tower. He had seen a surfaced Japanese submarine close to the Dragon. His immediate reaction was to swing the Dragon to head for the enemy sub, so as to fire torpedoes with zero gyro-angles. There were two continuously ready torpedoes in flooded tubes for an "emergency snap shot."

The captain had foreseen just such a situation and had rehearsed with all the officers how to handle a suddenly disclosed submarine. His doctrine assumed that all submarines seen, while in the present patrol area, would be enemy ones. It was shoot first and think afterwards. The captain recognized that a submarine running on the surface would be spotted through the scope at no more than about two thousand yards, giving little time for well-thought-out reactions. As the captain climbed into the conning tower he asked, "Where's the sub?" Hoskins indicated it was out ahead of the Dragon's bow. And added that, "The sub's broadsides were to me and it looked as though he was going real slow." Just after the captain ordered "Up periscope," the soundman reported, "The submarine's screws are making 120 rpm, about eight knots." The sonar operator had failed to hear the enemy sub's screws until well after it had been spotted visually.

When the captain jammed his eye into the scope's eyepiece and quickly swung the scope back and forth across the dead-ahead bearing, he was unable to pick up the Jap sub. "Where the hell is he at?" he snarled at Hoskins, who looked frantically at the illuminated compass repeater alongside the helmsman in the conning tower. "He's at 325° True." Hoskins barely got the words out in a shaky whisper. He was so nervous he was trembling. Then Hoskins noted that the Dragon was still swinging to port, well past the enemy submarine's bearing. After giving the order, "Left full rudder" to head for the sub, he had forgotten to follow his order with a "Steady on 325° True."

The captain, becoming aware that the Dragon was still swinging to port, ordered, "Steady as you go." To me he directed, "Put the scope on the correct bearing of the sub." And to Rollo, "Pass the word to have the outer doors on the forward ready-tubes opened."

I grabbed the periscope handles and swung the scope so that the captain was looking on the proper bearing. It was far around to starboard. Precious seconds were then wasted trying to locate the Jap sub. By the time the captain spotted it and savagely said, "Mark the bearing," the sub had turned away and was moving out of range.

With a disgusted, "The angle-on-the-bow is 170° and he's going over the hill," the captain snapped the periscope handles together and backed away from the descending periscope while gritting his teeth and glowering at Hoskins. The captain's displeasure was only too evident. Hoskins meanwhile fluttered around, trying to smile, but knowing that he'd blown it.

Back in the wardroom a short time later, with all the officers there, awake and agitated by the turn of events, the captain, after staring at the table top for a few minutes, gravely said, "They've sent the dogs out to get us. We've got to do a helluva lot better than this or we'll all be dead." The rest of us just sat there, numbly.

At about ten that night, the Dragon was back on the surface and charging batteries while making five knots on the diesel donkey engine. A bright moon made her highly visible. A Hearts game was in progress, with Johnson on watch on the bridge. Suddenly, an urgent cry of "Torpedo to starboard" was chillingly heard by the card players in the wardroom. The collision alarm immediately followed, its high-pitched shrillness galvanizing the men throughout the boat into slamming shut all watertight doors between compartments, then dogging them down tightly. The crew's reaction was automatic. Unfortunately, this action temporarily trapped all of the officers, except for Johnson, in the forward battery compartment. Undogging the door to the control room was out of the question—a torpedo hit with rapid flooding of the forward part of the Dragon and the sub would go to the bottom nose first.

The Dragon was vibrating with greatly increased power as we sat there helplessly. It was nerve wracking—waiting to hear if Johnson had avoided the torpedo. Seconds seemed as long as minutes. I noticed there were gray hairs in Smokey's scraggly beard. I also wondered why I was the only clean-shaven officer on the boat. My heart was racing, and all my senses were tuned for an ear-splitting, crashing explosion. I had the momentary thought that the lookouts had spotted the torpedo's wake about forty seconds ago and that there were probably only about twenty seconds left before it hit or missed. It wouldn't be a slow affair like waiting for depth charges. So I started counting the seconds. The captain was stony-faced as he hesitatingly picked up the phone to call the bridge. But then he thought better of distracting Johnson from dodging the torpedo. Rollo and Smokey looked stunned and ill. They had such worried looks that I muttered "grimmo." At which Rollo for a moment allowed a small smile to lift the corners of his mouth.

Then the wardroom telephone rang and Johnson reported to the captain that the torpedo had passed astern and that the Dragon was clearing the area at maximum speed on the batteries. Johnson also emphasized that a special look was being kept for another torpedo coming up from astern. But it never materialized.

The Jap sub had cleverly attacked from down moon where its skipper could clearly see the Dragon riding on the surface. At the same time, the Dragon's lookouts hadn't seen the enemy sub's periscope against the dark land background at the side of the channel. Luckily, the Japanese sub's skipper evidently thought that the Dragon was dead in the water. So the torpedo missed.

The Hearts game was ended and was not resumed that night.

When I relieved the bridge watch at midnight, I jokingly said to Johnson, about his dodging the torpedo, "Hey, for a reserve officer that was pretty well done." The captain, who was getting a breath of fresh air on the cigarette deck, overheard this questionable praise for Johnson's handling of the emergency. Stepping forward and acting mad as hell, he snapped, "I don't want to hear any distinction made between regulars and reserves ever again on this boat. Is that clear?"

I mumbled my assent, thoroughly chastened by the captain's ferocious dressing down of my attempt at some light humor. It wasn't funny to him. He unquestionably thought that we were in for a long war and that we'd lose many regulars and have to depend on many good reserve officers to win the war.

On the eighteenth after dark, a destroyer on a northerly course and at high speed, passed about six miles off. A few hours later, a five thousand ton tanker was sighted. The Dragon was then dived to periscope depth and an approach started. The bright moon had made a surface attack impractical although the captain wondered out loud whether he shouldn't "try this one on the surface."

Despite using up a great deal of battery, the Dragon never got closer than 4,500 yards. Thus, with only two hours left for a charge before dawn, the approach was abandoned.

Shortly after noon on the nineteenth, a small freighter escorted by two destroyers was sighted on the horizon. And at nightfall a large number of explosions were heard to the north indicating more bombing of the ships in Rabaul harbor.

The considerable number of destroyers being seen, even for escort of single ships, seemed very profligate and odd. It probably meant that the Japanese had their entire first team on hand to be readied to win a major fleet battle to win back Guadalcanal.

Sunday the twentieth was another "third day." Still, it remained ominously quiet until after the Dragon was surfaced at nightfall. Shortly, four large gray shapes with big bow waves loomed out of the haze. With the cry of "destroyers astern" from a lookout, I rang the diving alarm and the Dragon was crash-dived—passing fifty-four feet as the shears went under, in forty-seven seconds. On these bright nights, the Dragon rode the surface with decks awash and was trimmed heavy overall. With the help of negative she went down fast.

Battle stations were manned on the double. After a few quick looks by the captain, three torpedoes set on two feet depth were fired from the forward tubes at the rear destroyer, as the column of destroyers charged on by at about one thousand yards range making at least thirty knots. As before, Hoskins yelled up from his Mk 1 Torpedo Data Computer station that the gyros were not following in automatic. And as before, even when the torpedomen up forward were matching the gyros by hand, the gyros in the torpedoes were sticky and not responding properly to the settings. But all three torpedoes were fired and went out at queer angles with all three torpedoes missing.

Apparently, the wakes of the torpedoes were never seen by the destroyers for without changing course the four destroyers sped off toward Munda. And even though the torpedoes exploded as they sank deep at the end of their runs, the destroyers just kept opening out and shortly disappeared from view.

At 0700 on the twenty-first and shortly after diving, the captain took a final periscope look around before going to the wardroom for supper. To his surprise he spotted an enemy submarine running on the surface and heading home for Rabaul. This sub was apparently the one that shot at the Dragon on the seventeenth at the foot of St. George's Channel, eighty miles away. Now, only twenty miles from port, the oncoming Japanese sub, according to the captain, was acting "fat, dumb and happy." Then he added, "If we can only make our torpedoes work right, we've got him." He was rubbing his hands in pleasant expectation.

The skipper of the enemy sub had apparently decided that no American submarine would risk patrolling so close to the Japanese stronghold of Rabaul, which had continuous air coverage over the entrance to its harbor. As far as the Japanese skipper was concerned, the American sub that he'd shot at four days earlier had either been sunk or was chased away by the great amount of Japanese submarine activity.

"Is he zigagging, Captain?" I asked.

"No," the captain answered, while taking a second long look at the Jap sub. "He's not worried about a thing, the dumb cluck." The captain chuckled smugly as he slapped the periscope handles together to have the scope lowered.

"Can you describe the sub, Captain? Is he going fast?"

"He's a big one . . . a really big one. And I'd say he's making at least fourteen knots by his bow wake."

The soundman reported, "He's making about 200 rpm." This verified the captain's fourteen-knot guess.

As the captain continued to stare into the scope, a smile crinkled the skin around his eyes. "There are men in whites out on the sub's cigarette deck shining their shoes and getting ready to go on liberty when they get to port." The captain was enjoying this attack.

"How about a plane, Captain?" I reminded.

"I'll take a good check for planes," he promised and swung the scope all around while elevating the scope's eyepiece to look into the skies. With an "All clear" he ordered the scope lowered.

During the scope's descent, the captain had four forward tubes made ready. "We'll fire three fish and hold one in reserve in case the first three miss." And, "Set four feet on the torpedoes and the gyros on 357°, 000°, and 003°. The second torpedo with the zero gyro angle will be aimed just aft of the sub's conning tower.

To minimize his chances of failure he said to me, the assistant approach officer, "We'll use Franz's TDC solution and you do the firing of torpedoes at eight-second intervals."

On the next look, as the scope broke the surface, the captain swung it rapidly around, reporting "No planes." Then he zeroed in on the straight-running enemy sub. Showing only a foot of scope he carefully evaluated the set-up. "His angle-on-the-bow is forty-five degrees port and he'll pass us at less than a thousand yards. This is perfect!" he gloated.

To the captain, it wasn't a matter of revenge so much as the thought of getting a tough job successfully accomplished. He knew he was good at the business of fighting his submarine but he felt that the damned, rotten torpedoes had kept defeating some of his best efforts.

The Dragon was on a normal approach course at three knots, so all I needed from Rollo was the lead-angle that would be translated into a firing bearing for the captain's use.

The captain's single-range estimate, taken from the scope's estimate, taken stadimeter of about eight hundred yards, confirmed a point-blank firing range for launching the torpedoes.

For the final look, I swung the scope to seventeen degrees so that when the captain saw the conning tower of the sub pass the scope's cross hair he would fire the first torpedo. The captain, with his eye glued to the scope's eyepiece waited and waited and waited.

I never ceased to wonder about how much dead time there was in every submerged submarine attack. I, too, waited and waited. Then with the order to "fire the torpedoes" I punched out three fish while counting to eight between the ejection of each torpedo.

Eighteen seconds after firing the first torpedo, a tremendous explosion was heard and felt by all of the crew in the Dragon. Its detonation swished a surging wave of water through the Dragon's superstructure.

"That was probably a pre-equate to a hit," the captain said, disgustedly. "A run of only eighteen seconds doesn't equate a hit on our sub."

The captain, while keeping the scope on the enemy sub, chanted, "The lookouts are staring in our direction. They can't figure out what the explosion was."

Then, following a muffled explosion, the captain doubtfully noted, "We might have hit him deep in his middle." But he sounded unconvincing.

On the next loud explosion, however, there was no doubting the sound in his voice. "There goes his stern in the air." His voice rose half an octave and was loud. "We really got him! The lookouts on the sub are staring aft wondering what's happened. Men are jamming the bridge and some are jumping into the water." The captain was as exultant as a radio announcer describing the finish of an Olympic one-hundred-meter dash with an American hitting the tape first.

Suddenly, the tragedy of a sinking submarine made my stomach feel sick. I held my breath waiting for the captain's description of what was happening to the Japanese submariners as their sub began sinking by the stern. The *Seadragon*'s crew might have had their war ended in just the same way four days earlier——when this same sub had shot a torpedo at the Dragon. There was no feeling of elation, only pity for those little guys ready to go ashore for a liberty.

For an instant, the enemy were real human beings, badly scared and just trying to stay alive. For an instant the impersonal nature of submarine war had been interrupted. Momentarily, I worried about their fate. But with the announcement by the captain that, "She's sunk from sight," the Japanese became once more robots making their ship function.

The captain's voice sounded happy. He wasn't being heartless, he was just reflecting a knowledge that the Japanese were inflicting a lot of pain and death on our submariners as well.

Then Smokey yelled up from the control room that somethng was mighty wrong with the Dragon. "I can't hold the bow down. We're broaching with a large up angle." He followed this with, "Captain, we're at thirty feet and the bow is sticking out of the water."

The first big explosion had not been a premature of the first torpedo fired, but rather a bomb dropped close to the Dragon's bow. It had blown the forward main ballast tank partly dry. And this was confirmed by Smokey's "I'm flooding everything possible up forward to get us down."

I could visualize a Jap bomber making another run over the now visible bow of the Dragon, so I urged the captain to take a look for aircraft.

The captain was in the process of searching the skies once more for planes when a frantic report came over the conning tower's speaker. "A torpedo is running hot in number four tube and we can't close the outer door."

That was bad news. It meant that the exploding bomb had tripped the starting lever of the torpedo in tube number four up forward and the fish had moved partially out of the tube, getting pinched there. The torpedo's engines were burning up. But what was worse was that the arming fan for the torpedo's exploder was out in the stream of water moving past the bow of the Dragon. It might have fully armed the torpedo before any action to eject it or bring it back into the tube could be taken.

The day before, the captain had made me the gunnery and torpe-do officer. The captain had assigned me that job after he'd missed the destroyer with three wildly running torpedoes. Thus, the jammed torpedo was my responsibility. So I told the captain I was on my way to the forward room to try to get rid of the torpedo.

As I scrambled down the ladder to the control room and raced forward, I felt the captain right behind me as he pushed me through the door to the forward battery to get both of us to the forward room faster. The Dragon was in a state of crisis!

As we crawled through the watertight door leading to the for-ward room, the captain ordered, "Everyone out of the room except for the chief and Ruhe." Then, "You, Ruhe, dog the door and put pressure in the compartment to check the flooding if the torpedo blows."

After three torpedomen had moved aft, I dogged down the door and bled air from the high pressure air-line into the room until my ears popped and began hurting. The forward room was full of smoke from the hot-running torpedo. But no more smoke was issuing from the tube vent on the number-four tube, indicating that the torpedo had run out of fuel. What was worse, enough time had elapsed to fully arm the torpedo so that a slight jolt would trigger the exploder and blow up the torpedo. Along with the bow of the Dragon! But everything was happening too fast to feel any anxiety.

"What do you think Chief?" the captain asked as he pushed his way up to the narrow space between the forward tubes to check number four's vent. It was closed. So the tube should be fully flood-ed behind the jammed torpedo, making it easier for Smokey to trim the Dragon. Sweat poured from the captain's body, soaking his rum-pled khaki shorts and leather sandals, and chunks of cork, with which he'd been showered when the bomb exploded, clung to the matted hair on his chest.

The chief's shoulders slumped and his voice shook as he told the captain, "We can't suck the torpedo back in. Any jar at all will blow her up. We couldn't even use a diver outside to pull the fish clear." Chief Howard was an old hand, so that his firm positiveness called for some other solution to the dilemma.

"Let's go deep and flood out the warhead," I foolishly suggested, feeling very helpless.

The captain dubiously shook his head, reminding that, "Sometimes they explode when they go deep, like they did the last time we fired. Remember?"

The captain was groping for a solution. His hand shook badly as he tried to scratch a match on a paper matchbook to light a cigarette.

"We might just keep going and never jolt the fish," I muddily thought. But then I remembered that rough weather would cause the Dragon's bow to pitch and it would trigger the warhead of the torpedo. A better idea seemed to be to blast the fish out while backing down, thus getting a bit more distance between the Dragon's bow and the torpedo before it exploded. I was surprised about how practical this solution seemed, so I mapped it out to the captain.

The captain nodded contemplatively. Then he went over to the talk-back speaker and called the control room. "How's your trim Smokey?" he asked, without even a shade of nervousness in his voice. But I saw his hand trembling on the speaker's switch.

Smokey reported back, "I can handle the boat OK, but I'm using lots of speed and pumping lots of water out of forward trim."

The captain stroked his chin and puffed on a moist cigarette. To light that cigarette had almost cost him his eyebrows. Then, "Bring us up to one hundred feet and tell me when you've got a good trim. Then we'll back full."

It was evident that for the captain the problem was solved. His voice had lost its edginess as he ordered the chief, "Build up the impulse air for number four to the maximum. We'll blast the torpedo out even if she breaks up in the process."

"The firing mechanism will only stand about six hundred pounds," the chief said. But that was enough. When six hundred pounds of air hit the back of the jammed torpedo it would hurl it forward at a terrific rate and break it apart. Yet it might be far enough from the Dragon's bow when it exploded that the bow wouldn't be blown off.

Smokey reported to the captain that the boat was in good trim and at one hundred feet. So the captain ordered, "All back full."

The Dragon's propellers went into reverse with a great surge of power thrown into the shafts, making the forward room shudder and shake.

"Let me know when we're making full speed astern," the captain told Smokey. He followed with, "Rig the boat for collision."

With all the watertight doors dogged tight, ventilation flappers sealed off and sea valves all cranked tightly shut, the Dragon was prepared for a heavy beating.

The captain's next order, when Smokey reported that the Dragon was going full speed astern, was, "Stand-by number four tube."

The chief put his hand on the firing key. I took a tight hold on the torpedo skid alongside me, and the captain hunched his shoulders firmly back against the smooth side of a tube.

"Fire!"

The chief slammed down the key.

I counted, "one . . . two," WHAMmmmmm!

The shock of the explosion hit the Dragon like a well-aimed punch on the nose. I bounced away from the empty torpedo skid and was knocked to the deck. The captain was downed between the tubes.

Flame seemed to shoot through the tube door into the room and engulf it in a fiery red light. But the brilliant light might easily have been caused by the heavy concussion to my head.

Water poured into the room through a large jagged crack in the thick bronze door of number-four tube. Dazed, I fought my way through a heavy stream of water and pushed past the captain to help the chief crank shut the outer door and stop the flooding. With loud grunts and using all the muscle we could muster, the two of us slowly closed the badly damaged outer door. It was a miracle that it still existed and that its closing mechanism could be mule-hauled by the two of us.

As the outer door to the tube sealed itself, the water, flowing into the room through the cracked door, subsided. Although there was water swirling over the deck plates, that was it.

The bow had held!

The captain groped through the haze of spray still in the room. There were more numerous small leaks shooting water into the room as he called for all compartments to report their damage.

Smokey was the first to answer the captain. "You almost did us in, Captain. But we're now making two thirds ahead and I can hold the boat OK at this depth. Congratulations." Smokey's voice had a little croak in it as though he'd been given a reprieve from death.

I just felt numb.

Reports flowed to the captain from all over the submarine. The circuit breakers had tripped out. But the chief electrician had snapped them back in so rapidly that I hadn't noticed the lights going out. Sea valves had backed open, but were easily shut. Men were knocked down all over the boat with nobody badly injured. The gyro compass was out and there was minor damage reported from all over the Dragon but everything was under control.

When we adjourned to the wardroom the captain put on a detached smile and sat back to listen to the excited jabber. Quack quack was easy. In torrents of talk the pent-up tensions of the past hour were let loose.

Relieved of the diving watch, Smokey slumped on the wardroom's transom. He wearily told of at least five physical ailments that should disqualify him from submarine duty. "I've had it," he sighed. "My teeth hurt all the time. They're rotting out and poisoning my whole system." I stole a look at Smokey's mouth and couldn't see any sign of decaying teeth. "And my back hurts so much that I can't get any sleep. I'm a walking zombie."

I thought that Smokey's football days as a blocking back were just catching up to him. Then I had the unpleasant thought that his five patrols were changing him into a malingerer. But that wasn't being charitable to a guy who'd been a Rock of Gibraltar during the past hour as diving officer.

Hoskins continued to chatter, drowning out Smokey's moaning complaints. I didn't pay much attention to what Franz was saying because it was about what had happened to the *Sargo*, and that it was much worse than whatever happened to the Dragon. Johnson, who had been talking at the same time, was praising the performance of his engineers and electricians. And I was trying to tell what happened up in the forward torpedo room. But nobody was really listening to each other. Then Rollo dashed into the wardroom from the control tower.

"How about that, Hoskins?" Rollo shouted into Franz's ear.

Hoskins was coolly poised, mentally preparing to compare the *Sargo*'s bomb damage to that experienced by the Dragon's bomb and torpedo damage. He raised his eyebrows in thought, weighing the effects of what he'd just gone through versus the experience of the *Sargo* in February. A smile crept over his face. Self-assured, he bared his flashing teeth. He was ready for Rollo's assault on his veracity and flawless judgement.

"Come on, Hoskins," Rollo said, roughly grabbing him by the arm and yanking him out into the passageway. From there, he steered Hoskins toward the forward torpedo room. I followed.

Once in the forward room, Rollo yanked open the door to the officer's head and propelled Hoskins around to force him to look inside.

"Now let's see what happened to our toilet bowl," Rollo crowed—fully aware of the dramatic elements of the moment.

Hoskins, who had always claimed that the violence of the *Sargo*'s bombing had been well illustrated by the cracking of the officers' toilet bowl, didn't move a muscle as he was forced to look into the head.

I crowded up behind them to act as referee. There was no need however. Our toilet bowl was gone. Only a pile of porcelain slivers and white dust remained.

We were certainly earning our extra fifty percent pay for sub duty: seventy-five dollars a month.

The remainder of the night the Dragon moved south to be clear of the area. The captain felt it would be well searched for the next few days by "the dogs from Rabaul."

On the twenty-second, the destroyer activity in the north indicated that the Japanese were taking the Dragon seriously. In the afternoon, a destroyer was sighted, escorting a medium-size cargo ship that the Dragon was unable to close. At tea time (the Hearts players were now drinking tea), four destroyers were tracked on-by at a minimum range of 4,600 yards. After dark another DD passed the Dragon, but out of torpedo range. And then, just before midnight, two more DDs passed ahead, again out of range.

The nuisance value of the Dragon seemed high at this point. She was tying up large numbers of destroyers for antisubmarine searches and more for escorting ships down the channel. Just letting the Japanese know that the *Seadragon* was still around had its merit.

During the afternoon of the twenty-third, there was an unforseeable experience that almost caused the Dragon to fall victim to the vagaries of war. At 1551 a distant explosion was faintly heard. And logged. At 1606 there was another far off explosion. Then at 1621 the same thing happened. At 1630, a small freighter identified as the *Tomitsu Maru* of three thousand tons, with two small destroyers as escorts, was sighted in the general direction of the previous explosions. Six minutes later one of the escorts rolled over a depth charge that exploded just aft of the three ships.

Battle stations were manned for torpedo attack. By 1646, the stern tube doors for three torpedoes were opened. Two torpedoes were ready to fire at the freighter. One was held back for a threatening destroyer. All three fish had two-foot depth settings.

Again the gyros in the Mk-10s would not follow in automatic, and as reported by the afterroom, they were sticking in hand operation.

A periscope observation showed that, with only torpedoes in the after room, to bring the stern tubes to bear on the freighter required a large turn to port. On the next look, four minutes later, the freighter had zigged radically, necessitating more maneuvering by the Dragon. The captain ordered, "Right full rudder" and then added, "I'm taking us close under the stern of the port escort. Then we shoot."

The regularity of the explosions every fifteen minutes had occurred to me. However, it didn't seem important until I noticed that the clock was approaching 1651. A glance at Bueb's log showed that another depth charge could be expected shortly and that a depth charge might be rolled off the port escort, just as the Dragon was passing under it.

When I hastily explained to the captain the probability of being blown up by a casually dropped depth charge, rolled over for its nuisance value, the captain stopped the swing of the Dragon and ordered "All stop" on the motors.

Twenty seconds after 1651 there was a hull-rattling explosion uncomfortably close. It swished water through the Dragon's superstructure, indicating that it had missed the Dragon by only a few yards.

On the next look the captain was forced to another radical course change. Using stern tubes and zero gyro angles was no cup of tea. By the time the tubes were lined up for firing, the track angle was so great and the range increasing so rapidly that the captain gave up on that approach. But he later observed another depth charge being rolled off the stern of an escort.

On the twenty-fourth, close to noon, the Dragon made an approach on a small freighter but got no closer than 3,900 yards. It seemed that the Japanese knew the Dragon's poition so well that they could steer their ships to avoid her killing range.

Later, after surfacing in bright moonlight, a DD was spotted at nine thousand yards. When the DD closed to six thousand yards, headed for the Dragon, the plug was pulled and the Dragon went deep. The DD came close, shifted to short-scale pinging and then dropped a single depth charge fairly close to the Dragon. It was as though the DD was telling the Dragon not to underestimate the Japanese capability to sink her if she got too aggressive. Then the DD put on high speed and went over the hill.

Christmas Eve, 1942, seemingly had no significance on board the Dragon as the officers sat down to their Hearts game at 2100. I was catching the Queen of Spades with an infuriating regularity from all the players, and particularly from the captain who wasn't letting up on me for a second. There was no mention of Santa Claus or any intimation that there might be some gift-giving on Christmas day.

In the middle of the game, the radioman delivered a message to the captain. Originated by Admiral Nimitz, Commander in Chief of the Pacific, it was addressed to all submarines on patrol. The message economically said, "I wish you all a big, fat Jap ship for Christmas." At this I had the thought that "at least our top leaders have some heart."

The radioman also told of Tokyo Rose's broadcast that evening; of how she made fun of the American submariners' "holiday revelry," because they would have nothing to celebrate. Her words suggested that the Japanese intended to sneak a lot of their ships past U.S. submarines on Christmas day when their crews had feelings of good will and "were dreaming of sugar plums" (her words). And just plain doping off.

The Hearts game was adjourned a few minutes before the midnight dinner. I left to take over the mid-watch on the bridge.

As I entered the control room I noticed a washline with many black stockings hanging from a line stretched across the darkened, red-lit room. A note was attached to each stocking. I would have ignored this childish Christmas-eve display but the chief of the watch, standing by the trim manifold, said, "You'd better look at the note on your stocking, Mr. Ruhe." I thought I heard a snicker from behind me as the chief handed me a battle lantern and pointed at the approximate location of my stocking.

The first note I shone the lantern on wasn't mine. It said, "Dear Santa, Please bring Chief Bueb a hip-pocket negative tank so he won't have to keep reminding the captain to 'use negative' every time things get hot." That was sort of humorous so I tried the next note.

It said, "Dear Santa, bring Mr. Hoskins a metal toilet bowl." That made sense.

The men standing around the control room were waiting for the reaction to my note, so when I read: "Dear Santa, Please bring Mr. Ruhe a lot of Hearts hands with twos and threes so he doesn't have to take any tricks and can win occasionally," that hit me wrong. I unfortunately snarled, "Wise guy! Whoever wrote that is being too cute." There were some restrained guffaws at the way I flared up. I realized that, just as the officers had ganged up on me because I was an advertised Hearts expert, the crew were equally ready to needle "the new officer on board." I should have passed it all off but I snapped, "I can win, with or without the low cards."

Before climbing the ladder to the bridge I read the last note on the line. It said, "Dear Santa, Please bring Captain Pete a big, fat Jap ship for Christmas." That echoed my sentiments.

There was still another note hanging on the line beyond Captain Pete's note. But there was no stocking to which it was attached. Curious about it, I read, "Dear Santa, give the Dragon a Presidential Unit Citation." She deserves it, I strongly felt. She was doing her part of the job nicely, but the damned torpedoes were dragging her down.

When I arrived on the bridge to relieve the watch, I told Johnson about the notes but he didn't see any humor in them. Perhaps he was disappointed that the crew hadn't wished him anything for Christmas.

Near the end of the mid-watch, the soundman reported distant pinging on two different bearings. The two pinging vessels indicated by their use of their active sonars that they were sanitizing an area at the bottom of the channel. They apparently expected to scare away submarines so that important ships could move safely through the area, and not be torpedoed on Christmas day.

I called the captain away from his Hearts game to make the decision to either run away from the oncoming ASW vessels or to keep the Dragon in a position to block the channel.

When he joined me on the bridge, he'd already made up his mind. "If they get much closer we'll dive and try to work our way around them and go back into the channel." Then he went below to resume his Hearts game.

Twenty minutes later it was evident that the vessels were much closer. The moon was on the wane but there was a good deal of light, so I could vaguely see their light-gray shapes. They were small, probably Chidoris, the one-thousand-ton ships like the new U.S.

Destroyer Escorts, which were single-purpose, deadly antisubmarine warships. The Chidoris were similarly the most feared of the Japanese ASW ships.

I called the captain at his Hearts game and reported we could see the two searching vessels, out at about ten thousand yards. He instructed me to "go ahead and dive before they see you." So I pulled the plug. I was not taking any chances of spoiling the Dragon's opportunity "to make history"—an optimism generally shared by the entire crew.

The captain adjourned his Hearts game and came to the control room, ordering "150 feet, head for Cape St. George's and call away 'Battle Stations.'" The latter order was designed to have the plotting team keep track of the two ASW vessels so that the captain could maneuver the Dragon around them undetected, and move into a good position to intercept the now expected "big, fat Jap ship."

By daylight of the twenty-fifth, the Dragon was free of the two searching Jap ships but had to remain submerged for the day to ensure a totally covert attack when an important ship hove into sight.

Rollo had mentioned earlier that to celebrate Christmas there would be a big meal at noon, even though dinners were normally served at midnight. And of course turkey with cranberry sauce was on the menu.

The dinner at noon of Christmas day with its dried-out turkey, ersatz mashed potatoes, reconstituted powdered carrots and onions and over-baked pumpkin pie, at least provided some cranberry sauce to make the turkey moist and palatable. The numerous cans of cranberry sauce available late in the patrol had been found in the emergency stores locker in the afterroom. Somebody had helped himself to the Spam and other life-sustaining food stowed there for an emergency and substituted lots of jelly, two cans of tomato juice and lots of cans of cranberry sauce. It was the similar poor fare for men trapped in a sunken submarine as was found in the S-37's emergency lockers.

At 1900 a large ship, a troop transport of about eight thousand tons, was sighted to the northwest. She had two escorting destroyers. They were the big ones. The group was on a southerly course headed for The Slot. And loaded with troops, I hoped. The Dragon was promptly swung to have her stern directly in front of the oncoming ships in order to make the final maneuvering easier. When the range to the targets had closed to a few thousand yards, the captain moved the Dragon off the transport's track to offer a good stern tube shot with zero gyro angles on all torpedoes.

The range at firing proved to be 2,550 yards. It was greater than had been planned for, but stern-tube shots were clumsy to execute against a continually zigging target. All four torpedoes were set on two feet on the assumption that they would run deeper. Also, if a DD presented a good set-up we'd split fire, with two torpedoes for the transport and two for a destroyer. But eventually, all four were shot at the transport using the Mk VIII Angle Solver solution generated by Rollo Miller.

After the first torpedo had been launched, the captain reported it traveling wildly far out ahead of the transport's bow. The torpedo appeared to be an erratic, and according to the captain was "going into right field." The wakes of the next two torpedoes indicated that they were passing ahead of the troop transport as well. But the last torpedo from tube ten was observed to hit just forward of the ship's bridge with its explosion loudly heard a minute and forty seconds after it had been fired. The range estimate had been a good one. The transport quickly listed to port, sank deeper in the water, and the soundman reported her screws had stopped.

The captain kept the periscope raised, figuring that it was sufficiently dark so the destroyers would not spot it. That was evident when he saw one of the destroyers three thousand yards away push over two depth charges. After another four minutes he watched the same destroyer push over two more. However, by 1950 a moonless darkness had closed in and all three ships were lost from view.

The captain felt certain that a single Mk-10 torpedo with its light warhead was not going to sink the big ship, so he opted to remain close to the damaged vessel and try to finish her off.

The soundman was reporting destroyer screw noises that indicated that the two destroyers were circling the transport defensively. Then one of the DDs, as he swung in the Dragon's direction, evidently made contact on the Dragon. He shifted to short-scale pinging, speeded up and headed directly for the Dragon. The captain ordered, "Take her deep" and nodded his assent to Bueb, who promptly yelled down the hatch, "Use negative." But Christmas wasn't over yet, and there were no depth charges dropped on that pass or on subsequent passes for the next fifteen minutes.

Certain that the destroyer had lost the scent, the captain brought the Dragon back to sixty feet, only to have a destroyer regain contact on the Dragon, forcing her back down to 250 feet. Doggedly, the captain ordered the Dragon back to sixty feet when it seemed that the DD had lost its contact. And just as persistently, a destroyer re-attacked, losing contact as soon as the Dragon went deep.

Finally, the captain decided to stay deep until the destroyers' screw noises were faint. Then he would try to close the position of the damaged transport. By 2130, the skipper, after assuring that the destroyer's screws sounded distant, ordered, "Sixty feet."

By this time, the moon had started to rise, with a half slice of moon showing over the rim of the horizon. It produced a shimmering light on the glassy-smooth water, making it possible to see the outlines of a very large ship that was very close and no more than four hundred yards away. The ghostly light made it possible for the captain to also vaguely see a smaller, dark shape alongside the transport—a destroyer taking off troops was the captain's guess.

An ideal set-up.

However, as the Dragon was being swung to open out the range and bring the stern tubes to bear, the soundman reported that the other destroyer that had been protectively circling the transport, had speeded up and was heading suspiciously for the Dragon. The captain ordered, "Two hundred feet" but conned the Dragon for a good stern tube shot when the Dragon had opened out to about one thousand yards.

"This is it," the captain snapped. "Sixty feet, Smokey, and do it smartly."

On the way up, the captain outlined his tactics. "I'll take a quick, final look. Ruhe, you call out the bearing and you, Rollo, call out the course to steer for straight shots with zero gyro angles on our last four torpedoes. I'll give course changes to spread the torpedoes a little, and you, Ruhe, punch them out as I call 'Fire seven, fire eight,' etc." Then after a bit of thought, "If that one destroyer is as close as I think he'll be, we'll be going deep after the 'final bearing and shoot' order." It was nervy stuff but the captain described it in a matter of fact way. My throat was dry and my breathing was speeded up, plus I felt pretty dizzy. But all of this could have been from the bad air in the boat. She had remained submerged far too long.

When the captain guessed that the Dragon had opened out to one thousand yards he brought the boat up, took a quick look, announced, "Final bearing and shoot." Then the captain kept the scope up for an agonizingly long time. Everything was in automatic as though we'd practiced this half-baked way of firing a thousand times. But not so for the torpedoes that promptly went astray after they entered the water. Still, one luckily hit. An explosion was heard a minute after the fourth torpedo had been fired and the captain reported seeing a flash of fire spread up to the transport's bridge that "clearly outlined the topworks of a destroyer alongside."

He was so enchanted with watching the results of the lucky torpedo hit that he failed to look for the other destroyer.

"Where's the second destroyer?" I pleaded.

A quick swing to the bearing of the closing DD's screws made him curse, "My God! Down express—emergency!" And in seconds the destroyer was dumping four depth charges over the Dragon that shook her badly but only smashed light bulbs.

As the scope was lowered, the captain extended his hands with the palms up which signified, "That's it. Now we head for home." Yet it wasn't that simple. The destroyer kept darting about, dropping a string of four depth charges each time he crossed over the Dragon. But the charges shook the boat so slightly that it was evident the destroyer had lost sound contact.

The soundman could hear breaking up noises in the direction of the transport. He turned up the volume of his receiver so that we could all hear the groans and internal explosions of the transport as she grudgingly sank.

"Let's get the Hearts game going," the captain snapped. And to Johnson, "Keep headed east and go dead slow. We have to conserve every last little bit of juice in the battery."

When the game started, my head was fuzzy from the foul air in the boat. I really needed the twos and threes to keep from taking tricks. Hoskins was very polite when he dropped the old lady on a trick of mine. "And that's thirteen more points against you, chum," he said pleasantly.

When the captain slugged me once too often with the Queen of Spades, I protested, "Don't you realize it's Christmas, Captain?" The captain merely smiled while Rollo explained that Christmas comes on the twenty-sixth where the Dragon was, across the international date line. So I shouldn't be begging for mercy too early. And none was shown, as they all ganged up on me, driving me deeper into the hole, which wasn't all that deep since I was only down about twelve dollars at that point.

By 2330 the searching destroyer sounded distant, as reported by the soundman. The captain responded by breaking up the game, bringing the Dragon up to fifty-eight feet, and then taking a deliberate long look all around. The transport was gone and the sea appeared empty, but there wasn't enough light to be certain. He ordered, "Surface."

As the Dragon broke the surface the captain scrambled up through the hatch and into the warm night above. After one fast look he shoved the lookout, coming up behind him, back down the ladder and dropped back into the conning tower. "Two destroyers are shooting at us," he yelled, as the hatch was slammed shut above him. Heavy reverberations of gunfire were vibrating the inside of the conning tower as though someone was hitting a steel drum with a sledge hammer. The diving alarm that started the Dragon plummeting downward once more, could scarcely be heard over the din.

In the sudden quiet as the water enfolded the boat, the captain explained, "They were lying there, dead in the water, waiting for us to surface." More destroyers had come out from Rabaul to join in the hunt and that meant a long haul until the Dragon could break into the clear. "As of now we go into a state of emergency," the captain said soberly. "Take all measures to conserve the very little electricity and air left in this boat." There had been no replenishment of air in the boat during the brief moment on the surface.

All lights, instruments, and power devices, including the coffee-makers, were secured. The bow and stern planes and the helm were put in hand operation and the Dragon was balanced at dead-slow speed or even stopped for long periods of time. The air conditioning was shut off. And all men not on watch were ordered into their bunks to conserve oxygen. The blacked-out submarine gave one the sense of slowly dying.

Operating the planes by hand took its toll of the men at the diving stations. The heavy exertion in the bad air caused stomach cramps and collapse after only fifteen minutes of work. As each man was carried back to his bunk, another slid onto the bench before the depth gauges and laboriously cranked the ponderous hand wheels that moved the planes.

From midnight on there were no further depth charges. But the beat of the destroyers' screws and the yelping "pings" from their sound gears showed that they were using hold-down tactics designed to exhaust the Dragon and eventually drive her to the surface.

A small amount of oxygen was bled from the emergency tanks each hour, and carbon dioxide absorbent was spread on the deck to keep the air purified. The white powdery substance absorbed the most damaging part of the air and kept most of the men from feeling no worse effects than a dull headache.

At the end of my mid-watch I rejoined the Hearts game. Breathing had become difficult, and my head was splitting. I noticed Hoskins panting like a dog with his tongue hanging out. I realized we were all breathing more than thirty breaths a minute in order to get sufficient oxygen from the air. The test-tube checks showed the oxygen to be something less than ten percent of the air we breathed.

Shortly after I'd picked up my first Hearts hand, an electrician popped his head into the wardroom and reported: "The average gravity of the battery is 1.070. The cells have begun to reverse."

The Captain's jaw sagged. His cards dropped to the table. "Jump out the bad cells," he growled, "and keep a careful check on every cell from now on." He stared vacantly at the overhead before adding, "How many hours have we got left?" "About three, sir—or perhaps longer. We're using less battery power each hour," the electrician said hopefully.

"And are we generating much hydrogen gas?" the Captain asked.
"No, sir!"

At least hydrogen gas wasn't a worry. Then I began wondering when certain people would realize that it was now Christmas day, officially.

The captain rubbed his head thoughtfully. Shortly it would be daylight topside and planes from Rabaul would be flying tight searches overhead to deny the Dragon even a few scant minutes to replenish her batteries or get fresh air into the boat. But when the batteries went flat we'd have to surface and keep the planes at bay with our guns. With luck we might surface far enough from the aircraft and destroyers to get in a good charge before being forced back under.

A few more Hearts hands were slowly and methodically played. Then the captain eased himself upright and slowly moved out of the wardroom. His body was getting only enough oxygen for small amounts of effort. I followed him up to the conning tower, where he explained his plan of action. "We'll come to periscope depth and take quick looks; if there aren't any planes close to see our scope we'll stick up the SD antenna and check for planes. If there are no planes within ten miles we'll surface. If we work it right we might get in enough charge to last out the rest of the day."

A check with the duty electrician showed that the gravity of the battery was down to 1.040. "And many cells are reversing. The batteries are just about flat."

By 0900 of the twenty-sixth, the situation was truly "grimmo." Dully I thought, "Let's do something." For almost thirty hours we'd been without fresh air and my diaphragm felt as though it was crammed up into my shoulders. And, the Dragon was ready to sink from lack of power. But the captain continued to put off his decision to surface. He only remained upright by leaning on his elbows on the chart table.

At 0920 with the gravity of the batteries averaging 1.029 specific gravity and fading fast, the captain finally said, "OK, we've got to surface, Smokey, get me up to fifty-eight feet."

It was a slow process and exhausting work for the planesmen to bring the boat up to periscope depth. But finally, at 0930 the captain was looking through the periscope and reporting "no planes close by and only the tops of destroyer masts are visible far out on the horizon." Coolly, he said, "come up to fifty-two feet and operate the SD radar." A quick beaming of the SD showed a single plane at eighteen miles. "This is it," the captain mumbled. Then, "Stand by to surface."

Johnson, Miller and I had been directed to act as lookouts when the Dragon hit the surface, with Smokey taking over the bridge watch and the captain remaining in the red-lit conning tower to coordinate the very risky evolution. He would keep a periscope check on the doings of the destroyers that were trying to pin the

Dragon down until exhausted. Four of us were bunched together at the foot of the ladder leading to the bridge when the captain ordered, "Surface."

As the upper hatch snapped open, Johnson, Miller and I shot up the ladder and out into the blazing, blinding sunlight and cool, fresh air. But we had to grope our way to our lookout posts because we were totally sun-blinded. Waiting around in the darkness of the conning tower without wearing red goggles had not adjusted our dark-oriented eyes to see in the sunlight. We were blind as bats!

The two engines, throwing an emergency charge into the batteries, thundered into action, as the captain shouted up through the hatch, "Is it all clear topside?" His voice was indistinct in the hurricane of air pulled down into the boat through the upper hatch instead of through the main induction. The elegant fresh air replaced the foul air in the boat as it rushed aft to feed the engines.

"I can't see a thing. I'm blinded," I yelled forward to Smokey. I was feeling like one of the three blind mice, just as dumb and just as pathetic. The glare of the sun was unbearable as I pried my eyes open to no more than a slit.

"How about it Johnson and Miller?" Smokey shouted at the other two who had groggily groped their way up to their perches on the shears.

"I can't see anything, yet," Rollo complained, defensively. But soon Rollo yelled back, "The skies are all clear to port." Johnson also had the same agonizing delay in making his check for aircraft. Then he reported, "None in sight to starboard."

When I finally got my smarting eyes fully opened, I scanned my sector aft of the shears with my sun-dazzled, heavily squinted eyes. There was not even a small black speck visible in the cloudless deep blue tropical sky. But, using my binoculars, by continuously blinking to force the obscuring tears from my eyes, I was able to make out the topworks of two destroyers at least twelve thousand yards off. At that range, they weren't menacing. There was no urgency in my voice as I reported to Smokey the two DDs astern of the Dragon. He passed that information down to the captain who was now concentrating solely on the SD plane contact, at fourteen miles and closing.

With the plane contact at ten miles, Johnson had it in sight and reported, "The plane's headed right at us."

As the SD radar operator sang out, "Plane at eight miles and closing," the captain ordered, "Take her down Smokey—to 280 feet."

Johnson and Miller crowded behind me as I ran forward to the hatch and dropped below.

The Dragon had been on the surface only eight minutes. This was not enough charging time to make much difference in the flat batteries. The captain disgustedly grumbled, as the Dragon was taken deep, "That doesn't help. We'll have to try it . . ." He was interrupted by the blast of a bomb that harmlessly exploded high overhead. It did no more than rattle the Dragon. The captain continued, "We'll need more juice in the battery to last out the day."

The destroyers rushed toward the Dragon but were unable to make contact with their sound gear. Like an airplane hidden behind a cloud, the Dragon was safe under a cold, dense layer of water that blanked out the destroyer's "pings."

After thirty minutes of waiting, with the destroyers' screws having faded out and no more bombs, the captain took the Dragon to fifty-eight feet. No planes were in sight and a single destroyer could be seen out on the horizon. At fifty-four feet the SD radar showed a plane at eighteen miles and one at twenty-two miles. The captain then instructed, "We do the same thing. Two engines on emergency charge. Stand by to surface."

Again the Dragon shot to the surface with the same sterling three-some as lookouts, but now well light-adapted from staring at naked electric light bulbs.

That session on the surface gave the Dragon nineteen minutes of battery charge before a plane, streaking towards the Dragon, closed to six miles. That was dangerously close. Once more it was "280 feet, express."

But this time there was enough charge put into the batteries to sustain the Dragon in its dead-slow, blacked-out operations for the rest of the day, staying deep. In fact, the specific gravity of the battery, although only a few points higher than when the Dragon was first surfaced, actually increased a few points more in the next hour.

Of course the lights in the wardroom were turned on in order to restart the Hearts game. My head had cleared. As I picked up the first hand of cards, I hoped that I could finally work my way out of the hole. But I held so many high cards that I was forced to take trick after trick.

On one such trick, the captain without a sign of emotion, began pulling a card from his hand. I was watching him closely. Then he hesitated, undecided whether to dump it on me or not. I guessed it was the Queen of Spades. My heart sank. But he thoughtfully pushed it back into his hand.

On the next trick, Hoskins played high. This time the captain yanked the Queen of Spades from his hand and triumphantly slapped it on Hoskins' trick. Hoskins and Miller gazed in amazement at the queen while the captain chuckled loudly. "Merry Christmas, Merry Christmas," I kept muttering to myself because the spell was broken. I was no longer the outsider—the new man on board. It was every man for himself from then on. I knew that, as Hoskins gathered in the trick, his cheeks flushed and his jaw set tightly.

I had to rub it in. "You won't need that metal head bowl, Chum," I said snidely. "We're on our way home."

The Hearts game was adjourned after a few more hands by the captain. The strain was gone. No more worry about the battery and the air in the boat. The captain had gotten his big, fat ship (later identified as the troop transport *Nankei Maru* of 8,416 tons and credited to the "savage red submarine" by Tokyo Rose). The captain returned to his cabin for a well-deserved long and uninterrupted sleep, with the Dragon at 280 feet and heading east.

As surmised, Jap ships were very active on Christmas Day and almost every American submarine on patrol shot at "a big, fat, Jap ship." The *Tautog* sank a five-thousand-ton troop transport; the *Spearfish* heavily damaged two seven-thousand-ton cargo ships; the *Thresher* got a seven-thousand-ton cargo ship; while the *Sailfish* hit a Jap sub, and the *Grayback* sank a landing craft with gunfire. And, of course, the Dragon got her ship. It was, to date, the biggest single-day haul by U.S. submarines since the war began.

Later, well after the Dragon was surfaced after darkness had settled in, I was in my bunk sleeping soundly. All signs of searching destroyers had disappeared at about 1600. So I had gone to bed, convinced that the Dragon was in the clear and that for a long time to come the war was over for the Dragon. Dimly, I had heard the surfacing alarm with a half-awake awareness. Then it seemed as though immediately thereafter the diving alarm was sounding and within seconds there were first many far off explosions, then two violent ones close beside my bunk. They made me bang my head on the bulkhead and almost tossed me out of my upper bunk.

What had actually happened, however, was that the Dragon was surfaced into a very dark and empty sea. After more than two hours of charging the batteries, two destroyers loomed up out of the darkness and challenged the Dragon with signals on small searchlights. Then they charged at the Dragon. Down she went to two hundred feet. The two DDs shortly passed overhead, dropping ten depth charges in quick succession. Then two more with greater care. The last two charges shook the *Seadragon* violently and caused the electric contacts for the motor controls to jump out, with loss of power to the screws for a few seconds, until the electricians reclosed the contacts.

To evade these destroyers, the captain steered the very slow Dragon between the two DDs and out the other side. This gave the Dragon a nice breather. The destroyers kept up their hunt until after midnight and then took off.

Finally, at 0130 on the twenty-seventh the Dragon resurfaced. There was nothing in sight. So four engines were bent on the line and at eighteen knots the Dragon was headed up around the north end of Bougainville Island. Then, with only a few miles behind the Dragon, the number two Winton diesel engine failed with a cracked cylinder head. It seemed to be the greatest damage sustained on the patrol, despite the many depth charges dropped by the Japanese "first string" and the blow-up of the Dragon's own torpedo.

At one of the Hearts games on the way to Pearl Harbor, the captain showed by his lack of concentration on the game, that something was particularly worrisome to him. He took a moment to discuss his concern. "That last salvo of torpedoes we shot at the dead-in-the-water troop transport didn't go haywire because of the gyros. And they didn't look like erratics. I think something went wrong with our fire-control team and I want you, Ruhe, to analyze why the final shots proved to be so bad." Also, four hits for the nineteen torpedoes fired was going to be severely criticized by the admirals when the Dragon arrived at Pearl. It would take a lot of explanation.

In checking all the data used for the final salvo of torpedoes and each individual's role in the fire-control party, I was amazed to find that everyone except Hoskins had made at least one foolish error. Nobody seemed to get it through their head that the torpedoes were being fired at a ship that was dead in the water. Not even the captain had seemed to remember that. So lead angles were produced, the wrong final course was steered, and the spread on the torpedoes was produced by changing the bearing set on the scope rather than changing the course of the Dragon accordingly. Being down too long breathing foul air was apparently the culprit. But it was not then properly realized.

Days later at a lull in the Hearts game, the captain went to the conning tower to study through the scope a merchant ship that was hugging the coast of Makin Island. He spotted a large gun mounted on the stern of the ship and so decided not to try a gun attack. Giving the ship a wide berth, he conned the Dragon towards Pearl.

In the interim, the rest of us were discussing what we were going to do when we got to Mare Island for overhaul. To our surprise, Rollo said, "I'm getting married as soon as I get my month's leave."

I was certain that Rollo had no girl waiting for his return and that none of his previous girlfriends seemed like good prospects. So I challenged his optimism about finding himself a wife in such a short period of time—only one month, the extent of our leave. I said, "I'll bet you ten dollars you won't be married when you get back from your leave," Rollo accepted the bet.

Smokey was just as eager to take Rollo's money but showed some caution. "I'd like to take you for ten bucks, Rollo, but I don't think I'll be around after we get to Pearl Harbor."

At this I had the thought, "He still thinks he's going to get all of his teeth pulled out and that he's finished in submarines."

Enroute to Pearl Harbor there was a good deal of time on watch to think about the lessons of submarine war to be learned for this patrol. As I stood my watches on the bridge staring out at the calm and empty seas flowing past the Dragon, I kept wondering about what had gone wrong, and even more so, what Captain Pete and the Dragon had actually accomplished.

It made me angry to think that the admiral back in Brisbane who had assigned the Dragon to St. George's Channel, the hottest patrol area in the South Pacific at that point in time, had nevertheless loaded the Dragon with worn-out Mk-10 torpedoes, relics from the first World War. They were trouble makers! There should have been some decent torpedoes available for the Dragon, somewhere.

The admiral, I did have to admit, had used good judgement in sending the stolid and brave Captain Pete to play a key role in the Battle for the Solomons. In fact, when the admiral had seen the battered, red-mottled *Seadragon* arrive in Brisbane earlier, he might have decided that she was the most expendable of the submarines under his command, and to be sent into the lion's mouth for nuisance value and little else.

Having a submarine in the Rabaul area had tied down a high proportion of the Japanese ASW assets of the South Pacific and had seriously delayed the transits of her cargo and troop-carrying marus. Her effect on the tempo of Japanese warship operations could not be measured. But it was evident that great numbers of high-speed destroyers carrying troops and emergency supplies for beleaguered Japanese troops, and which had to get past the Dragon, had lost precious time in carrying out their assignments. This disrupted carefully planned and precisely timed operations. Having to avoid the Dragon with radical course changes, and taking the time to lay patterns of depth charges before proceeding onward, caused delays that increased their hazard of being bombed or intercepted by American warships.

At the same time, however, the very high speeds used by the Japanese first-line destroyers and the radical maneuvering of the merchant ships made it almost impossible to get off a decent torpedo shot at such targets. This was particularly true with torpedoes that required the most primitive of ways to shoot them, with gyros set by hand and with very shallow depth settings to compensate for their incorrect running depths. Moreover, the highly visible give-away wakes of the torpedoes made them poor weapons against alerted highly mobile ships. Why weren't U.S. subs getting wakeless, electric torpedoes like the Germans were using?

What impressed me most was the captain's high-risk strategy of lying in wait for the enemy submarine in such an unlikely and dangerous location that the Japanese submarine's skipper was fatally lulled into a false sense of security. A big risk produced a big payoff!

Several questions about the patrol were disturbing. Why were we using torpedoes with only 385 pounds of explosives in the warheads? Why did we pay so little attention to the ill effects on our thinking processes due to low percentages of oxygen in the air we breathed during our major emergency?

Perhaps of greatest importance was the Dragon's demonstration of a submarine's ubiquitous quality. The Japanese seemed to think that the Dragon was anywhere and everywhere in the channel area. The large number of depth charge explosions heard at great ranges from the Dragon showed the enemy's tendency to expend large amounts of ordnance on imaginary contacts.

The entry into Pearl Harbor was most impressive, particularly when compared to the small amount of military activity I had observed when I left Pearl Harbor in early April of 1942. I spotted about fifteen planes in the air at all times, with most on antisubmarine patrol, along with twenty-four patrol vessels outside the harbor. All necessary precautions were taken to ensure that the Dragon was not misidentified as a "Japanese cruiser" and bombed, as had been foolishly done by some silly pilot, who at high altitude had spotted one of our subs returning from patrol. Inside the harbor most of the damage to ships and installations from the bombing of Pearl Harbor had been repaired.

When the Dragon was tied up at the Submarine Base, a member of Admiral Lockwood's staff came aboard to discuss the Dragon's patrol results with the captain. He told the captain that messages had been intercepted that indicated that the *Seadragon* had possibly sunk two ships on Christmas day. He wanted the captain to closely describe the destroyer that was alongside the transport when it was torpedoed the second time. The captain said he couldn't. Still, he was encouraged to claim a destroyer either sunk or damaged in his patrol report. But he didn't.

Smokey got a physical checkup at the dispensary, soon after the steaming watch was secured. When he returned to the boat, he reported that most of his teeth were abscessed and loose in their sockets and would have to be pulled. (Later, when back in the States, the doctors found that Smokey also had some rotted discs in his back, and he never recovered from his back troubles. That finished him for submarine duty.)

The endorsements to the patrol report, with its claim of two ships sunk and one damaged, were nevertheless highly critical of Captain Ferrall's performance. Getting only four hits for 19 torpedoes fired was not considered satisfactory. The admirals who signed the endorsements felt that "the sticky gyros were the result of excessive daily routine procedures which caused the gyro-setting gears to be badly worn and caused the torpedo problems experienced." And, "setting only two feet on torpedoes aimed at a big ship" was considered to be poor judgment on the part of the captain. But the upshot of it all was that when the Dragon pulled into Mare Island in California to start her overhaul, Captain Pete was transferred to the Bureau of Ships in Washington and a new captain reported aboard the *Seadragon*. There was no indication that Captain Pete would get a Navy Cross for this patrol, so the hopes for even getting a Navy Unit Commendation for the Dragon faded.

As for Rollo getting married, we should have known better than to risk ten dollars on the duplicitous Miller's marriage prospects. He took leave after the Dragon's arrival in Mare Island and went back to his home in Williamsport, Pennsylvania. So far, so good. Then twelve days later I received a telegram from him. "HAVE MET THE UNDERLINE THE GIRL STOP AM PROPOSING MARRIAGE." Fourteen days after the first telegram there was a second. "AM RETURNING WITH WIFE JANE STOP YOU OWE ME TEN BUCKS." This didn't make sense until a year later when Rollo revealed that back in Brisbane before we went on patrol, his great pal Chuck Leigh had told him that his wife Dottie's best friend was the perfect girl for Rollo Miller to marry. Chuck had emphasized, "Snap her up before she gets too restless." And Rollo had great faith in Chuck Leigh's good taste relative to women. So I was out ten bucks.

The overhaul of the battle-damaged Dragon at the Mare Island Shipyard in California wasn't completed until mid-April. After a horde of tests for seaworthiness, and several returns to the shipyard to have things corrected, the Dragon, under Lt. Cmdr. Royal "Foo" Rutter, sailed to Pearl Harbor for a workup before going on her sixth war patrol. She wasn't "like new" as hoped for and still had sticky valves, balky operating levers, leaking glands, and unexplained battery shorts. Evidently the greatly expanded work force at Mare Island—with its quota of 4-Fs and with its young-girl helpers who wore sweatshirts and no brassieres—wasn't up to the standards of workmanship that had made Mare a preferred shipyard to be overhauled in.

Thus, when I received orders in late May 1943 to report to "new construction" at Kittery, Maine, it was with relief at not having to suffer through another war patrol fighting the equipment.

After almost a month of leave, spent with my wife and son back in Allentown, Pennsylvania, I reported on board the *Crevalle* (SS 291), just after her commissioning, for duty as Torpedo and Gunnery Officer. By late August, the *Crevalle* (pronounced KRE-valley) was headed for the Pacific to make her contribution to the war effort.

4

Baptism

The first war patrol of the U.S.S. *Crevalle* officially began on October 20, 1943, at 0800 when she backed away from the tender at New Farm Wharf, Brisbane, Australia and proceeded into the Brisbane River. A few silent workmen on the dock and on the tender *Pelias* paused for a moment to casually watch the *Crevalle* get underway. They offered no good-bye waves or shouts of "good hunting" to liven a morning that was gray, windless and dreary. It was not an auspicious moment for starting on patrol. But on the bridge of the *Crevalle* the anticipation for a bang-up baptism of Japanese ship-sinkings had everyone in excellent spirits. "Now we can go get 'em," our expert baseball player Luke Bowdler, said, like a baseball coach sending his team out onto the playing field. It expressed how the *Crevalle*'s officers and crew felt.

It had taken the *Crevalle* a long time to finally be ready to go into action against the Japanese. Commissioned on June 24, 1943, at the Portsmouth Naval Shipyard, she'd started her sea trials on July 11, then twenty days later headed for New London. When she was hurried through the Cape Cod Canal in what was claimed by the *Crevalle*'s captain, Lt. Comdr. Henry G. Munson, to be "in the record time of forty minutes," he excused his impetuousness by admitting that "perhaps I was overly eager to get back into the war." The giggling with which he followed this remark suggested that he thought this was very humorous.

At New London, eight work-days were devoted to repairing discrepancies and installing alterations in the *Crevalle*'s equipment. Then, twelve more days were spent in at-sea exercises, mostly practicing torpedo attacks. When the captain allowed the *Crevalle*'s crew to sleep in until 0800 on the first day of underway training, it was an unheard of act in the submarine navy or, in fact, in any navy except for Munson's Navy. The crew loved it but the sarcastic, morose George Morin, the first lieutenant, growlingly commented that "The old man is show-boating to make bucks with the crew." Yet, this was only one in a long series of "thoughtful" actions taken by Munson for "his crew." They made for a great loyalty to their skipper and great enthusiasm to be the best fighting-crew in the submarine navy.

Then, twelve days were spent practicing gun and torpedo attacks. During this period the captain made even more "bucks" with the crew when he routed out the base paymaster from a deep sleep on Sunday morning—three days before the *Crevalle*'s departure—"to pay the crew what they have on the books." The captain's position on this wild act, as he told it in the wardroom, was that he felt the men should leave some money with their dependents before they shoved off for Panama. Then he slyly added that the crew needed money for some good binges during their last three days in New London. The crew was paid before noon on Sunday but the paymaster, not liking Munson's officious, heavy-handedness, reported the incident to the base commander. Thus, at four in the afternoon the base commander, reinforced by a delegation of other base officers, arrived on board the *Crevalle* and threatened dire consequences if Munson didn't apologize to the paymaster who accompanied the delegation of base officers aboard. With jaw working furiously, Munson grudgingly admitted he had gone overboard in his concern for the crew's needs and duly apologized to the paymaster. Next day, Captain Munson smugly told the officers in the wardroom that he "heard that the paymaster had been transferred off the base." Munson's "thoughtful concern for his men" was much appreciated by the crew.

The trip to Panama took seven days, with the only real problem in the transit being posed by the overly eager "Sighted Sub, sank same" U.S. aircraft pilots. They were bombing surfaced subs, without bothering to properly identify the sub's nationality. They regarded every submarine sighted as a German U-boat.

After five days of refit work in Panama, the *Crevalle* headed across the Pacific on a twenty-five-day trip to Brisbane, Australia. Enroute there were two, one-day stopovers; at the Galapagos Islands and Pitcairn Island of *Bounty* fame. According to the captain, the stop at the Galapagos was "to relieve the boredom of the very long, nine-thousand-mile trip." Cleverly, he used the weak excuse of needing more fuel "to make it on two engines." So after only six hundred miles of steaming, the *Crevalle* was topped off at the Galapagos Islands even though she started from Panama with enough fuel to go at least twelve thousand miles at two-engine speed. Then when he saw the name of Pitcairn on the chart and realized the *Crevalle*'s course would take her within seventy miles of that island he sent a message saying he was changing his planned course "to go into the lee of Pitcairn Island to make some critical repairs." What repairs? The captain made bucks with the crew by describing over the loud speaker system how the *Bounty* mutineers had hidden out on this island for ten years to avoid being captured by searching British warships. Then when Fred Christian came aboard, a fifth-generation descendent of Fletcher Christian, the leader of the mutineers, the crew marveled at his size-eighteen feet, his huge hands and his muscularly large Polynesian body. A never-to-be-forgotten moment in the pause before war action.

At Brisbane there were eight more days of intensive training at sea. And then the *Crevalle*'s readiness to go on war patrol was finally going to be verified by Comdr. Chester Bruton, Commander of SubDiv 81 and a winner of three Navy Crosses while skipper of the *Greenling*. He was aboard the *Crevalle* as she headed for Moreton Bay for several four-inch gun shoots and many submerged torpedo attacks against a small "convoy" made up of a corvette, the submarine *Blackfish* as the main target, and two patrol chasers. If Commander Bruton OKed the readiness of the *Crevalle*'s battle team, he'd be transferred to the corvette and returned to his headquarters on the tender *Pelias*.

After clearing the swept channel through the mine fields that protected the approach to the Brisbane River, the four-inch gun crew gave a superb exhibition of hitting the cloth target that was towed behind the corvette. Commander Bruton was well impressed with the speed of manning the gun and then getting actual hits in the first few rounds fired.

But the torpedo attacks were a different matter for Commander Bruton. He seemed to feel that Captain Munson's organization of the fire control team for periscope attacks was all wrong. The *Crevalle* was using Dudley "Mush" Morton's "Wahoo method," wherein the executive officer was on the periscope while the captain roamed around the conning tower, free to make tactical decisions without the pressure of making judgements from what was seen through the scope. Captain Munson felt, that like Mush Morton he might be too excitable when faced with the actual battle picture as seen through the periscope. Commander Bruton, on the other hand, like most submarine skippers, felt that Munson was dodging the responsibility of being the periscope observer. Others had frankly said about this method that a skipper "just doesn't have the guts to do the scope work and begs off with the claim that he needs the latitude to properly think about the developing fire control problem." Added to this criticism of how Munson had structured his torpedo attack team was his use of a sound shot against a troop transport during the battle for Guadalcanal, when Munson had the S-38 boat. Then he had apparently decided it was too dangerous to stay at periscope depth and opted to go down to ninety feet and fire his torpedoes by sound bearings alone. Though the transport he sank was a critical element in the United States defense of Guadalcanal, Munson was rarely credited with having shown good sense and the requisite bravery to be a good submarine skipper. It was a cloud over his record, and I felt he was incorrectly evaluated since the end achieved certainly justified the means. I felt very strongly that this first patrol would tell a different story about Munson's guts and his judgement as to organizing his fire control team in this off-beat fashion. Frank Walker, the exec, had proved extremely good on the scope in the many torpedo attacks which the *Crevalle* had practiced.

During the torpedo attacks on "the convoy," Commander Bruton stood in the conning tower and critically watched every action of both Captain Munson and Frank Walker. The many successful attacks against the major target, the *Blackfish*, brought no smiles or signs of approval from Commander Bruton. Then, with the fire control team in the conning tower getting less nervous about having the commander observe their performance and with everyone feeling more certain that this *Crevalle* team was one of the best, things got pretty relaxed. In fact, on an approach lasting many minutes, Frank began humming "Nelly Kelly" in between looks. Then just before ordering "Up periscope" he began softly singing, "It's the same old song they sing, I love you. The boys are all mad about Nelly, the daughter of Officer Kelly. And it's all day long . . . ," As the scope moved upward, I noted that all of the *Crevalle* officers in the conning tower except for the captain were singing along with Frank, and trying to harmonize, in the bargain. The look on Commander Bruton's face changed to a black, clenched-jaw, disapproving frown and before Frank started calling out the situation as he saw it through the scope, Commander Bruton turned away and climbed down the ladder to the control room. From there he went to the wardroom where he angrily ordered Willy Gregory, the officers steward, to give him a cup of coffee.

When the captain noticed that Commander Bruton had left the conning tower, he hurried to the wardroom to find out what was wrong. The commander merely said, "Send for my boat to take me ashore."

When Commander Bruton had nothing more to say, Captain Munson edgily ventured, "Are we ready to go on patrol?"

"You're ready," the commander snapped. He then remained silent while waiting for the *Crevalle* to be nosed alongside the corvette. Then he jumped to the main deck of the corvette and didn't even wave good-bye to Captain Munson.

With the *Crevalle* headed north into the Coral Sea after 1600, the captain cautioned the crew that "We are now in enemy territory and moving into action. All men must stay alert and ready for all emergencies. I aim to make this patrol one which you'll remember for a long time to come." There was nothing bashful about our captain.

A little after midnight I was awakened by Frank who read me a message from Admiral Fife's staff that read: "Bill Ruhe is father of a baby daughter." I knew that it was Commander Murphy with whom I'd played much tennis who originated this message. It was a nice gesture. Frank then congratulated me, noting that "girls are a whole lot harder to get these days." But that didn't sound right because previous wardroom checks of this statistic had shown that submariners apparently had about twice as many daughters as sons. And this was attributed to a theory that battery gas inhibited the production of male sperms. But it was nice to know that my wife Carol would now have a little girl to fuss with and put into pretty dresses.

The first full day of the war patrol was most pleasant for the men on the bridge standing deck watches. The sun was hot, the seas were smooth and the soft breeze signaled that spring had come to those who were "down under." The Coral Sea was normally a choppy, mean body of water. But the *Crevalle* charged ahead with only a slight pitching of the boat. Down below it wasn't quite so idyllic, as the captain moved restlessly back and forth through the submarine, congratulating men on their efficient repair work and the reliable operation of the gear in the compartments where they were standing watch. He also asked them about the well-being of their wives and children. He knew most of the men by their last names, making more important his conversations with them. And he was a nervous bundle of energy as though he was fully charged with high-voltage electricity. He confronted one man after another to show his great interest in their professional performance.

On the other hand, the captain remained aloof from his wardroom officers. He spent most of his time behind a drawn curtain to his stateroom where he swiftly did crossword puzzles from many-page crossword puzzle books—an unlighted cigarette dangling from his lip on the right side of his mouth. Occasionally, he ventured into the wardroom "to get a bridge lesson," asking Frank to arrange a foursome, with me included to do the instructing. Invariably, both Luke and George had some poor excuse to get out of playing bridge with the captain. So Frank would get Jerry to be my partner and Luke McDonald to be the Captain's partner. Jerry was such a miserable player there was little fun in having him as a partner, and Lucien "Mac" McDonald, the engineering officer, with his crinkly eyed, perpetual smile offered no help towards making the captain play a decent game. Despite his considerable intellect, the captain seemingly had no card sense and always seemed to do the irrational thing, which I was supposed to comment on and ensure that it shouldn't be repeated. But it never worked that way.

The captain was an enigmatic person to deal with, volatile one moment and the next, calmly deliberate in dealing with a situation. It was difficult to guess how to best get along with this man.

Overall he was a fine warrior and more deadly because of his exceptional intellect. His Nordic heritage showed in his wiry frame, pale white skin, chiseled features, and his intense blue eyes. Adding his wispy blond hair, he seemed to be a modern-day kind of Viking.

After supper in the evening, I played some of the classical records that had been bought with wardroom funds, with Frank's approval. The Mozart, Grieg, Haydn, and Beethoven symphonies were glorious things to hear. But only Luke Bowdler and I stayed in the wardroom to hear the first couple of records. The captain didn't wait to hear the start of the first record, going to his room "to do a puzzle." While the other officers listened to a record for a few moments, did some unappreciative snarling, and then disappeared.

Friday, October 22, there was much discussion and worrying about how to enter The Great Barrier Reef off the northeast edge of Australia. The *Crevalle* was carrying an Australian Coast Pilot, Captain Bruce, who knew the area well and suggested using Grafton Passage to go through the reefs. But he admitted to being concerned about entering the passage through the reef after nightfall. So at noon, the captain bent on all four engines at full power to give the pilot an hour of daylight for identifying the reefs that marked the *Crevalle*'s path through this dangerous area of reefs and shoals.

Captain Bruce said that the *Crevalle* would retrace the trip made by Captain Nemo in his submarine *Nautilus*, as described in Jules Verne's book, *Twenty Thousand Leagues Under the Sea*.

The winds and currents were against the *Crevalle* as she raced towards Grafton Passage, arriving off the passage an hour after dark, and unsure of her exact position. Captain Bruce recommended that the captain anchor the *Crevalle* and wait until morning before entering the reef area. But Captain Munson went ahead with the penetration of the reef, using only one engine and conning the sub through the treacherous area, using continuous soundings taken by the fathometer. The depths were checked against the bearings taken on the beamed light from the lighthouse at Cairns to keep the *Crevalle* on a safe course.

As the *Crevalle* entered Grafton Passage, she passed two small Australian vessels on patrol off the entrance. They seemed totally unaware of a submarine passing close by them. After much blinking of the *Crevalle*'s searchlight in their direction they finally exchanged recognition signals, mystified at how the now disappearing submarine had slipped undetected through their patrol line.

Early on Saturday morning, the twenty-third, the *Crevalle* entered Torres Strait beyond the Great Barrier Reef. The water was a luscious coral green and the reefs everywhere sparkled with lapping

water. Some of the reefs shown on the chart were clearly marked
but couldn't be sighted because they were evidently submerged.
There were other reefs well above water that didn't show on the
chart. It was quite confusing. But on went the *Crevalle.*

Late in the evening we passed Point Restoration where, according
to Captain Bruce, "Captain Bligh of the *Bounty* first touched land
with his open boat that had been set adrift in the mid-Pacific by the
Bounty mutineers." Forgotten was Captain Nemo's path through
Torres Strait, as Captain Bruce pointed out first where Bligh had
landed, then where Bligh had spotted unfriendly natives shaking
their spears at him, and then, later in the day, where Bligh had
passed up a landing to get water because of his fear of hidden head-
hunters. And finally, how he had adjusted his courses through that
area of the Strait by noting the reflections in the sky of water breaking across reefs.

By 1800, as the *Crevalle* was proceeding out of Torres Strait,
Captain Bruce suddenly remembered that it was there that Captain
Nemo had run his submarine *Nautilus* aground. When this happened, Nemo was faced with a horde of threatening, spear-shaking
and war-painted aborigines who had paddled out to the *Nautilus*
and boarded her. But Captain Nemo had all the hatches closed and
dogged down so that there was little damage actually done by the
natives' spears against the iron sides of the deep-diving *Nautilus.*

On Tuesday at sunrise, with the *Crevalle* about to enter the swept
channel leading to Darwin, George Morin, just after being relieved
of the deck watch, saw a periscope close to the *Crevalle.* He immediately ordered the helmsman to put on left full rudder and increased
speed to eighteen knots. His quick thinking probably saved the
Crevalle from having a torpedo shot at her. The rapid maneuver
must have ruined the Japanese submariner's aim. The submarine
contact was quickly reported to Darwin. Within two hours several
planes flew out from Darwin and spotted an unidentified submarine
on the surface that dove on the approach of the aircraft. It was then
guessed that the Jap sub was laying mines at the head of the swept
channel and that extensive minesweeping would be required before
anymore U.S. submarine transits in and out of Darwin would be
allowed. By noon, two minesweepers had hurried north past the
Crevalle as she headed in to Darwin.

When the *Crevalle* tied up at the pier in Darwin, Commander
McGregor came aboard to deliver to Captain Munson his patrol
instructions. The commander said that Red Coe's *Cisco,* the first
boat of *Crevalle*'s division was "overdue and presumed lost." She'd
left Darwin on September 19th after getting her hydraulic system
repaired, then failed to answer a message from headquarters on
September 28 and for several days after that.

After supper I ambled about the well-bombed town of Darwin. Many of the buildings had been reduced to piles of rubble. Other buildings had their sides torn off. An Aussie flyer whom I joined on my walk pointed out where the main bank had been. Only a pair of broken columns on top of a marble stoop with marble steps leading up to it remained to mark the spot where there had been a bank. In the midst of all this destruction grew many gorgeous flame trees, poincianas, and cascara bushes. And there was a delightful smell in the air being wafted over the wreckage by the blooming of many wildflowers everywhere. It was truly spring down under.

The Aussie flyer said that on the last Japanese air raid, eleven British Spitfires had been shot down while the escorting Zeros lost only four of their aircraft. It had been quite a shock for the veterans of the Battle of Britain, to be outmaneuvered by the more agile Japanese fighters. In fact, the Aussie flyer noted that the entire British wing of Spitfires that had come to Australia "to help the Aussies win their air war," had been grounded for a month after that debacle so that they could learn the tactics to properly deal with the Japanese fighter aircraft.

Later, I drifted out to the Army barracks outside of Darwin. There, a mob of Army officers were having a party for eight Army nurses. Frank Walker was there, lifting a few drinks and singing some Army songs, not to impress the nurses but just to sing. The Army officers were incoherently telling dirty stories for the questionable entertainment of the shy nurses, who were not risking being friendly. At some point in the party, Frank received a call from Birck, the signalman, who asked, "Does the Navigator (Frank) desire the routine midnight time check?" Birck, when drunk, would pull that sort of foolishness.

The *Crevalle* departed from Darwin early the next day and headed north towards the island of Timor. It was quite unsettling to be proceeding up the buoyed channel while not knowing if the channel had actually been swept free of mines by the Australian minesweepers that had passed *Crevalle* before her arrival at Darwin.

Twice during the morning, the *Crevalle* was forced to dive by closing aircraft, even though they were thought to be Allied ones.

On the twenty-eighth the *Crevalle* crossed the Timor Sea where fat, green water snakes with black stripes lay on the surface in dense packs of many thousands of serpents wriggling around and ruffling the otherwise smooth water. The tropical sun bore down with such a blazing ferocity that three hours of the bridge deck watch left me light headed and physically exhausted.

At 1430 the *Crevalle* was submerged so as to go undetected as she went through Wetar Passage at the eastern end of Timor. The captain was certain that there were Japanese coast watchers on Timor to spot a transiting submarine. In actuality, the *Crevalle*'s route was so far from the coast that coast watchers would never have seen a surfaced sub moving at that distance from the coast.

On the next day, the *Crevalle* was steered towards several puffs of what appeared to be smoke from ships over the horizon. This produced a feeling of excited anticipation amongst the bridge watch. As the *Crevalle* was raced in the direction of the possible ships, the puffs of smoke turned out to be big clouds of spray blown into the air by several schools of large whales.

On the thirtieth, while officer of the deck, I had to dive the boat three times at hourly intervals away from what appeared to be the same low-wing monoplane. It was most likely an antisubmarine aircraft on patrol. Each time with the plane clearly in view through my binoculars, in accordance with the captain's orders I dove the *Crevalle* when the radar range had closed to eight miles. Each time there were no bombs dropped and it seemed evident that we had not been sighted. On the first dive, due to the excitement of getting under before being sighted by the plane, I left the portable bridge microphone topside. It proved to be flooded out when the *Crevalle* was resurfaced. The captain was much annoyed by this lapse in routine and said I was in "his dog house."

After my watch, when I went below, I pored through the intelligence material that Commander McGregor had brought along with him from the submarine headquarters in Perth. There was a lengthy description of the antisubmarine methods used by the Japanese, compiled from many submarine patrol reports and intercepted Japanese messages. In sum, the information was quite discouraging because it suggested that the Japanese were proving to be a lot more capable and smarter than had been guessed. But then I felt that despite the Japanese antisubmarine capability most of our submarines were coming back from patrol and were also sinking lots of Japanese ships. So they couldn't be as good as their methods indicated.

Then I listened to a radio broadcast that reported that Navy had beaten Duke and that Notre Dame had lost to Great Lakes Naval Training Station. Evidently, the best football players were being recruited into the Navy, some to go to Annapolis and some to oddball teams like the Great Lakes outfit. There was also a message reporting that the submarine *Dorado* had been lost while enroute to Panama from New London. Remembering that the *Dorado* had been commissioned back in New London as she lay alongside the *Crevalle*, my stomach began to knot up and it stayed tight for the next couple of hours.

Late in the afternoon, the air turned cool and frequent rain squalls hurried past the *Crevalle*. A radar contact at a distance over the horizon caused "Battle Stations" to be called away. The *Crevalle* then raced at high speed on the surface, in the direction of the contact. It was moving at thirty-five knots and never materialized into a large ship. So the captain decided it was a cloud being tracked, and gave up the chase. Biehl, the radar technician, had done such an excellent job of fine-tuning the surface search radar that it was likely that even wet sea gulls would be tracked as valid, small-ship contacts.

On the morning bridge watch on November 1, I dove the boat on a fast-closing radar contact that seemed to be a plane but that was never sighted by anyone on the bridge, even though the skies were clear and the last range to the contact was "five miles," as the *Crevalle* went under. The captain, when I came down from the bridge, was waiting at the foot of the ladder in the control room with a disgusted look on his face. With an ugly, grimacing smile showing lots of teeth, he then cackled at me like a chicken and flapped his arms as though he was a bird. He was insinuating that I was acting "chicken" and had dived away from a bird. But throughout his condemnation of my actions as an officer of the deck, I kept reciting to myself one of my many litanies to stay alert and alive. "He who spots a plane and dives away will live to see another day."

The captain had done this flapping of his arms and cackling business on Jerry Gromer, who took the *Crevalle* down on a contact he never saw on the previous day. Then, later after my incident, the OOD, Luke Bowdler, received the same treatment when he dove the *Crevalle*, having seen no sign of a plane but with the radarman claiming that the contact was "at five miles and closing."

Later, as I was readying to go to the bridge and take the midwatch, Mac McDonald, the OOD, upped the *Crevalle*'s speed to eighteen knots and was matter-of-factly talking down to the captain in the conning tower about the situation topside. "I've got him in sight now. He's some sort of small ASW warship, and doesn't seem to have seen us. He's moving only slowly through the water. Doesn't have much of a bow wake." The radarman in the conning tower gave the range to the warship as "3,200 yards."

The *Crevalle* was at the top of Sibutu Passage which led into the Sulu Sea and had apparently successfully avoided the Japanese patrol invariably encountered in the passage somewhere.

The captain had misgivings about passing up a possible torpedo target, so he questioned Mac as to the warship's size.

"He's no more than a subchaser of about six hundred tons." Small? "But no torpedo target, Captain," Mac reported. The captain stayed in the conning tower, not bothering to go to the bridge and have a look for his own satisfaction, because he admittedly had "poor night vision" and couldn't have seen anything, anyhow.

On the second, the *Crevalle* was on the surface crossing the Sulu Sea, when Luke, the OOD, dove the boat on an unsighted contact "at six miles." The captain sneered at Luke as he dropped into the control room. "Another bird?" the captain asked, contemptuously. But as the *Crevalle* passed seventy feet, going "down express" to one hundred feet, there was a teeth rattling "Whammmmm" as a bomb exploded close overhead. Light bulbs were shattered and cork flew off the overhead. Luke looked very pleased, while the captain turned on his heel and went silently to his stateroom, where he pulled his curtain closed.

Over the next five days the *Crevalle* conducted all-day submerged patrols close to the southern coast of Luzon. Ferry boats, motor launches, and fishing boats in great numbers were almost continuously in sight. None, however, were worth shooting at. They were too small and too shallow in their draft to even hit. On one night, I was on watch on the bridge and in complete darkness when a lookout shouted, "Torpedo on the starboard bow." My instant reaction was to order "Right full rudder," turning towards the incoming threatening wake that was clearly visible as a bright luminescent streak moving towards the *Crevalle*. The wake should have passed ahead of the *Crevalle*'s bow because of her swing to starboard. But at the last moment the wake hooked around. And out of the water, framed by a luminescent swirling wave that rose above the sea, shot a dolphin that was just playing a game with another big sea animal, the *Crevalle*. My knees shook throughout the encounter and I recognized that I'd been so paralyzed by the situation that I'd forgotten to dive as soon as possible to avoid a possible second torpedo fired down the same track.

Late on the ninth, the captain brought the *Crevalle* alongside a large sailing banca. Wanting information on the ship traffic in that area, he threatened "We'll shoot up that banca if the people don't cooperate." He had expressed a certainty that such sailboats were on patrol for the Japanese and should be destroyed. I as gunnery officer, disagreed, not wanting to see native Filipinos slaughtered. The captain remained quiet. So I wasn't sure whether he felt that I was insubordinate.

Luckily the captain changed his mind when he saw that the boat contained four women, eight children and only four men, topside. Several of the people in the banca kept jabbering, "Me Filipino." When the captain said, "This is an American submarine," they all laughed delightedly. Then there was more jabbering on the banca that the captain interrupted by asking, "Do any big ships sail along this coast?" A tiny man who was barefooted and wearing only a pair of ragged dirty pants answered the question haltingly. "There are fifty Japanese soldiers there." He pointed to the dark land lying close by to the north. "No big ships ever sail this way," he added, pointing up and down the coast. "No big ships," the little man repeated. The captain, convinced that he'd heard the truth, had thirty pounds of rice sent topside. When the big bag of rice was passed over to the banca, the women pushed several bunches of fig bananas at the *Crevalle*'s crewmen down on the main deck. Satisfied now that everyone was happy, the captain pulled the *Crevalle* clear and resumed a surface patrol. He even smiled at me.

Then, next morning while the *Crevalle* was submerged, and only a few hours after getting the "no ships" information, Jerry sighted a wisp of smoke out on the horizon. Observations through the periscope soon confirmed that there were three large, coal-burning merchant ships headed towards the *Crevalle*. They were being led by an eight-hundred-ton, trawler-type escort. It was evident that they would pass several miles from the *Crevalle*'s present position. So the captain used full speed on the batteries in a long approach to get close to the track of the small convoy. The chase took more than an hour and by that time the batteries were within eighty points of exhaustion with their output within three volts of the low voltage limit. But the Captain ignored the imminence of the battery going flat and the sub losing all submerged power. He said, "We get off the torpedoes, then we think about how we're going to evade the trawler's depth charges." I asked if the trawler could be torpedoed first, but Frank assured the captain that the trawler was too shallow in draft and was too maneuverable to be a decent torpedo target. Thus the *Crevalle* would "be in the soup" if she fired at the trawler-escort.

When the range was 2,200 yards to the biggest ship, the second in the column of the three ships, the captain ordered six torpedoes fired from the forward torpedo tubes with a "quarter length spread, starting at her bow and moving aft." The target was identified from the Japanese Book of Merchant Ships as the *Meiyo Maru* of 5,600 tons. She was a very old cargo ship, but still in service. And it was expected that the fifth and sixth torpedoes would go astern of the *Meiyo Maru* and possibly hit the third ship in column, which almost overlapped the *Crevalle*'s target.

While the torpedoes were on their way, Frank reported that the three ships were a dirty gray and smoking heavily and that the escorting trawler was weaving out ahead of the merchantmen and was acting "fat, dumb, and happy." Disturbingly, Frank said, "There are many men in white uniforms, manning the rails of all three ships, and they're peering into the water looking for a periscope. They've been alerted to there being a submarine near this spot." Thus they should quickly spot the wakes of the torpedoes and alert the trawler to the *Crevalle*'s location. Evasion of that ASW escort was not going to be easy with the little power left in the batteries.

Frank then chanted, "The wakes of the first three torpedoes are running straight and on target." Then, "There's a premature! And, another premature! The geysers they've thrown up look a thousand yards away." The quartermaster confirmed this range, announcing that the two explosions, clearly heard through the hull, were thirty-seven and thirty-six seconds after the first two torpedoes had been launched. Shortly, there were two more explosions that sounded like hits, but Frank said that they were two more prematures about fifty yards short of the big merchantman. Then he called out, "There's a good hit aft of the midships structure on the following ship," identified as the *Kaisyo Maru* of 4,400 tons. "That hit threw a lot of ship debris and smoke into the air, and she's going down by the stern."

The captain meanwhile ordered the *Crevalle* swung around to bring the stern tubes to bear on the second ship in column. Unscathed, it was pouring heavy black smoke from its two funnels, trying to make a fast getaway. Unfortunately, when the stern tubes were finally in a firing position, the track on the big ship was large and the range was opening rapidly. Still the captain ordered, "Shoot all four stern torpedoes" and out they went. All missed.

Frank coolly said, "The trawler is headed for the *Crevalle* with a bone in his teeth." Then he cursed and "There's a premature! And there's another premature!" Meanwhile, many depth charges were being rolled off all of the ships and the sound of big deck guns firing at something could clearly be heard, yet Frank reported that there were no splashes near the *Crevalle*'s periscope. "This is wild," Frank grunted. "There's so much smoke and spray from their shallow-set depth charges that I can't tell what's happened to the last two torpedoes." Although there were more than thirty explosions, nobody thought that any of them were hits. Perhaps two were additional prematures.

Frank kept watching the trawler and noted that it had depth charged the spot where the *Crevalle* had launched her six forward fish. Then, the continuously raised periscope was spotted and the trawler swung towards the *Crevalle*. Over he came as the *Crevalle* was slowly taken deep, her nearly exhausted batteries forcing slow speed to be used. No depth charges were dropped. Soon thereafter, sound reported that the trawler's and one other set of screws were headed up toward Verde Island Passage.

The captain quickly had the *Crevalle* eased back up to periscope depth and Frank took a fast look all around. He reported seeing only one ship with the trawler, and they were retreating northward. Two of the merchantmen were missing. And couldn't be located.

With five more hours until dark it took much husbanding of the *Crevalle*'s battery power to remain submerged. All lighting was secured and battle lanterns were used exclusively. All fans, air conditioning and toasters were shut down. The *Crevalle* was kept at periscope depth with her speed at dead slow or stopped. The boat was balanced using compressed air to trim the boat by pushing water out of tanks.

Then there was a bomb explosion close overhead. The captain ordered safety flooded (for extra weight) to have the *Crevalle* sink down to 150 feet. Mac who was on the scope took a final look and said a Val-type dive bomber was circling the scope. Two more depth bombs were dropped. But they were set so shallow that nothing was shattered. The Val had apparently flown from Manila in response to the *Crevalle*'s attack on the three merchantmen.

Finally after dark, the *Crevalle* was surfaced to charge her batteries. Many of the cells had reversed and were shorted-out. This prevented them from draining the rest of the cells of the little capacity they had remaining. By putting two engines on charge, the batteries recovered rapidly and the *Crevalle* was ready for another engagement. But hopefully not one where six torpedoes would premature.

The torpedo performance was horrendous. Thus, as torpedo officer I recommended to the captain that all the magnetic exploders of the remaining torpedoes be shorted-out. My guess was that this was the feature in the torpedoes that caused the prematures. But the captain said, "No. But we'll report this problem to Admiral Christie and see what he wants to do about it." Admiral Christie was the man who had tested these torpedoes at Newport and was responsible for their performance. So perhaps he'd take the captain's report to heart and change the exploder mechanism in the torpedoes.

At the midnight lunch on the eleventh of November the captain declared: "Because it's Armistice Day we've got to celebrate it with a gun battle with lots of bullets flying around." Thus when Mac, the OOD, announced that he had a small, 750-ton motor vessel in sight, the captain hearing this report looked at me and said, "This is it" and ordered "Battle Stations, Gun Attack."

When I got to my spotting position on the forward twenty-millimeter gun deck and studied the cargo ship through my binoculars in the bright moonlight, it looked harmless and unarmed. But I still had an uncomfortable feeling that this looked all too simple and that something would happen to make this more than sharp-shooting a clay pigeon in a shooting gallery.

The ship had a spoon bow with Japanese characters inscribed on it. Thus I didn't feel guilty about sinking this harmless ship and possibly killing many of its crew.

Then as the captain conned the *Crevalle* close to the slowly moving cargo vessel, I cursed him under my breath for delaying his "Commence firing" order, as the range got dangerously close. The ship might suddenly unmask a big gun and blast me and my gun crews in their exposed positions. It was no fun standing out there in the open where an exploding shell could nick you with a piece of shrapnel. In fact, my shoulders felt cold and clammy because of the waiting.

With the radarman calling "1,500 yards to the target," the captain ordered "Open fire," and the captain of the four-inch gun crew signaled "commence fire." After three rounds had been pumped out at slow-fire and all three rounds were observed to be hits in the steel-hulled ship, I told the gun captain to "commence rapid fire." The shells going in along the water line were ripping jagged holes. Then I had the pointer and trainer put a couple of explosive shells into the vessel's bridge structure. That should have eliminated all personnel who were on the bridge. Moreover, the gaping holes through which I could look, showed no sign of life in the pilot house. After fifteen hits with the four-inch gun the captain ordered "Cease fire." During this period the twenty-millimeter gun beside my spotting position had poured at least fifty incendiary shells into the cargo ship. But no fires were started even though it looked like the deck of the ship was cluttered with oil drums, some of which had been pierced by bullets.

With the ship dead in the water and slowly settling, the captain nosed the *Crevalle*'s bow against the riddled ship's side. He then told me to jump aboard and find out what the ship was carrying in the way of cargo. I had the impression, as I jumped over to the main deck of the sinking cargo ship, that the captain wanted me to go below and look at her holds. But that seemed out of the question at the rate the ship was going down. Luckily, I was wearing sneakers, so getting around on the tilted deck was manageable although dicey because of the oil leaking from punctured oil drums. It was possible to ascertain that some of the drums were carrying coconut oil by the smell of their leakage. I thought to go to the bridge to find some Jap charts or records, but as I moved in that direction I spotted furtive movement in the pilot house. There was a chilling moment when I thought I might get a hand grenade tossed at me. Luckily, I was carrying a .45 caliber pistol that Frank had slipped into my hand just before I dropped down to the *Crevalle*'s main deck to go forward and jump across to the cargo vessel. If a Jap showed his head to aim a grenade at me I might get him first with my .45. But I wasn't feeling so brave that I wanted to have a shootout. So I yelled at the captain, "There's still somebody up there in the pilot house," hoping that my search of the ship would be terminated. He immediately shouted back at me, "Come back aboard, Ruhe. That ship won't stay afloat much longer."

When I sheepishly climbed back to the *Crevalle*'s bridge I sensed that the captain was chuckling about my imagined "live Jap" up on the ship's bridge. But I felt certain that I'd seen a human being moving around in the pilot house.

As the *Crevalle* was pulled clear, the small freighter's bow was thirty degrees in the air and water was over her main deck as she settled fast.

Before going below I noticed that the faces of my deck-gun crew were blackened by the gun smoke. Firing had been into the wind and the advertised "smokeless" rounds were anything but. I also saw that Jerry Gromer, the battle officer of the deck for gun action, was well supplied with weapon power. He had two hand grenades and a carbine lying in front of him on the bridge combing and at his hip he'd strapped a .45 caliber revolver. Jerry was at least fifteen years older than the other junior officers and was a few years older than the captain. Short, chubby and pink-cheeked he still seemed "old" as he stodgily moved around the boat, or sat around the wardroom boringly discussing inconsequentials. Jerry played an occasional game of acey-ducey or cribbage with the wardroom officers but preferred to spend his time back in the crew's mess chatting with the enlisted men. Jerry was a former gunnersmate who'd been commissioned an ensign after the start of the war. He was termed a "Mustang"—an officer who had formerly been a career enlisted man. Captain Munson had picked Jerry up as a knowledgeable gunnery expert who the captain felt would be a great asset on a submarine where he, the captain, expected to use his submarine's gunfire against a lot of ships. To his credit, Jerry did stand an alert watch and he was scrupulously careful to keep his books correct as commissary officer.

Jerry's arsenal of weapons made him seem a bit blood-thirsty. So I didn't like the way he was studying the waters around the sinking freighter, looking for survivors. With none in evidence, I risked leaving the bridge as the captain pulled the *Crevalle* clear and headed her north up the west side of Luzon.

On the twelfth, the *Crevalle* began a patrol off the entrance to Manila. To the north were the high mountains of Bataan and Mariveles. Both were ominously visible in the bright moonlight. It was there that U.S. soldiers were treated so brutally by the Japanese. It made me think of General MacArthur's words "I shall return" and get some revenge for the way the Japanese had mistreated the men who were captured there.

The all-day dive was almost unbearable as the heat in the boat rose to ninety-seven degrees. With the air-conditioning system badly misaligned, the only favorable thing about this faulty condition was that it still reduced the humidity in the boat. I still slept in a pool of sweat, much as I had in the 37-boat.

During the day small steamers were sighted, hugging the coast. But all were too distant and too small to waste battery in closing them.

On the fourteenth, the *Crevalle* moved to a spot off Cape Bolinao, at the entrance to the bay where the Japanese had made their initial invasion landings for the conquest of the Philippines. Storm warnings were received after midnight that indicated that a typhoon was heading towards the *Crevalle* and would sweep over her in the next twenty-four hours. The barometer dropped to 29.20 inches and the seas grew mountainous. Many of the men became seasick despite the fact that the OOD was allowed to use whatever speed and course was necessary to minimize the rolling and pitching of the *Crevalle*. On the early morning watch on the bridge, I watched the bow of the sub head down into the trough of a wave at a steep angle, so steep that the waves rose high above me on either side of where I stood. Water poured over the bridge, and it looked like we would go deep. But with all the tanks blown dry, the *Crevalle*'s bow would shiver and shake, and start rising upward to point high in the air before she started down another steep wave. It was frightening to realize that a bad course and too much speed could submerge the sub under the waves for a dangerous period of time. But it was also comforting to realize that if things got impossibly rough the *Crevalle* could always be dived and operate below the force of the giant waves and high winds.

During the all-day submerged patrol that followed, and while I was asleep, the general alarm sounded, along with the call: "All men, man your Battle Stations, Torpedo Attack." Fortunately, the seas had abated somewhat so that the torpedoes could steer a reasonably steady course and not fluctuate too much in depth.

Racing to my station in the conning tower in my skivvies and barefeet, I recognized that the typhoon's heavy rains blanketed the seas around the periscope and that anything sighted would be close aboard. Jerry was on watch, but it was Doc Loos, the chief pharmacist mate, who had spotted a ship at about four thousand yards when Jerry gave him a look through the periscope. The unidentified ship was headed towards the *Crevalle* so only four torpedo tubes forward were made ready. There was no thought that perhaps there were more ships hidden behind the heavy curtain of rain. The captain and Frank arrived in the conning tower soon after I did.

Frank was able to take only three looks through the scope, with about three minutes between each look, before I called out, "We'll have to start shooting. It's now or never. In less than a minute the torpedo run will be too short to arm the torpedoes."

The captain yelled back at me, "I'm the captain of this boat and I'll decide when we have to shoot!"

Meanwhile, Frank chanted that the ship now identified as the *Tatukami Maru* of 7,065 tons, had "zigged towards the *Crevalle* and is showing a zero-angle-on-the-bow." To Frank's range of 1,300 yards to the cargo ship I loudly said, "Estimated torpedo run is nine hundred yards, decreasing rapidly."

The captain was slow in his reaction, but ordered the torpedoes to be fired "down the throat."

The range was below nine hundred yards when the first torpedo was launched. No spread had been ordered and none was used, with all four torpedoes aimed at the bow of the oncoming ship. The first torpedo hit with a tremendous bang and its heavy concussion shook the *Crevalle*. The second, third, and fourth torpedoes either missed or didn't arm. Frank lowered the periscope. He was certain that the fourth torpedo had run directly under the big ship. Cool and workmanlike, he suggested to the captain that the *Crevalle* be taken deep to avert a collision while full rudder was applied to swing her clear of the ship as it sank.

Through the sides of the conning tower we heard the ship's screws grind to a stop. Then there were loud creaks and groans and low-order explosions as the ship was torn apart, aided by the typhoon's powerful waves.

As the *Crevalle* was eased downward, sound picked up the light propeller beats of two escorts. So when a dense thermal layer was noted, starting at 350 feet, the sub was leveled off just below that depth and balanced in the layer with her motors stopped. This ensured an "ultra" quietness so that even the best Japanese antisubmarine ships would not detect the *Crevalle* on their listening gear. Moreover, the high level of noise churned up by the typhoon should prevent detection by sound means. Yet an escort, pinging rapidly, chugged over the top of the *Crevalle*'s forward room and a discharge of six depth charges was heard. The six explosions that followed indicated that the ASW ship had straddled the sub with her pattern of charges but that they were all set too shallow to have any effect. The ASW warship had been on short-scale pinging when he made the run. As the attacker swung away in a wide arc, he continued pinging on short scale. And back came the first escort, but not pinging, as though he was being coached onto the *Crevalle* by the pinging ASW warship. But no depth charges were dropped. This Japanese tactic had been described in Commander McGregor's intelligence material. It was most worrisome. I guessed that the explosions of the first six depth charges had created so many reverberations that the active ping-returns were absorbed into the background of confused noise.

The captain, feeling that the bow planes were making too much noise in their hydraulic-power operation, had them shifted to hand operation. This seemed to be the correct action since the two escorts scurried around futilely and finally shifted back to long-scale pinging. Shortly, all contacts were lost and the *Crevalle* was brought back to periscope depth. A good look around by Frank showed nothing. We carefully surfaced to minimize the force of the seas pouring over the bridge. A large shot of water, however, poured down through the upper hatch when it was opened. But from then on the OOD merely closed the hatch and stepped on it until a breaking wave had passed over. The hatch would then snap back up of its own accord when foot-pressure was released.

The waves washing over the periscope had prevented any good looks. So the captain decided that the *Crevalle* should ride the surface in order to have a good chance of getting another ship. By going at one-third speed and heading two points off the wave direction the bridge could be kept fairly dry. And by wearing goggles, the stinging rain, accelerated by winds of over eighty knots, became bearable. But little was seen since the goggles had to be wiped continually.

The radio reported that the typhoon was sweeping over Luzon and doing much damage. Fortunately, a continual check of the wind's direction showed that the eye of the typhoon had passed the *Crevalle*'s position and was slowly moving north and away. That meant that conditions on the bridge would tend only to get better. And as they improved I thought about Frank and his performance in the typhoon attack. He stayed even-handed and had suppressed his talkativeness and tendency to want to sing when things were going right. He was like a finely trained athlete who performs well under pressure and effortlessly. Frank was no athlete. But he had been manager of the Naval Academy's football team, back in 1934.

Once below at the wardroom, I noticed that the captain was the only officer to order coffee. The rest of the officers had shifted to tea. But that shortly proved to be in short supply since much of the *Crevalle*'s stock of tea had been brown-bagged ashore and given to new-found Aussie friends, who were unable to get any due to the war.

On the night of the sixteenth, the *Crevalle* headed south to a patrol area off Manila. The captain felt that the ship-sinking off Cape Bolinao would cause all shipping to stay clear of that area for the next few days. Better luck was thus expected far from the scene.

Turning into my bunk after an early morning watch, I was so exhausted from battling the many waves that poured over the bridge, along with the pelting, driving rain that assaulted my body, that I slept all day. This was something I'd never done before. When I was awakened for the next watch, it was discovered that the captain had reduced all bridge watches to three hours, on the basis that four hours were too exhausting and that the OOD's efficiency in the fourth and final hour had become too low.

Within minutes after relieving Mac of the watch, I picked up a very large dark smudge on the horizon. Through the binoculars it looked like a long tanker riding high in the water. The captain was called to the bridge. Without hesitation, he called away the radar tracking party. The gathering darkness made it increasingly difficult to define the type of target that was out there. The radar held the target initially at sixteen thousand yards with the range decreasing slowly. To simplify the tracking solution being obtained on the Torpedo Data Computer (the TDC), the captain ordered the *Crevalle* stopped for a few minutes. Rapidly, it was ascertained that the big ship, now almost invisible in the moonless blackness of the night, was making nineteen knots and was zigzagging wildly while slightly closing the *Crevalle*'s position. Small zigs of the target about every four minutes were superimposed on large zigs every twenty minutes. The general direction in which the target was moving was northwest and would carry the ship six thousand yards clear of the *Crevalle* and out of shooting range. So the captain put on all four engines and rang up flank speed, and had all ballast tanks blown dry to increase speed a knot or two. The Bendix Log showed 20.5 knots.

At this time, an escorting warship was barely visible on the near quarter of the big ship. His bow wake was more evident than his haze gray hull.

At about ten thousand yards range, Luke said softly to the captain, "It looks like a flat-top. But it doesn't have an island midships. And it isn't a big tanker because there is no bridge or any funnels aft." The captain merely grunted. With his very poor night vision he probably saw only a blank wall of blackness. He thus must have wondered about Luke's assessment.

"A flat-top . . . An aircraft carrier!" The thought of bagging an air-craft carrier put the captain on an exhilarating high. His warrior instinct made him chuckle with undeniable enjoyment. And his body surged forward as the *Crevalle* rode down a long swell. Then he reared backward as *Crevalle* climbed out of the trough of the wave. He acted as though he was on a galloping horse, riding with a posse that was overtaking a speeding train carrying a gang of bandits. Although I imagined this, the captain's great interest in trains and railroading would tend to make him think in terms of train situa-tions. The captain was known to take a week's vacation each year and ride the caboose of a freight train that was pulling many box cars. It was his hobby. His wife Ann also complained that the toy train set that her husband had bought for his son, John Henry, was played with far more by "Hank" than his son.

The two ships were out on the *Crevalle*'s port beam as she headed on a collision course with the track of the ships. This course took her to a spot far ahead of the warships' present position. It was apparent that with the very small differential between the speed of the *Crevalle* and the big ship, it would be necessary to run a great distance while reducing the separation range at only about fifty yards a minute. More than two hours thus elapsed while the initial radar contact range of sixteen thousand yards was reduced to ten thousand yards separation.

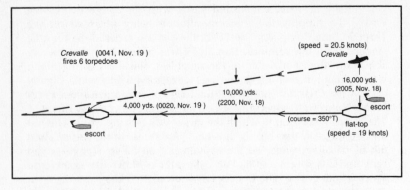

Figure 4.1 Crevalle's attack on flat-top (November 18–19, 1943)

Occasional radar ranges were taken on the target ship, however only very cautiously. The radar's antenna was aligned with the bearing that Luke fed from his bearing transmitter on the bridge. Then the radar was triggered for an instant to get a single radar echo return. It seemed certain that two such Japanese warships would by this point in the war, have electronic intercept equipment for picking up radar emanations from U.S. warships. But a single squirt transmission of the *Crevalle's* radar would be difficult to detect. And if detected it would be difficult to get a bearing on it, not to mention determine if the characteristics of the signal matched that of a U.S. submarine radar.

George maintained a plot of bearings and radar ranges to the ship along with a plot of the *Crevalle's* moving position. His plot clearly indicated that if the ship on one of its big twenty-minute zigs turned radically away, the *Crevalle*, might be all night getting into an attack position. The plot also showed that if the captain became impatient and tried to head for the target to close the range more rapidly, that *Crevalle* would wind up far astern of the speeding target. And well out of torpedo range.

The patience required for this approach steadily increased the tension within the men on the bridge and in the conning tower. Minute after minute the clock moved slowly ahead with an almost unnoticeable improvement in the *Crevalle's* chances of getting in for a torpedo attack.

Frank wandered silently around the red-lit conning tower, checking the fire control solution and periodically transferring the *Crevalle's* position from the plot kept by George to the navigation chart. Frank wanted to make sure that the *Crevalle's* course took her clear of any shallow areas. This was no time to run aground. Frank wasn't even humming a tune.

The captain dropped down into the conning tower occasionally to study George's tracking plot. Then he checked Frank's navigation chart. Finally, he studied the firing solution that I was generating on the TDC. Nothing was said. Then back to the bridge he climbed to stare blindly out into the darkness.

The ten torpedo tubes made ready at the start of the chase were drained down and were not to be re-flooded until it was certain that the *Crevalle* was headed in to launch her torpedoes at close range.

The captain's total dependence on Luke to tell him the situation out in the darkness was an aberration of this submarine war. Additionally, the radar bearings and ranges that the captain needed to assess the situation were supplied by Lt. George Morin. Both of these men, so important in this night surface attack, were naval reservists commissioned shortly before the war. Luke took his twelve-week indoctrination course at the Naval Academy, and George at Prairie State in New York. They were both quick thinking, and good athletes full of vitality. Luke was talkative like the manager of a baseball team while George was silently moody much of the time except for short moments when he turned on his great charm with rapidly delivered words that were softly spoken as though great confidentiality was involved. Both were indispensable.

Two more hours went by, slowly grinding away at the distance of separation between the hunter and the hunted. There was no sign that the warships knew there was a submarine getting dangerously close to their track. The range to the ship had been whittled to four thousand yards. At this point the captain started to imagine that he could see the big ship as a dark smudge out in the blackness and ordered that all ten torpedo tubes be flooded and the torpedoes made ready for firing. Then the two warships began a rapid exchange of blinked lights, and zigged towards the *Crevalle*. A large searchlight beamed close to the *Crevalle*'s bearing. The captain yelled, "Get Old Glory run up to the top of the shears. I want that carrier to know who's attacking him."

It seemed certain that the *Crevalle* had been spotted. But how?

"We're coming in," the captain shouted at the flat-top. The *Crevalle*'s course was changed to head for a spot just ahead of the bow of the carrier.

At this point, Jerry, the OOD, ordered the rudder put hard over, then quickly corrected that, having the *Crevalle* resume her course. He was avoiding a sailboat.

With the range to the flat-top at under three thousand yards, the captain, peering through the murky haze, incredulously yelled, "Hey. This is an aircraft carrier." Then he ordered "All stop," to reduce the *Crevalle*'s speed for launching the torpedoes. If fired at over twelve knots, the torpedoes would tumble and run erratically.

When the TDC indicated a torpedo run of 1,500 yards and with the *Crevalle*'s speed dropping to twelve knots, the captain ordered that all six torpedoes up forward be fired. The torpedoes were set on six-feet depth and a target length of six hundred feet was used for the spread of the torpedoes from bow to the stern. All six torpedoes were launched.

Luke thought the flat-top was a merchant ship converted to an aircraft ferry. The captain, with his doubtful identification said it was an escort carrier of some sort, "And big!" The escort resembled a Fubuki destroyer and was on the far side of the flat-top—temporarily out of action.

Before a minute had passed, there was what the captain called, "a perfectly catastrophic explosion which threw flames and corruption a thousand feet in the air." Three more hits were heard by people inside the *Crevalle* but were not observed by anyone on the bridge. The flat-top began to frantically toot his whistle in short blasts. It was a signal that the carrier was under submarine attack. At this, the Fubuki appeared from behind the flat-top's stern.

Within seconds the tooting was interrupted by the bangs of big guns aimlessly shooting at ghosts in the pitch blackness. Machine gun fire chattered away and twenty-millimeter tracer shells were sprayed like water out of a garden hose. Tracers were directed at each other as probably were the shells from the big guns, which were fired with little observable flame. It seemed certain that the Japanese were using smokeless powder with their big shells. In many ways they were well ahead of the United States in their weapon technology.

The inside of the conning tower reverberated and shook from the concussion of the gunfire from big guns. Every now and then a white-hot shell would pass overhead leaving a trail of disturbed air. It didn't seem that the gunners on the two warships had the *Crevalle* in their sights but there was one instant when the sub's bow was badly shaken. A torpedoman up forward excitedly reported, "I think we've been hit in the bow by one of those shells."

When the *Crevalle*'s stern was bearing on the flat-top the captain ordered the bridge cleared and "Dive, dive." As he hit the conning tower deck he yelled at me to fire the stern tubes. But I had no bearing on the carrier. Luke having ducked down below the combing for protection from the shells being sprayed in the *Crevalle*'s direction was not providing any bearings. When I asked the sound man for the bearing of the target's screws, he reported that the carrier had come to a dead stop. But he said he held the destroyer's screws loud and clear and "They're closing fast."

The captain ignored the fact that I wasn't firing the after torpedoes because we did lack data and a good solution. When I looked at

Frank for help, he merely spread his hands outward in a hopeless gesture while negatively shrugging his shoulders.

Jerry had failed to close the lid on the bridge microphone box when he dropped below and that meant that it was going to be flooded out and ruined for the rest of the patrol. He would also be in the captain's "dog house." But leaving the box open allowed everyone to hear over the 7 MC speaker system the cacophony of machine gun bullets hitting the *Crevalle*'s tough steel sides and the loud booms of big guns in rapid fire. There was lots of noise and for a moment I felt that perhaps submariners did sometimes get wounded in battle and earn Purple Hearts. But actually submarining was an all or nothing sort of thing. Lots of people lost. But no paraplegics were produced.

The dive proved agonizingly slow as the vents failed to open hydraulically. Mac, as diving officer, yelled over the 7 MC system "Hand dive, hand dive." And the men in each compartment swung into action and mule-hauled the vents open with inspired, strong-armed tugging. It was evident that having a strength club aboard would be a good idea for future patrols. Old Pop Bridges, the chief of the boat, who was stationed on the ship control manifold during battle, had inadvertently shut off the hydraulic system when he thought he was closing a valve for the seawater to the depth gauges. Old Pop was older than Jerry and looked a lot more weather beaten. His seamy, worn-out leathery face showed that he'd seen better days. Though Pop seemed over-the-hill, the captain had selected him as "a figurehead from the old Navy to father the present crew of lively young men who need somebody to look up to." But I felt Pop's days were numbered aboard the *Crevalle* after hearing how he'd doped off. The *Crevalle* couldn't afford much of that kind of stuff.

At this point I noted in my journal that I was beginning to identify our boat as "*Crevalle*" rather than the popular way of calling her "the *Crevalle*." It was as though our submarine, which had once seemed an inanimate structure of welded steel, had become a living entity with a character of feminine sensitivity and with female idiosyncrasies. Subs normally were referred to as feminine, and surface warships as masculine.

Luke said that his last look topside had showed the Fubuki hooking around towards us but that the *Crevalle* was inside the turning circle of the destroyer and shouldn't get any well-placed depth charges. Then, the first string of depth charges was so distant that it had to be guessed that all the shooting had totally confused the Fubuki. At no time had his sonar pings zeroed in on the *Crevalle*.

Close at hand were the grinding, agonized noises of a damaged ship being torn apart in the long swells that pushed her up and down and sideways. Since the screws of the Fubuki seemed distant, the captain ordered the *Crevalle* back to periscope depth. But Frank couldn't see a thing on the very dark ocean surface. A check had been made of George's plot to ascertain where the flat-top had stopped so that the *Crevalle* wouldn't ram him on surfacing. But our position proved well clear of the damaged ship. The only unusual incident that followed the surfacing was Mac reporting that although he had blown bow buoyancy tank to get a good up-angle on the *Crevalle* while surfacing, nothing had happened. "All the air seemed to be escaping from the tank," he reported.

The captain had me drop down to the main deck and go forward to see what the trouble was. Using a flashlight, it was determined that a large jagged hole had been ripped in the bow where the bow buoyancy tank was located. Evidently, a large caliber shell had hit the *Crevalle* during the wild shooting of the Japanese warships. Luckily, the tank was forward of the pressure hull. Had the shell hit a little further aft it would have pierced the pressure hull, preventing the sub from diving.

After the bridge watch had done much peering out into the gloom around us, with nothing in sight the *Crevalle* quickly cleared the area at seventeen knots.

Later in the wardroom, the captain argued with Luke about the size and shape of the flat-top. Jerry, the OOD, said nothing, as though unaware of what had happened topside. Luke insisted that the ship was no bigger than ten thousand tons and didn't have any aircraft tied down on her top deck. But he thought, as configured, she'd be excellent for carrying a large load of aircraft. The captain insisted that the flat-top was an escort carrier of at least eighteen thousand tons displacement. And that was what Luke feared would be put in the patrol report.

The next four days were fruitless. Four torpedoes remained and those four were in the stern tubes. So it could be difficult to expend them before heading "back to the barn."

The *Crevalle* maintained a daily submerged patrol near the east coast of Luzon just south of Manila where lots of small cargo ships, sailboats and small motor launches moved around on irregular courses as though they were on antisubmarine patrol. But all were of too shallow a draft to be torpedo targets. It had become evident that the Mk-14 torpedoes were running considerably deeper than set, and would merely miss by going under a shallow draft vessel.

Later in the evening of the twenty-third, the *Crevalle* struck a submerged object that bent the rodometer of the Bendix log, the device for measuring the boat's speed. Thus, it couldn't be retracted into the boat. Then at midnight, the *Crevalle* hit something else that knocked the holding dogs off the stern planes. Since Frank's navigation chart showed no underwater obstructions in the *Crevalle*'s location, it appeared that she had struck submerged wreckage from a recent ship-sinking.

Wednesday, the twenty-fourth, was bath day for the crew. Showers were allowed only weekly as a water conservation measure. Food handlers, however, were required to bathe daily. There was no below-decks griping about this shower routine because the air-conditioning system had been worked on and reduced the sweating, while submerged, to a low level. After dark, a Japanese hospital ship, brightly lit and with red crosses on the sides, passed a few thousand yards from the *Crevalle*. Too many of these privileged vessels were being observed by U.S. submarines, making suspect their actual use for other purposes like carrying troops and war supplies. But the hospital ship was allowed to pass without inspection.

Thanksgiving Day, the twenty-fifth of November, was a day on which we hoped to shoot the four torpedoes. Then we could be thankful for being able to start home. But that wasn't as important to the crew as being able to thank God that all were still alive, and "successful in their trade," as Frank expressed it. The dinner at noon was very good with ice cream and pumpkin pie for dessert. Then, just before the end of the day, smoke was sighted on the moonlit horizon. It proved to be a freighter using the same route as the *Crevalle*'s previous two victims. The Japanese were not rerouting their ship traffic; they were merely sending out a horde of small patrol boats to scare enemy submarines out of the area.

For the next hour, the freighter was tracked to determine her zig plan. It was only a simple one with small changes of course. She was making eight knots, and there was no sign of an escort! An attack on the surface in total darkness seemed dictated but incredibly the captain dived the *Crevalle* a thousand yards off the unidentified maru's track. There the *Crevalle* waited at slow speed for the approximately four-thousand-ton ship to cross her stern. Perhaps the captain's decision to make an attack, based purely on SJ radar data, was predicated on his awareness of many patrol boats having been sighted in the area.

Shortly, with an 1,800 yard torpedo run, all four torpedoes were fired from their stern tubes in quick succession. They were spread to get at least three hits. The first torpedo exploded within a few seconds. A premature! The second and third hit with heavy detonations. The fourth missed the ship. The radar echo on the first hit mushed out into a huge blob while the screws of the torpedoed ship immediately stopped. In the process of coming to a stop the ship had rolled over two depth charges and their explosions were heard just after the second torpedo was heard to hit. Then the radar pip of the maru disappeared from the radar screen. Through the periscope, nothing definite was observed. The *Crevalle* was quickly surfaced but nothing was found. Not even a lifeboat was detected on the surface of the sea. But a medium-size patrol boat roared towards the *Crevalle* and passed close aboard, as though unaware of the *Crevalle*'s presence.

With all twenty-four torpedoes expended, the captain bent on three engines. Following which, a message was transmitted to Perth that told of the *Crevalle*'s patrol results: "Four ships sunk and one damaged," and that she was heading for Fremantle. It was a great feeling to be on our way, but it was still a long way home with many narrow and dangerous passages to be transited. Reports from other boats indicated that the Japanese antisubmarine effort in these passages had become more efficient, intense, and worrisome.

On November 29, while crossing the Celebes Sea an unescorted freighter was sighted, bound for Tarakan. Without any torpedoes on board, and with heavy air activity over the Celebes Sea, it seemed too risky to sink the ship with the deck gun. And since there were no U.S. submarines near at hand the captain decided there was no need to track the cargo ship. So the *Crevalle* proceeded on her way.

The *Crevalle* entered Makassar Strait on the thirtieth, running on the surface on three engines. That evening while on watch, what seemed to be a submarine was sighted at 3,500 yards closing the *Crevalle* on an opposite course. The *Crevalle* was swung away on the possibility that it was an enemy submarine or a patrol boat with a very low silhouette. The captain thought that what was being evaded was definitely a U.S. submarine and insisted upon blinking a recognition signal at the unidentified vessel. There was no reply. So the captain had four engines put on the line and steered the *Crevalle* away to continue on south. This was risky business, showing a light towards a dark menacing shape on the ocean. When the quartermaster started flashing the identification signal, a cold chill ran down my spine and I felt jittery for a few moments.

On December 1st, two bancas were investigated. They were loaded with what looked like Javanese fishermen. The men wore only loincloths and colorful red, orange and yellow bandannas around their heads. The captain called away the twenty-millimeter gun crews and said he intended to destroy the native craft if its occupants appeared to be disguised Japanese spies. Jerry had his hand grenades ready to toss at the bancas' crew if they acted like the enemy. The captain also had the American flag run up to the top of the shears in preparation for gun action. Again it was "We've got to have Old Glory at the main when we go into action."

When the *Crevalle* closed the nearest banca it promptly dropped its sails. At this, the captain, feeling that lowering the sails of a foreign vessel showed a mark of respect for the United States, sprang to attention, snapped his heels, turned to "Old Glory" and saluted the flag. But the sixteen men on the banca merely looked smug, as though they were out on a lark away from their womenfolk. The Javanese, it was understood, let their women do all the work at home so that the men could at any time dash off on long ocean fishing trips. Without further investigation, the *Crevalle* went on her way.

At 1400 I was awakened by a frantic cry of "Dive, dive." Then, appealingly, "Get her down—fast." Luke had spotted a plane less than two miles away and high in the sky, about to dive at the *Crevalle*. There were some agonizingly long, drawn-out seconds before the sub passed sixty feet, going deep. At this my breathing got easier. Then at 130 feet a depth bomb exploded overhead. It shattered light bulbs but was set too shallow. Probably one hundred feet. A second bomb went off with a "pop" as though it was a dud. The delay in receiving the first bomb indicated that the plane had overshot the *Crevalle* on its initial dive-bombing run. Luke turned to me and gasped, "That was no bird." If nothing else, the dive bombing of the *Crevalle* made the lookouts far more alert.

The *Crevalle* charged through Lombok Strait at flank speed on the surface during the early morning of the third of December. Two patrol boats sighted us and gave chase. Apparently they couldn't match the *Crevalle*'s speed and fell far behind her as she shot out into the Indian Ocean before dawn.

The remainder of the transit south should have been a delight, yet I found myself being irritated by almost everything. Jerry's desire to get off the boat and join a relief crew in port made me boil. Luke's prolonged sleeping in the bunk above me seemed an utter nuisance. The seas, running very high, thoroughly soaked me on each bridge watch. And then the cooks had all sorts of rotten excuses for serving miserable meals. I decided to refrain from talking with anyone more than I had to, in order not to show how I was smoldering. Then George gave me the silent treatment. I wondered whether I was suffering from lack of vitamins or just plain loss of weight. Or was it letdown from the excitement of the patrol?

The captain indicated that one of the officers would have to leave the *Crevalle* and go to new construction. I was afraid that I'd be fingered to go. Then the captain, with a wide toothy smile showed me my fitness report. All 3.6's. My heart sank. It was the worst fitness report I'd ever gotten. Normally, Academy officers got straight 4.0's from their submarine skippers. So 3.6's looked like I was going to be transferred off the boat. But I discovered that Frank had gotten the same marks as mine. Frank explained that "Our captain thinks that 3.6 is a 'starring' mark, and we should feel flattered that he rated us that high." I hated to think what marks the "fresh caught reserves," Luke and George, were getting. But then Frank indifferently said that fitness reports in war weren't all that important and wouldn't affect our future assignments.

Again finding myself with some thinking time near the end of a patrol, I tried to summarize what might be learned from the *Crevalle*'s first patrol.

The performance of the torpedoes was so dreadful—about half prematures, deep runners, or duds—that in addition to reporting the many failures, I felt the captain should get all the skippers at his rest home to go to Admiral Christie and insist that something be done about the torpedo situation right away. All the skippers were reporting similar torpedo failures in their patrol messages summarizing the results of their war patrols. So Admiral Christie should be firmly pressured to realize that his excuse was not valid that: "The torpedoes aren't the problem, it's the skippers who can't shoot straight that need to be worked on."

The considerable number of aircraft, closing the *Crevalle* from long distances away, that flew directly at the sub and forced her to dive, indicated that the Japanese aircraft had some sort of electronic intercept receivers that could give them a good bearing on the *Crevalle*'s air-search radar emanations. Warships also seemed to have electronic intercept equipment that was able to detect submarine surface-search radars. How else to explain the radical maneuvers of the flat-top and her escorting destroyer? This meant that the *Crevalle* would from now on have to use its radars sparingly and in such manner that meaningful electronic intercepts by enemy aircraft and ships would be unlikely.

There didn't seem to be any broad strategy for deployment of the *Crevalle*. Were U.S. submarines being assigned strictly to areas where merchant ships might be encountered and sunk? What about going after the Japanese fleet, particularly her destroyers and big escorts? This attrition war looks like slow business and things might be speeded up by selecting warships as primary targets.

The captain's continuing efforts to create a crew with high morale, while paying less attention to the officers, was questionable. Fortunately, Frank gave frequent pep talks to the wardroom officers, for which he was labeled "the Coach." But the captain might better have delivered such morale-boosters.

The day before arriving at Fremantle, Frank rounded up most of the crew for lectures that included "Drinking in Port," "Personal Hygiene," "Information Security," and "Relations with Civilians." On the other hand, I had to spend most of the day censoring stacks of mail. Much to my surprise, the men were feeling particularly good due to the results achieved on the patrol and hence were writing letters to show it. As I studied letter after letter, enlisted men who were passing the wardroom would stick their heads in and ask if I would arrange to have a ship's party "to celebrate our good patrol." Since no one had been designated as recreation officer, the enlisted men seemed to think I'd get the ball rolling and Frank would help me. They did deserve a party.

Off Fremantle early on December 7, a submarine was sighted out on the horizon. It promptly dove. No message had been received concerning a U.S. submarine in the *Crevalle*'s path, so the captain gave the unidentified submarine's diving position a wide berth as the *Crevalle* headed for Fremantle Harbor.

Having the deck watch entering the harbor, I was allowed to put the *Crevalle* alongside the pier where a large crowd of people, workmen, civilians, and submarine officers lining the pier produced much cheering as the *Crevalle* tied up. A band on the dock was playing "Anchors Aweigh" and "Pack Up Your Troubles in Your Old Kit Bag." There were a few good-looking women in khaki dresses who were soon identified as the drivers of the recreation cars that were assigned to the *Crevalle* during her stay in Fremantle. Just getting this recognition for a job well done put me in a good mood to start the two weeks of rest period ahead. For a moment, I thought that everyone on the pier was ordered there to welcome a returning boat in order to keep the morale high in the fighting boats. And that was important, because many of the submarines were having a rough time of it.

Captain Munson had arranged by voice radio to have a beer party on the pier immediately after arrival. And what confusion that generated! The *Crevalle* men were rushing over to the pier while staff officers, relief crew, and tender personnel were coming aboard. People swarmed all over the *Crevalle* trying to determine what repairs were necessary and where the job orders were that covered the work—as though it was all going to be done in the next twenty-four hours. Few of the *Crevalle*'s crew who had written the job orders could be located. Then, when finally located, they proved to be too beered-up to give clear explanations about the specific jobs that needed doing.

It was a great relief for Mac, George, Luke, and me to climb into our assigned car and head for the rest home, Lucknow, in Cotesloe, Perth. The volunteer driver of the Chevrolet was Joan Darcy, who was rapidly determined to be married, and with her "bloke" out at Tobruk, North Africa.

On arrival at Lucknow we were confronted by two women who stood on the stoop at the entrance to Lucknow as a questionable welcoming party. Matron Vance who supervised the rest home had a stern, disapproving look as she surveyed her guests. Beside her, a tiny bird-like creature who chirped, "Welcome, welcome, welcome," was identified as Lucknow's hostess, Ricki. She was dressed in a black taffeta cocktail dress and had overly rouged cheeks, making me wonder at the sort of establishment being run for the submarine officers. Matron Vance, on the other hand, standing ramrod straight, all six feet of her, with arms folded under her massive breasts and wearing a slate gray dress that formlessly fell to her ankles, appeared to be supervising a Temperance Union, a society of abstainers from hard liquor. I hoped this wasn't another dismal

Brisbane-type rest home. And it wasn't, despite the Matron's frowning visage and Ricki's smothering fluttering around, "trying to do whatever I can to make you boys comfortable." Ricki kept apologizing for making each officer pay fourteen Aussie pounds, (about fifty dollars), for the two weeks of food and for the liquor and beer rations. But when twenty-four quart bottles of Emu Bitters beer arrived in a packing case that was big enough to double as a coffin, we knew our stay was going to be a great bargain.

Early the next morning, the captain sent word out to Lucknow that Mac had been chosen to get "new construction" back in the States, and to pack his bags because he was leaving on the afternoon plane for Sydney. That meant a lot of farewell drinking and toasts to Mac and much well-wishing that he'd get a good boat. Mac, always the congenial anything-to-please guy, got groggier and groggier as the time approached to be escorted to his plane by two carloads of officer friends. Then he barely made it to the top of a portable staircase that was alongside the aircraft. At the last step he stumbled forward, collapsed onto the top of the stairs and passed out—to the loud cheers of the rowdy send-off party. Two stewardesses emerged from the open door leading into the plane and grabbed Mac's prostrate body by the feet and dragged him into the plane. With that, the door was closed, the stairway pulled clear and the plane started down the runway to the wild waving and yelling from Mac's friends.

I decided that Mac had been chosen because the captain didn't want to change his fire-control party in any fashion. He was happy with it. A battle diving officer would be needed. Jerry? It seemed more likely that the *Crevalle* would get a veteran submarine officer from another boat in Fremantle for the next patrol.

Admiral Christie noted in his endorsement to the *Crevalle*'s Report of her First Patrol: "Such aggressive attacks demonstrate what a powerful and versatile weapon our standard submarine can be under the intelligent direction of the commanding officer and a well-trained crew." On reading this, I had the disturbing thought that with Admiral Christie thinking that submarines were "weapons" he wasn't recognizing that the rotten Mk-14's were actually the weapons being used. This might well contribute to the unsatisfactory torpedo situation.

Captain Munson's claim of four ships sunk and one damaged earned him the Navy Cross, while the crew was given authority to wear the Submarine Combat pin for having had a "successful patrol."

5

Mutiny?

At 1700 on December 30, 1943, the *Crevalle*'s lines were cast off from her pier in Fremantle Harbor. She was underway for the open sea and her second war patrol.

Just before sailing, a disquieting report had been given to Captain Munson that the *Capelin* had been last heard from on December 10th and was finally being written off as lost. The *Cisco*, the lead ship of our division of four boats built at Portsmouth, New Hampshire, had been lost in October. Two out of four boats lost on their first patrol. Did this mean that there was a structural weakness built into these boats that would do the *Crevalle* in far more easily than a normal fleet boat? A sudden failure at deep submergence then sudden flooding of the boat?

There were only a handful of people on hand to say farewell. The unusually small send-off committee up on the pier, a few of Frank's drinking friends, three women drivers of the cars used on rest-leave, and "The Boomer" Tom Suddath, the staff mines officer, who seemed less than enthusiastic about the *Crevalle*'s prospects.

The Boomer had just left the *Crevalle* after checking on the eleven Mk-12 mines stowed in the after torpedo room. His last instructions to me were relative to readying the mines for the mineplant. His undue concern for simple mines seemed misplaced. But then he knew something about mines carried on submarines, and he also knew where we were going to plant the minefield. It was something *we* wouldn't learn until the sealed orders for the *Crevalle*'s special mission were opened when the boat was well clear of Australia.

Crevalle's Op Order read: "Proceed via Exmouth Gulf (for fuel), Lombok Strait, Makassar Strait, Sibutu Passage, Balabac and thence to Dangerous Ground after special mission, and patrol between Dangerous Ground and the coast of Indochina." This wasn't Siberia we were being sent to. Yet the subdued, quiet send-off we were getting seemed ominous.

There were no friendly shouts from The Boomer, who stood apart from the small gathering on the pier. It was so uncharacteristic that I began feeling that our mineplant was going to be a lot tougher than I'd contemplated. And more hazardous.

Then two busloads of sightseeing schoolboys led by their headmaster were emptied close to where The Boomer stood. Some fifty "little nippers" rushed to the pier's edge to watch the *Crevalle*'s departure. Dressed in gray flannel jackets and sawed-off britches and wearing tiny blue caps and blue ties they surrounded The Boomer, to see their present heroes, the American submariners, go off "to kill Japs."

Recognizing the opportunity presented, The Boomer quickly formed the boys into a straight line close to the pier's edge while he, like a consummate cheerleader, took a position before them and led them in three "Hip, Hip, Hoorays!"

Suddath's deep, bass voice boomed, "Hip, Hip!" Then, the boys answered with high-falsetto "Hoorays!" while thrusting their little blue caps into the air for emphasis. It was the most spirited send-off to date. It would be great to have them on the dock to cheer our return.

On the way out to sea, the *Crevalle* passed Rottnest Island, where the fleet tug *Chanticleer* had laid a hundred feet of four-inch transocean cable that the *Crevalle* severed in a practice test. The test was to demonstrate a readiness to cut the Japanese telephone cable laid across the bottom of the Java Sea from Surabaja to Borneo—a vital section of the Indonesia-to-Japan communication system.

From the bridge I looked down at the *Crevalle*'s bow, noting with a relieved, quiet satisfaction that the cable-cutter had been removed just prior to sailing.

The cable-cutter had been flown out to Fremantle from Washington and was received on board the *Crevalle* on December 22. Evidently, all radio traffic from the Indonesia area had stopped at the beginning of December. Messages relative to warship and merchant ship traffic, whether in plain language or encoded, were eliminated. The portion of the Java Sea where the cable lay was no more than two hundred feet in depth, though cutting this cable had not appeared to be an easy job for a submarine, because the cutting exposed the sub to enemy countermeasures.

The cable-cutter looked like an inverted mushroom, with four pairs of twelve-inch-long saw-toothed knives that were articulated to begin a sawing action when a heavy strain was put on the wire that towed the cable-cutter.

On the twenty-eighth, early in the morning, the sample cable laid off Rottnest Island was easily snagged. The cutting knives went into action and chewed their way through the cable in a jiffy. And when the cable-cutter was hauled up, it was gripping one end of the cable, as was expected from our instructions.

Happily, on return to port the captain was notified that he was to dismantle the cable-cutting rig and leave it ashore.

After leaving Rottnest Island well astern on the thirtieth, the captain suddenly ordered what he called "a routine dive before proceeding north." This was madness after two days of loading stores, spare parts, and provisions, along with topping off of fuel and replenishment of lube oil. It was too risky to dive fast with so many changes in weight. The *Crevalle* was dived off two-engine speed, making about fourteen knots.

Luke Bowdler, who took over the engineering officer job from Mac, had made the compensation calculations as best he could. But something was dreadfully wrong as the *Crevalle* started under. As acting diving officer, I was shocked to have the *Crevalle* nose sharply down and head for the bottom—out of control.

There was no time to feel any doubt as to what needed doing. In that freezing moment, with an instinctive reaction stemming from experience, I yelled, "All back emergency!" And I followed this with, "Blow bow buoyancy and blow safety." The safety tank held several thousands of pounds of water that when blown to sea compensated for the boat being heavy overall. What a comforting sound it was to hear the loud hiss of high pressure air rushing into the safety tank, which was just below my diving station.

The *Crevalle* awkwardly shot back to the surface and lay there motionless with motors stopped, like an injured duck. The captain, now in the control room was muttering something about "some of us should learn how to dive the boat correctly." He said this with what sounded like a titter and with a troubling, wild-eyed silly grin on his face. He seemed to love the excitement he had created by his ill-considered "running dive."

Then another dive was tried but more cautiously. And a good trim was gotten before she resurfaced and headed north.

On December 31, a large number of man-hours were spent checking all parts of the *Crevalle* for structural weaknesses that might have sunk the *Capelin* and *Cisco*. Quite by chance, I was able to identify what might be a fatal flaw in the *Crevalle*'s construction. While running my hand over the flange in the vent-riser (the piping for venting the air from a ballast tank and which was under sea pressure when submerged) for the after main ballast tank in the after torpedo room, I felt a loose, jiggling, hold-down bolt. It was out of sight between the vent-riser and the hull. Sliding my finger further behind the riser I discovered an empty bolt hole. I tried the other side of the flange and found an empty bolt hole along with two bolts on that side not being tightly secured. Evidently, the yard workmen at Portsmouth had found it too difficult to screw down all bolts on the flanges because they were poorly designed and denied any use of leverage for tightening the bolts or even getting some of them into their bolt holes. As a result only about 200° of the flanges' circumference was bolted tightly. Further investigation revealed that the flanges on the vent-risers in the forward torpedo room were similarly only partially bolted down. Since these vent-risers were exposed to sea pressure, the shock from a nearby depth charge might easily cause the flanges to open up and flood the room uncontrollably, particularly when the submarine was at deep submergence.

Two of the auxiliarymen went to work fashioning a ratchet wrench with a bent handle that could tighten bolts in the most constricted area of the flange. But even before the *Crevalle*'s flanges were securely bolted, the captain sent a message to the *Cabrilla* alerting her skipper about the structural problem that had been uncovered.

New Year's Eve was almost forgotten until Frank Walker flipped some water from a drinking glass into my face at midnight and quietly chuckled, "Happy New Year, Ruhe."

At New Year's breakfast, Jim Blind, a new officer on board and who had relieved Luke Bowdler of his commissary officer duties, proudly announced that he'd been able to draw so many boxes of cigarettes that each regular smoker would have more than two packs a day to feed his habit. Blind, in his show-boating gesture, had grossly over-stocked the *Crevalle* with cigarettes. But what was worse, when I asked for milk I got instead a reconstituted powdered milk. Unsympathetically, I snarled at Blind, "Where's the fresh milk we always get before sailing?" Blind looking embarrassed called for Westmoreland, the commissary steward. Westmoreland poked his head into the wardroom and reported that all the milk cans had been used at the last ship's ball game to ice the beer, and that they'd never been returned to the boat. So there was no fresh milk. That was obvious. A great start for 1944!

Things were quiet all through New Year's Day, with no drills or training sessions.

On Sunday, January 2nd, the *Crevalle* stopped off at Exmouth Gulf to top off the diesel fuel oil tanks. As the *Crevalle* passed the bleak, sun-scorched hills on the way in, Frank Walker remarked prophetically that "only an oil strike here could justify this God-forsaken place." (Actually, in 1956 a major oil strike was made in those arid brown hills.)

The ballast tanks in the mid-part of the boat had been converted to fuel tanks so that by topping-off, the *Crevalle* could travel on patrol more than sixteen thousand miles at ten knots on the surface. Evidently, the *Crevalle* was expected to stay out at sea a mighty long time and "go all over hell."

Captain Munson was a veritable dynamo of movement, buzzing around the boat, "full of good ideas."

George Morin was smilingly told "to build a gun target from four oil drums tied together, then paint them yellow and put a red flag on a pole attached to the oil drums." With an intense seriousness the captain said, "We're going to need a good target for the four-inch gun because I intend to use her a lot."

Jim Blind was directed to "get the new cook squared away so we can get a decent meal once in a while."

Jerry Gromer was to "add fish to the menu." The captain seemed almost overcome by his clever idea: "You supervise the fishing over the side by many of the crew, so we can have fresh fish for supper."

My instructions from the captain were less exciting: "Search out any cause for rattling in the superstructure while we're running submerged, and eliminate the source." And, as an afterthought, the captain chortlingly added, "When you're finished with that, I want you to make a sketch of how we can camouflage the *Crevalle* with black striping so the Japs won't be able to figure out our angle-on-the-bow, or even know whether the *Crevalle* is coming or going."

Shifting from the black-painted hull the *Crevalle* had on her first patrol to an all-gray one had forced a major concession from the captain that "gray is better." When the visibility of the black *Crevalle* had been compared with the *Flasher*'s light gray paint job, on the way back together from the last patrol, it seemed certain that gray was much more invisible on moonless, as well as moonlit, nights.

I was convinced that black stripes on the *Crevalle*'s light gray topworks would only make her more visible at night and fool nobody. But I had to humor the captain on this ridiculous project. So that evening I drew several submarine silhouettes, painted them light gray with my watercolors, and then tried several patterns of black striping: random, slanted, vertical, zig-zag, and of varying width.

Before I turned in for some sleep, the captain studied my sketches. He chose the zig-zag one and giggled about how it would fool them. He kept repeating, "This will fool them, this will fool them, this will fool them," like a broken record. Then he told me to "supervise the painting of the *Crevalle* from this sketch of yours."

"But I'll be on watch then, Captain," I protested.

"That's OK, you don't do the painting. Just show a couple of your men what they're supposed to do with their buckets of black paint. What's so hard about that?"

"Nothing," I thought, but it wasn't that simple.

Next morning, Niemczyk and Enright reported to me on the bridge with their buckets of paint and brushes. I showed them the chosen sketch and gave them the general idea of how the topsides should look. Then they climbed down the ladder to the main deck, whistling and joking as though off on a happy lark. I thought that these men weren't treating their painting assignment very seriously.

After half an hour of slopping paint over the side of the conning tower and the exposed part of the ship's hull, the two men climbed back up to the bridge. They were acting silly, as though their work had been all fun and games. I found out a few days later that perhaps I should have been suspicious of how well their unsupervised paint job resembled my sketch.

In the afternoon, the twenty-millimeter guns were given a good test. They were tried out against two small oil drums that were pushed over the side. After the *Crevalle* opened out to five hundred yards from the drums, they were easily riddled by bullets and sunk, using the new, recently installed gun sights.

Later, I asked the captain if I could disconnect the magnetic feature of the exploders in the torpedoes' warheads. The captain without further thought gave me an unequivocal "No." Then, in explanation, he said that Admiral Christie had insisted that all magnetic exploders were to be continued in use. "But I think the Admiral will change his mind shortly about this matter."

From January 4th through the 6th, the *Crevalle* approached Lombok Strait. A timed approach (in order to take advantage of the darkness, the currents, and the positions of the ASW ships) to Lombok Strait, and a passage through what was called "The Barrier" was made with some trepidation. The Barrier was created by the chain of islands that stretched from Sumatra on the west to Timor on the east. Penetrating The Barrier was a risky thing because of the great concentration of Japanese ASW forces in each major passage: Malacca, Sunda, Lombok.

Noting that Jerry as an officer of the deck was acting listless and exhausted and disinterested in maintaining an alert lookout effort, I discussed his attitude with him. He complained that he wasn't feeling well and asked to be taken off the watch list. When I suggested this to the captain he laughed, reminding me that this would cut the watch list to only three watch-standers.

Jim Blind was still acting as my junior OOD. His learning pace was slow because he was always talking when he should be listening. Many of my watch-standing suggestions to him were countered with, "But that wasn't the way we were taught to do it at Sub School." Perhaps he had no respect for my experience as a wartime submarine OOD. Then when he told me he couldn't swim because he hadn't been near much water during his upbringing in Idaho, I wondered what was wrong with the system for letting a guy who can't swim get into the submarine service? Jim was a bright radar expert, yet I felt edgy about his role on the fire-control team.

Very early on the sixth of January, the *Crevalle* entered the strait between Lombok and Bali. The mere mention of Lombok Strait gave me a queasy feeling because of the efficient depth chargings experienced when penetrating this hole in the Japanese fence. However, with the moon having set, the expected surface and air patrols didn't materialize in the pitch darkness as the *Crevalle* raced through on four engines at 18.5 knots.

The *Crevalle* then continued on the surface all day, moving north through the Java Sea and into Makassar Strait.

Just before midnight, a lookout reported a shape out on the horizon that looked like a submarine. I could feel my skin contract as I verified this contact through my binoculars.

When called to the bridge, the captain, without trying to see the contact through his binoculars, insisted that I quickly close the friendly submarine because he wanted to "talk" to her skipper by blinker-gun light. He was certain that it was Selby's *Puffer* coming south off patrol.

I wasn't so sure of that and didn't like the situation. My throat had gone dry and my legs were beginning to shake a bit. As a precaution I steered the *Crevalle* to stay well clear of the approaching submarine. Then without challenging the unidentified contact, he told the quartermaster to blink "This is Munson, This is Munson, This is Munson." My heart started thumping because the quartermaster's blinking light was making a good aiming point for a Japanese torpedo.

By the time the *Crevalle*'s radar picked up the low-lying contact, it had closed to under four thousand yards. With still no reply, I swung the stern towards the unidentified submarine. But then a tiny blinking light from the other submarine's bridge asked "Is Frank aboard?"

I called this message down to Frank in the wardroom and his response was, "Send back, 'don't drink it all.'" The message was definitely from Gordon Selby, on the *Puffer*, one of Frank's favorite drinking partners.

As the *Puffer* moved on south out of blinker range, Captain Munson kept sending words of advice to Selby on how to go through Lombok Strait without being detected.

When I went below after midnight I was much worried about the captain's lapse of good sense in dealing with an unknown submarine contact. Hence, alongside the captain's instructions in the night order book, I wrote, "Call Commander Walker and Mr. Ruhe for any ship contacts made during the night." What might seem to be a small patrol boat in the darkness could be another submarine—an enemy one.

At 0530 a messenger shook me awake from a deep sleep and urgently said, "We've picked up another submarine on the surface, Mr. Ruhe." He then said that the captain was on the bridge and that Commander Walker had been notified. I jumped out of my bunk and raced barefooted and in my skivvies to the bridge.

As soon as I poked my head over the bridge combing my stomach turned over. There was a submarine, clearly visible in the dawn's early light and not far off. It had a starboard angle-on-the-bow and was running almost parallel to the *Crevalle*. I pushed Jerry, the OOD, aside and pulled his binoculars over to my eyes. The submarine, at about two thousand yards was definitely not a U.S. fleet boat. The unidentified sub, in fact, looked like possibly a Dutch K-class submarine or more likely a small Japanese RO-class sub. Then I spotted a Japanese flag painted on the side of the submarine's conning tower. At about the same instant, a lookout shouted, "He's got a rising sun flag painted on his side."

The captain was back on the cigarette deck blissfully standing beside the quartermaster who was blinking on his signal gun, "This is Munson, this is Munson, this is Munson."

I asked Jerry if the unidentified submarine had been challenged and whether he had replied satisfactorily. Jerry evasively suggested that the sub had answered with the correct reply to the challenge and that he was a "friendly submarine."

As Frank Walker moved alongside of me, having climbed through the hatch to the bridge, I told him that we had a Japanese sub out there and that he should get on the TBT, and take bearings on the sub. Then I dropped down into the conning tower to set up the TDC for an attack with two stern torpedoes. I noted that Frank was swinging the *Crevalle* to bring the stern tubes to bear.

The Captain was off on a cloud somewhere. But then when he felt the sub heel over on the turn he started shouting, "What's going on?" and a moment later, "Who's changing our course?" I heard Frank's voice answering, "It's a Jap sub, Captain and we're turning to fire torpedoes."

Frank then yelled down to me that the Jap sub had swung around and was now showing an eighty degree port angle-on-the-bow. The Japanese sub's maneuver showed that he was confused by the situation.

The after room announced that tubes number seven and eight were ready to fire. Frank's TBT bearings indicated that the enemy sub had steadied on a course of 160° True, so I gave the after room the order "Standby to fire." The radar range had closed to 1,650 yards and her speed was tracking at fourteen knots. When Frank held down the buzzer on his bearing transmitter, indicating that he was steady on the aiming point, I ordered both tubes fired, with about six seconds between the two torpedoes. Then I raised the number one periscope to see the results. The captain was still yelling, "What's going on?" from back on the cigarette deck.

The two torpedo wakes were easily followed as they streaked to head off the Japanese sub. But short of the enemy sub the first torpedo suddenly exploded, throwing a huge geyser of water and torpedo fragments into the air, hiding the Jap sub from view. The second torpedo blew up in the same spot, triggered by the premature explosion of the first fish. I thought, disgustedly, "Those damned magnetic exploders have done it again." Then I wondered why I hadn't gotten the torpedo men to disconnect the magnetic feature on all the torpedoes without telling the captain about it.

When the mass of water thrown into the air had subsided, the enemy submarine was seen to be submerging with a dangerously sharp down-angle. The sub was either out of control from sheer fright or was getting deep as fast as possible before more of the Crevalle's torpedoes were launched.

The whole situation was incredible, especially the enemy sub supposedly using the correct reply when challenged. Strangely, the camouflage paint-job on the Crevalle seemed to have confused him completely. The captain's "This will fool them" seemed to make more sense than I was willing to admit. But why hadn't the enemy sub shot his torpedoes first?

The enemy sub giving the correct reply to the Crevalle's challenge really bothered me. So, I cornered the quartermaster who'd sent the Crevalle's challenge, and asked what reply he had received back. He said nervously that he wasn't sure what the letters were that he'd received. "Were they the same letters that you used for your challenge?" I shot back at him. The quartermaster said he didn't think so, but he couldn't swear that they weren't the same. Moreover, the captain showed no interest in my questioning.

Frank and I went below, just shaking our heads.

When the captain came below and went into his cabin he called me in and menacingly snapped, "What the hell were you and Frank Walker pulling on me up there on the bridge?" His eyes flashed dangerously. With a snarl he added, "You guys just took over my command and fired at that sub. It might have been one of ours you know." Apparently, he still didn't seem to recognize that it was actually a Japanese submarine that had been fired at, even though a Japanese flag was painted on the sub's conning tower. Later, in a message to headquarters, the captain told a simple story of how the *Crevalle* had encountered a Japanese RO-class sub running on the surface that correctly replied to the *Crevalle*'s identification challenge and how the two torpedoes fired had prematured at six hundred yards, letting the Japanese sub escape unharmed.

When I was alone with Frank, after this wild scolding, I asked him what was going on with the captain, and were we in real trouble?

Frank said that Hank Munson was always a rough guy to serve with. And that over the long period he had known Munson, he was at times erratic in his treatment of officers. Frank's indifference to this problem of our meddling with the captain's command wasn't very comforting. At least there were two of us involved, and not just me. Frank also predicted that the two of us were going to catch a lot of hell and then be praised for our actions by Munson, on a regular basis.

All day of the eighth, the *Crevalle* ran on the surface, moving up through Makassar Strait. The usual air patrols out from the Celebes never materialized. But it was a tense business running exposed in broad daylight.

After dark, the twenty-millimeter and .50-caliber gun crews were called away to tackle what appeared to be two small patrol boats. Luckily, they proved to be two piles of wreckage, verified after a few rounds from the twenty-millimeter guns had blasted them with explosive bullets.

Jerry had to be taken off the watch list after this gun action. He claimed that he was feeling terrible. But Doc Loos, the hospitalman, couldn't find a thing wrong with Jerry. Nor would Jerry take the medicine that Doc Loos felt would relax him and get rid of his aches and pains.

At 1300 on Sunday, January 9, the *Crevalle* was closed to investigate what the captain evaluated as a suspicious-looking two-masted sailing banca that was "probably manned by Japanese and was being used to report American submarines transiting Makassar Strait." The captain observed that the banca was too well positioned to be anything but a lookout for the Japanese.

When the *Crevalle* was steered close to the sailing vessel, the single man on deck, dressed in an orange, red and brown shirt, red pants and wearing a red kerchief on his head, looked very much like an Indonesian native. He seemed thoroughly terrified and not brazenly surly like a Japanese sailor. Although the banca also looked like a friendly native craft it sank like a rock after only a few twenty-millimeter hits were scored. Bancas like this were usually unsinkable. But this one quickly went down as though loaded with ammunition, radio gear and heavy power equipment. Moreover, there were six heads in the water in the swirl where the banca had disappeared from sight. The captain seemed proud of the results. But I felt no exhilaration from killing men and sinking such an unarmed craft—particularly on Sunday.

At the end of the gun action when I dropped down to the main deck to retrieve some of the spent cartridges to use as ash trays, I was horrified to see that my camouflaging team had painted rectangles with large black dots in the center, on both sides of the conning tower. In the dawn's early light they would have looked like rising sun flags. But even more bizarre were the words "Fuck you—you Japs" printed in block letters along the side of the *Crevalle* just below the main deck. Had the Japanese read that, they'd have been tipped off for certain that the *Crevalle* was an American submarine.

Later, after darkness, I brought a bucket of black paint topside and furtively painted out the flags and the lettering. And I kept the matter a big secret.

The *Crevalle*'s transit of Sibutu Pass on the evening of the tenth was the most rugged watch I ever stood. Standing out in the open, the rain pelted down so hard for two hours that my face was beaten raw and bruised. It took all my willpower to uncover my face for frequent looks through the binoculars. Since the *Crevalle* was going through a narrow and dangerous passage it was necessary to keep peering into the driving rain because the SJ radar's scope was saturated with echo returns from the blanket of rain. In these conditions, nothing could be detected.

Jim, on watch with me, was a pitiable sight. He stayed hunched over most of the time, protecting his face. When he had to raise his head for a quick look around, his face showed such agony that I was tempted to let him go below. But his whimpering annoyed me, so I decided he'd just better tough it out.

All through the eleventh, the *Crevalle* crossed the Sulu Sea. Yeoman Dempster, I had heard, was so sick with appendicitis that the pharmacist mate had recommended he be transferred to a submarine coming off patrol.

A radio message was sent to Submarine Headquarters in Perth regarding the need to get Dempster back to port for an immediate operation. In the meantime, Doc Loos felt that if Dempster took a lot of sulfa pills he could withstand a rupture of his appendix. Then, a rendezvous with the *Cabrilla* was arranged as soon as the *Crevalle* entered the South China Sea. The *Cabrilla* was heading home after having sunk only one small ship, on a very long patrol.

But first the *Crevalle* had to transit Nasubata Channel to the east of Balabac Island on her way to meeting the *Cabrilla*. Philippine guerrillas had reported seeing mines being laid by a Japanese minelayer on either side of the very deep Nasubata Channel. Consequently, it was imperative that the *Crevalle* be carefully navigated through the channel at night, making certain that she stay in its deepest part at all times.

During the western transit through the channel, Frank Walker took bearings on identifiable peaks on Balabac Island using the TBT while I plotted the positions generated and recommended course changes to keep the *Crevalle* in the deepest part of the narrow, winding channel carved out by strong currents moving east. One-third speed was used in order to allow plenty of time for getting fixes and changing course as necessary.

When the channel was cleared and the *Crevalle* moved into the deep water just east of Balabac, Frank slipped down into the conning tower and folded up the plot I had made. "We might need this plot to show the admiral where we went without getting blown up," he noted.

On the morning of January 12, the *Crevalle* closed the *Cabrilla*, while Dempster, strapped into a stretcher and wrapped in blankets, was hauled up through the engineroom hatch. He was then placed in a rubber boat on the main deck, joining Pace, the torpedoman who would paddle the inflated boat. At this, the *Crevalle* was then flooded down until her main deck was awash. Then the boat was pushed off into the choppy seas, with Dempster waving a weary and painful farewell to his pals who thronged the cigarette deck to see him off.

The *Crevalle* was circled at ten knots some distance away while the *Cabrilla* closed in to pick up the boat and Dempster. Captain Munson was taking no chance that the *Crevalle* would prove to be an easy torpedo target for a patrolling enemy submarine.

Doug Hammond on the *Cabrilla* shouted over to Captain Munson that the South China Sea was a bummer and that he was glad he was heading home.

The last seen of Dempster was as he was being lowered through the *Cabrilla*'s engineroom hatch.

The *Crevalle*'s patrol didn't look promising. But at last orders were received that afternoon from Commander Task Group 71 to inactivate the magnetic feature on all torpedo exploders. It was finally official. Admiral Christie had actually admitted that it wasn't the fault of his skippers that they were getting a lot of misses but rather the torpedoes for not being triggered when passing under a ship. Juggling sixteen torpedoes around the forward torpedoroom, to deactivate the exploders was rough going. But it was joyfully carried out by the *Crevalle*'s torpedomen.

On the thirteenth, the mines were readied in the after room to carry out the special mission. And as suggested by The Boomer, "Problems should be expected"; this proved true.

After one of the mines in tube number ten had been pulled back into the room and suspended from the overhead by a chain fall, the second mine that had lain deep and unseen in the tube was pulled partially out of the tube for a pre-firing check. Shockingly, it revealed the round silver protecting plate over the exploder pot to be merely a depression of gray, frothing and mushy metal. The intricate exploder mechanism had become merely a smoking, shapeless, pudding-like substance. "Acid musta got in there and ate the stuff away," commented a bewildered torpedoman. All of the parts for arming and firing the mine were totally decomposed. The safety features were gone! Thus, there was a long discussion with the "old hands" in the room as to what to do about this dud mine. Should it be pulled back into the room and stowed there until the *Crevalle* returned to port or should it be the fourth mine to be launched while keeping our fingers crossed?

When I presented the problem to the captain he said, without giving much thought to the danger involved, "Go ahead and launch it with the rest of the mines in its proper sequence."

Was the captain acting irrational or was he right, as he was most of the time? But at least I'd see to it that the mine was eased out of the tube gently. It seemed that our lives would be in the balance.

These mines the *Crevalle* carried were of a new and insidious type. They were simple-looking eight-foot-long cylindrical black cans, almost two feet in diameter and packed with more than one thousand pounds of high explosives. But it was the delicate mechanism inside that made them so effective. This device blew up the mine when a ship with a strong magnetic field passed overhead. But it didn't do this the first time. The mechanism had a setting for a certain number of ship passes, between three and nine, before it actually triggered the mine's exploder. Ejected with compressed air from the torpedo tube, this type of mine settled on the bottom, sank into the mud and waited. It took many days of minesweeping before the number of passes over the mine added up to a moment of detonation. How could the Japs guess that it would take three or more passes before a mine let go?

After the mines were all checked out and I'd reported their status to the captain, he had all available officers report to the wardroom for a briefing on the *Crevalle*'s special mission. A chart of the Saigon River and its approaches was spread out on the wardroom table. The captain first paused to allow for a careful study of where the mines were to be placed, a few miles up the Saigon River.

"Here's where the admiral wants those mines put," he indicated. The big blue vein on his forehead protruded noticeably. "If we get chased out of this spot, we can lay them along the coast further north. But he *wants* the mines placed in the middle of *this* river," the captain emphasized.

When the captain peered at the chart, his threadlike, silky blond hair and boyishly absorbed face made him look like an Oxford professor studying a rare insect collection. The hazards he described seemed more pleasing to him than the calculus problems he worked on in his cabin daily for relaxation. His voice was excited and his thin, craggy face brightened as he pointed out that a Japanese fort commanded the right bank of the Saigon River at its mouth; that an island obstructed the river passage on the left side, forcing ships to make a sharp jog in the channel; that the water was between thirty and sixty feet deep; that fishing craft crowded the area where the river emptied into the sea; and that we could expect patrol boats weaving a continual pattern of search near the entrance to the river.

"If we get to a position up past this fort and lay the mines in an S-curve about two hundred yards apart," the captain noted, "the minesweepers will have a tough time sweeping across more than one mine on their straight-line sweeps. It will make their job almost endless." It was a good assumption. "And we'll make the final run-in during darkness so we can be upriver before the moon rises. The plant will be finished before there's enough light to distinguish the *Crevalle* from the many fishing boats expected close to the fort." The captain's plan sounded simple.

Frank mentioned that, "The sun sets at 1846 and the moon rises at 2234," and "that will give us a little more than three hours of darkness. If we surface about forty miles from the coast and average seventeen knots on the run-in, we'll get in undetected in the blackness. There's only about two knots of current to buck, according to the Coast Pilot Instructions." It all sounded easy.

All day the *Crevalle* crept submerged toward the coast of Indochina until after sunset. Then she surfaced in time for Frank to take star sights and calculate the *Crevalle*'s exact position without using radar. He reported that she was many miles further from the coast than planned. Then, after two hours of full-power running, a cautious single-sweep of the radar alarmingly showed that the nearest land was still eighteen miles ahead. Something was wrong. Evidently, heavy rains up-river were creating a current of over five knots at the mouth of the Saigon River where it emptied into the ocean.

Another half hour of pounding ahead on four engines showed that the *Crevalle* had only made six miles good. The current being bucked was much stronger than expected.

"We're licked," Frank told the captain gloomily as he reported his latest position. "We can't make it now until well after moonrise. Then we're going to look like a clay pigeon at a shooting gallery."

The captain didn't waver. Some minutes later he called the after torpedo room to warn that there was going to be a delay, but that planting the mines would start in less than an hour. At this, I went back to the after torpedo room to check the readiness of the mine-planting team.

The reload and firing teams were stripped to the waist, prepared for six minutes of back-breaking, furious mule-hauling of the heavy cylinders. Wedged between the tiers of tightly stowed mines and hampered by the additional three torpedoes in the skids, the men waited patiently. Only their eyes questioned the frequent lurches of the *Crevalle* as she was being steered around fishing boats.

"Ten more minutes," the captain was heard to comment to Luke. The button for the bridge mike was apparently stuck in a down position. Thus all conversation on the bridge was broadcast over the ship's loudspeaker system.

Back in the after torpedo room it was easy to follow the feverish confusion being created by fishing boats that had to be dodged. The captain's commands, which were shouted down the hatch to the helmsman in the conning tower, told of the difficult time the captain was having maneuvering the *Crevalle* upstream.

Then there were a rash of observations from Frank concerning the rapid cuts on hills, islands and structures that he was taking in order to keep a steady plot of the sub's position. "We're only making twelve knots good, Captain," he was heard to report.

The lookouts also maintained a steady flow of reports: "There's a light on the right-hand side of the fort, sir"; "Lights are being turned on over on the beach to port"; then, excitedly, "There's a big dark shape that looks like a destroyer on the starboard beam"; "Two fishing boats are one point on the starboard bow, sir"; "There's a small object in the water dead ahead. Looks like a log, or something."

"The moon is just beginning to rise," was heard. Frank's alarmed voice sounded as though he was resigned to a very bad situation.

"The fort on the starboard side is abeam, sir," a lookout reported. That meant that the *Crevalle* was well into the river's mouth and only a mile from the initial planting position. The men in the after room were smiling, eager to get on with the job.

"The destroyer is blinking a light at us," a lookout quietly reported, as though he was fearful of being heard over the several miles of water that separated the *Crevalle* from the patrolling warship. But Captain Munson rejected the imminence of this threat. "Somebody doped off and opened a door by mistake," he was heard to growl.

"We're there, Captain," Frank's voice announced.

"You give the orders to the helm, Frank, from now on," the captain ordered, "I'll only take over if necessary to avoid something." This was in accordance with the captain's prearranged plan. Frank would steer the *Crevalle* along an S-curve and control the speed, dependent on how well the after room gang could achieve a thirty-second interval between mine launches.

When the captain ordered, "Commence the mine plant" I breathed a sigh of relief and a "Here we go"—for six minutes of frantic juggling and firing of mines in the overcrowded torpedo room.

I thought then of Luke Bowdler's words just before the run-in for the laying of the *Crevalle*'s minefield. "If anyone goes overboard during this operation, we should include a Japanese grammar with the life ring we throw him and include the course and distance to the closest neutral country." Since there was that damaged mine back in tube number ten that might blow up after being launched, I should have relayed these words to the torpedomen in the after room.

The first three mines were launched at the required thirty-second interval. Then the mine in tube number ten was gently eased into the water using only 150 pounds of pressure to move it out of the tube. The sub's fourteen-knot forward motion helped it clear the stern. Down it went to the bottom and into the mud, to lay there inertly. It was useless. But it did remove the tension from the mineplant team. The loading crew momentarily looked back at me with broad smiles. Then they went back to work with a vim that resembled the offensive line of a football team trying to get a score from the one-yard line.

After three more mines were ejected on schedule, the captain impatiently called the after room. His voice was high-pitched and pleading, "Try to speed things up back there, it's getting real hot up here."

Hot! The captain should have seen the rivers of sweat running down the backs of the mine-planting team.

Then I heard the captain call to Frank, "Is the water deep enough to dive in?"

Frank answered, "Affirmative, Captain." He added, "There's eighty-four feet of water here."

The captain's next call to the after room questioned whether the mineplant could be continued submerged, I said, "Affirmative, Captain." It should be even easier to do the job with the submarine going at a much lower speed and being more stable.

"OK, we're going down," was announced, along with the diving alarm being sounded. Through the racket of the topside people dropping into the conning tower, the captain could be heard directing the diving officer to "ease her down slow with very little dive angle," and Frank adding, "We don't want to stick the *Crevalle*'s nose into the mud. There's only eighty-four feet of water here."

With all eleven mines planted accurately, the *Crevalle* was swept rapidly out to sea by the strong current pushing her along. The *Crevalle*'s escape was made on a beeline for the deep waters of the South China Sea.

Ten mines were deep in the Saigon River's mud. They were counting the magnetic passes overhead and waiting to blow up under an enemy ship. The eleventh mine, by the grace of God, had proved a dud.

The last act of the mine-plant gang was to push the three remaining torpedoes into the tubes, finally giving the men in the room some empty torpedo skids to sleep on. Real luxury.

With all the energy, emotion, and skill put into this special mission, it was a shame that the results of this effort would not be known for a long time, if ever. And no medals would be awarded if ships were sunk by the *Crevalle*'s mines.

When the officers adjourned to the wardroom, there was the same relieved every-one-talking-at-once routine that existed after every attack or close depth charging. (Long after the war's end, a rundown of the American submarine mine campaign indicated that the *Crevalle* had sunk one ship in the middle of the channel that proved unsalvageable, and had damaged two other ships, one of which sank but was later salvaged and the other ran itself aground on the shore and was left there until the end of the war. The damage to these ships, it was reported, closed the Saigon River to merchant ship traffic for more than two weeks—another bonus for the *Crevalle*'s minefield.)

The *Crevalle* then headed to the vicinity of Cape Varella. Some of the biggest ships had been sunk there by U.S. submarines in 1943. But there were no ships moving along the coast to break up the monotony of all-day periscope patrols. The captain was annoyingly nitpicking everything we did, and left a turbulent wake as he produced "good suggestions" all over the boat.

In the late afternoon of the seventeenth a message was received telling of the *Redfin* to the south of the *Crevalle* running across a convoy of four cargo ships with a Fubuki destroyer escorting them. When the Fubuki made contact on the *Redfin*, the *Redfin* sank her, but the four ships got away and were headed in the *Crevalle*'s direction. Their course and speed were given in the message.

What did the captain do? He headed the *Crevalle* straight for the spot where the Fubuki had been sunk—like Gary Cooper striding up the main street of a western town at high noon to get the bad guys. An expanding search-curve would have made a lot more sense. Of course nothing showed up. And the captain defensively rationalized that the information wasn't good enough. But as Frank put it, "The captain just didn't have his heart in this one."

Early on January 18, the *Crevalle* was headed into the coast to gain what the captain termed "negative information" and "to rest the men," who didn't need rest. They needed action.

The waves were so mountainous close to land that the *Crevalle* frequently broached as attempts were made to take looks at periscope depth. Even at eighty feet, between looks, the *Crevalle* rolled heavily.

In the middle of the afternoon, a bomb exploded fairly close to the *Crevalle*, after a plane had apparently seen her broach. Luke, who was on watch in the conning tower, ordered the *Crevalle* to be taken deep when he felt the effects of the bomb, and advised the chief on watch in the control room to use negative. But Pop Bridges, the chief of the boat, who should have responded, was nowhere around to open the flood on the negative tank. Thus, without the extra weight of the negative tank's water, and with the waves trying to lift the *Crevalle* out of the water, going deep proved agonizingly slow. A follow-on bomb was expected but didn't materialize.

After an hour at two hundred feet, periscope looks were resumed.

The next few days without enemy contacts were interminable and distressingly long.

On the twentieth the *Crevalle* moved thirty miles off the Indochina coast "to intercept merchant ship traffic." What traffic?

On the following day, the *Crevalle* was taken out into the middle of the South China Sea. The captain claimed that the Japanese were so smart that they "run their ships way out here, and so this is where we'll get them." But that was a loser.

The acute boredom of the crew was well illustrated during an inspection I made of the forward torpedo room. As I entered the room I noticed a torpedoman sitting in a camp chair between the torpedo skids. He was reading a comic book and was unaware that his left hand was casually stroking the arming fan of a torpedo that lay in the skids beside him. I watched this for a few seconds and determined that his hand was actually rotating the water-wheel-like blades on the torpedo's arming device. The fan was recessed in the top of the torpedo and turned a threaded rod in the detonator as the torpedo traveled through the water toward its target. After 150 yards of run, the threaded rod would then be withdrawn from the detonator, freeing it to be triggered if the torpedo was jolted.

When I yelled at him to "Stop it!" he looked up with surprise, unaware that he was doing something wrong. He couldn't believe that he would have armed the torpedo with only a few more strokes. And, that became evident when the exploder assembly was carefully withdrawn from the torpedo. It was apparent that the torpedoman's relaxed way of killing time had gotten the crew close to being blown up by a slight jolt of the fish.

In the afternoon, the *Crevalle* was moved towards Dangerous Ground, a large area in the middle of the South China Sea with a myriad of tiny islands and reefs. Some were charted and some not. Coral, moreover, produced new ones yearly. The names of ships that had blundered onto hidden reefs littered the navigational chart. The sunken ships were grim reminders for the *Crevalle* to stay clear of the hazardous reef areas.

For the next four days, the *Crevalle* uneventfully patrolled on the surface about thirty to fifty miles to the west of the reefs on the western side of Dangerous Ground.

On January 23, I blew up at George for his heckling of one of my men. I ordered George to "Knock it off." George unmirthfully laughed at this then went silent and glared menacingly at me. From then on he gave me the silent treatment. It was foolish and childish. On the bridge when he relieved me of the watch, he pointedly told the quartermaster, "Tell Mr. Ruhe that I'm relieving him of the watch." In the wardroom at meals he would politely tell someone sitting beside me, "Please tell Mr. Ruhe to pass me the butter." Or whatever. Both of us were disgusted with the way this patrol was developing, but that was a poor excuse for all the irritability.

In the evening after my blow-up with George, the captain suggested a bridge game. But Frank had "to check his navigation." Luke had "to catch up on his engineering logs," Jim couldn't play bridge, and George, disdainful of the captain's bridge-playing capability, had vacated the forward battery area.

Then, the captain started worrying about Spratly Island, just at the western edge of Dangerous Ground. He was certain that it had been occupied at the beginning of the war and that it had both a radio and weather station on it. Frank checked the chart and noted that Spratly Island was only eight feet high and thirty feet long and uninhabited. He also observed that "a small typhoon would sweep this island clean."

The captain insisted with a fluttering and unnerving laugh, however, that it should be investigated and then bombarded with the four-inch gun, "to destroy the Jap installations on the island."

Frank didn't relish taking the *Crevalle* in close to Spratly because it was well surrounded by reefs. But the captain insisted that Spratly be investigated, submerged. Sneak in on a deserted island? And blast a coconut from a coconut tree?

Quite obviously, all Japanese ships were steering well clear of Spratly, so the *Crevalle*'s mission of destruction meant nothing to shoot at and two days of patrol wasted.

Early on the following morning I was awakened by the call, "Radar tracking team man your stations." Two radar contacts had been picked up at over ten thousand yards. The contacts tracked on a westerly course and were making eight knots. When their range was under eight thousand yards and they were still not visible in the moonless darkness, the *Crevalle* was submerged to radar depth to commence an approach on the targets.

Shortly, a large course-change by the two contacts put the *Crevalle* over four thousand yards off their track, robbing her of the opportunity to shoot torpedoes. Then, instead of pulling away from the enemy ships to get back on the surface and run out ahead of them so as to try another attack before dawn, the *Crevalle* was kept submerged until daylight.

I inwardly cursed the captain for his poor judgement, and got madder and madder as time ticked away, while the *Crevalle* was doing nothing. The captain kept glancing at me with a venomous look. It was obvious he was sensitive to my disapproving shadowed eyes, as I kept the TDC generating, hoping for an eventual shooting solution. I also mumbled, "We've got to show some desire to get this guy." The captain must have heard this caustic aside because the muscles in his jaw started working and his eyebrows raised a fraction, menacingly.

When we surfaced two hours later, the ships had vanished. Almost frantically, the captain had all four engines bent on the line and headed the *Crevalle* westward, hoping to regain contact. But it looked hopeless.

I argued with Frank that the captain was acting weird and that he, Frank, had to make more of an effort to convince him of the tactics to get those two ships. Frank merely growled that it was no use. I think the captain, who was on the bridge and standing near the hatch, must have overheard this conversation because the next time he dropped down into the conning tower his piercing blue eyes regarded Frank and me quizzically and a deep frown creased his forehead.

By great good luck, shortly after noon a lookout spotted a puff of black smoke far out on the horizon. It was on a bearing so radically different from where the two ships were expected to be that there was some doubt that the puff of smoke marked the location of the two ships that had earlier been threatened with an attack by the *Crevalle*. The *Crevalle* was maneuvered out ahead of what proved to be the same two ships, and then submerged for an approach.

When the ships had closed to less than four thousand yards, every succeeding periscope look by Frank showed both ships headed straight for the *Crevalle*'s periscope, even though an effort was made to get the *Crevalle* off the enemy's track for a good shot.

Frank after a long look described the ships he saw. The escort was "a gray-painted naval auxiliary and looked like a converted whale-killer." The other ship identified from the Japanese Merchant Ships Book was the *Taibun Maru* of 6,581 tons, a passenger-cargo ship. Frank reported that her decks were loaded high with armored vehicles, trucks, small jeep-like autos and lots of crates, while the decks were also crammed with khaki-clad men who were apparently soldiers. It appeared that the ship was transporting an entire garrison of troops and equipment to another outpost.

On the final look before shooting, Frank excitedly said that the escort was at 250 yards and headed for the *Crevalle*. So the captain ordered the boat to be taken deep, "emergency," and gave up on the attack, much to the amazement of everyone. There were no depth charges dropped.

Again, the *Crevalle* dawdled around for far too long. She remained deep until the sound of the target's screws had been lost for more than an hour. So when the *Crevalle* was surfaced at twilight there was no sign of the two ships anywhere. Not even a puff of black smoke.

Frank wouldn't even talk to me, he was so disgusted.

On four engines the *Crevalle* was again raced out to the westward to regain contact. And this time the captain's "intuition" paid off. Radar contact on the two ships was regained well after dark. Moreover, the captain seemed like his old, fire-eater self. He told the fire control party that the *Crevalle* was going in to the attack "like a motor torpedo boat," at top speed on all four engines. Attacking on the surface at high speed ensured a good firing position when shooting. But the risk was certainly higher. Yet all of the crew were behind the captain on this attack. They'd gladly accept the chances of the *Crevalle* being hit by gunfire.

With the range to the target ship at 2,500 yards and with the naval auxiliary escort well clear on the starboard bow of the *Taibun Maru*, the *Crevalle* was slowed to ten knots and four torpedoes were fired from the forward torpedo tubes with a one degree spread between torpedoes. One torpedo hit inside the bow of the *Taibun Maru*, disintegrating the forward part of the ship. It sank from sight in three minutes with a thirty degree down angle. The other three torpedoes missed because the ship was in the act of a large course change while the torpedoes were in the water.

The escort swung into action. He charged down the port side of the sinking transport and dropped depth charges where he thought the *Crevalle* might be. This was certainly no help to the many men who had jumped overboard and were being killed by the underwater exploding depth charges.

The naval auxiliary was firing a big gun all around the horizon as the *Crevalle* departed the scene at twenty knots. A few of the bangs of what sounded like a five-inch gun uncomfortably rattled the inside of the conning tower. Yet there were no signs of shell splashes nearby. It was a noisy, exhilarating finale to many days of tedium.

In the wardroom later, the captain was very proud of his strategy that resulted in finding the ships. He said that "by returning to the knuckle where he had picked them up we had successfully regained contact." Nobody said a thing. But I felt he should have stuck around and gone after the escort.

Nothing happened for the next twelve days. The only thing to worry about was running aground on a reef in Dangerous Ground. Hence, someone in addition to Frank was always helping to navigate, ensuring a good check for every fix that Frank calculated.

But again, the grumbling and impatience with the captain's erratic behavior had infected the officers. George stopped eating meals in the wardroom and took his meals back aft with the enlisted men. He also started regarding me as though I was no more than an expanse of wallpaper before his eyes. Jerry seemed physically wretched and mentally exhausted. Frank was so peeved with the captain that he wouldn't answer me, but would merely grunt an assent. Luke was averaging over fourteen hours a day in his bunk. And my reading program was without any concentration. When the captain held field day throughout the boat for three days straight on the basis that the ship was dirty, even the crew joined in with incessant complaints.

At about 0300 of February 2, Hein, a lookout, reported two torpedo wakes to port, heading for the *Crevalle*. Down the *Crevalle* was taken, emergency, to get under the torpedoes. Then when she was leveled off at one hundred feet, both the bridge watch and the sound man indicated that there had been no sighting or hearing of attacking torpedoes.

The captain decided that Hein had probably seen the phosphorescent trails of a pair of dolphins.

Two nights later, Hein, up on the shears as a lookout, again reported two torpedo wakes headed for the *Crevalle*. Down the *Crevalle* dived. And again no one else saw the wakes.

At this point Frank decided that Hein was hallucinating and took him off watch.

When called to the wardroom, Hein swore that he saw the torpedo wakes on both occasions. When questioned further, he revealed that he had been on the cruiser *Juneau* when she was sunk by torpedoes east of Guadalcanal in November of 1942. He told about being an after lookout on the cruiser and of seeing a pair of torpedoes race toward the ship and then explode near his station. He was then trapped in the wreckage of the sinking ship but was released at some great depth, with his life jacket helping him regain the surface.

He remembered that 240 of the *Juneau*'s crew had survived the sinking. But after twelve days in the water, all but seven had died of exposure or were eaten by sharks. Then he was finally rescued by the destroyer *Ballard*. Despite a broken leg and a fractured skull, while he was in the water he kept praying that he'd survive so he could go to the Naval Academy. That brought tears to the eyes of Frank and me.

The *Ballard* carried him to Pearl Harbor where he thought he was going to be assigned to a group of enlisted men being shipped to the States to be part of a bond-selling tour. But the next thing, he found himself in a draft of men flying to Australia to join a submarine. Hein was a rosy cheeked, handsome, bright young reservist who seemed to be excellent officer material and didn't deserve this heartless treatment.

I listened to Hein's account with consternation, particularly at the unthinking indifference of the shore establishment for the fellows who were fighting the war.

After hearing Hein's story Frank promised to put him ashore at the end of the patrol, accompanied by written instructions to send him to the Naval Academy Preparatory School, "at the earliest."

(Very sadly, I heard after the *Crevalle*'s fourth war patrol, that Hein, after being transferred off the *Crevalle*, had been put on another submarine that was going out on patrol. His sub was lost on that patrol.)

Also that day, the *Crevalle* began using the four-hundred-horsepower donkey diesel engine for surface patrolling, to save fuel.

February 8th was the ordered last day on station for the *Crevalle*. But the captain requested a five-day extension, hoping to expend the fifteen remaining torpedoes and "to help the morale of the *Crevalle*'s crew." They needed it.

The reply from headquarters in Perth not only granted the extension but also ordered the *Crevalle* to proceed via the Celebes Sea over to the Molucca Sea for a short patrol, and from there return home to Fremantle with a stop off at Darwin.

On February 9, at 2300, the *Crevalle* carefully retraced her path through Nasubata Channel, east of Balabac. Frank made certain to keep the sub from blundering into any of the Japanese mines planted on either side. And not by coincidence, there were two native bancas within the confines of the channel that the captain suspected were lookouts reporting transiting submarines. But he wasn't inclined to use the twenty-millimeter guns on them. He wanted to concentrate solely on precise navigation through the narrow, winding channel of deep water.

On the eleventh, the *Crevalle* settled down to a submerged patrol in Alice Channel, a narrow pass from the Sulu Sea to the Celebes Sea and through the Sulu Archipelago. This was another of the captain's wild, intuitive guesses. He sensed that merchant ship traffic would use this restricted, difficult-to-navigate passage instead of the wider Sibutu Passage to the southwest. But the rest of us thought it would be a quiet day. So George and I played chess in the ward-room. At 1500, the captain called from the conning tower to have me come up to look at a small warship which was patrolling across the upper end of Alice Channel.

When I got to the conning tower the periscope was down and the captain seemed overly eager to tell me all about "the gunboat out there." His wild blue eyes were dancing around without focusing on anything and the blue vein in his forehead was swollen and throb-bing. He looked like he had a bolt of lightning trapped inside him. "We've got to sink this critter with our big gun," he chuckled inane-ly. Then he stared at me mischievously as I was directed to have a look at "the gunboat." Focusing on the warship moving away from the *Crevalle*'s position, I had the feeling that the captain was testing my guts. After looking at the small warship, he thought I'd get chick-en and want to back out of any gun action. I could see why. The war-ship was of only a couple hundred tons, but it had clean lines, looked fast and maneuverable, and had what appeared to be a three-inch gun in her waist. There was also a towering pile of red-painted depth charges stacked on his stern, proving that the warship was particularly designed to fight submarines. Also his shiny, newly painted gray sides along with the white uniformed men who were on his decks suggested that the *Crevalle* would be tackling an efficient, dangerous enemy warship. When I lowered the scope and turned to the captain to see what he really felt about engaging the gunboat with the four-inch gun, he was quivering with what looked like a crazy eagerness to sink the ASW warship. I felt it was a dumb idea to risk a submarine for such a relatively unimportant Japanese ship. One hit from that big gun on the enemy warship could mean a hole in the *Crevalle*'s pressure hull. Then it would be almost impossible to extricate the *Crevalle* from the Jap-held area and get her safely out into the Indian Ocean. The captain knew that as well as I did.

But I just said, "OK, Captain. We can sink her," and went down to the control room while the captain ordered "Battle stations, gun action." Then the general alarm started clanging through the boat.

I had some qualms about having to stand out in the open to spot the four-inch shell fire. The gunboat had to be destroyed far from the *Crevalle*. Without further concern, the positioning of my gun crew in the access trunk leading up to the main deck was checked. Red Tackett was at the top of the ladder. He carried a mallet to knock open the outer door to the main deck when the *Crevalle* was sur-faced. Next to him on the ladder was Ducharme, the wiry, smart, veteran gun captain. Then Enright, the second loader. The rest of the loading team formed a chain down the trunk and to the shell maga-zine below the control room. The fuse setter was correctly the fifth in line. Tense silence was shown by the gun crew as they were coiled to spring out on deck the moment Tackett hammered the lugs free on the outer door. A deadly slugging match was about to start.

I took my place, just behind the captain in the line leading up to the bridge from the conning tower. The twenty-millimeter gun crews, with their bandoleers of cartridges around their necks, were behind me in line.

Frank took a last look through the periscope and then ordered, "Surface." High pressure air roared into the ballast tanks sounding like a drawn-out war cry.

At "twenty-three feet and holding," both hatches were pounded open and the crew erupted onto the bridge and main deck. After climbing over the bridge combing to the twenty-millimeter gun deck, I studied the gunboat through my binoculars. He was at five thousand yards and was heading away. Below me the four-inch gun crew unlimbered the gun and the first shell was rammed home by Tackett. Ducharme closed the breech block and shouted, "Ready to fire" toward the bridge. The captain shouted back, "Set 5,200 yards on the sights, and commence firing when ready."

This looked easy. A hit in those red-painted depth charges and the gunboat would go up in a cloud of smoke.

Ducharme barked "Fire" and the pointer on the gun tramped on the firing pedal. The gun roared.

I watched the shell wing its way out towards the retreating gunboat. It dropped about fifty yards short. "Up a hundred," I ordered.

The sight-setter quickly reported, "Set" and a second shell went sailing across the water and hit close to the bow of the warship. At that, tiny figures raced across the gunboat's deck and bustled around their big gun. "We've got to get him now!" I muttered to myself.

Ducharme looked like an efficient machine as he yanked the breech door open, snapped out "Load," then slammed the breech block shut after Tackett had jammed the next shell home. This man was a "fire eater."

The third, fourth and fifth rounds were fired and there was still no sign of a hit by an explosive shell. What was worse, the target had spun about in a sheet of sun-tinted spray and was headed back at the *Crevalle*. His broad, white bow-wake arched outward from his sharp nose. It made him look like an angry bird-of-prey attacking across the water.

Then I observed that the fourth round had gone right through the warship's bridge, leaving a clean hole, without exploding. There were more hits as the gun kept firing in rapid succession every four seconds. But they produced similar small holes through the hull and superstructure. Ducharme was nervously glancing back down the line of shell passers. He realized that something was dreadfully wrong. There was no "punch" in the shell hits. So I yelled "Cease fire," and jumped down to the main deck to examine the shells being handled. The shell in Tackett's arms was set on "safe." Enright's shell was set on safe. That was all wrong. Evidently, the fuse-setter, who used a wrench to turn the shell settings from "safe" to "armed" had thoughtlessly twisted an "armed" shell back to "safe." The next man aft of him carried an armed shell. In fact, all the shells coming up from the control room were armed. One man in the loading team banging a shell against the bulkhead would have blown up the whole loading line. Somebody down below was twisting the fuses to "armed." And the fuse-setter, not realizing this was twisting his wrench in the wrong direction. I yelled down the gun access trunk to keep the shells on "safe," as Ducharme twisted the first couple of rounds back to "armed." Firing was then frantically recommenced. (An investigation later showed that a new man deep in the shell-passing line, on seeing the shell in his arms set on "safe," inexplicably took a pair of pliers out of his pocket and turned the fuse setting on each shell he passed to "armed.")

The range to the gunboat was down to two thousand yards. Wisps of smoke drifted back towards his stern as his big gun barked sharply across the water. Ominously, a geyser of water jumped into the air a scant fifty yards from the *Crevalle*'s bow. Ducharme, thinking that the *Crevalle*'s four-inch gun had sloppily dumped a round into the ocean ahead, yelled at the gun-pointer: "Stay on the target, Fritchen, or we're all dead meat."

Fritchen shouted back, "I'm right on, Gunner."

Ducharme added: "Keep your mind on your job, Fritchen. Don't let a couple of close enemy shells spoil your aim."

Fritchen didn't even glance back at Ducharme—ignoring the reprimand being dished out.

Then a mountain of water rose into the air a few yards to the left of the four-inch gun crew, and some of the shrapnel from the exploding shell pinged against the *Crevalle*'s sides.

Ducharme's reaction to this was instantaneous. He turned towards me with an alarmed face that was now a greenish-gray color. "They're shooting at us, Mr. Ruhe," he growled, incredulously. Then he savagely turned back towards the gun to ensure a killing hit on the enemy warship before he got his head torn off by an enemy shell.

The clang of a big piece of shrapnel on the conning tower just aft of me produced a sickening feeling in the pit of my stomach. It made me glance around my exposed position to see if there was some part of the bridge I could put between myself and the next shell, which was due shortly. But there was no sort of shielding anywhere. There wasn't even the usual plate of protective steel in front of the twenty-millimeter gun-mount. It had been eliminated from submarine guns because of the great drag it produced when the submarine was submerged. I had to admit to myself that I wasn't as brave as I wanted the captain to think I was. I even considered jumping down to the main deck where I might direct the gunfire from the side of the conning tower, which was away from the direction where the enemy shells were landing in the sea close to the *Crevalle*. But I rejected that and just prayed that we'd start hitting the gunboat and silence his big gun.

The gun crew pumped out shell after shell at the warship in feverish haste. "Sink him," I heard the captain beg. Then the shells began to hit with explosive violence, tearing large jagged chunks from the gunboat's hull and bridge.

"Whooooooommm!" A thunderous explosion on the gunboat rocketed across the water. Debris and flame mounted several hundred feet in the air as the gunboat's stern disintegrated. The four-inch gun had finally placed a shell into the big, red-painted pile of depth charges. The twenty-third round from the four-inch gun had finished off the gunboat at a range of 1600 yards. It was too close for comfort, particularly since the Japanese had opened-up with a scary chatter of machine guns.

My gun crew went crazy. They thumped each other on the back. They yelled into the air. They laughed and danced about. I just crazily shook my fist at the enemy ship. The captain was all smiles. And this produced an irresistible feeling of well-being relative to the captain and myself. Ducharme looked nervously exhausted as he accidentally leaned his arm on the red-hot barrel of the gun then quickly pulled it away and slumped against the pointer's seat.

The remains of the gunboat were well down in the water. But he wasn't sinking. He was stopped, however, and his topside was cleared of his white-clad crew, while many oil-covered heads floated in the water near the shattered wreckage of the gunboat.

The captain eased the *Crevalle* close to the dazed survivors hoping to get a few prisoners. He instructed the *Crevalle* crewmen on the main deck to "try to haul a couple of live ones aboard." But the Japanese in the water floated motionless. Their eyes glared at their enemy with what looked like pure hatred. Their powder-blackened heads resembled charred coconut masks with ash-gray hair and inset mother of pearl eyes flecked with red. Their clothing had been blown off. Their only flicker of life was evidenced by the occasional blinking of their staring blood-shot eyes. None tried to swim close to the *Crevalle*'s side.

So the captain moved the sub close to a Japanese survivor while Howard climbed over the side to offer a helping hand to the man in the water. The Jap, however, ducked his head downward, gulped mouthfuls of water and then sank from sight.

Another survivor near the *Crevalle*'s stern tried to pull himself up onto the *Crevalle*'s slimy, curving side. But his handhold slipped and without a murmur he sank into the *Crevalle*'s slowly turning screws.

These men in the water were the enemy. We were seeing them close at hand and closely observing how they acted. It was evident that they would rather die than be humiliated by being taken prisoner. Such people were going to be very hard to beat and they promised a long war before the job could be finished.

More of the heads in the water choked down gulps of the oily water, causing their heads to plummet from sight—like punctured cans of rocks filled with water.

"Holy God," Enright swore. "What a bunch of wild men." He turned his massive, peanut-butter-filled body away from the scene of hara-kiri being performed in an inhuman and unreal style. Then he moved over to Red Tackett's side and began to shadow box with his pal. Enright had regained his high spirits once more. To him, the suicidal actions of the Japanese survivors were easily forgotten.

During the rescue attempts, Jerry had rested his tommy-gun on the bridge rail, aimed in the direction of the heads in the water. When the captain noted this he shoved Jerry's gun aside and snapped, "There'll be none of that. Those men are no threat to us." That brought considerable relief to me because I'd been worried about somebody vengefully taking a pot-shot at one of the helpless survivors. There was no place for that in submarine war.

On the next day, the *Crevalle* cruised east through the Celebes Sea. Nothing was sighted.

On February 13, a 750-ton sea truck was overtaken. This small merchant ship was a new, efficient cargo-type of ship that the Japanese had found easy to construct and that was appearing in greater and greater numbers as more of the big Japanese merchant ships were sent to the bottom. The captain wanted to sink her with guns but decided that the seas were too high for gun action.

By Valentine's Day, the *Crevalle* was on the last day of her patrol. She had moved to the top of the Molucca Sea, responding to another one of the captain's hunches. He felt that there he would find sea traffic going to New Guinea. But his wild guess seemed without foundation. So I took the time to write a love letter to my wife.

By midnight, when the *Crevalle* was supposed to leave station nothing had materialized. Yet, instead of bending on four engines and heading home, the captain decided that nobody would be any the wiser if he stayed a day longer.

The fifteenth seemed another wasted day, but then smoke was sighted out to the east. Through the high periscope, the topmasts of a seven-ship convoy steaming towards the Philippines, could be seen. And behind this group of ships was still another hair-like mast. A trailing escort? This was the moment in submarining every submarine skipper dreamed about. Close at hand were a considerable number of marus plodding across an uncluttered sea with little ASW protection, and the skies were clear of aircraft. What a set-up for a night surface attack!

Thus, despite a glaring sun and a smooth sea, the captain decided to stay on the surface and run parallel to the convoy while staying about sixteen thousand yards off the convoy's port beam. His strategy was to track the ships, using the high periscope during daylight. Then when darkness closed in he planned to put the *Crevalle* up ahead of the convoy for a night surface attack, depending on radar for his attack information.

With sixteen feet of periscope raised above the shears, it was possible to determine the make-up of the convoy. There were three small cargo ships in column leading the convoy. In a second column on the starboard quarter of the three lead ships, were a large and two medium-size freighters in column. On the port quarter of the lead ships was another column of two ships, a large freighter and a trailing escort that looked like a merchantman converted to a naval auxiliary warship. The escort was painted warship gray and carried several big guns that looked like six-inchers. The spacing between ships was about one thousand yards. All were making ten knots and were zig-zagging on a base course of 350° True.

In the early afternoon, when a four-engine Emily-type flying boat appeared over the convoy, the people topside started acting jittery. The lookout who first spotted the aircraft, had a tremor in his voice as he reported, "There's a big airplane above the middle of the ships out there, Captain."

The bomber wove a cloverleaf pattern over the merchantmen, and swung out periodically for a short leg of about four miles in a westward direction. On one sweep towards the *Crevalle*, the Emily started blinking a light at the *Crevalle*. The plane had evidently spotted an unidentified ship on the ocean's surface that he felt needed to be challenged. The captain immediately cleared the bridge of all personnel except for Frank and himself. Frank meanwhile, guessing that the plane wasn't sure as to the kind of ship it was challenging, grabbed a blinker gun and sent back some meaningless flashes at the aircraft. Frank's blinked response to the plane's challenge, plus the *Crevalle*'s gray and black camouflage job apparently did the trick, because the plane winged over and returned to the convoy. The air-search radar showed that the plane had closed to four miles before turning away. Yet the captain and Frank stayed resolutely on the bridge. Then Frank's voice elatedly yelled, "We fooled him. He thought we were a fishing boat." I felt certain at that point that everything was going to go right and that this would be a banner day. Forced to dive, the convoy could have been lost.

It was very gutsy of Frank to try this ploy to fool the aircraft and it was very nervy of the captain to hold off diving until absolutely the last second.

Later, a second Emily appeared over the convoy and relieved the first one, which went home. But the *Crevalle* was not bothered again by a suspicious enemy aircraft.

At this point, the captain told Frank to work out a maneuvering board solution to move the *Crevalle* from her position on the port beam of the convoy to a position eight miles out ahead of the convoy. "Use fifteen knots for our own speed," the captain advised.

The maneuvering problem given to Frank was a simple one and one he had solved many times before. But under the stress caused by the threatening Emily aircraft, Frank's capability to think "relative movement" had disappeared. He stared uncertainly at the maneuvering board for several minutes then passed the job to me. He admitted, "With that Jap plane hovering around out there, my mind draws a blank." Normally good at this sort of thing, my mind also drew a blank. I was of no help. So Frank advised the captain, "Just keep going this way and swing to the east after dark."

As night closed in, the *Crevalle* arrived at a position eight miles ahead of the convoy. Then with a "Here we go," and without a silly laugh, the captain swung the *Crevalle* south to close the convoy at high speed and attack with a high degree of surprise.

At this dramatic moment the captain was admirable for his decisiveness. It generated in me a feeling of affection for him. He was wound up like a tight spring and his warrior-like enthusiasm for battle was infectious. It produced an infusion of a this-is-what-you-were-made-for sensation of well-being in me. Any concern for what might happen when the *Crevalle* charged into the convoy was pushed into the back of my mind.

When the nearest ship in the lead column was at four thousand yards, all the ships were showing a zero angle on the bow and heading straight at the *Crevalle*. Luke, the battle TBT operator, began describing the ships ahead, despite the darkness. The captain, significantly, with his near-zero night vision, still couldn't see a single ship.

As Luke described each ship, the quartermaster jotted down the details on a pad and passed his notes down to George Morin in the conning tower. George then tried to identify them from the Japanese Merchant Ships book. But George failed to find a single ship that matched the descriptions of the ships observed by Luke. So he thrust the book at me and growled insolently, "You see if you can identify any of these foolish ships? Luke must be taking dope."

But I was no more successful. "They probably aren't Japanese ships," I doubtfully noted. "They could be ships captured by the Japanese at the start of the war; British, Dutch, French, perhaps some of our own."

That satisfied George who called up to the bridge that the ships didn't seem to be Japanese ships but rather ships of the Allies that had been seized by the Japanese.

The *Crevalle*'s course took her close down the port side of the first three cargo ships. Then, with the set-up too poor for firing at the big ships in the far column beyond the lead ships, the captain swung the *Crevalle* out to westward to open the range an additional thousand yards.

All six torpedo tubes were reported ready to fire as the captain swung the *Crevalle* back to head for the big freighters in the far, trailing column.

The small lead ships had begun tooting their whistles frantically, warning of submarine attack. One of the ships, blew two short blasts to signal that the attack was coming from its port side. The three ships were also using bright signal lights to alert the ships astern of the existing emergency.

I heard Luke being directed to aim the first three torpedoes at the biggest freighter—which was second in the far column and the next three at the leading ship in the far column. The captain then called down to me to apply a 2 1/2° spread for the torpedoes fired at each target.

The *Crevalle* was slowed to ten knots just before firing the six torpedoes so they wouldn't tumble on being launched.

When fired, the wakes of the torpedoes, as observed by Luke, indicated that the first and second torpedoes hit in the big ship that was following the lead ship of the far column. The two torpedoes caused tremendous damage in that ship, according to Luke. The third torpedo, he said, missed astern. The fourth torpedo he saw hit the lead freighter, while the fifth missed ahead and the sixth plowed into the small cargo ship at the end of the lead column.

At the explosion of the first torpedo the Japanese gun crews on the merchant ships began wildly shooting their big guns out into the darkness. Some sounded like six-inch guns by their deafening blasts. Heavy concussion from the gunfire rattled and reverberated the *Crevalle*'s conning tower, like huge boulders being bounced off a massive steel drum.

Bedlam had taken over. Whistles tooted, red tracers streaked across the sky, machine guns chattered, shells screamed close overhead and horns moaned complainingly.

With the discharge of the sixth torpedo, the captain ordered right full rudder to bring the stern tubes to bear on the lead freighter in the trailing port column. When the range to this ship had opened to one thousand yards the three remaining torpedoes in the after room were fired.

Luke saw the first torpedo from the stern tubes miss ahead of the close freighter. The second torpedo, according to Luke, had an unexplainable hit in the third ship of the far column. While the third torpedo exploded under the close freighter's bridge.

It was a wild, reckless, imprudent time to be on the bridge. Everyone up there was yelling warnings to the captain: "The escort is swinging to port. He's cutting us off to the westward.". . . "The near target we just torpedoed is being hit by shellfire from ships in the far column.". . . "The two small ships to starboard which were leading the convoy are scattering in different directions and smoking heavily." . . . "A ship astern is shining a big light at us."

The captain started swinging the *Crevalle* to get some breathing room for a reload of the last six torpedoes in the forward room. But the naval auxiliary changed course and charged at the *Crevalle*. This forced the captain to keep her swinging until she was able to pass close ahead of the freighter just damaged. Then he drove the *Crevalle* down through the center of the convoy to block the escort from an intercepting path.

Luke observed several flashes of exploding shells on the naval auxiliary. She was apparently taking the brunt of the convoy's crazy, indiscriminate reaction to the *Crevalle*'s surface attack. But with the *Crevalle*'s phosphorescent wake evidently visible to some of the gun crews on the freighters, not surprisingly Luke saw and reported a shell hitting in the water close off the *Crevalle*'s port quarter.

With Japanese ships still moving slowly north and the *Crevalle* headed south on four engines, it looked as though the captain would extricate her from this mess of wild and confused shooting.

The naval auxiliary, however, was reported to be swinging back towards the fleeing *Crevalle* in order to ram her. The warship was closely following the sub's maneuvers.

At this point, with many shells whistling past and with the escort's big guns apparently trained on the *Crevalle*, the captain decided to pull the plug and go deep to four hundred feet. For sheer daring this attack would be difficult to match!

I thought of the great courage that was shown by our men who were exposed topside, and how they had maintained their self-control despite the dread of being blown up by a shell hit. In the conning tower, I didn't have a spare moment to think about the dangers involved. But I did note that my heart was beating hard and irregularly. And my breath was being held in long pauses. I was too busy to even breathe regularly.

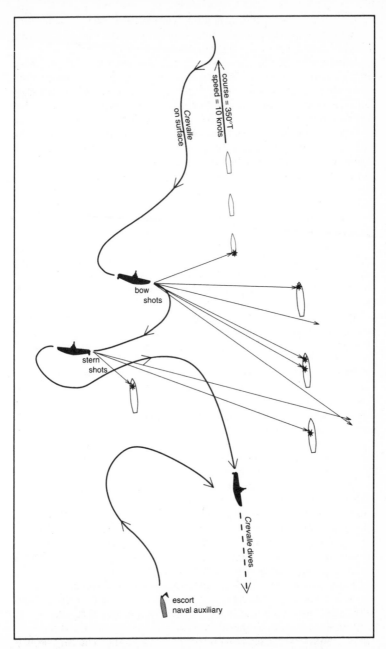

Figure 5.1 Crevalle's attack on convoy, February 15, 1944.

Once submerged, the turned-up sonar receiver was broadcasting a cacophony of boiler explosions and loud groans and creaks from ships breaking up, on several bearings.

Within minutes the escort was churning over the *Crevalle*, carelessly dropping eight improperly depth-set but powerful charges. By their deafening booms it was likely they were one thousand-kilo charges and their depth setting was probably only one hundred meters as they managed to smash only a few light bulbs, but nothing else.

The captain up to then had certainly been at his fighting best. So for the moment, I forgave him for his vacillating actions earlier in the patrol. But the captain kept the *Crevalle* at four hundred feet for an exorbitantly long period of time, a good hour after the soundman had reported that the escort's screws had speeded up and then faded out to the north. The escort was leaving the scene to catch up with the remnants of his convoy. In fact, all convoy noises had also disappeared as the *Crevalle* crept south away from the surface action.

Still, there were some damaged ships up there on the ocean somewhere, that should be finished off with the *Crevalle*'s six remaining torpedoes. Moreover, the naval auxiliary was too valuable a ship to let off the hook. And worse, the captain kept everyone at their battle stations, making the waiting infuriating and intolerable.

Both Frank and I strongly urged the captain to get the *Crevalle* back on the surface and resume the attack. But he acted exhausted by the violent surface action and gloomily said, "I've done enough for one night."

When we finally surfaced an hour before midnight, the captain put only one engine on the line and nonsensically headed the *Crevalle* eastward. He said he was going to "mop up on the damaged ships." But it was recognized that they were actually to the north of the *Crevalle* and getting farther away by the minute.

Holding the eastward course for only a few minutes, the captain then turned the *Crevalle* to the south. This moved her even more distant from the scene of action and the crippled ships.

While the captain remained on the bridge, Frank and I stayed in the red-lit gloom of the conning tower. So it seemed safe to complain about the tactics the captain was using which certainly weren't designed to regain contact on any of the remaining ships of the convoy. "We can't quit now," I argued. Then I tried to persuade Frank to get the captain to chase the escaping ships. "You can't let the old man stop now," I urged, "even if he is tired."

Frank said darkly, "He's off the beam again, and you know it."

Sure I knew it, so I suggested, "Let's just steer the *Crevalle* north. While he's up on the bridge, he will never know the difference."

Much distressed at the idea, Frank muttered, "This whole business is hopeless." Then, even more discouragingly, "The captain is in no mood for any further attacks. And I don't want to cut him out of the action like we did with the RO-boat."

I pressed Frank again, "But we can't quit now. You've got to go up to the bridge and get the captain off the dime."

Frank sounded even more disgusted. "It's hopeless."

At this point, a dark shadowy figure in the front of the conning tower, that I assumed was the quartermaster, moved into the light of the chart desk. It was the captain! He had slipped down into the conning tower unseen and had overheard our conversation. He absently glanced at the chart beside Frank's elbow for a few seconds then sarcastically said, "All right, you fellows go ahead and conn my boat wherever you damn well please." Bitterly he added, "You seem to know exactly what I *should* do. Now *you* do it." And he climbed back to the bridge leaving both of us dazed and aghast.

My body felt like a punctured gas bag with the air rushing out of it. I was too shocked to even consider the captain's invitation to take over and get the *Crevalle* back into action.

But Frank didn't hesitate. He ordered the helmsman to come to course 350° True and had flank speed rung up while having all for engines put on the line. Frank reacted like a floored boxer who was back on his feet chasing his opponent around the ring.

Off went the *Crevalle* in pursuit.

At a little before midnight, with the moon a narrow sliver peeking through heavy, threatening storm clouds, a lookout sighted the shapes of two small ships out on the horizon ahead. As the two ships were being closed, the naval auxiliary detached itself from a dark area of rain clouds off the *Crevalle*'s starboard quarter and came into view. He seemed to be hurrying to catch up with the remains of his convoy.

The *Crevalle* was in a good position to attack the ASW warship, so she was submerged to radar depth and the approach was commenced. The captain stood quietly by the chart desk, scowling at Frank who was going right ahead with the attack.

All six remaining torpedoes were readied.

The firing set-up looked good, with the escort making sixteen knots. But then he started slowing and blinking a light at the two ships up ahead. Frank, worried that shortly the warship would start maneuvering radically, decided that it was necessary to torpedo the enemy warship without any further delay.

With a range of 2,600 yards and the warship making about ten knots, all six torpedoes were fired on a fifty-degree port track. But that wasn't very smart, for although the first torpedo hit the naval auxiliary up forward, he was turning towards the *Crevalle*. So the other five torpedoes, according to Frank who was watching their wakes through the periscope, passed harmlessly down his starboard side.

Then the enemy warship, seriously wounded but still able to use his engines, churned slowly over the *Crevalle* and dropped some very big depth charges that violently shook the *Crevalle*. The escort was like a lumbering bear in its death-throes trying to give his enemy a fatal, powerful hug.

Fortunately, there were no reports from the seven compartments of any serious damage that might require immediate emergency action.

Even deep, and the *Crevalle* had been taken to four hundred feet, the warship could be heard firing his deck guns. Then, ten minutes after he'd been hit, his propellers stopped. That was easily heard through the hull, with great relief. Over at the chart desk, the captain was malevolently frowning at Frank and me. But with uneasy smiles, we still felt a bit of satisfaction.

Frank promptly brought the *Crevalle* back to periscope depth for a quick look to see the status of the warship. He was, according to Frank on the periscope, barely visible with what looked like a giant cloud of steam around him. Several more looks seemed to confirm that the warship was listing heavily and down in the water. Then in between looks he was suddenly gone with only a pile of smoke where he'd been.

The Captain went silently to his stateroom and pulled the curtains shut. Frank turned the periscope watch over to George and decided to keep submerged a bit longer. Frank was not convinced that the warship had actually sunk. "He might still be up there, inside a rain storm," Frank noted, "and ready to fire his guns at the *Crevalle* when she surfaces." Frank said that heavy rain had cut his visibility to the target and cautioned that there was a risk "of being blind-sided."

When we gathered in the wardroom there was no hand slapping or continuous chatter. Frank and I went over all of the descriptions of the ships in the convoy that Luke had dictated to the quartermaster. We also listened critically to what Luke said he saw during the firing of the nine torpedoes at the convoy.

Only the escort proved identifiable. It was the *Tatusake Maru* of 7,065 tons, a naval auxiliary that readily fit Frank's periscope observations of his characteristics.

There was some bitter discussion about having a bigger warhead on our torpedoes so that a single hit would sink a big ship outright. I wondered out loud, "Why are we using 680-pound warheads on our Mk-14's when reportedly the Germans are using a torpedo with an 1100-pound warhead?"

The captain, when he finally decided to come to the wardroom, said that he could only claim the escort and the big freighter that had taken two torpedoes as having been sunk. The others, having sustained only one hit each, had to be assumed as only damaged.

And that's what he sent in his dispatch to headquarters in Perth, putting "waffle bottoms" as padding for the encoded message. "That's for Admiral Christie's do-nothing staff," the captain gloated.

All day of the sixteenth of February, the *Crevalle* hurried south through the Molucca Sea, headed for Darwin. The captain brooded in his cabin, keeping the curtains closed. He finally called for me, and after studying me steadily he said maliciously, "You know, Ruhe, that was mutiny you pulled on me last night."

Mutiny? My heart sank until it hit my shoe tops.

"And I also heard you griping to Frank about me letting that ship out by Spratly get away," he accused. Then, with a sly, ugly smile, "I also remember how you guys took over and shot torpedoes at that Jap sub without letting me know what was going on. And that was inexcusable." He wasn't finished. "I've felt all along the dissatisfaction of both of you on how I've been running this boat." He stared off into space, then came to a decision, "I'm going to court martial you and Frank for insubordination when we get back into port."

I protested that Frank had nothing to do with questioning his authority. At this the captain, chuckling inanely said, "You're both in this together. I've been carefully watching you two guys all this patrol."

Startled, I began to realize that the captain was actually in an overstressed state and wasn't making much sense. When he dismissed me, at first I couldn't take his weird accusations seriously. I didn't feel any self-pity. But his threats weren't helping my sleep.

I told Frank about the conversation with the captain and Frank merely said, "Don't worry about it. He'll cool off."

Then, later in the day, with five officers in the wardroom, the captain praised both Frank and me by name, and gave recognition to our contributions for making this patrol a great success. He mentioned that Frank had pushed him back into combat when he was tired out and had lost his fighting spirit. And that Frank was "the best executive officer in the whole submarine business."

But I didn't feel off the hook until next day, when, all smiles, he praised me for putting up with his "vacillations" and for helping to hold the *Crevalle* together as one of the best fighting ships in the U.S. Navy. But was he rational? What was his actual state of mind?

On the sixteenth, two Jap bombers were sighted some distance off, but the *Crevalle* wasn't dived.

Next evening, the *Crevalle* was crossing the Ceram Sea below the equator, when a large schooner was spotted ahead. Hoping to gain some intelligence on ship movements in that area, the captain steered the *Crevalle* near the sailing vessel. Then Frank, the acknowledged expert on speaking Spanish, shouted through a megaphone, *"Pare y baja las velas."* But the schooner sailed on, ignoring the order to stop and lower the sails. Frank repeated the same order several times but without result. Then, impatiently he yelled, "Dammit, drop your sails." And the sails came tumbling down.

The captain then eased the *Crevalle* against the schooner's side and told Frank to ask the cowering natives on board whether they had seen any ships lately. There was so much racket being made by little brown-skinned men, naked children, pigs, chickens, and dogs that Frank had to bellow, *"Basta! Quedo quieto."* Which simply meant, "Shut up!" The people and things on deck went silent. When Frank questioned the native men about ships, they only shook their heads meaninglessly. But the men were insistent in trying to force a peace offering on the captain. Some tiny women had come up from below and were trying to offer fruit to the men on the *Crevalle*'s topsides.

Magnanimously, the captain climbed down to the main deck and accepted a scrawny little dirty-gray chicken, while indicating that that was all he would accept because he didn't want to deprive them of such precious food. He bowed gratefully for the gift of the miserable little chicken. The people on the schooner all answered with deep bows and broad smiles.

The bird was so emaciated that it didn't look as though it would live very long. Nor that anyone would want to eat it. The captain handed the chicken up to Howard, the chief torpedoman, and told him in a low voice to take it below while all the natives were watching. When the captain backed the *Crevalle* away from the schooner's side, he suggested with a whispered aside to the men on the bridge to have big smiles on their faces and to look grateful.

Howard took the weak little chicken to the after room and gave it to Crowley to take care of. When later I went aft to look at the chicken, Crowley was feeding it bread crumbs, which the bird ravenously gobbled up. Crowley then revealed that this was no labor of love because he figured that the little starved thing would shortly start laying fresh eggs. For him.

Late on the eighteenth, a large cargo ship was sighted heading slowly towards Ambon. It had a small, rusty, heavily smoking vessel playing the role of escort. The vast amount of smoke pouring out of the small ship's stack was suspicious. It was also weaving around the larger ship at a greater speed. The crummy little ship fit the description of "Ambon Charlie," a Q-ship that had attracted several U.S. submarines into an attack. When torpedoes had been fired at Ambon Charlie, they ran under him and the subs then had received a highly efficient and damaging depth charging. The captain temperately gave the two ships a wide berth. I was happy that there were no torpedoes left because the captain might have, in one of his moments, insisted that we had to "get that Q-ship."

As soon as the pair of ships were well clear, the captain tried to raise by voice radio any submarine in the Banda Sea, to pass on contact information. But his helpful gesture backfired. Within minutes a Japanese plane came in low from the east headed straight for the *Crevalle*. Luckily the *Crevalle* was submerged so rapidly that no bombs were dropped by the plane.

In an hour the *Crevalle* was back on the surface heading home. But shortly, a Lilly-type bomber sneaked in so low from up-sun that the bomber was able to lay a bomb that exploded close off the stern. Then the bomber opened up with machine gun fire as the upper hatch was being closed and before Jerry, the OOD, had started the *Crevalle* submerging. Inside the conning tower it sounded as though the plane's bullets were tearing up the main deck and blasting holes in the *Crevalle*'s hull up forward. As she was taken deep, the forward room reported that there were no signs of hull damage up there but that they'd heard lots of hits above their heads. The after room reported they'd heard fragments of the bomb hitting in the stern. But nothing else.

After a short wait the *Crevalle* was taken back to periscope depth. Quick looks through the periscope confirmed that the plane had not lingered in the area. When the bow buoyancy tank was blown on surfacing, the hissing of high pressure air through holes in the tank indicated that the machine gun hits had actually done some important damage to the *Crevalle*. From then on, this forward tank would have to remain flooded, making it difficult to dive fast during the rest of the trip home. The machine gun hits in the main deck flooring merely created lots of gouged and torn up boards. That wasn't important, except that the *Crevalle* would look as though she had been through the war with a vengeance when she pulled into Fremantle.

When two planes were sighted on February 19th, at the extreme south of the Banda Sea, it was necessary to rapidly submerge for each one as they closed the *Crevalle*. But the punctured tank being flooded, the boat was unthinkingly trimmed to be light forward. Thus, without a functioning bow buoyancy tank, the diving officer had every available man run speedily forward to bring the *Crevalle*'s nose down. It was a circus, with clowns diving through the compartment doors and piling on top of each other up by the forward tubes. When the bow had taken a sharp down angle, the men were then raced back towards the stern. Submarining was never foolish, but this business was approaching the ridiculous.

When crossing the Banda Sea, it appeared to be covered by huge patches of yellow seaweed. The yellow patches, on closer examination, proved to be millions of wriggling black sea snakes with wide yellow bands around their bodies. They were the highly poisonous

Banda Sea Snake, one of the most deadly of reptiles in the world. When I recited this fact to Frank, he suggested that "it would be a dirty trick to sink a Jap ship in this area." I agreed.

The *Crevalle* entered Darwin on the twentieth, just after dawn, to top off with fuel and pick up mail. On the way in, the men on the bridge saw a large flight of U.S. Liberators headed north towards the Halmaheras. Not having received a message from Darwin acknowledging *Crevalle*'s arrival time, the captain was afraid that the she might be bombed by a U.S. plane as she closed Darwin. Apparently, the staff in Perth didn't like the captain's padding of his message with "waffle bottoms" and decided to let the captain just stew in his own juice.

Late at night, after leaving Darwin, George reported from the bridge that there was heavy bombing going on over to the eastward and that searchlights were beaming all over the sky. Apparently, the *Crevalle* had missed a big air raid against Darwin by only a matter of hours.

It was a six-day trip to Fremantle and all seemed peaceful until the third day when the captain started brooding. He took his meals on his desk in his stateroom, claiming that he had to concentrate on writing the patrol report. He kept the curtain to his room drawn. He also failed to show up for the field days he had instituted for the boat, "to clean up all the dirt."

On the fourth day, the captain called me into his bunkroom and with the same wild-eyed approach, he told me he was going to see that I was court-martialed when we got in for my insubordination during the patrol. "You think I've forgotten about how you and Frank tried to take over my command. That's mutiny, you know!" he snarled.

When I protested that he'd praised Frank and me for making the patrol a great success, it just made him angrier.

"You'll never go back to sea on my submarine and I'll see that you're bounced out of the Navy," he emphasized. There was much more invective as my legs got weaker and weaker.

I saw that things were bad right now, but he should soon snap out of this dark mood and return to his mercurial but rational personality. With no more stress and after he had gotten a Navy Cross for his exceptional patrol, he'd probably forget about pressing charges against me. At least I hoped so.

When I related this session with the captain to Frank he said we'd just have to go to Admiral Christie when we got in and lay our cards on the table. And pray.

On the way south from Darwin, I had a great amount of time to reflect on the war patrol just being completed. Aside from my conflict with Captain Munson, there seemed to be some valuable lessons of submarine warfare to be learned from this patrol. Most importantly, night surface torpedo attacks were the way to go. The high tempo of operations inherent to surface attacks gave a wide margin of advantage to the attacker over the defensive actions of enemy ships.

As illustrated by the *Crevalle*'s night surface actions against a convoy of many ships, from the time the *Crevalle* was committed to the attack—just ahead of the lead ships in the convoy—to the time she was dived to escape from the enemy's counterattack, was only a matter of nine minutes. The *Crevalle* completely controlled the tempo of operations and the surface action itself. By comparison, the earlier submerged attack on the *Taibun Maru* took over sixty minutes with the enemy surface ships, at times controlling the action and dictating the tempo of the *Crevalle*'s attack. The enemy ships' countering actions time and again frustrated and neutralized the *Crevalle*'s offensive tactics, resulting in no torpedoes being fired. However, when the *Taibun Maru* group was attacked by the *Crevalle* on the surface and at night the action took only fifteen minutes. The *Crevalle* remained on the offensive throughout the attack and totally controlled the tempo, with decisive results accruing from calculated risk-taking and aggressive actions.

An important consideration was that in the short surface actions, the captain's responses were unwavering. From start to finish, the captain's decisions were consistent with his aggressive actions. Whereas with submerged operations, the great span of time involved tended to create vacillation on the captain's part.

The attack on the RO-class Jap submarine with two torpedoes, seemed to indicate that the magnetic feature of the Mk-14 torpedoes in use was the likely producer of the premature explosions of the torpedoes. The explosion of the first torpedo had probably countermined the closely following second torpedo. Whereas, when using contact exploders, prematures and countermining were not likely to happen.

Very significantly, the captain, instead of giving up with fifteen torpedoes remaining, and disgustedly terminating the patrol in accordance with his orders, asked for a five-day extension to the patrol and even stuck around for an extra day to try to "get rid of all of the torpedoes." The results justified his tenacity and endurance. Also the sixty-one day patrol and the thirteen thousand miles steamed illustrated the great endurance of a fleet boat.

The *Crevalle*'s mineplant might have been the most significant and successful feature of this patrol. But it is hard to tell if this is true. That's the nature of a mining offensive. Its success might only be measured in terms of the delays created in the movement of shipping until the discovered minefield was thoroughly swept.

On the day before arrival at Fremantle, a loud cackle was heard, coming from the after room. Crowley's little, but fatter, chicken was announcing that an egg was being laid. Out came an egg with Crowley catching it as it emerged. All he got was a handful of yoke as a shell-less egg broke all over his hand. Though his hopes seemed dashed, Crowley was a man of action. He went forward to the galley and got a lot of egg shells, which he pulverized and then fed to his chicken. The scrawny little bird, starved for calcium, gobbled up Crowley's offering. The next morning, there was another cackle and the little bird deposited an egg with a nice white, but fragile, shell into Crowley's hand. He was the envy of the crew at breakfast as he ate his fresh egg.

When the *Crevalle* tied up at 0800 after two months of steaming, Admiral Christie was on the dock and pinned a Navy Cross on Captain Munson when he went ashore to greet the admiral. In his remarks, the admiral said that four ships sunk and three more damaged made this an outstanding patrol. The admiral then came aboard for only a few seconds, nodded to the men standing on the main deck, looked them over approvingly and then turned around and went back across the gangway. Frank intercepted him on the dock as he was about to get into his car and said, "Lt. Ruhe and I have to talk with you about this patrol." Scarcely showing that he'd heard Frank's request, the admiral said, "You two be in my office at nine." Then his staff driver whisked him away.

I looked hopefully around the dock for The Boomer and his crowd of little schoolboys with the blue caps, but there was no sign of them. However, there was a big crowd of refit people, women drivers, and even a few staff people out from Perth. It was a buoyant moment as lots of enthusiasm was shown along with great interest in the bullet holes through bow buoyancy and the splintered decking on the main deck. As was observed, "At least you made it in one piece."

At 0900, Frank and I entered the admiral's office in his headquarters in Perth. He greeted us warmly and said he had expected that we would want to see him, and he guessed that it should be before Captain Munson had paid a call on him. "I've known there was something wrong going on aboard your submarine," he said, "from the messages I received as well as a few things I heard about— Selby's encounter with your sub in Makassar Strait, your yeoman's version of what happened when you shot at a Japanese sub and the way Munson acted when he was in Darwin." Then he added, "What's the story?"

When Frank told about the periods during which the captain was irrational and how he'd zeroed in on us as troublemakers, the admiral merely nodded and quietly said, "Don't worry about this. Just stand easy. I'm seeing your captain in a few minutes and he'll probably tell me the whole story of what went on."

I had to add, "He's threatening to court martial us for mutiny, Admiral." The admiral looked amused by Captain Munson's threat. Then an aide entered and told the admiral that Commander Munson was waiting outside to call on him. At this, Admiral Christie slipped us out through a side door and we went back to our rest home, Lucknow.

Within an hour the captain drove up and asked to see both Frank and me privately in the reception room. We waited for the axe to fall. But the captain, all smiles, said, "I told Christie about how I had periods during the patrol when I wasn't putting it all together, and even blanked out at times. Then I told him about how you two, taking a big risk, carried me through those periods, and did a superior job despite my problems."

This made me feel like the lowest of heels for not being totally loyal to this high-strung man who had suffered from the terrible strain of a very trying submarine patrol. The captain's eight combat patrols as a skipper had taken a severe toll, psychologically.

"I also told the admiral," Captain Munson explained, "that I needed a rest to recoup and wanted to spend a couple of months in a relief crew in Fremantle before I'd be ready to get another submarine command." Expansively he mentioned that he'd recommended that Lt. Comdr. Frank Walker relieve him and take the *Crevalle* back out to sea. And that he was recommending Silver Stars for Frank, Luke, and me. At that, both Frank and I sagged down into our chairs. It was all too unexpected. Luckily for us, we'd managed to hit one of those really good days for the captain.

Shortly, Commander Hank Munson was relieved of the *Crevalle*'s command by Lt. Comdr. Frank Walker. Munson then remained ashore as head of the Refit Detail, working on submarines between their patrols. In July, Admiral Christie sent Munson back to sea as Commanding Officer of the U.S.S. *Rasher*. Munson soon ran into a very large convoy of ships off the west coast of Luzon. In a night surface action, much the same as the one on the *Crevalle*'s last patrol, he sank five ships totaling 52,600 tons, one of which was a 28,000-ton aircraft carrier, and damaged four more ships totaling 22,000 tons, for a total patrol tonnage of 74,600 tons of ships sunk and damaged. It was the most sunk and damaged tonnage on a single patrol for any U.S. submarine in World War II. Luke Bowdler, having left the *Crevalle* after her third run, was with Munson as his TBT operator on the *Rasher* and acted as Munson's eyes in the night surface attacks.

6

Shallow Waters

The third patrol of the *Crevalle* was markedly different from previous war patrols in that it was conducted for the most part in shallow waters. Good sense and a submariner's instinct should have dictated trying not to hunt enemy ships in the shallow waters off Borneo, the *Crevalle*'s assigned patrol area.

In such coastal waters, planes could frequently spot a submarine all the way to the bottom. In addition, a slight blunder in navigation could cause a submarine to run aground. But what was most worrisome was that shallow waters simplified the antisubmarine problem for Japanese destroyers. They could use a single, shallow depth-setting on their depth charges and have a good chance of being right-on-target. Moreover, in shallow waters the tactic of going deep to evade depth charges would be eliminated from a submariner's bag of tricks.

It was evident that at this stage of the war, the Japanese had decided to move their convoys close to the shore lines of their newly captured territories. They were willing to risk the loss of their ships to reefs and mines rather than to the torpedoes of U.S. submarines in deep waters far out to sea.

It was a rough way to initiate a new skipper, Lt. Comdr. Frank Walker, into his first submarine command. It was evident that operation in shallow waters would demand a high level of risk-taking to get favorable results. By taking his submarine close to a coast Captain Walker was also running the risk of inadvertently having his boat blown up in a minefield.

The Japanese were, according to several pre-patrol briefings, laying many minefields to protect their coast-hugging ships from the U.S. submarine threat.

Thus, the psychological strain on the captain's mind from the shallow-set depth charges and the mine threat might reduce his aggressiveness considerably, while diminishing the gung-ho spirit of the *Crevalle*'s crew as well. But for this patrol, the *Crevalle*'s wardroom contingent of eight officers and the crew were eager for action. They were anything but the brooding, overly intense type of submariners who would lose a lot of sleep over the dangers involved. In fact, the three officer newcomers, Walt Mazzone, Dick Bowe, and Howie Geer promised much lighthearted fun and would help to take the strain off Capt. Frank Walker's back. Hank Munson and Jerry Gromer had been transferred off the *Crevalle*. I was now the exec, Walt became the diving officer, Dick took over the plotting job, and Howie just "assisted."

The *Crevalle* was scheduled to finally shove off on patrol at 1300 on April 4, 1944, after more than four weeks in port. The incomplete work in the conning tower had kept delaying her departure. Adm. Ralph Christie drove out from Perth to see the new conning tower arrangement that had been designed by Hank Munson the departing skipper, and to wave good-bye to the departing *Crevalle*.

The admiral, after studying the rearrangement job, said that he thought it worthwhile. He voiced his approval of the periscope hoist-motor being shifted from the conning tower to the pump room. And he liked the new PPI scope for viewing the radar picture. But he questioned the need for the newly installed plotting table. "You don't need a plot any longer," the admiral noted. "It's just a holdover from the old days." I suggested, however, that having a plot in the conning tower was actually necessary. I cautiously argued that, "for night surface attacks against many ships it is about the only way for the captain to keep the picture of what is happening on the surface of the ocean." This failed to convince the admiral who curtly said to Captain Walker, "I guess your rearrangement job is a good thing. But . . ." and his voice trailed off. Then with a handshake for only the captain, the admiral climbed out of the conning tower and departed the *Crevalle* to see the *Rasher* arrive from her just completed patrol.

Finally at 1600, the *Crevalle* quietly pulled away from her berth in Fremantle Harbor and headed for sea at high speed to be well clear of two other subs that were also leaving port on schedule to go on patrol. There were no well-wishers on the tender or on the pier to cheer or wave farewells. It was as though it was good riddance getting the *Crevalle* out of port.

As at the start of the second patrol and just after heading north beyond Rottnest Island, the new commissary officer, Lt. Walt Mazzone, proudly announced that he'd drawn seven cartons of cigarettes for each crew member. Then what really dimmed Mazzone's supposed coup was his discovery that he'd forgotten to draw match-es for lighting this vast number of cigarettes. The only alternative was to light the cigarettes from an electric hotplate—a face-searing, dangerous business.

In defense of his cigarette fiasco, Mazzone announced that Westmoreland, the first class commissaryman, had brought many large cans of fresh milk aboard. Mazzone added that he'd requisi-tioned many cans of Hershey chocolate syrup as well as a large amount of ice cream mix.

The patrol was off to a good start.

Walt Mazzone had been transferred to the *Crevalle* from the *Puffer* after she'd taken a frightening and punishing depth charging at the hands of several Japanese destroyers. The thirty-seven hours of relentless antisubmarine attacks against the *Puffer* had made his skipper so terrified and morose that he'd become "a useless pussy cat during the depth charge attacks and caused the crew's morale to be shot to hell." Consequently, Admiral Christie had relieved the *Puffer*'s skipper of his command and reassigned more than half of *Puffer*'s officers and enlisted men to other boats. A new skipper and many new crewmen, the admiral felt, would "give the *Puffer* a new outlook."

Despite being one of those chosen to leave the *Puffer*, Mazzone, a light heavyweight boxing champ from San Jose State, showed no signs of having been fazed by the experience. To Walt, having his submarine leaking badly, bottomed, out of oxygen and with a skip-per immobilized and unable to make a decision, was just part of the "war in the boats." And the retelling of his ordeal was full of chuck-les and Italianate gestures.

Walt, with his sloping, muscled shoulders, and a neck like a vigor-ous tree was a reassuring shipmate for what lay ahead. His presence was a great morale booster. His pasta-polished, big white teeth which frequently flashed in a wide grin, his walrus mustache, swarthy complexion and cleat-grooved, bananalike nose gave him the appearance of a friendly Sicilian bandit who would help the *Crevalle* traverse a host of treacherous spots in the shallows off the coast of Borneo.

For the first few days after the *Crevalle* left Fremantle, Captain Walker was in a foul mood, griping incessantly about things not working right. What particularly infuriated the captain was that both periscopes stuck when in train or got totally jammed. Grit from the conning tower work had sifted into the periscope bearings. In addition, there hadn't been sufficient time to thoroughly clean up the dirt left by the tender workmen before the *Crevalle*'s departure.

The captain also mercilessly criticized the performance of the crew at the many drills held each day. In particular, he felt the fire and collision drills were carried out too casually. He seemed to have forgotten how he sang "Nelly Kelly" between firing looks on the periscope when, as exec, he was making practice approaches on destroyer targets. He also raised hell about the hand dives and crash dives which he said "needed a lot more speed." To this I was fully in agreement. But the *Crevalle* was getting there, and they'd be ready when we met the enemy.

The captain was apparently uptight about his new role as a skipper. But he was too experienced in war operations to feel inadequate in his new job.

The day before entering Darwin was spent on final drills that prepared the *Crevalle*'s crew for going north into Japanese territory after topping off with fuel at Darwin.

In the afternoon, several hours were spent practicing the "Battle Surface" drill. It appeared that Captain Walker was contemplating using the guns a great deal. But that made little sense if the *Crevalle* was going to do most of its fighting in shallow waters. Surface gun action was very risky because retaliation by aircraft attacking from the cover of land would occur with little warning. Yet George, the new "Gun Boss," having taken over as the torpedo and gunnery officer, drove his gun crew relentlessly as though the sinking of all enemy ships would be done by using the four-inch deck gun. He even used a one-by-two board to whack the backsides of men who lagged after they'd emerged from the gun trunk leading to the main deck from the control room.

The new four-inch gun captain, Chief Fred Sutter, a chief gunnersmate and now the chief of the boat replacing Old Pop Bridges, watched with disapproval George's use of force. Sutter's narrowed eyes and tight jaw indicated that this wiry, youthful chief found such training methods unacceptable. Later, he appealed to me to put a stop to this ruthless driving of the men to their gun stations.

Chief Sutter had been transferred to the *Crevalle* when Captain Walker, feeling that Old Pop needed a relief, went searching for a young, tough chief who'd fit his style of managing the *Crevalle*'s crew. Left ashore by the *Scamp* because he needed a rest from several strenuous patrols, he was in a refit crew when Captain Walker located him, and borrowed him "for only a single patrol."

Known as "The Hook," Chief Sutter with his sharp, beak-like nose, raw-boned face and tough lean frame looked like a cowboy who'd spent most of his years in the saddle. But The Hook would be a great asset on the *Crevalle*.

By the end of the Battle Surface drills, George had his gun crews manning their guns in under fifty seconds from the instant that orders were given to "Stand by to surface" and, finally, to "Open fire."

In the evening as the light faded from the skies, I took some star sights that produced a navigational fix that was so accurate that next morning the *Crevalle* was at the rendezvous point on schedule to meet the pilot boat sent out from Darwin. The pilot, a Lieutenant Umpleby, jumped aboard and climbed to the bridge to guide the *Crevalle* down the swept channel leading to Darwin.

The town of Darwin lay on the east side of a large, shallow bay lined by mangrove swamps. Darwin itself lay on a low bluff and looked more like a tropical outpost than a thriving seaport serving the islands of the East Indies to the north. Gray, unpainted wooden houses on stilts and with verandas on all sides were on the seaward side of the town. From afar it showed few signs of the bombing by Japanese planes flying out of the Halmaheras. Lieutenant Umpleby explained that the Japanese had actually aimed at the ships lying alongside the single large pier below the town and that the buildings in the town had been accidentally hit.

When in the harbor of Darwin, the *Crevalle* was forced to lay at anchor until 1400. Then, the single pier was vacated by a large ammunition ship that had been off-loading bombs prior to sailing to Fremantle. The captain had been unwilling to risk tying up along-side a potential disaster in order to take on fuel. If a Japanese bombing raid had materialized, the only place for the *Crevalle* to be was out in the bay, safely on the bottom, and free of the tremendous overpressures an ammo ship would create when blowing up.

As soon as the *Crevalle* was tied up and began topping off with fuel oil, the captain and Luke went out to the airfield to have a drink with the British flyers. Then, well after dark and with the fueling completed, the captain arrived back at the *Crevalle* with some fifteen drunken RAF pilots in tow "to see a submarine." They lurched around the *Crevalle*'s insides and loudly claimed that "a submarine is too dangerous to be in during a war." One pilot insisted that the captain on his return to Darwin should come out to their airfield and get flying lessons so that he could join their wing "and really enjoy the war."

I had the feeling that this swaggering bunch of walrus-musta-chioed flyers were taking their war against the Japanese too lightly. One pilot, as I shooed the whole crowd off the *Crevalle*, said on departing that "We've got the Japs on the run. You're not going to see anymore air raids on Darwin. The Japs will be scared away." I hoped so, but I didn't think so.

Back at sea, the *Crevalle* ran into a steady, drizzling rain as she headed north towards her patrol area off Borneo. Despite the bad weather, the radar had phenomenal performance getting extremely long ranges of thirty to forty miles to land. A ducting of radar waves was evidently in effect. Unusual atmospheric conditions were holding the radar waves close to the earth's surface and bending them along the earth's curvature, as though they were trapped inside a curved pipe. So instead of only line-of-sight detections, the radar was getting returns from objects well over the horizon. The freakish radar conditions were also evident when the radarman tracked a target making twenty-seven knots heading towards the *Crevalle*. With the range down to one hundred yards and still nothing in view, the captain thought he might be chasing a ghost. But then the cry of a sea gull was heard and the captain decided the *Crevalle* was chasing a rain-drenched bird that produced very good radar echos. Most importantly, this "chasing of birds" put him into a fine humor. He ordered the quartermaster to bring a sou'wester rain hat to the bridge to protect him from "the bird's bombing run" and he told me to colorfully write up this incident in the ship's log because "your line of crap sounds good in print." I was in the captain's good graces and that was evidenced by the captain's barely noticeable smile as he gave me these instructions.

Captain Walker was now comfortable in his element of high risk, nervous excitement, and aggressive action against a dangerous enemy. He enjoyed being there and he showed it. His expansive smile had returned along with his hurry-up way of talking, as though he couldn't wait to get to the punch line, which he always thought was highly interesting and a bit amusing.

All day, sea gulls flitted around the *Crevalle* as she headed up past Timor and into the Banda Sea. One sea gull had the effrontery to perch on the top of the shears and shrilly scream at the lookouts.

Once in the Banda Sea, the seas were so rough that the large yellow masses of Banda Sea snakes had disappeared from the surface.

The *Crevalle* raced past Ambon in the Celebes and through Manipa Pass in the dark of night. As expected, there was a patrol boat in the center of the pass that forced the *Crevalle* to circle the small warship, remaining three thousand yards from the craft to prevent being seen. But radar interference on the radar screen and much flashing of lights on the shore close to the *Crevalle* indicated she had been detected as she transited north.

On the following morning, a submerged patrol was initiated in the hopes of intercepting ship traffic to Ambon. But more periscope trouble was the only reward. The number one scope jammed and couldn't be budged. It took four men working sixteen hours with pulleys and crowbars to break the scope free and get it back into operation.

On the same day, a message was received telling of the *Scamp* being bombed to the north of the *Crevalle*, above Molucca Passage. The bomb had caused so much damage that Captain Walker would not have to worry about returning Chief Sutter to the *Scamp* for several months to come.

When the *Crevalle* passed the location of the *Scamp*'s bombing, a Japanese plane suddenly burst through heavy rain clouds and almost nailed the *Crevalle* before she dove beneath the sea. The plane had headed straight at the *Crevalle* as though it was homing on a radar contact. But there had been no radar interference on the *Crevalle*'s radar screen. No bombs were dropped.

The *Crevalle* was resurfaced in fifteen minutes, but then quickly dived as three, twin-engine bombers flew in low over the water and rushed across the *Crevalle* while she was still on the surface. The planes barely missed the *Crevalle*'s shears. Still no bombs were dropped.

A few hours later a burn-after-reading message was received that gave the position and course of a Japanese Mogami-class cruiser. Thus when a radar contact was reported that checked with the cruiser's predicted position, I felt a spine-tingling thrill. But nothing materialized. The contact had apparently been made on a dense rain cloud.

After transiting Sibutu Pass, a "contact message" was received from the *Redfin* saying that a Japanese tanker was headed through a narrow passage in the Sulu Archipelago. The *Crevalle* was close to the passage and headed at high speed to close the tanker's reported position.

The *Redfin* message had also said that she'd sunk four ships and was headed "for the barn and to drink some Moose Milk." A favorite beverage of the *Redfin* officers, Moose Milk was a barely drinkable mixture of Advocat (a Dutch liqueur), milk and the poor whiskey that was issued as a ration for all submarine officers on rest-leave.

On the evening of April 19, the *Crevalle* arrived off Nasubata Channel, to the east of Balabac Island in the Philippines. Current and tide tables were closely studied to calculate the swing of moored contact mines on their cables, while all watertight doors were dogged tightly closed so that even a mine hit might not prove fatal to the *Crevalle*. Transiting the channel took two tense hours of nervously waiting for the violent shock of a mine exploding against the sides of the *Crevalle*. At least the open hatch to the bridge promised a chance of getting out of the sinking submarine, and staying alive. Then the *Crevalle* was out in the clear and headed for Balembangan Island to the south of Balabac Island.

On the twentieth, the *Crevalle* began her patrol at "Point Easy" off Balembangan Island above the northern tip of Borneo. The offshore water depth was about 150 feet while the one hundred-fathom curve was some thirty miles to the west. It was too distant to be used for evasion of ASW warships.

At noon a "burn message" was received ordering the *Crevalle* to patrol off Balabac Island to intercept a Japanese force of warships that were expected to pass through Balabac Strait that night. Nothing materialized.

By April 22, the *Crevalle* was back off Balembangan and inflicted with a Zeke-type plane that zoomed out from land several times trying to catch the *Crevalle* on the surface. It was at about six miles that the plane was spotted coming out from the land background. This gave only 1-1/2 minutes of warning. But that was enough time to get the *Crevalle* submerged and below any surface-exploding bombs that the plane might use.

Soon the plane was named Borneo Barney and was expected on a regular basis starting at about 0900. Barney was persistent. He kept the lookouts on their toes.

On the twenty-fifth, while on the surface, smoke was sighted to the east. It was a freighter hugging the coast of Balembangan inside the twenty-fathom curve. By using the number two high periscope, her superstructure could be discerned. It was ascertained that the ship was accompanied by two small sea trucks and an armed yacht that patrolled off the freighter's bow. The large merchant ship was identified as the *Lima Maru* of seven thousand tons. The captain, moreover, observed that she was carrying two aircraft on her main deck, but didn't mention this to the fire control team in the conning tower.

The *Crevalle* was then dived at twelve thousand yards ahead of the group of vessels and when the range was two thousand yards to the freighter, the captain fired all six of the forward torpedoes. It was really a case of overkill but the captain wanted to make sure to sink his first ship as CO.

Throughout the approach he'd left the periscope raised, ignoring the possibility that one of the escorts might see it. And how about aircraft? Where was Borneo Barney? I kept begging the captain to take a careful look around the skies to make sure there wasn't a plane nearby that would drop a bomb on the periscope. But he ignored my pleas to look for aircraft. He was too intent on studying his target and its three accompanying small vessels.

The captain was all business. No sign of nervousness. No quaver in his voice. There were only small smiles when he pulled himself away from the scope's eyepiece and let George have a look. The captain's unfluttered confidence and all-in-a-day's-work attitude was infectious. I quietly hummed "Nelly Kelly" and George whistled softly.

As George started pumping out the torpedoes I took a fathometer reading: "105 feet." The *Crevalle* couldn't move much closer to the beach and still remain submerged.

The first torpedo hit the maru amidships with a tremendous explosion. The captain's first words after the hit were, "We got an airplane. We blew her sky high."

"An airplane? Borneo Barney blown up by a torpedo? What a neat trick," I commented to the captain with awe in my voice.

"Hell, no, Ruhe," the captain snorted. "There were two planes sitting on the ship's main deck and one of them went up into the air and over the side." As an afterthought he added, "And the planes didn't look like Borneo Barney."

Then as the second torpedo hit, the captain reported, "That fish tore her bow off and she's sinking with a big down-angle."

One more torpedo exploded in the ship and the next three evidently went through the wreckage and exploded harmlessly when they hit the beach.

"How about the yacht-escort, Captain?" I tried to keep the concern out of my voice. But the captain kept his eye on the submerging cargo ship. He ignored the armed yacht.

"The sea trucks and the yacht are fleeing towards the beach," the captain said disgustedly. "Stand by to surface . . . And man the twenty-millimeter guns."

Evidently, the captain intended to scare the hell out of a lot of small-craft Japanese sailors. But why risk taking a bomb delivered by Borneo Barney, who should by now have been alerted by the torpedo explosions?

Still, the *Crevalle* was surfaced and with an "All clear" from Luke on the bridge, the captain ordered "Ring up flank and bend on four engines." He was going to risk a bombing just to get a few rounds of incendiary bullets into the wood hulls of the three small vessels. It was sort of crazy.

I raised the number one scope to watch the *Crevalle* plow through the wreckage of the torpedoed ship. There were about fifty survivors in the water with some already beginning to swim to shore, a mile away.

At the report, "The fathometer reads fifty-eight feet," the captain promptly ordered "Left full rudder" and turned the *Crevalle* to the westward to race for deep water, since at any second she might be forced to dive away from an enemy aircraft.

When Howie Geer, the assistant gunnery officer, came below he protested, "Submariners shouldn't be trying to shoot up ships so close to the beach." I noted that Howie obnoxiously pronounced submariner like "sub-mariner," and gave him an icy look. We definitely were not sub-par sailors.

In a few minutes, a plane with a screaming whine, came in low over the water and straight at the *Crevalle*. Without taking the time to study the plane to see if it was Borneo Barney, the captain dove the *Crevalle*, pushing everyone ahead of him down the hatch. The upper hatch was dogged shut only a moment before the seas closed over the submerging sub.

A bomb exploded overhead as the *Crevalle* scrambled for eighty feet—as deep as could be risked without slamming the *Crevalle's* nose into the muddy bottom. When the bomb detonated there was only twenty-five feet under the keel. It was a close thing.

Within a minute another bomb, probably set for ten-meters depth, exploded much closer to the *Crevalle's* shears. But the damage was slight.

With the *Crevalle* working her way westward, three distant explosions were heard in the direction of Balembangan Island. They sounded like depth charges and indicated that an ASW warship was trying to scare a U.S. submarine away from ships sailing close to the beach. The *Crevalle* was surfaced to find out what was going on.

Through the high periscope I was able to spot puffs of smoke and shortly could make out the tops of six merchant ships heading south, escorted by a ship with warship-like masts.

The *Crevalle* officers in the conning tower looked exhausted from the tension caused by the recent torpedo attack in shallow waters. But the captain saw no alternative to going in for an attack on this new group of enemy ships.

It became evident that the merchantmen were traveling tight against the coast, in waters of about fifty-foot depth. Yet the opportunity to shoot all remaining fish and head home couldn't be missed. It would be a great coup for the captain on his first war patrol.

Remaining out of sight of the ships, the *Crevalle* was worked to a position south of the convoy and well ahead of it. She was then dived for a submerged attack. But with the range to the leading ship at about four miles, the convoy headed into Marudu Bay to hole-up for the night. Hence, the *Crevalle* was surfaced.

The waters inside the bay were no more than fifty feet in depth and ruled out a submerged attack. While the escort, a Wakatake-class destroyer, stood guard at the narrow entrance to the bay like a sheep dog protecting his flock from wolves.

The captain, after some soul searching, decided it was too risky to fight the Wakatake in order to get into the bay on the surface and sink a few cargo ships. He might have gotten a Congressional Medal of Honor if he'd done that. But he chose to have the *Crevalle* lay off the entrance to the bay during the night and to keep track of the Wakatake as it patrolled back and forth across the narrow entrance to the bay.

Then, just before dawn, the *Crevalle* was dived off the entrance to await the exodus of the convoy. At daylight the Wakatake left the entrance to the bay and began patrolling well to seaward while weaving a pattern of continuous course changes. Thus, every cautious periscope look showed the Wakatake on a different course. Periscope looks were taken with only six inches of the scope showing above the flat, calm sea. The looks were very brief and infrequent. However, despite the captain's careful use of his periscope, the Wakatake seemed to know exactly where the *Crevalle* was at all times. He would beam his sonar directly at the *Crevalle*, its loud whelps sounding like the barking of a sheep dog telling a wolf to stay clear of the flock of sheep being protected.

An hour later, when puffs of smoke appeared above the jungle of trees surrounding the bay it was evident that the convoy was underway and exiting from its overnight haven. It was also evident that to get at those cargo ships required eliminating the sheep dog. So the captain headed for the Wakatake, and ordered, "Battle Stations." Four torpedoes were readied.

The Wakatake, at 2,700 yards and headed for the *Crevalle*, had his sonar on short scale when the captain decided to fight it out. "We'll shoot a down-the-throat salvo. Use three torpedoes," the captain ordered. It was a desperate tactic but other subs were having good luck in sinking overly aggressive destroyers in this fashion.

When the range was under 1,500 yards and the Wakatake was still showing a zero angle-on-the bow, the captain said, "On the next look we'll start firing."

But then between periscope looks, the soundman reported that the destroyer had wheeled around and was heading away. A quick look confirmed this. He was rejoining his flock of merchant ships.

The convoy remained out of range and proceeded south inside a protective line of reefs. Hence, the *Crevalle* was surfaced and on three engines raced at flank speed to the southward to catch the ships when they emerged from the protection of Saracen Bank, a reef area off Borneo that the *Crevalle* couldn't risk crossing, and that extended many miles to the south.

All day the *Crevalle* skirted the outward edge of the bank. Fathometer readings were taken to check the accuracy of the old 1900 Dutch charts being used. They seemed accurate except that some new coral islands were visible. These were added to the obsolete charts.

Early the next day, the *Crevalle* was driven under by a twin-engine float plane that placed a bomb directly over the *Crevalle*'s conning tower but was set too shallow to do any damage. Radar interference had showed on the radar scope indicating that the plane had held the *Crevalle* on its radar as it came in low over the reefs. While cautiously observing this plane through the periscope, a second plane appeared. Both circled the spot where the *Crevalle* dove. Then at noon, there were four planes searching the same area. Consequently, from then on the *Crevalle* remained submerged until dark. At this point, the captain decided that the convoy had slipped by and that there was no guessing where it might have gone. So the *Crevalle* was headed back north towards Balembangan Island.

On April 29, the *Crevalle* was once more off Balembangan. Like clockwork, Borneo Barney showed up at 0900 and headed straight towards the *Crevalle*. Down she went. And no bomb. Barney hadn't missed a day harassing the *Crevalle*. Although not efficient, he was certainly persistent.

With the *Crevalle*'s presence in the area definitely established by the Japanese, the captain decided to take a few days off from his shallow-water patrol and move to the eastern edge of Dangerous Ground where there was deep water. But that proved to be a waste of time since Japanese shipping continued to stick close to land while transiting the South China Sea.

Unfortunately, the day-after-day routine of patrolling up and down across a flat, waveless sea and under a blazing sun without the sign of a single ship spelled intense boredom. So, although the *Crevalle* operated safely over a hundred miles from the coast of Borneo where planes didn't bother to patrol, she was doing nothing.

During this period of aimless patrolling, I was annoyed at the way Luke slept every possible minute when he was off watch. So I kept a log of when he was sacked out. Then after three days I presented it to him as proof that he was spending far too much time in his bunk, doing nothing. "The log shows that you spent fourteen and three quarter hours in your bunk," I slyly noted. It was pure meanness on my part. Luke's sleeping wasn't any of my business but it just ate at me that he was isolating himself from the usual wardroom camaraderie and fun.

When I shoved the result in front of Luke's face I acted as though it was a bit of a joke. But it wasn't.

Luke angrily stomped off to the bridge. However, when he came off watch and we played an hour of cribbage together, he was cheerful once more and seemed to have forgotten the incident. Luke wasn't even nervous about not getting back into his bunk.

Fed up with nothing happening, the captain decided to head for Miri, an oil-loading port on the western coast of Borneo where there were bound to be some tankers. Tankers significantly headed the U.S. priority list for merchant ships to be sunk. Cutting down on the oil flowing to the Japanese mainland, it was felt, would do maximum damage to the Japanese war effort.

By May 3d, the *Crevalle* was close to Miri, and a few hundred yards from a mined area that showed on corrected charts of the waters off Borneo.

Reassuringly, a black can-buoy half a mile to the east marked the seaward end of the Japanese minefield and the swept channel out of Miri.

An all-day submerged patrol was then initiated close to the buoy to make certain that any exiting tankers could be readily attacked.

Late in the afternoon, the masts of several ships were sighted near the shore. Their change of bearing indicated that they were traveling north and hugging the coast. There was also a plane weaving search patterns over the tops of the ships' masts. When the plane departed at sunset, the *Crevalle* was surfaced and headed in towards the ships, which were moving behind a continuous line of offshore mines.

Just before darkness closed in, a large cargo ship identified as the *Syoyo Maru* of 7,500 tons was discernible at 8,500 yards. On her port bow was a small escort and much further astern of the *Syoyo Maru* were the tops of a small tanker on the same course.

A check of the chart showed that there was a break in the offshore minefields a few miles to the north. So the *Crevalle* headed at high speed for this opening. Though it was bright moonlight, the *Crevalle*'s gray paint job kept her invisible to the Japanese ships while it was easy to keep them in sight and get radar ranges on them periodically.

While paralleling the course of the ships, the radar range to the small escort was at one time as low as 1,700 yards but the big ship remained at over four thousand yards range. Unfortunately, during the *Crevalle*'s dash to get into position for a good torpedo attack she moved into heavy rain squalls that were punctuated with long jagged streaks of lightning. Part of the time the rain clouds were so heavily charged with electricity that St. Elmo's fire was produced on the upper part of the shears. Thin, intermittent flames licking upward were frighteningly visible. While blinding flashes of light, like flash bulbs exploded before one's eyes, were accompanied by deafening cracks of thunder. The lookouts were brought down on deck to keep them away from the St. Elmo's fire because no one had the faintest idea how dangerous this phenomenon might be to men close by.

At times, flashes of lightning near the shore revealed the ships in black silhouette and made the *Crevalle* as visible as she would be in broad daylight. Yet the ships steamed on, apparently oblivious of the developing attack.

In the midst of all the fireworks and deafening noise, the *Crevalle* was submerged twelve thousand yards ahead of the three ships to make a radar approach on the unsuspecting vessels. The depth of water was 150 feet. And that was a luxury.

Just before midnight, although heavy rain obscured the targets, the lightning had stopped. The SJ surface search radar clearly showed all three targets, with the *Syoyo Maru* in the lead. When the range closed to 2,700 yards to the big ship, four torpedoes were fired from *Crevalle*'s stern tubes. Then, within two minutes there were two heavy explosions, out in the blanket of rain. Hits? Three minutes later there were rumbling sounds that might have been the agony of a ship breaking up. But the curtain of rain had become impenetrable, even to the radar.

Within ten minutes, the *Crevalle* was surfaced. Then there was a tremendous explosion from the direction of the ships that rocked the *Crevalle*. People on the bridge felt a pressure wave momentarily flatten the skin on their faces while those in the conning tower had their eardrums compressed and then released with a pop as the force of the explosion passed across the *Crevalle*. And there were only two small contacts left on the radar. Had the *Syoyo Maru* blown up?

Again the *Crevalle* commenced an end-around of the two remaining ships. The larger of the two radar pips was presumed to be the small tanker. But when the range had dropped to 1,400 yards to the bigger target, it was identified as a small engines-aft freighter, the *Takosan Maru* of 1,400 tons. Momentarily visible through the rain squalls, a visual bearing was ground into the TDC and four torpedoes were fired from the forward tubes. The tracks of all four torpedoes were easily seen from the bridge as their motion through the water stirred up the phosphorescent biomatter of the tropical waters.

The first two torpedoes missed ahead. The target was going much slower than estimated from the TDC solution. The third seemed to pass under the bow of the small cargo ship but didn't explode and the fourth torpedo swung erratically to the right and missed astern. The freighter had apparently slowed radically, possibly to avoid a reef, when the torpedoes were fired.

Meanwhile, the *Crevalle* was maneuvered hard to port to miss colliding with the freighter that had swung around to ram the *Crevalle*. After the merchantman missed the *Crevalle*'s stern she kept swinging and headed back towards the Borneo coast. Miraculously, she steered across the nearby Champion Bank, which showed such little depth of water on the chart that she should have gone aground. But she kept going and disappeared into the darkness. Earlier the escort had fled across the same reef area.

The night's work was most discouraging, though the *Crevalle* probably bagged a good ship.

By morning, the *Crevalle* was headed back to the Balembangan area where at least she would be unhampered by mines in prosecuting an attack.

On the way back north, *Crevalle*'s radioman copied several broadcasts of Class E, unclassified radio-traffic. One message concerned an enlisted man on board whose wife had just died. Navy Relief was requesting that the man be transferred back to the States as early as possible because his three children were without relatives to take them in. Before showing the message to the enlisted man, I took it to the captain to see what he wanted to do about it. He read it gravely. Then he told me to handle it. He said that it was hard enough for him to have to worry about risking the lives of his entire crew while making his attack decisions without also having to think about three little homeless kids.

Soon after diving off Balembangan Island on May 6, smoke from several ships was spotted to the south through the periscope. Shortly, the topmasts of eight ships became visible. The ships were headed towards the *Crevalle*'s submerged position.

The convoy was tracked making eight knots. Its ships were in a single column and not closely spaced. The lead merchant ship was small. The next ship in column was an odd one, with a flat, unencumbered main deck and two fort-like structures at both ends. The captain guessed that "it might be a type of motorized dry-dock." The next two ships were nondescript but the fifth ship in column was described as "a huge cargo ship." The eighth and last ship was "the biggest tanker in the book, and that's the one we'll shoot at." Captain Walker's description of this ship tallied with a two-stack whale factory that the Japanese had converted into an oil tanker at the start of the war. It was the seventeen thousand-ton *Nisshin Maru*, and had a big slanted opening in the stern through which speared whales were hauled into the ship. There, they'd be chopped up and the blubber converted into whale oil.

Actually, the others in the conning tower were more interested in where the escorts were and what they were doing to threaten the *Crevalle*. Patrolling along the seaward side of the column of merchant ships were, according to the captain, many escorts. The lead escort was a Shinonome-type destroyer. His sound gear was pinging away while the next escort, a Wakatake-type destroyer, remained silent. There was also a Shinonome patrolling on the inshore side of the convoy's column. Making matters worse, the captain spotted a Sally-type aircraft circling over the ships. The enemy's first string was present in force.

The *Crevalle* was kept headed towards the shore to reduce the shooting range. Soon she was directly in the path of the Shinonome. The pings from his sound gear swept across the *Crevalle* without making contact. In shallow waters a destroyer's sound gear was frequently overwhelmed by reverberations. Also, in the tropics the dense thermal gradient near the surface of the seas allowed a submarine to duck into the thermal layer that extends down to about one hundred feet. In this layer, sonar pings failed to penetrate. Consequently, the *Crevalle* was taken to eighty feet. Going deeper could not be risked.

After the Shinonome's screws were heard passing overhead, the *Crevalle* was quickly returned to periscope depth to watch the

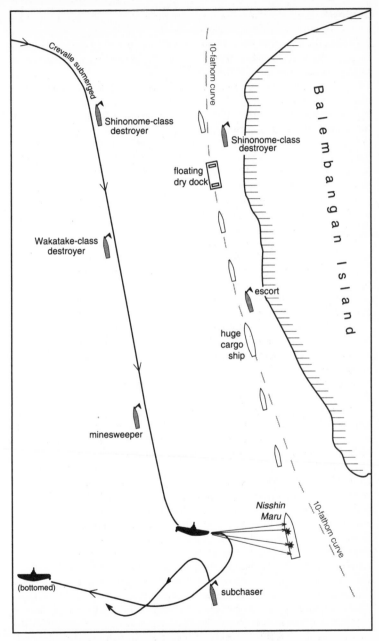

Figure 6.1 Crevalle's attack on convoy, May 6, 1944

destroyer moving clear. The captain then shifted to the Wakatake that was approaching at three-thousand-yards range. He wove his way past the *Crevalle*, which was forced back down to eighty feet. On the next look at sixty-five feet, the captain spotted another escort, a minesweeper. By careful maneuvering, the minesweeper was avoided without contact being made on the *Crevalle*. Then on came a sub-chaser escort.

The captain was cool and businesslike, seemingly unimpressed by the changing threats posed by the escorts as they protected their flock of ships. And there wasn't a single display of nerves or pause in work by the other members of the fire control team. They were like journeymen practicing their trade; hardly the popular image of warriors flailing around in battle.

Luke was the diving officer and his trim control was flawless as the *Crevalle* was taken down and back up between the evasions of the escorts.

When back at sixty-six feet, the whale factory was observed to be at four-thousand-yards range with a seventy-five-degree port angle-on-the-bow. This put her on a dangerous course, soon to put her aground.

On the next look the captain reported that the tanker had zigged to her left and had become "an ideal target."

Four torpedoes were launched from the forward tubes with a torpedo run of nine hundred yards. The other two readied torpedoes were held in reserve to shoot the oncoming escort, if necessary.

At the moment of firing the subchaser was headed for the *Crevalle*'s periscope, but the captain left it up to see the results from the four torpedoes fired.

The first torpedo "hit amidships and lifted the tanker's goal posts into the air." The captain's voice rose several notes and several decibels in pure delight for what he was observing. "The second torpedo hit under the tanker's bridge and it blew off her bow."

Seconds later there were two closely spaced explosions that the captain observed through the scope. He explained that the Sally-aircraft had dropped bombs on the wakes of the *Crevalle*'s next two torpedoes—hoping to explode them before they reached the tanker.

A third hit was heard on the tanker. But the captain didn't spot where it had struck since he had swung the periscope to see what the subchaser was up to. Moreover, there was so much noise being created by the fatally damaged tanker that it sounded as though she was sinking on top of the *Crevalle*. This reminded the captain to head the *Crevalle* westward before she ran aground.

On a course of due west, at full speed, and just below periscope depth, the *Crevalle* was raced toward deeper water. The rapid sh-sh-sh-sh-sh of the subchaser's screws increased in volume until the conning tower was filled with noise. Then the escort was over the *Crevalle*, dropping three depth charges that exploded so close that the concussion of each charge caused me to see what appeared to be a mass of flames engulfing the inside of the conning tower. As the bright redness subsided, I looked towards the upper hatch to see if it had been blown open, thus letting in the flames from an exploding depth charge. It was still tightly dogged. Others in the conning tower experienced the same effect. Much glass was shattered. Wrenches went flying around. It was only the start of a bad shellacking for the *Crevalle*.

A minute later, ten charges were laid down the length of the *Crevalle* that exploded within a foot of her hull. The *Crevalle* was shaken violently. I noted that everyone in the conning tower had a firm grip on something to prevent being slammed into the protruding equipment that crammed the tiny space.

There were two more charges. Six more. Seven more. Counting the depth charges ceased to be important. As each depth-charge attack began, the screws of the attacking warship could be heard through the hull. The captain would order full speed and try to move the *Crevalle* off the destroyer's track. Then he'd stop the sub's screws after the last charge had exploded. He hoped that the Japanese would think that they'd destroyed the *Crevalle*.

Unfortunately, the great precision of each depth-charge attack over the next twenty-five minutes indicated that the *Crevalle* was stirring up an easily followed trail of mud, which was being churned to the surface. But Luke, the diving officer, warned: "Don't reduce your speed, Captain. We're taking great amounts of water into the sub. If you cut the speed, the *Crevalle* will sink fast and hit the bottom hard." Luke added, "I've got the drain pump going full bore but I can't catch up with the great amount of water leaking into the *Crevalle*."

Consequently, the captain decided to bottom the *Crevalle*. He also ordered a fathometer reading be taken—despite the noise it created. It showed the bottom at 174 feet. So with the sound dome and the Bendix Log retracted, the *Crevalle* was eased down onto a muddy bottom and with a gentle shudder she came to rest with a two degree down angle.

All equipment throughout the boat was secured except for the motor generator which ran the JT listening sound gear. The drain pump was no longer running. The *Crevalle* then lay so quietly and motionless in the mud, that according to the captain, "Drawing water from a spigot would sound like Niagara Falls."

Three ASW vessels remained close to the bottomed *Crevalle* and wove search patterns overhead. Their echo-ranging had stopped. They were evidently listening intently for the slightest sound coming from the *Crevalle*. The lack of noise was ominous.

Report on damage came by telephone from all compartments of the *Crevalle*. They were reported to the captain in little more than a whisper. The captain received the reports stone-faced. All leaks were felt to be under control. Since the air conditioner had been secured, the conning tower quickly heated to well over ninety degrees. Only low-wattage red lights were in use. No one moved about. It was like being inside a huge, silent broiler.

Soon there was a first warning of serious trouble. A loud clanking, like something being paid out from a vessel nearby was heard. Then a series of metallic sounds indicated that something was being dragged along the bottom of the ocean. We stared quizzically at each other trying to guess what the strange sounds meant. The quartermaster suggested that it might be a grapnel being dragged along the floor of the ocean to snag the *Crevalle*. The captain laughed at this idea. But I visualized the *Crevalle* as a huge fish being trawled for. A cold tingle went down my spine at the thought.

Soon a set of screws was speeding up in a different direction than that of the metallic clangs. The propeller noise of this new contact remained on a steady bearing and increased to a loud roar as a warship passed overhead. But there were no depth charge explosions. The run at the *Crevalle* was evidently made on some sort of noise that had come from our bottomed submarine. Still, the warship didn't want to chance a poor depth-charge drop that could create a blanket of reverberating explosions that would mask the *Crevalle*'s movements for a short time. The ASW ships seemingly knew that the *Crevalle* was sunk in the mud where their active sonars couldn't touch her. But they could hear the slightest noise and pinpoint the sub's location.

Whirring noises were heard on several bearings. Someone hazarded the guess that more grappling gear was being paid out by other ASW vessels. The captain smiled indulgently at this suggestion. Uncharacteristically, however, he remained pensively silent. No wise cracks. No tune hummed. And no orders to anyone. He just sat on the conning tower's deck, out-waiting the enemy. His passiveness was nerve-wracking, because he was normally a man of action, not the motionless, worried guy that I watched closely for some sort of instructions to break the spell of inaction.

Then, a dull thudding and scraping of iron on the ocean floor's outcroppings moved towards the *Crevalle*. Unnervingly, there was a harsh grating noise close to the *Crevalle*. This was followed by a loud "clank" as something hit the sub's hull. There were lesser clanks as the object bounced up the side of her hull and passed over the top. I watched the captain's dull eyes follow the sounds across the *Crevalle* and into the waters beyond. The helmsman whispered "They're dragging for us." That was not the product of an overwrought imagination! Barely audible nervous reports came from every room that something had been dragged over the top of the *Crevalle*. The captain chuckled ironically at such a fantasy but his laugh was not convincing.

Fear was seeping into the bones of all the men. The simmering hot atmosphere of the conning tower held a deadly chilliness.

The captain was still doubtful about what was happening. He told me to walk through the boat and see if some nervous guy was trying to "repair some metal thing with a hammer." He added, "And make sure nobody wears shoes!"

In each compartment I passed through, men gave me questioning looks and invariably asked, "What's happening, Mr. Ruhe?" or, "How bad is it?" To such questions I merely shrugged an ambiguous, "Who knows?" I recognized their nagging fear.

At the officer's pantry, the stocky, black officers' steward, Willie Gregory, plaintively asked, "Is this the end?" and admitted he "didn't like this business." A reasonable and honest reaction.

It seemed that what was happening to the *Crevalle* could only get worse. I had the thought that men suffer more from imagined dangers than from a hard-headed realization of the actual peril being posed. The men on the *Crevalle* were beginning to think we were in extremis. But I didn't agree with that. I felt we could work our way out of this situation as we'd done in the past.

When I reported back to the captain that there was no explanation for the clanks except for the guess that they were caused by a towed grapnel, he finally agreed that this was a possibility.

The captain took this to heart and ordered an axe sent to the conning tower to destroy all equipment and told Jim Blind to begin burning all the secret codes. However, the use of the axe was deferred on the basis that it would make too much noise.

Then there was a terrifying "clang-ng-ng-ng" as a grapnel coming from a new direction hit the side of the *Crevalle* and stuck there followed by the high-pitched whine of a wire suddenly put under heavy strain. A hook had caught on some part of the hull making the sub shudder and rocking her to port. Then the *Crevalle*'s keel started to scrape along the bottom. She was being towed, as evidenced by the depth gauge that jerkily moved from 174 to 177 feet. Then the *Crevalle*'s bottom sounded like it was being torn apart. Dragging a submarine with the gear of a small warship seemed incredible. But it was recalled that a submerged submarine at neutral buoyancy had literally no weight. Evidently, Luke had pumped all of the excess water out of the *Crevalle* and had gotten her back into a good neutral-buoyancy trim. So she was being towed easily.

It seemed that although snagging a submarine might possibly be a new Japanese technique, there could be additional deviltry involved. "Perhaps," as someone suggested, "they've got a device with a lot of explosives in it which the Japanese fasten to the tow wire and then slide it down until it hits the submarine and explodes." George estimated that only twenty pounds of TNT exploding in direct contact with the *Crevalle*'s hull would rip a large hole in her and finish her off.

The captain had a weak, tolerant smile for what he thought was the men's imagination. But it had stirred him up a little. He began to believe that the *Crevalle* might be in deep trouble and that something had to be done.

There was more groaning of the hull as the sub was being dragged unwillingly into deeper water. The depth gauge now showed 178 feet. At least the *Crevalle* was being towed in the right direction.

"OK. That's it." The captain had finally snapped out of his lethargy. "No more of this crap. Let's get out of here."

He nodded at me, indicating he wanted me to swing into action. So I called down to Luke, "Put a bubble in safety and do it slowly so that there isn't much noise." Then, when I heard air hissing into the safety tank, I told the helmsman to ring up two-thirds speed. That would slowly break the *Crevalle* free of the clinging-mud bottom, while not creating a brown trail of mud on the surface of the sea.

I watched the depth gauge in the conning tower for over a minute before the hand at 178 feet began to quiver and then jerkily move to 176 feet, then 175 feet. The *Crevalle* was free of the mud and moving ahead and upward. At this I called down to Luke to bleed the air from safety into the boat to get the *Crevalle* back to neutral buoyancy. My look at the captain for his OK to put on high speed so the *Crevalle* could break loose from the grapnel, got an assenting nod. So I had the helmsman ring up flank speed, and held my breath.

Within seconds, along with the loud churning of the *Crevalle*'s screws, there was suddenly a shaking of the boat and a tremendous clatter that sounded as though the shears had been torn off. The *Crevalle* had broken free of the grip held by the ASW vessel and surged forward—like a fish that had had the hook in its mouth torn loose.

Two-thirds speed was ordered once more. The ASW warship would realize that his grapnel had lost its hold but he couldn't be sure that the *Crevalle* was trying to escape from her mud-enclosed prison.

The whirring and scraping noises continued. Still, there were no speeded-up screw noises to indicate that the *Crevalle*'s escape had been recognized. Ten minutes later, a destroyer passed no more than one hundred yards ahead of the *Crevalle*, oblivious of her presence.

Silently, the *Crevalle* glided out into deeper water until by noon all screw noises had faded out.

The captain then risked going to sixty-six feet. With only a foot of scope showing, he made out the topworks of a single vessel that was well astern. Not until dark did the captain decide to transmit a contact message on the convoy just attacked.

When the upper hatch was opened and fresh air pulled into the boat by the started-up diesel engines, my stomach protested with a wave of nausea—a normal reaction to the inrushing cool air.

The message sent to headquarters in Perth told of the *Crevalle*'s attack on the Japanese convoy and summarized the patrol results to date, along with the number of torpedoes remaining. Four were aft and two were forward, but one of the torpedoes up forward had a bulge in the warhead and wouldn't go into a tube, so it was unusable.

The captain's message was cleared on the first transmission. Then the *Crevalle* was headed towards Dangerous Ground for a breather and to await further orders. Getting away scot-free rated a bit of celebration so it was suggested that our four quarts of medicinal brandy be "confiscated" for the benefit of the crew. But Captain Walker felt that the patrol was far from over and that the liquor should remain under lock-and-key until all of the *Crevalle*'s fish were expended.

All day of May 7th, the *Crevalle* rode the surface far from land. Nothing was seen. Just before midnight, orders were received that terminated the patrol and ordered the *Crevalle* to proceed back through the mined Nasubata Channel. At this, I suggested that the boat's stock of Old Overholt brandy could now be consumed. But then another coded message arrived that instructed the *Crevalle* to head for the island of Negros in the Philippines to pick up thirty-five refugees and carry them back to Australia. However, as our little black-skinned steward later noted as he reflected on the *Crevalle*'s escape from the Japanese grapnels, "That was only the beginning."

The day following, the *Crevalle* raced up the east side of Balabac Island and later at night barreled through Nasubata Channel with its threatening minefields on both sides of the channel. Navigational fixes derived from bearings taken on Balabac's mountain peaks checked nicely and promised an uneventful passage. But at the narrowest part of the channel, a native banca was seen dead ahead of the onrushing *Crevalle*.

The captain called down from the bridge, "Can we safely clear the banca ahead to one side or the other?" I checked the chart which showed the channel to be at its narrowest part and yelled back to the captain, "Go by him as close as possible and don't let him drive you off course and you should make it O.K." Then I climbed to the bridge to have a look at the unexpected hazard. Was it friendly or an enemy?

Luke was arguing with the captain that the banca should be rammed or sunk with machine-gun fire. But the captain insisted that the banca was native and shouldn't be harmed.

As the *Crevalle* passed the small vessel, the *Crevalle*'s heavy bow wake nearly swamped the craft. Three men were visible on her top deck despite the darkness. They stared up at those on the *Crevalle*'s bridge without a sign of friendliness. Then when the banca was bobbing a mile astern in the *Crevalle*'s wake, two green "Very" stars—like Fourth of July rockets—were shot skyward from the banca's deck. They were a signal to the Japanese on Balabac that a U.S. submarine was transiting the channel. At this, the captain beat himself on the side of the head and kept disgustedly muttering, "What a Patsy . . . What a Patsy . . . What a Patsy is Walker." He'd been royally fooled and he knew it. But it was for the last time, since when I saw him writing his daily notes on the patrol he recorded: "We have just joined the Gun Club."

The *Crevalle* hurried across the Sulu Sea for her special mission.

Westmoreland, the commissary steward, was instructed to save whatever ice cream mix was left so that there'd be ice cream for the refugees when they were picked up. What a treat that would be for people who had been hiding out in the jungle for the past two years.

Early in the afternoon I was awakened by a heavy jolt and felt the *Crevalle* shudder in agony. It seemed that the *Crevalle* had rammed a ship or gone aground. I raced to the bridge half dressed to find everyone there staring at the body of a large badly injured whale of at least thirty feet in length, that was drifting down the *Crevalle*'s starboard side. The whale had a huge rent in its body from which vast quantities of blood flowed and that washed up on the sub's sides, staining her hull with a diluted, bright red coloring. Howie Geer said that the whale had playfully cruised around the *Crevalle*'s bow as though trying to make love to another whale. But then the whale had misjudged the threat of the *Crevalle*'s sharp bow. With a heavy pitch it crashed down on the whale's mid-section, almost chopping the whale in half—it was whale-love carried too far.

Later in the day the *Crevalle* arrived near the coast of Negros and was submerged several miles offshore to make sure that she was not spotted by Japanese coast watchers. Great caution was counseled. After closing the beach to about a mile, the *Crevalle* was headed north submerged and paralleled the coast. Through the periscope the captain studied the dense green jungle on the hill that rose from the sea and he looked for Japanese activity of any sort. Additional instructions had been received that directed the captain to spot on May 11 an "All Safe" signal of two white squares separated by at least thirty feet that would be visible on the hillside above the passenger embarkation point. "If no safe signal is displayed, the

Crevalle shall remain submerged during daylight so as not to reveal the point of rendezvous." The latitude and longitude of the evacuation beach was included in the message. "Further instructions will be sent, if necessary, to shift the place of embarkation or to terminate your mission. It is possible that the Japanese are aware of your mission and might take measures to trap the people and destroy your submarine."

After dark, the *Crevalle* was surfaced far off the coast of Negros and waited through the night for the prearranged rendezvous at dawn.

Just after first light on the following day, the *Crevalle* approached the rendezvous point submerged. No safety signals were visible on the side of the hill. But within two hours, two white squares appeared on top of the dense mass of green trees. The only activity seemed to be two fishing boats offshore that drifted back and forth. There were no Japanese patrol boats in evidence, and the day dragged on with nothing further happening.

Then late in the afternoon boats were suddenly dragged from the jungle that hugged the sandy beach. Tiny figures were seen moving out of their hiding places to flock around the boats. Loading of the boats was commenced. Two sailing bancas and an oared boat then left the shore and headed out to sea. But they were a mile south of the rendezvous point.

A mile off in the plan didn't seem to matter since there were no signs of enemy activity. Additionally, the three small craft were crammed full with what looked like a legitimate load of refugees. Hence, the captain ordered the *Crevalle*'s security detail to be readied in the control room preparatory to surfacing. The security detail was armed to the teeth and was formed to prevent a sudden takeover of the *Crevalle* by a disguised team of Japanese.

When surfaced, the *Crevalle* had her ballast tanks fully blown so she would ride high and dry for the embarkation of the passengers. Out of the first banca that pulled alongside, bounded two Filipino guerrilla officers. They nimbly climbed to the bridge and perched themselves on the cigarette deck's rail. The remainder of the banca's occupants waited quietly. Lieutenant Colonel Abcede, in charge of the operation, promptly introduced himself. He was dressed in fresh, unwrinkled khakis. He wore no insignias nor carried any sidearms and looked no more than fourteen years old. His crinkly-laughing, clean shaven, light-brown face exuded confidence. On the other hand, his assistant, Major Andrews, wore filthy, sweat-stained khakis, had a half-grown nondescript beard and carried two .45's at his waist along with a bandolier of cartridges strung across his chest. Abcede did all the talking while Major Andrews kept peering around looking for trouble.

"We have forty passengers for you, Captain," Abcede said. "A few more than you expected? Can you take that many?"

The captain shrugged a "Why not?"

"Seventeen are children and eleven are women," Abcede qualified.

I watched the captain's face as he considered the problems of privacy, showers, toilets and berthing spaces for this mix of passengers. A slight smile eased across his face and with an "OK, we'll take all of them, just hurry them aboard," Abcede swung into action.

Using a walkie-talkie he coached the boats alongside the *Crevalle* and berated two boats that lagged behind the first three boats arriving at the sub. Carrying additional passengers, the two extra boats had stayed well clear until it was ascertained that the surfaced submarine was indeed a U.S. submarine.

Two of the couples, herding a flock of children ahead of them, were identified by Abcede as American missionaries, the Lindholms and the Fleischers. Their fair-haired children scrambled rapidly down the ladder into the *Crevalle*'s after battery compartment. But the many brown-skinned Filipino children drew back from the hatch, terrified at the idea of entering the mouth of the black sea monster that they'd seen emerge from the deep an hour earlier. The native children evidently hadn't understood what a submarine was until this moment. The security detail nevertheless firmly shoved them into the after battery trunk opening. Later, it was reported by men who had been sitting in the crew's mess, that when the children arrived below several of them vomited all over the mess deck. Four of the dark-skinned young passengers were shy, bosomy, teenage Filipino girls. Their big, liquid brown eyes had the frightened look of does suddenly discovered in a forest by a hunter. They would certainly compound the problems below decks so I suggested to the captain that we put them in Chiefs Quarters in the after part of the forward battery room, and keep them up forward throughout the trip back to Darwin. The captain OK'd that.

The situation was precarious as the evacuees boarded the *Crevalle* and were stuffed below as quickly as possible. Speed was of the essence. A Japanese bomber might suddenly fly out from the nearby jungle allowing little time to have the decks cleared and get the *Crevalle* submerged.

As for the physical condition of the passengers, the children and women looked healthy but pale from hiding out in shacks away from the sun. A few suppurating sores were evident on some of the children; nothing more. But all the men were crippled in one way or another. Some limped, some couldn't carry their belongings, some needed help easing down into the submarine, and all were tanned a dark brown, indicating that they'd been out in the open battling against the Japanese on the island of Negros.

In the middle of the loading operation, I watched a heart-rending situation develop down on the main deck. Mrs. Lindholm, after watching her children disappear down into the submarine and her belongings handed below by men helping on the ladder, had suddenly turned around to discover that her husband was not following her. They began to argue loudly with each other. She was pointing towards where the children had gone and he was waving towards the beach as though that was where he intended to go. Mrs. Lindholm was wearing woven grass sandals and a white cotton formless dress with its flower-print faded badly. Her husband, on the other hand, was wearing a denim shirt, open at the neck, and knee-high rubber boots. Mrs. Lindholm should have guessed that her husband was not going with her to Australia. But she hadn't, as evidenced by her sharp cry of anguish when her husband pushed her away and stepped over into a banca. Dejected and crying bitterly, Mrs. Lindholm made her way unsteadily to the open hatch and unassisted climbed below.

Abcede quietly explained to the captain: "She thought that her husband was going to Australia with his family but he decided to stay here. The people on Negros badly need his spiritual and medical help. These are hard times, Captain."

While the fugitives were being hustled into the *Crevalle*, large amounts of .45 ammo, flour, tins of ham, playing cards, and magazines were brought topside and swiftly handed to the Filipinos remaining in the bancas. Just as swiftly, Abcede had the bancas break loose and head back for the beach.

With the disappearance of the last passenger into the *Crevalle*, Abcede saluted Captain Walker in farewell and then curtly told Major Andrews, "Let's go." With that, the two guerrilla officers dropped to the main deck and jumped into the single banca still alongside. "Happy hunting, Captain," Abcede shouted.

Below, the refugees were distributed throughout the boat. The men were quartered in the after torpedo room and in the enlisted men's quarters. The women were told to "hot bunk it" in the four-bunk Chiefs Quarters. And some would have to sleep in the forward torpedo room with the children, using the empty torpedo skids as makeshift beds.

Many of the evacuees promptly got seasick even though the *Crevalle* was steaming through calm seas and only pitching gently. Even some of the seemingly tough, war-damaged guerrillas turned greenish-white and fled to the crew's head.

Before taking star sights, I spotted Mazzone in the wardroom, holding two tiny kids on his lap. He was telling them a story and they were gazing at his face attentively, showing no sign of fear for this big, strong piratical-looking officer. Four-year-old Fritzy Real and his two-year-old sister Nancy recognized that Mazzone was a soft-hearted guy, despite his swarthy face with its large scarred nose and beetle brows. Unchecked, Nancy pulled on his unkempt, shiny black beard in a gentle loving way.

The midnight meal in the wardroom was a pleasure to watch. All seventeen of the children were jammed around a table that normally sat only six officers. The children seemed well disciplined as they calmly waited for their food to be served by several mothers who stood behind them and ladled the food onto their plates.

The *Crevalle*'s two wardroom stewards, however, were very disturbed when they saw tiny sand crabs scurry across the white tablecloth. They had come from shells that the children had as playthings. Willie Gregory, in an agitated state protested, "Mr. Ruhe, they can't have those things in this wardroom. You won't be able to eat here if you don't do something about all those animals creeping over everything." Gregory was right. So I told the mothers to keep the sea shells up in the forward room.

One of the little kids looked up at me with big, innocent eyes and squeakily said, "Are we going to kill Japs real soon?" The rest of the kids all turned towards me to hear my reply but I kept quiet.

Then, the children refused to eat mashed potatoes until their mothers demonstrated that mashed potatoes tasted good. The vanilla ice cream, moreover, stayed uneaten as the kids recoiled from the coldness of such a dessert. But the other food with which they were familiar was eaten ravenously. They had certainly lost their initial fear of their strange new home.

In the morning Gregory was back, complaining that the officer's head in the forward room was stopped up with "something that one of the women put in it." He said he wouldn't try to blow it clear because he didn't understand "things like this." So I told Howie Geer to brave the terrors of a head clogged with Kotex and, "just flush the #%@#*%$@ thing out to sea." Then I assembled the mothers and teenage girls in the wardroom and told them about the crisis created by the misuse of the toilet plumbing. I left it up to the women to devise their own plan for disposing of "things," without trying to flush them through the toilet. Mrs. Osario said she'd handle the matter. And that was that.

All the mothers wanted to understand what made us officers tick and asked many questions of anyone they could buttonhole, as though their lives depended on it. They were estimating their chances of making it to Australia with their children intact. They had heard Japanese radio broadcasts telling them that America was a beaten country, and had been advised to turn themselves over to the Japanese forces on Negros. But as Mrs. Lindholm, the missionary's wife noted, "You all look so well fed, so supremely confident, and so efficient that I can see you are really winning this war." Then she added rhetorically, "It won't be long now until its over. Don't you think?"

All next day I listened to the stories of our passengers. The stories they told of Japanese atrocities and of the role the guerrillas played in winning the war on Negros were unbelievable. They made the *Crevalle*'s crew feel guilty for leading a life where nobody was ever injured and everyone was well fed and got plenty of sleep.

The *Crevalle*'s crew was told to remain quiet about all details of her patrol and none were allowed to talk about the *Crevalle*'s route from Negros to Australia. It seemed certain that stray information that the passengers picked up while on board would be blabbed when the evacuees went ashore in Australia. Being a Silent Service made sense.

On May 12, two small bancas were sighted dead ahead of the *Crevalle* as she headed south through Laparan Pass, which was a channel of deep water between reef areas in the Sulu Archipelago. The vessels of only a few tons displacement floated threateningly in the middle of the pass. And since the captain was now a declared "member of the Gun Club" he had the twenty-millimeter guns manned.

As the *Crevalle* neared the two small craft with their lowered sails, the black-skinned men topside who were acting like fishermen, began paddling furiously to get out of the way of the onrushing *Crevalle*.

"Those guys don't belong here," the captain snorted. "Go ahead and fire several rounds ahead of each boat." He directed this order to George who was in charge of the gun action. The gunfire, however, only made the occupants of the two boats paddle more frantically.

At this, the captain told George to have the forward gunner empty a pan of ammunition into the larger of the two vessels. When the explosive shells started ripping chunks of wood out of the banca's sides, the occupants of both boats stopped paddling and jumped overboard. The big banca, which had been low in the water before firing, began to sink slowly. It seemed that she was full of heavy gear: radios, transmitters, ammunition, guns, and "Very" pistols.

The captain conned the *Crevalle* to slowly circle the bancas while studying the topsides for signs of antennas or gun mounts. But nothing was observed.

"There's no question but that they're acting as sentinels to report the passing of U.S. submarines," the captain stated, "If we hit them quick enough, we might get a free ride down through Sibutu Passage." He was trying to justify his actions.

One of the Filipino guerrillas who was a passenger on board the *Crevalle* had been called to the bridge to talk to the natives who were floating in the water. He asked them what they were doing and in Moro they answered that they were fishing there.

"Do you think they are Moros?" the captain asked, uncomfortably.

"All of them look like Moros. But they're a treacherous lot who'll do anything for a little money. You can bet they're employed by the Japs. Don't worry about them, Captain. They can swim over to Laparan Island without any trouble." Then, as an afterthought, he recommended that the *Crevalle* finish sinking both boats as a lesson. But the captain had rung up flank speed and headed south towards Australia.

When I went below and headed into the forward battery compartment to check on how the women and children had reacted to the gunfire, I was mobbed by a horde of little kids who stood by the door waiting for news about all the shooting they'd heard. "Were you killing Japs? . . . How many Japs are dead? . . . Are we getting into lots of trouble?" their high-pitched, excited voices shrilled at me. The bloodthirsty little devils had to know all about the gun engagement.

"There were two boats carrying spies which we shot at," I lamely explained. "So now they won't warn the Japanese about where we're going." I didn't deceive them into thinking we were a big bunch of heroes, slaughtering Japanese.

"But did you sink their boats?" one little child persisted. The children had heard the captain pass the word over the 1MC announcing system that there were "two Jap boats dead ahead" and "twenty-millimeter gun crews to the bridge for gun action."

When Mrs. Osario asked with some concern, "Was it quite bloody?" I merely shrugged noncommitally, leaving the question unanswered.

Mrs. Lindholm told me that a torpedoman in the forward room had given the women and children, who were there during the gun action, a blow-by-blow account of what he guessed was happening to "the spies in the two bancas." This forced me to tell the children that we didn't actually "kill any of the spies" but that we'd done a good job of preventing them from warning the Japanese that the *Crevalle* was on the surface and moving south. I never mentioned that the occupants of the two bancas were Moros.

The gun action proved to be justified as there were no air patrols and only one ship contact on radar that the *Crevalle* was maneuvered around as she raced past the Tawi-Tawi naval base.

Just after dawn on the following day, I was awakened by a bomb exploding close off the stern. A two-motored bomber had stealthily closed the *Crevalle* through a heavy low-hanging cloud and under the air-search radar's pattern. Luke, with the bridge watch, was caught napping. The diving alarm sounded, but too late. The door to the control room was jammed with little children who had zipped out of the wardroom on hearing the explosion to see what was happening. They momentarily blocked my way aft, making me realize that these kids were a real menace in case of an emergency.

In the control room I listened to a report from the after torpedo room that told of bomb fragments striking the hull. But a close inspection later showed no hull leaks or any damage to the torpedo tube shutters.

The captain seemed highly irritated by this near fatal lapse in vigilance and scowlingly asked Luke to account for what had happened. The captain was indicating that one more strike and Luke was in trouble.

After an hour of submerged running, during which I instructed the mothers to keep their children in the wardroom when the alarm sounded, the *Crevalle* was surfaced and then entered Molucca Strait, headed for Darwin.

But within minutes, the air-search radar operator reported a plane at eight miles and closing. A two-engine bomber was sighted by Luke who was back on watch and who guessed it was the same plane encountered earlier. But this time Luke got the *Crevalle* under, with a bomb exploding harmlessly overhead as the *Crevalle* was leveled off at one hundred feet.

Two minutes later there was an explosion far below the *Crevalle*. It was a depth charge set to catch the *Crevalle* when she went deep. Luckily she didn't go deep this time. The new tactic by a wily and capable ASW aircraft was a new Japanese ploy to worry about.

Two close shaves should have made Captain Walker apprehensive about the safety of the passengers. Yet instead of quietly creeping away from the area, well below the thermal layer recorded by the bathythermograph, the captain ordered the *Crevalle* back up to sixty-five feet for a look. He seemed impatient to get on the surface and back to port without any further delay.

The first periscope look showed empty skies and no trace of the bomber. But with dense, dark clouds hanging close to the sea, the risk of running on the surface seemed too high. So the captain decided to stay at periscope depth and to move steadily at low speed toward Australia.

Soon smoke was sighted. This was followed by a sighting of the topmasts of six ships that were heading north beyond Trifore Island. "Do we risk going after these ships?" the captain asked the assembled fire control team. Then he answered himself, "We've still got four good fish back aft in the tubes. So we might as well." But the same two-engine bomber was now spotted hovering over the convoy of ships. This created many minutes of soul-searching doubt for the captain. But he finally ordered, "Man your battle stations. Torpedo attack."

The captain identified at least five escorts running with the six-ship convoy; two Shinonomes, one minesweeper, and two Chidoris. The Chidoris were the most feared of the Japanese ASW warships. They were designed solely to sink submarines. They were like the U.S. Destroyer Escorts that were running up a big score of kills against Nazi U-boats and Japanese submarines.

The group of ships was moving slowly and heading up Molucca Strait towards the Philippines.

The captain hummed "Nelly Kelly." He had a nerveless easiness that spelled danger. The captain should have been cautioned to forget the convoy and think about slinking away, sparing the women and children more of the horrors of war. But the captain's self-confidence was brimming to overflowing. I sensed that he was perhaps showing off a little for the women carried aboard.

The approach on the convoy developed so slowly that I started to feel nervous and began worrying that this wasn't going to be a simple attack. It seemed that the *Crevalle*'s destiny was foolishly being controlled by those four damned torpedoes that were begging to be shot.

Then, the captain reported that the convoy had zigged directly at the *Crevalle*. She was swung hard to port to bring her stern tubes, with the four remaining torpedoes, to bear on the ships. The captain expected the convoy to zig shortly.

But on the next periscope look, the ships had not zigged and all five escorts were converging towards the *Crevalle*'s scope. With a grunt the captain said, "What the hell is this?" as he swung the scope for a look all around. "Jesus, it's a smoke pot just about on top of our scope." He cursed some more. The bomber had laid a smoking marker on the water for the escorts to zero in on. And a Chidori a few hundred yards off was leading the charge.

At this point the captain grunted, "Everything has gone to hell in a basket." With which he ordered "350 feet, down express." Then, with his voice at least an octave higher, he shouted, "Rig for depth charge!" And not a moment too soon, as the Chidori's screws were heard thundering overhead while the *Crevalle* passed 130 feet. Seconds later eight depth charges exploded close to the *Crevalle*'s hull. Two exploded so close to the conning tower that their concussion blinded me as though I'd been slammed on the side of the head by a sledgehammer. It was the same effect I'd experienced earlier. Then I thought that the conning tower was engulfed in flames—as though the upper hatch had snapped open and fire from the charges had swept down into the confined space around me. The great noise of the explosions seemed to smash my eardrums. Moreover, my head kept ringing for the next several days. The blinker gun was thrown out of its holder and struck the captain on the side of his head. All lights were shattered. I automatically flipped on the battle lantern alongside the TDC. Its dim light showed water shooting across the conning tower in a heavy jet-stream. The water was pouring in through a hole where the steering wheel shaft went through the forward part of the conning tower.

Somebody yelled, "The conning tower is flooding." That started a rapid exodus from the conning tower, leaving only the helmsman and myself isolated in the tiny compartment as someone below slammed the hatch to the control room shut. The helmsman was knocked to the back part of the conning tower and was uselessly gripping the steering wheel which had its shaft sheared off. Reflexively, I helped the helmsman guide the stump of the shaft, which was still attached to the wheel, back into its hole leading to its outside linkage. It took a lot of strength to shove the shaft into the hole against the heavy stream of water flooding into the conning tower. But once we'd managed it, the hull compressed around the shaft as the *Crevalle* kept going deeper, while the flow of water was reduced to a trickle. It was a neat job of damage control.

A look around the conning tower, using the emergency battle lantern, showed both radar receivers smashed and only small leaks around the cables that passed through the hull. There was nothing further to be accomplished in the conning tower so I hammered on the lower hatch until it was finally opened from below by Mazzone, the diving officer. He was surprised to see me unhurt.

Leveled off at 350 feet, the *Crevalle* then caught another string of depth charges. They exploded almost as close as the previous string of charges, but a little more above the hull. I noted that the explosions indicated that the Japanese were now using a one-hundred-meter-depth setting on the charges. The prior charges had exploded close overhead as the *Crevalle* passed 170 feet, indicating that the first string were set at fifty meters. The *Crevalle* was thus operated at 400-foot-depth so as to straddle the charges with their 50, 100, and 150 meter depth settings. There were more close charges, so the captain ordered "Go to five hundred feet." He was taking the sub well below the 150-meter setting on the Chidori's depth charges. Five hundred feet was eighty-eight feet below the *Crevalle*'s test depth of 412 feet and seemed very risky. Yet the faces on the men who heard the command showed only indifference. They all knew that the *Crevalle* was built with a 150 percent margin of safety and they were trusting that Portsmouth Naval Shipyard had built the *Crevalle* well.

The Christmas-tree lights at the diving station, showed a red light for the torpedo loading hatch up in the forward torpedo room and Mazzone complained that the *Crevalle* was getting steadily heavier up forward. Though pumping water out of forward trim to sea, he couldn't catch up with the increasing weight. At this report, the captain told me to go forward and see what was happening. There'd been nothing reported from up forward. My look into the forward battery room by shining a flashlight through the glass port in the door, indicated that the room was totally demolished. All the false bulkheads that surrounded the chief's quarters, the wardroom, the pantry and the officer's staterooms had collapsed. Evidently, the metal pins that held them together had been sheared by the force of exploding depth charges near the hull. Still, there was no sign of water on the decks. So I had the dogs on the door hammered open and stepped into the compartment. Then, by shoving the sheet metal bulkhead panels around, I was able to ascertain that none of the teenage girls were under the wreckage. The officers' staterooms proved just as quiet and abandoned. I was afraid what I might find when I shone my flashlight under the collapsed sides of the wardroom.

All of the books had cascaded out of the bookshelves onto the metal panels and the cork insulation inside the pressure hull had flaked off, showering the books like a heavy fall of snow. All was deathly quiet. Then my light caught several pairs of glittering, tiny eyes staring at me. But there wasn't even the sound of a whimper coming from the children buried under the mass of debris. When I asked whether they were all right, one child started to whisper something but others immediately "sshhed" the little kid. These children had great self-discipline. No groans. No crying. It would take a good deal of work to extricate them from the wreckage, so I went aft to ask the captain to detail some men to pull the kids free of the junk on top of them. Then I moved forward to check the forward torpedo room.

Shining my light through the glass port set in the door to the torpedo room, I was able to see that the room was jammed with people, all of whom looked very much alive. Many women were standing between the torpedo skids in black oily water that had flooded the room well above their knees. The edges of their cotton dresses swirled out over the surface and mingled with a litter of floating chunks of cork. Woven baskets with their clothing floated on the slimy sea of water. The black scum had stained the few bits of female wear they'd brought aboard. A check of the vent from the forward room showed a good deal of air pressure in the room. So I bled this off before I could push the door open and enter the forward room.

Once in the torpedo room, I spotted three of the guerrillas up by the torpedo tubes along with Chief Howard. He was examining what looked like the dead body of another one of the guerrillas. The man was stretched out on a mine skid and had a bloody gash on the side of his head. He was white as a sheet. "I had to hit him with a wrench when he tried to go out through the upper hatch," Howard explained. "The guy went berserk and was trying to undog the hatch to get out of the submarine." Howard showed little concern for the man he'd hit. He reassured me that, "He's still breathing and his heart's beating."

"Can't we get some light in here, Howard?" I asked.

The Chief explained that all the battle lanterns were smashed and the emergency lighting circuit was drowned out.

My check of the torpedo loading hatch, which had showed a red light on the Christmas tree in the control room, showed that the long, rectangular hatch was dogged down and only a small stream of water flowed into the boat around the deformed edges of the hatch.

"The hatch was lifted by one of the depth charges and a lot of water poured into the room," Howard explained while watching me shine my flashlight around the edges of the hatch. Then he directed my attention to the dished-in hull just forward of the deformed hatch. "We're lucky the hull didn't fracture from the force of that depth charge," Howard soberly noted. The inner side of the hull at the top of the torpedo room looked as though a giant sledgehammer had caused a two-yard dent in the hull of about ten inches in depth. "The scariest thing, though," Howard added, "was to have the dogs on the hatch to the escape trunk shear off and zing around the room like ricocheting bullets. One of those hitting your head and you're a dead man."

All of the women appeared to be uninjured and were stoically standing in the water. No hysterics. No signs of being frantic about what had happened to the children. I guessed that all seventeen of the kids were under the pile of debris in the wardroom area.

Before leaving the room, I told Howard to send everybody aft and that I'd get Doc Loos to see about the injured man. "But you keep stopping the leaks up here while I get Mr. Mazzone to use the drain pump to get the water out of the room." Howard went to work, putting a patch on the submerged vent of the number six torpedo tube. The tube had suffered a smashed outer door and its vent had backed open and couldn't be shut. This allowed a lot of water to flood into the room. No wonder Mazzone was having trouble with holding a trim while so much water continued to flow into the forward room.

As I went aft to report to the captain about the mess up forward, I saw that several of the *Crevalle*'s crewmen were uncovering the little children in the wardroom and that Doc Loos was there ensuring that none were badly hurt by the collapsing bulkheads. There was still no sobbing or noise of any sort. The kids were good submariners!

When back in the control room, I reported to the captain that things looked manageable up forward, I also noted: "The passengers don't even seem mad at us." This produced a weak, guilty smile on the captain's face.

"We'll get them home," the captain muttered. But how was another question. Both periscopes were mangled. Both the master and the auxiliary gyro compasses had spilled their mercury and were inoperable. The two sound gears were dead and the radio transmitter was a pile of junk. And the radars no longer resembled electronic gear. The trim pump had stopped functioning. This forced Mazzone to move water from forward to after trim by putting air pressure in the forward trim tank. He reported that he had moved over eighteen tons of water from the bow to compensate for the great amount of water in the forward room, and that he was being forced to use two-thirds speed to prevent the *Crevalle* from sinking deeper. All hydraulic pressure was lost so the *Crevalle*, to get home, would have to utilize the high pressure air from the 3,000-pound air banks. Fortunately, the bow and stern planes and steering gear were still usable in hand operation, although it took a great amount of strength to operate the balky mechanisms.

Mazzone, remembering how I'd been isolated in the conning tower when the first charge exploded, said, "I don't know what happened to you up there, but down here all of the men in the control room were knocked to the deck, including me." Mazzone decked by the Japs? A good story to be retold.

A check on the batteries showed that their specific gravity was down to 1.140 and that meant there was little juice left. Consequently, all ventilation was shut down while the temperature in the boat soared to over one hundred degrees. It looked as though we were going to have a replay of the exhausted-battery incident on the *Seadragon* back in 1942 near Rabaul.

Yet things didn't appear all that grimmo. Members of the crew kept arriving in the control room reporting minor injuries to personnel and the leaks generally under control. Several battery jars in the forward battery room had been cracked but there was no sign of chlorine gas from leaking battery acid. Better yet, there were no sounds of searching destroyers audible through the hull.

By noon, the soundman reported that his JK sound gear was once more operable and that he was able to track the screws of enemy ships and could hear the pinging of the escorts. "But no ships hold any contact on the *Crevalle*," he declared with a note of relief in his voice.

Happily, throughout the afternoon the destroyers moved further away. And the Lord was thanked that there were no more depth charge attacks. A few more close charges might easily have spelled the end of the *Crevalle*.

Mazzone requested that all movement of people in the boat be reduced to a minimum. A slight change in the angle of the boat would cause the free water in the forward torpedo room to shift sufficiently to throw the *Crevalle* badly out of trim.

I offered to relieve him as diving officer for a while but he felt that he was so sensitized to the *Crevalle*'s trim problems that he shouldn't take a rest until most of the water was removed from the forward room. Since the drain pump was out of order, plans were made to bail the water out of the room with a bucket brigade up through the forward escape trunk, once the *Crevalle* was back on the surface. I cursed the lack of a portable electric sump pump for just such an emergency and vowed to get one before the next patrol, even if I'd have to steal it from another boat.

George's ingenuity in jury-rigging damaged equipment and his tireless driving of his auxiliarymen without let-up, resulted in the drain pump being put back in commission and the water in the forward room pumped to sea.

Shortly after dark, the *Crevalle* was surfaced from ninety feet depth. "We'll get up fast and hope there is no plane overhead to drop a bomb on us," the captain said. He recognized that with the scopes and radars demolished there was little sense in going to periscope depth first. Luckily, when the lookouts arrived on the bridge their looks all around in the hazy darkness revealed nothing close to the *Crevalle*. With the diesel engines operable, and with an undamaged armored tank-compass in the control room to steer by, it seemed certain that the *Crevalle* would make it to Darwin, even if it took a long time to get there. Having the Army-issue magnetic compass used in U.S. tanks was a great stroke of luck. I'd met an Army colonel in Brisbane who was assembling supplies to be sent to Army units in New Guinea. When I spotted the tank compasses he had in a pile, I asked for one and got it and took it back to the *Crevalle* where I mounted it beside the steering gear in the control room. Then I compensated it for all the surrounding metal. The compass deviation card was a wild 360° recording of deviations that varied as high as twenty-two degrees from a true heading as recorded by the master gyro compass. But it seemed certain that with it a course could be steered within a couple of degrees of what it should be.

When the moon rose and with the *Crevalle* peacefully running south on two engines through Molucca Strait, I went to the main deck to assess the topside damage. The depth charge that sheared off the steering wheel shaft had torn the forward twenty-millimeter gun platform into a jagged hole. The charge that had lifted the torpedo loading hatch also tore away all the decking around the four-inch gun and sliced about ten inches off the muzzle of the gun. The topside JT sonar was gone. In assessing the damage, it seemed certain that five-hundred-pound depth charges were used and that they exploded within two or three feet of the *Crevalle*'s topsides. Somebody called to me from the bridge to get a look at the bow planes which wouldn't rig in. But there was too much deck damage to risk going forward. This wouldn't be a critical handicap unless the *Crevalle* ran into heavy seas. Then, slow speed would be necessary or there'd be an unmerciful pounding on the planes with heavy shocks produced in the forward part of the *Crevalle*. That would be mighty rough on the passengers.

All day of the 15th of May, the *Crevalle* ran submerged. The vents had been hand operated to get her down. Only the forward vent to the number one main ballast tank was hard to open. But it was jury-rigged with a block-and-tackle to force it open. Then it seemed to take forever to get the *Crevalle* under. And once under, the captain ordered only three knots speed, both to conserve the battery and to make little noise. He figured that he'd pressed his luck too far already and couldn't risk being picked up by an antisubmarine patrol boat out of Ambon. There was deep water all the way to the Banda Sea so there was little chance of the *Crevalle* going aground even though she was running blind.

Under George's direction the panels for the wardroom and bunkrooms were put back in place using regular nuts and bolts. The children, along with the two mothers who had remained with them when the wardroom became a shambles, had been herded to the crew's mess. There they were entertained by the enlisted men who had them on their laps.

All women and children were moved out of the forward part of the sub for twenty-four hours, to live with the crew while the fiasco up forward was taken care of. Then their same living arrangements were restored. But the officers were so busy getting things back in commission and just trying to keep a badly crippled *Crevalle* headed for Darwin that they had little time to find out any more about the passengers. Additionally, they didn't want to pick up their gripes for the bad treatment they'd been put through. Understandably, the captain kept the curtain to his stateroom pulled shut. He didn't want to talk about what had happened.

Without a workable radio transmitter there was no way to tell Admiral Christie that the *Crevalle* was going to be long overdue in her arrival with the passengers. And that was bad.

With the seas increasing during the night, the *Crevalle* was forced to slow to eleven knots because of the heavy pounding of the waves on the pitching bow planes. A chain-fall was then rigged to both planes and they were hauled in by brute force so that sixteen knots speed could be enjoyed when running on the surface.

At daybreak of the 19th, the *Crevalle* unexpectedly met a motor launch sent out from Darwin to pick up the passengers. The skipper of the launch shouted through a megaphone, "What's the name of your sub?" Every man on the bridge shouted back, "*Crevalle*." Back through a megaphone came, "I've been waiting out here for three days to pick up your passengers. What happened?" But that was left unanswered as the motor launch came alongside the stopped sub and an Australian Army officer jumped aboard. He explained to the captain that MacArthur didn't want anyone to find out how the refugees had been brought to Australia and that as soon as they arrived in Darwin they'd be flown to Brisbane to a quarantine camp for two weeks of internment. Then the women and children would be flown to the United States.

When all of the passengers were brought topside along with their baskets and packages of meager belongings, the captain asked me to get the sub's camera and take a snapshot of the whole group with the captain standing in the center. His family.

Amazingly, they all seemed genuinely thankful for their "nice" treatment aboard. Mrs. Lindholm said, "You're such wonderful men and so kind. I hope you can all live to the end of the war and go home to your wives, who must miss you terribly." I choked up at that. Several of the women openly cried as they said good-bye to the captain. One might have thought that just getting off the *Crevalle* would have been the happiest moment in their lives. But nobody was smiling as they climbed down into the motor launch. The kids stood up on the launch's seats to wave at us. And one woman blew a kiss back at us. That was too much. Even the captain had a drop of moisture in his eyes.

Debarking the passengers at the entrance to the channel through the minefields made particularly good sense, since the *Crevalle* was finally tied up alongside a Liberty ship at the boom-jetty in Darwin. The Liberty ship had five thousand tons of bombs aboard plus a lot of gasoline and black powder. Having the *Crevalle* alongside this powder keg was nerve racking. So while the captain was visiting his RAF friends out at the airbase, I had the *Crevalle* moved to the other side of the jetty.

Then I felt like a dodo when I discovered that an enemy bombing raid had cut all freshwater lines on the jetty, requiring that a hose be run to the Liberty ship to get freshwater from her tanks.

The Army officer who'd met the *Crevalle* on her arrival and taken the passengers to Darwin turned out to be an intelligence officer and came aboard the *Crevalle* after seeing the women and children off for their flight to Brisbane. The men, he said, would be flown to Perth for further Army assignments.

The *Crevalle*, although rapidly refueled and reprovisioned, was held over a day for her departure. Heavy U.S. bombing raids on Surabaja during the nineteenth had caused all submarine safety lanes, (where no bombing was allowed) to be eliminated until 1000 on the twentieth.

Late on the twentieth, with no pilot showing up to guide the *Crevalle* back through the swept channel, the captain said, "We'll shove off and head for Fremantle on our own." And did.

Next day, a thorough house cleaning of the boat was held, especially to remove the strong barn smell of the refugees. It was a pervasive, unpleasant odor to men who'd become adapted to the diesel-oil smell that was always there and accepted like the presence of an old friend.

Back in the crew's mess I saw a sign saying, "Mr. Morin has taken over navigation today. Instruction in using the escape lung as a life preserver will be held in the forward torpedo room." Things were back to normal.

The *Crevalle* overtook the *Flasher* on the way south and ran in company with her the rest of the way to Fremantle. I was again amazed to observe that under clear but moonless conditions, the *Flasher*, painted a solid, haze gray was invisible to my excellent night-vision eyes.

In the last several days of the trip, my reflections on what might be learned from this patrol proved interesting.

It was evident that an enemy whose high seas shipping was being badly decimated by submarine attacks would gravitate his operations into shallow waters despite the serious shortcomings in using such waters.

Favoring ship operations close to the shore were: the protection provided by inshore minefields; the facility to move into small bays for protection against radar-equipped submarines; the threat of land-based aircraft attacking from a land background offered good protection for enemy ships; and the ability to concentrate antisubmarine protection on the seaward side of ships hugging a coastline made it more difficult for a submerged submarine to make a successful attack.

Importantly, sinking ships with submarine guns was relatively impractical since with gun crews on deck the sudden appearance of an aircraft would catch the submarine sufficiently unaware so that the probability of her being bombed while still on the surface or close under the surface would be greatly increased.

The shortcomings of enemy ships using shallow waters were: the danger of going aground; the possibility of being blown up by one's own mines; the difficulties of maneuvering; the poor sonar conditions for the antisubmarine protection efforts; and the loss of transit time in avoiding submarines by means of close-to-shore transits. What was observed during this patrol was that Japanese shipping using shallow waters was being forced to take almost double the time to get to their destinations than if they'd sailed across the deep seas.

The severe depth chargings and bombings that the *Crevalle* experienced demonstrated how tough a fleet boat is and how tough people are, women and children included. The extensive damage sustained by the *Crevalle*, while continuing to be functional, spoke well of how survivability is built into the submarine by means of its tough hull, its simple repairable gear, and the ease with which damage control measures can be quickly and effectively carried out.

Going deep, exceeding the advertised test depth to get below the maximum depth setting of the enemy's weapons reduced significantly the probability of depth charge damage.

Fortunately, the inefficiency of the depth charge as a weapon saved the *Crevalle* from greater damage or destruction. An antisubmarine homing weapon should be a far greater threat.

On the twenty-eighth, a lookout sighted the light on Rottnest Island, off Fremantle Harbor. Its sighting produced many long sighs of relief.

Admiral Christie was on the pier awaiting the *Crevalle*'s arrival when she tied up before 0800. And the three bottles of Old Overholt whiskey were won by Graham, the motor machinist, for his best guess as to the time for the first line being thrown over to the dock—a submarine version of an "anchor pool."

The admiral came aboard to greet the captain and shake his hand and say "Well done." His warm pleasantness indicated that he was happy about his decision to give Frank Walker command of the *Crevalle* and to let me stay aboard despite the possibility that I might be a trouble-maker.

The first thing every *Crevalle* officer asked on arrival was, "What is the liquor ration this time?" The answer: "One bottle of scotch per officer and the usual twenty-four quarts of Emu Bitters beer." It was also promised that each officer could draw eight quarts of whiskey at the Australian canteen. Significantly, the large wooden, pine box containing the bottles of beer still looked uncomfortably like a coffin.

A second order of business was to have Chief Sutter scout around quietly and locate, before he went on rest leave, a portable, electric, submersible sump pump. If flooding into the boat knocked out the normally used pumps, such a pump was a necessity to shift water around the boat to maintain a trim. "Requisition it, borrow it, or steal it," I told Sutter. "But let's not go back to sea without one!"

The admiral's endorsement to the patrol report read, "The third war patrol of the USS *Crevalle* ranks as one of the outstanding aggressive patrols of the war." Equally pleasant was the addition: "The *Crevalle* will require longer than the normal refit period to correct the damage sustained." That meant the crew would get more than two weeks of rest leave.

But not so. On schedule, the *Crevalle*'s crew and officers were ordered to leave their rest camps and return to the boat to help ready her for sea.

There was much interest in where the grapnel had caught on the *Crevalle* when she lay on the bottom. After much searching around the topside area, a ladder rung on the starboard side of the fairwater was found to have been fractured at one end. The one-inch, bent, iron rung had been almost straightened out before the grapnel had torn loose. It was difficult to believe that a huge thing like the *Crevalle* could be towed with such a frail grip by a small warship using its minesweeping gear. But the sub's virtual weightlessness at neutral buoyancy as she lay on the muddy bottom made this towing experience plausible. (Interestingly, a 1943 Japanese Ordnance pamphlet found after the war showed a nineteen-pound explosive device that could be slid down a grappling wire and which would explode on contact with the object snagged.)

7

Wolfpack

Departure for the *Crevalle*'s fourth war patrol was set for the afternoon of June 21, 1944. Her patrol was going to be coordinated with two other submarines, the *Flasher* and the *Angler*. The three submarines had been directed to operate as a wolfpack, the first such utilization of Fremantle-based boats.

Three-boat wolfpacks had operated out of Midway and Pearl for the past six months. They differed, however, in one essential way from the wolfpack the *Crevalle* would be a part of. Instead of having a division commander aboard one of the boats for tactical coordination of the wolfpack, an on-scene submarine skipper would be in charge. Hence, Lt. Comdr. Reuben Whitaker, the captain of the *Flasher* and senior skipper, was named "Tactical Commander of Whitaker's Wolves."

A short meeting of the skippers and the execs of the three boats was therefore convened on board the *Flasher* on the morning of departure, to finalize the tactics and communications for the pack's operations as a coordinated unit.

Whitaker, a short, aloof, elegant and supremely confident man with a blond, wispy mustache and lots of flair, made the meeting brief. He wanted to leave Fremantle as quickly as possible. He emphasized simplicity in communications and said in effect that "the skippers should use their good judgement as to when to use plain-language communications and how to disguise what they were saying, if necessary." He also said that he did not "contemplate having to encipher any of the communications," nor was he demanding precise radio circuit procedures.

"I'm using the call sign 'Dumbo.' Walker will be 'Patsy,'" and then Whitaker paused, giving Frank Walker a knowing suggestion of a smile. He had undoubtedly heard more than once how Walker had called himself a Patsy when he was fooled by the Japanese. Whitaker added, "Hess, you'll be 'Goatfish.'" Hess cringed at the sound of his call sign.

Whitaker looked at the other two skippers for their approval. They merely shook their heads in amusement while rolling the call signs around on their thirsty tongues. They were testing how such names might sound to the Japanese out in the South China Sea where "Whitaker's Wolves" would operate.

"Just do what's necessary relative to the information passed between the boats. And play everything by ear," Whitaker counseled with finality. The plan of action for his wolfpack had apparently been decided upon in his mind and nothing more he felt need be said.

However, Ray Dubois, his scrappy, aggressive exec, insisted upon discussing details. "Captain, we haven't talked about submerged communications as yet." But Whitaker, with an impatient wave of his hand cut Dubois off. Jake Bowell, the exec of the *Angler*, and I remained silent. So Whitaker turned to Captain Walker and Frank Hess and suggested that all three of them go to the Officer's Club for a farewell drink. This left Dubois, Jake Bowell, and me to discuss what concerned us about Whitaker's far too brief instructions. But none of us had much of an idea how best to operate in a three-boat wolfpack so the subsequent discussion bogged down into some foolish solutions to unlikely situations.

I'd read a few newspaper articles about what the Germans over the past two years were doing with their large wolfpacks of seven to eleven U-boats against Atlantic convoys. But the U-boat wolfpack tactical problems were markedly different from those confronting Whitaker's Wolves. Tactical command of a German group of U-boats was effected by a submarine commander at a shore command-center back in Europe. Thus, there was a large volume of communications flowing from the U-boats far at sea to the tactical commander ashore. Then his tactical instructions were radioed back to the German wolfpacks in encoded messages. By comparison, Whitaker's concept of wolfpack operations against Japanese convoys was so simple that I felt we were dealing with kindergarten stuff and trying to learn how to crawl before being able to walk. For Whitaker's Wolves, details weren't important.

After returning to the *Crevalle* and just before lunch, two shore patrolmen brought three *Crevalle* torpedomen on board, having picked them up at the train station in Perth where they'd drunkenly staggered off a train from Kalgoorlie. They'd missed muster on board at 0800 and were thus over leave. Hence, the shore patrolmen unceremoniously and without delivering a shore patrol report telling of the mens' offenses, dumped the men along with their duffle bags onto the *Crevalle*'s main deck and departed. Langfeldt, Locktov, and Niemczyk had many bottles of gin and whiskey in their duffle bags, that I felt should be destroyed. But with Langfeldt on his knees and blubbering, "Please, Mr. Ruhe, don't do that. Save our booze so we can celebrate after the patrol," I had second thoughts. Tears were in the three men's eyes and Langfeldt's drunken appeal was with pure anguish. So I relented and had the liquor secretly stowed in a locker with a padlock on it and had the men led to their bunks "to sleep it off."

At the end of this incident, Walt Mazzone who had become the engineering officer when Luke Bowdler had been transferred after the end of the third patrol, in a conspiratorial whisper suggested that he had something to show me. He then led me back to the after engine-room and told me to look into the bilges outboard of the port engine. There, Walt had stowed a portable, electric sump pump! To my questioning look, he explained that he and an engineman had stolen it from the *Jack* two days previously. "We used a punt to go alongside the outboard side of the *Jack*. Then, the engineman went down the engineroom hatch and stole it. Unfortunately, the *Jack*'s below decks watch saw him briefly and asked why he was in the *Jack*'s engine-room. The reply given was, 'I'm checking the damage *Jack* sustained on her last patrol.'" But this didn't sound very credible.

This could cause a good deal of trouble, I felt, yet I gave Walt a well-deserved, "Attaboy." It was also hoped that the *Crevalle* would get underway before Miles Refo, the *Jack*'s exec, discovered the sump pump's loss. He was a tough man to deal with.

Then just after lunch the messenger poked his head into the ward-room to say that the *Flasher* had gotten underway and was leaving early. Evidently, Whitaker was so eager to get on patrol that he couldn't wait until Walker and Hess returned to their boats.

When the three skippers had gone to the Officers Club, they had tentatively set 1500 as departure time. By 1445 I was sufficiently worried about Captain Walker and his timely return to the *Crevalle* that I called the Officers Club. The person who answered said that Walker, Hess, and Selby, of the *Puffer*, were having a last round of drinks and that they were preparing to leave. Was this last round a round before another last round? We waited.

Then at 1635, down the dock came Captain Walker, followed by Hess and Selby strung out across the dock. They were baying at each other like wolves. Selby with his silver white hair was easily distinguished from a mob of workmen going off their jobs at the end of the day and who had paused to watch the *Crevalle* and the *Angler* leave. Selby kept waving and baying at his two pals as they staggered and teetered across the temporary wooden planks thrown across the bows of the boats. The two skippers refused proffered helping hands from deck watch personnel as they made their way to their boats, which were singled up with all hands chomping at the bit to get going. When Captain Walker arrived on the *Crevalle*'s bow, I pulled her clear using full speed on the batteries. Then, rapidly shifting to the diesels, the *Crevalle* at flank speed sped past Rottnest Island making up for lost time. Nobody looked back to see if Frank Hess had made it to his *Angler* without falling overboard.

The first day out was one of recuperation rather than training. Later, with the *Angler* in company, night radar attacks were conducted against her until midnight. The *Crevalle*'s gray paint job made her so invisible at night that Captain Walker decided to keep the submarines at least three thousand yards apart at all times.

After midnight, I broke out two mail bags full of newspapers. There were about ninety daily editions of *The Morning Call*. At sea, the newspapers were eagerly read by the entire crew. The procedure was to dole out the twenty latest papers to the officers and the rest went to the forward room where Chief Howard had his torpedomen clip out the comic strips and paste them into scrapbooks. These were routed to the crew. What remained of the papers were well scrutinized for baseball scores and football results. As for the war in Europe and the Atlantic, the officers seemed more interested than the crew in such news. The campaigns in Europe were well covered and the new things being developed by the Germans were lengthily described; but news of the Pacific War was almost nonexistent. By the end of a patrol the newspapers would be in shreds, but there were still some men trying to read the pieces of the papers remaining.

Wednesday, June 23, was a calm, bright sunny day at sea. More training dives and a few periscope approaches on the *Angler* were held. The *Crevalle* would race ahead, submerge, then the captain would try to get a good firing set-up as the *Angler* passed by on the surface.

I observed that in between the simulated torpedo attacks on the *Angler*, all of the officers including the captain were busy writing letters to their wives to make up for their failure to produce many letters during the time in port. Moreover, it was discovered that George Morin was bilging all the other officers by writing one-a-day letters to his wife. Unfortunately, the wives back home when getting together had swapped notes as to letters received. They complained about their poor treatment as to numbers of letters from "their husbands." Hence, their husbands did some back-dating of their hastily written letters to make it appear that a good many letters had been written during rest leave. The mailing of all accumulated letters from Exmouth Gulf, where the *Crevalle* would refuel, should fool the wives, it was felt, into thinking they were being remembered just as often as the insidious George Morin's daily letters to his wife, Hope.

For the first two days, better meals were being served, thanks to Chief Emme, the new commissaryman. This indicated that the crew would put on some weight during the patrol instead of always arriving at the rest camps at the end of a patrol in a scrawnier condition. For lunch, however, Chief Emme served mashed potatoes made from dehydrated potato flakes and powdered milk. I ordered the chief to stop that and first expend all the potatoes stored in the after battery trunk leading to the main deck. Emme had also brought large tins of powdered onions, carrots, and eggs aboard so he wouldn't run out of food by the end of a long patrol. But sampling the reconstituted carrots and onions and tasting an ersatz omelet, forced me to order Emme to leave those items off the menu until there was a severe food shortage.

The *Angler* was the first to enter Exmouth Gulf on May 24th, and promptly bent one of her screws on a bottom obstruction near the fuel barge. Consequently, Jake Bowell, the round-faced, snaggle-toothed exec of the *Angler*, and I in a small boat, sounded the area around the fuel barge. But we failed to find anything shallow enough to cause trouble with submarines using Exmouth Gulf to top-off with fuel before going further on patrol. In addition, our hands were badly blistered by the sounding-line we used.

The *Angler* left before noon on one screw to return to Fremantle and have her propeller replaced; so there would be no opportunity to form the three-sub wolfpack very soon.

The *Crevalle*'s fuelling was completed by 1600. Then, while heading out to sea, it was discovered that the SJ surface search radar was out of commission and needed a part that couldn't be found on board. Thus, *Crevalle* was forced to return to Exmouth Gulf to wait there until the part was flown up from Perth. In the meantime, Manny Kimmel's *Robalo* and Charlie Henderson's *Bluefish* arrived and tied up alongside the *Crevalle*. They were enroute north for patrols.

On the following day at 1400 a spare part for the SJ radar, plus a radar technician arrived by plane from Perth. The radar technician was certainly not needed since the *Crevalle*'s masterful radarman, Biehl, could readily fix the radar by himself.

By 1535 the *Crevalle* was underway and headed back out to sea. On the way and at flank speed, the four-inch gun crew fired ten rounds at a derelict freighter that was aground on Northwest Cape near the entrance to the Gulf. Four brightly flashing hits at 4,200 yards range on the old hulk, indicated that the *Crevalle*'s 1919 vintage gun was well aligned for long range engagements. The *Crevalle* was finally on her way to see some action.

In the next three days, the *Crevalle* raced towards The Barrier. Then the *Crevalle* shut down both her radars as she entered Lombok Strait. Two small enemy patrol craft were sighted in the moonless blackness, but they completely ignored the *Crevalle* as she eased past them and moved into the Bali Sea without incident.

Just after dawn and south of Sakala Island in the Bali Sea, the *Crevalle* was forced to dive when another patrol boat was sighted. This was in the same spot where the *Crevalle* had been bombed on her first patrol. The *Crevalle* remained submerged and moved northwest into the Java Sea where the captain sighted through the periscope a motor sampan with a red meatball on the side of her pilot house. A similar Japanese flag was painted on the sampan's deck house and a tall radio antenna extended above the pilot house. The *Crevalle* was then quickly surfaced and eighteen four-inch shells were fired into the eighty-ton vessel. Many devastating hits sank her. But the sampan had remained on the surface sufficiently long to be able to transmit an emergency radio message before she went under. Within minutes, and not unexpectedly, out came a plane that forced the *Crevalle* to submerge.

June 30 was one of those on-edge, tense days of waiting-for-something-to-happen. The green-blue waters of the Java Sea were so shallow and crystal clear that it was a miserable place to encounter any of the Japanese first-string warships. Yet, in the morning, as the *Crevalle* was heading west on the surface across the shallow Java Sea, a "flash" contact message was received from a U.S. Black Cat flying boat on reconnaissance out of Darwin. It told of sighting a Tenryu-class cruiser and two escorting destroyers heading east across the Java Sea. The *Crevalle*, as she hurried towards Karimata Strait, was in the path of this deadly force of enemy warships. She'd meet them shortly along her track, which showed depths varying from nineteen to twenty-five fathoms.

My heart sank. The *Crevalle* was in the wrong place to encounter such a lethal force of ships. I dolefully had the thought, "If we tackle these ships, they'll beat us to death. It's been a good war so far—so why does it have to end this way?" Then I timidly decided that the smart thing to do was to submerge and sneak out of the path of the oncoming ships.

The captain, as he read the message, muttered, "Oh, shit." His clenched jaw and squinted sad eyes showed that he was just as concerned as I was about the situation.

Then, radar emanations were detected that indicated a closing aircraft. Even before it was sighted, the *Crevalle* was dived. Remaining undetected was the essence of survival in such brightly lit shallow waters. After a short period of running submerged, the *Crevalle* was surfaced and resumed her dash across the Java Sea. But within an hour, the *Crevalle* was again driven down by an enemy aircraft that first used its radar to locate the sub and then shut it off for the final run-in for an attack. But no bombs were dropped. George suggested that the plane was on a sweep out ahead of the three warships and that they would be sighted shortly. This sent a cold chill down my spine and the adrenalin started flowing.

Just before surfacing again, the captain spotted several hair-like masts jutting above the horizon out to the west. The *Crevalle* was planed up to fifty feet to examine the contacts with the scope extended fifteen feet above the water. As the captain studied the topworks below the masts there was another growled "Oh, shit." Then, "The ships seem to have sharp starboard angles-on-the-bow and are headed for us." The moment of truth had arrived. Shaking his head sadly, he muttered, as he lowered the scope, "We can't be chicken. Let's go get 'em."

I watched the captain's face closely. His knit brows and pensive stare at the conning tower deck showed little determination to do battle with the warships but also that he was puzzled by what he had observed. He kept the *Crevalle* at sixty-five feet for the next thirty minutes, periodically poking up the scope for quick looks. But he saw nothing on the bearing of the warships. They weren't arriving as fast as expected. While, sweat poured from my bare chest, soaking my shorts.

When the *Crevalle* was planed up to fifty feet for another extended periscope look, what he saw caused another "Oh, shit." But this was uttered with a note of self-flagellating disgust. "Those ships are only harmless sailing craft—a big one and two small ones. Christ! What a Patsy I am." He had let the Black Cat's message fool him into believing that what he vaguely saw out on the horizon had to be the threatening warships.

A heavy weight seemed to have been lifted from my shoulders as the *Crevalle* regained the surface and continued westward. And I was proud of the captain for not chickening out when he thought that a deadly battle was imminent.

For the next three days, the *Crevalle* uneventfully picked her way across the Java Sea, up through the shallow waters of Karimata Strait, and on into the South China Sea. But during the third day, the *Crevalle* was forced to dive away three times from sighted planes. She was running radar-silent. Yet on each dive there was radar interference on the *Crevalle*'s SD scope while no visual sightings were made, except at short ranges. Jim Blind had rigged the SD for a receive-only mode.

The *Crevalle* had moved into monsoon weather. The skies were leaden gray and mottled with swiftly moving storm clouds that produced occasional drizzling rain. Visibility was cut to less than three miles. The captain no longer worried about enemy aircraft spotting the *Crevalle*'s wake on the frothy seas churned up by gusty winds. Hence he pushed the *Crevalle* north at high speed. He was eager to join Whitaker and start operating as a partial wolfpack of two boats until Hess in the *Angler* could join up.

Then, another secret "burn message" was received. It told of the departure of several warships from Singapore that were headed northeast through the South China Sea. A second "burn message" which was received just before twilight gave the 2400 geographical position of the warships—a few miles north of the equator. The captain was understandably excited about the prospects of tangling in deep water with some of the best warships of the Japanese fleet. So he called on me to get a good "fix" to verify the *Crevalle*'s position and give him a good chance of intercepting the ships at their midnight position.

But getting a fix using star sights seemed quite hopeless. The rain-dimmed horizon and scudding black clouds sweeping across occasional patches of open sky, allowed only fleeting sextant sights to be taken on stars that were not clearly identified. Four sights were finally "shot" and seemed good enough to calculate their lines of position. But the "fix" generated by the four lines of position, produced a thirty-five mile triangle.

The captain said that such a position was next to useless. So the *Crevalle* had to be conned toward the 2400 warship position using the dead reckoning device, the "DRT." It was a "by guess and by God" method of getting there.

At midnight, a few short radar sweeps were made but no ships were detected. No wonder, because when I finally got a radar fix on a well-identified small island on the Fourth of July, I was dumbfounded to realize that the *Crevalle*'s position, as shown by the DRT, was forty miles north of where the *Crevalle* actually was. It was thus apparent that the star sights taken on the third were calculated for the *Crevalle* being north of the equator, not south of the equator, where she actually had been. All the lines of positions were wrong because the tables in the Celestial Navigation Book were different for north latitudes and south latitudes. I didn't admit this error to the captain but it certainly humbled me—"the compleat Navigator."

The Fourth passed without fireworks. Navy holiday food was served at supper time; turkey and minced pie. To help the holiday mood, I wandered around the boat and chatted with many of the crew, inviting their comments and feelings about serving on the *Crevalle*. To my great alarm, more than a few of the men said they wanted to get off the *Crevalle* and have shore duty in Perth, rather than being transferred back to the States for new construction. It was evident that some of the crew had become "Perth-happy" lovers. So I loudly observed that if being great lovers of Aussie women affected their on board performance, I'd have them detached and sent to the boats in the Aleutians. And I emphasized "the Aleutians!"

For the next eight days, the *Crevalle* was on station, patrolling on the surface across the Saigon-Takao-Formosa sea route and waiting for the *Flasher* to come up from the south and join the *Crevalle*. The *Angler*, meanwhile, had arrived on station to the east of the *Crevalle*.

On one surfacing into heavy seas, the OOD failed to put his foot on the upper hatch to shut it as a huge wave piled over the bridge. The resulting flood of water down through the hatch soaked much of the electrical gear in the control room and in the pump room below with salt water. The mess caused, plus no targets, drove the captain into moving the *Crevalle* over to the Indochina coast south of Cape Varella.

The day of the twelfth, the *Crevalle* conducted a submerged patrol off Hon Doi Island where the seas were even worse than out in the middle of the ocean. Deep swells bounced the boat around when at periscope depth and made periscope looks very dicey. Even with five feet of scope extended, the mountainous waves sloshed over the scope's window, blanking it. And then the spray off the top of the waves would douse the upper window and cause a blurring of images out beyond the scope. Predictably, when a two-thousand-ton steamer that was hugging the coast passed inboard of the *Crevalle*, it was not sighted until it was abeam. Its dark gray camouflage made the ship blend well with the jungle beyond. Moreover, a chase was rejected since the depth keeping performance of the Mk-14's in such violent seas seemed questionable.

When the *Crevalle* was surfaced at night after the seas had abated somewhat, the long swells churned up the waters making them glow brightly as a result of the high density of phosphorescent sea life near the surface. Large jellyfish littered the main deck showing spots of light and silvery streamers. Unfortunately, this marine life rotted and stuck to the *Crevalle*'s topsides, making the stink on the bridge decidedly unpleasant.

Between the thirteenth and the eighteenth of July, all-day patrols were conducted. But uselessly. First, a five-hundred-ton motor vessel too small for a torpedo was sighted on the fifteenth. Then a Dave-type aircraft spent a few hours flying back and forth across the *Crevalle* as though the pilot knew the *Crevalle*'s location quite accurately but wasn't able to spot her periscope. Again, the seas were so rough that the hull could not be seen when just under the waves. Then a "burn message" was received that said that a Japanese sub was hunting for an enemy submarine in the vicinity of Cape Varella. That wasn't close enough to the *Crevalle*'s actual position to cause even a slight chill down my spine. Then, on the seventeenth a small motor ship passed within two thousand yards. But it was no torpedo target, considering the high waves' effect on torpedoes.

Because of this lack of action all the men were in foul moods. The officers were no exception. George Morin had started sulking and was not speaking to anyone except members of his watch. Jim Blind was ignoring Mazzone, who was now in a bad humor at all times. And Ronnie Loveland, a newcomer, had refused to play cribbage with Dick Bowe. The captain inscrutably played solitaire in the wardroom. But that was OK because nobody was talking to anybody else while in the wardroom.

Only two full meals were being served with breakfast at 0700 and supper at 1900. Lunch was skipped and only soup was served if someone needed some sort of sustenance. The crew showed a lack of interest in eating, and their waistlines were getting slimmer.

Then on July 19 a message from Whitaker was received that said the *Flasher* had put two torpedoes into a Kuma-type light cruiser of 5,100 tons and that Whitaker had seen its mainmast topple after one of the hits. The cruiser got away, but Whitaker felt that it was badly damaged and would probably sink before it reached port. Whitaker's message also said the *Flasher* had six torpedoes remaining, having sunk two cargo ships and a tanker before she joined the *Crevalle* in the South China Sea. Whitaker requested the *Crevalle*'s patrol results to date.

That was easy to answer, "Nothing."

Whitaker also wanted Walker to cover the possible escape route of the Kuma cruiser in the direction of Camranh Bay where the cruiser might go to effect repairs.

Thus, the captain and me, using the position of Whitaker's attack on the cruiser, designed a retiring search curve for optimizing the *Crevalle*'s chances of finding the cruiser if it was limping in the general direction of the *Crevalle*. But after a day of futile search, Whitaker sent another message directing "Patsy" to discontinue his hunt for the cruiser and to begin patrol across the possible track of a fifteen-ship convoy of merchant ships that was headed down the coast towards Singapore. The message was vague and didn't promise much of a chance to locate the convoy. But all day of the twentieth was spent patrolling rapidly back and forth across the convoy's possible line of advance. Yet, as before, nothing materialized.

In the morning, while I was taking a sun sight to check the *Crevalle*'s position, I was amazed to find the sun in its first phase of an eclipse. I still had my childhood enthusiasm for this phenomenon, remembering how, many years ago, I'd watched the sun go through a total eclipse through a smoke-blackened piece of glass.

With only ten days left for wolfpack action, Whitaker asked headquarters in Perth for a change of station for all three of his submarines. Shortly, a ComSubs 212002 dispatch directed Whitaker's Wolves to head for Cape Bolinao on the west coast of Luzon above

Manila. Another message received at about the same time told of Hank Munson taking command of the *Rasher* and taking the *Rasher* back to Pearl for an overhaul at the end of his patrol.

On the afternoon of the twenty-fourth, the *Angler* hove into view and radar interference on the *Crevalle's* SJ scope indicated that the *Flasher* was nearby. So all three of the boats were finally on station off Cape Bolinao and the wolfpack was ready to function as a coordinated attack group.

Then another burn message was decoded. It detailed the route of a Japanese submarine that was making seventeen knots and proceeding on the surface to Japan, having left Germany several months earlier. It was transporting a shipload of the latest German technology and its ballast tanks carried mercury which was in short supply in Japan and necessary for their gyros and other instruments. The message emphasized that at all costs the Japanese submarine had to be intercepted and sunk. There was too much at stake. The Japanese war effort, rejuvenated by the latest German inventions, could prolong a war, thought to be won at this point, for many additional months. The message also gave a geographic position through which the Japanese submarine would pass at 0700 on July 25.

This time I felt that the burn dope was reliable. Thus, as I drifted around the boat to see if the men were ready for the impending action, several members of the crew cautiously asked, "Mr. Ruhe, when are we going to sink something?" My emphatic answer was, "Now!" Even George and Walt Mazzone began to be pleasant once more.

At 1700 a *Flasher* message ordered the three subs to form a search line at 0500 on the twenty-fifth, 252° True from the *Flasher* and with eleven-mile spacing between subs, with *Angler* in the middle and the *Crevalle* on the western end of the line. After forming the line on the surface, the three subs would then submerge just before 0700. The *Angler's* position was at 15° 03.5' North latitude and 117° 11' East longitude. It was the position of the Japanese submarine at 0700 and where she should pass over the *Angler*.

Before dawn on the morning of the twenty-fifth Whitaker's Wolves took station across the path of the Japanese sub, which was closing from the southwest. Blinker identification signals had been exchanged with the *Angler* and the *Flasher* before the *Crevalle* fanned out towards her westerly position relative to the other two subs.

As dawn began to break, with the *Crevalle* on the surface and her bow pointed toward the oncoming Japanese submarine, the number two high periscope was raised to carefully study the seas to the southwest, hoping to make a first sighting of the very important Japanese submarine.

At 0653, however, a plain-language voice transmission from the *Angler* said, "Goatfish has just sighted the masts of a large number of ships bearing 115° True from me, at about ten miles from my present position."

I swung the high periscope with its four feet of additional length over that of the number one scope, away from the bearing of the expected enemy sub and around to the eastward. After much slow scrutiny of the horizon, I was able to discern many tiny masts bristling just above the horizon. Their bearing was 105° True. This sighting was immediately sent to Dumbo.

He replied, "I've got the ships in view bearing 215° True."

Whitaker had a tough decision to make: keep waiting for the Japanese sub and ignore the convoy, or go with the bird-in-a-hand option. It was almost 0700 and there was no sign of the Jap sub. If the enemy submarine was late but still on her predicted track, she could get mixed in with the convoy and be difficult to sort out from the mass of ships and escorts. Moreover, Whitaker had mentioned in one of his messages that other American subs were being taken off their patrol stations to congregate along the Japanese sub's route to Japan; a defense-in-depth to back-stop Whitaker's Wolves. There were plenty of U.S. subs in reserve to make sure the enemy sub never got to Japan.

Consequently, Dumbo sent orders to Patsy and Goatfish by voice radio. "Leave your present stations and go after the big convoy you have in sight. I'll trail the convoy and give you information on its makeup and actions. I've only got six torpedoes left, so you fellows get in your licks first."

Whitaker's decision hadn't been easy to make. If the sub carrying the German technology got to Japan, Whitaker knew he'd be fried for not carrying out the orders he had received to have his wolfpack intercept the enemy sub and sink it. Even a lot of ships sunk from the convoy at hand would not be mitigating. But Whitaker, I knew, would brook no questioning of his decision. Nor would Ray Dubois, like a good exec, risk counseling Whitaker about the risk he was taking relative to his future career in the Navy.

Whitaker's use of plain language in wolfpack broadcasts seemed very cavalier. It invited the Japanese convoy commanders to intercept the wolfpack's radio transmissions and be alerted to the imminent attack of at least three U.S. submarines. Dumbo evidently hoped that such knowledge would so confuse and panic those who ran the convoy that they'd do dumb things and be easy prey to the attacks of his Wolves.

Shortly, Dumbo sent another voice broadcast to Patsy and Goatfish. "There are two outer columns each with five big ships and the center column has four even bigger ships. They've got many destroyer-type escorts in some sort of circular perimeter defense. All are valuable ships. Go get 'em."

Meanwhile, Frank Hess's *Angler* had bent on four engines to speed ahead of the convoy—paralleling the advancing ships twelve miles away to prevent being sighted while moving into a position where she could dive for a submerged approach. Frank Hess, a short, heavy-set, broad shouldered man with wavy, sandy hair and a broad face, promised a good start for the wolfpack's attacks.

Within minutes both the *Angler* and the *Flasher* reported that a four-engine seaplane was making sweeps out from the convoy in cloverleaf patterns. No attempt was made to authenticate their broadcasts. However, spurious and deceptive broadcasts might be heard on our voice radio frequency, originated by a clever, wily Japanese officer trying to fool and disrupt the communications of Whitaker's Wolves. Without authentication he could get away with such a ploy.

Goatfish reported: "The convoy is heading north on courses between 305° True and 010° True and seems headed for Formosa. The marus are all making eleven knots and zig-zagging frequently."

Then at 0752 *Goatfish* reported that his *Angler* was twelve miles ahead of the convoy and diving for an attack.

Three minutes later there was a frantic call from Dumbo. "I'm being forced down by a closing aircraft. But at the earliest I'll resurface and continue reporting the convoy's disposition. Good luck."

The *Crevalle*, in pursuit of the convoy, began her end-around on a slightly northeasterly course on the assumption that the convoy was actually heading for Japan and within hours would change her present base course to the right. Like Hess, Captain Walker conned the *Crevalle* to remain about twelve miles from the nearest ship in the convoy. Speeding to get ahead of the mass of ships, the *Crevalle* had three diesels pounding away with a heavy roar while the fourth was on battery charge to ensure a full battery at the start of the *Crevalle*'s submerged attack.

Of first concern was the seaplane hovering over the convoy. It eventually swung towards the *Crevalle*, having evidently spotted "a stranger" that it had to investigate. When the range to the aircraft had dropped below six miles, the captain pulled the plug and down the *Crevalle* went. No bombs were dropped.

After half an hour of staying deep, the captain brought the *Crevalle* to periscope depth, ascertained that there was no plane nearby, and after surfacing, resumed the chase, keeping the convoy's masts in sight.

Two planes were now hovering over the convoy. A second anti-submarine aircraft had joined the seaplane.

There was an exhilarating feeling of excitement on the bridge as the *Crevalle* raced once more up the port flank of the convoy.

The day was one of a brilliant sun that beamed on a scarcely ruffled, silvery blue sea. Occasional large masses of low, dark clouds

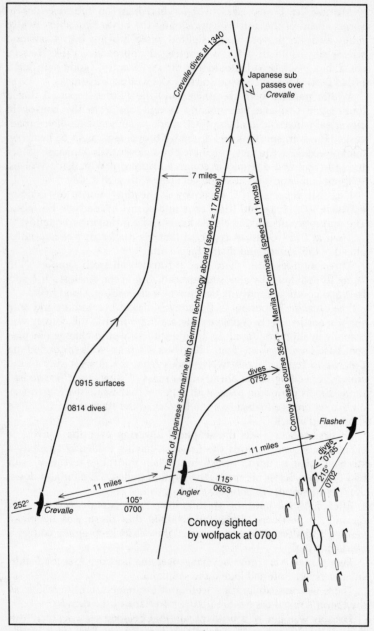

Figure 7.1 Wolfpack's day action, July 25, 1944

drifted across the sky, blanking the sun for a few minutes as they passed. When the sun was shut off from the surface of the ocean, strong breezes were generated that whipped the sea into a choppiness that caused the *Crevalle* to bounce along as though on a rough road. Some of the clouds were so black and full of moisture that it was only a matter of time until one of them dumped its rain on the ocean.

Before arriving at the planned diving position to commence an attack on the convoy, the *Crevalle* ran through a heavy downpour that fell too suddenly to get rain clothes up to the bridge watch. Hence, those on the bridge, including the captain and myself, were quickly soaked by the tropical rain. But we felt pleasantly warmed as the rain took the chill out of our bodies—the fear that the two patrolling aircraft might spoil the *Crevalle*'s hunting day.

Prior to diving at 1340, Patsy had received reports from Goatfish and Dumbo. Dumbo broadcast that the ships were "on a base course of 350° True and making zigs of up to 60° every half hour." Goatfish had sent a discouraging report. "After I went in for my attack the convoy had a big zig to the eastward which left me out in left field. The closest I got to a ship, an escort, was four thousand yards." Then Dumbo explained that the big zig that frustrated Goatfish "caused the convoy to head directly at me. Two destroyers passed directly over me. They held contact on the *Flasher* and kept her deep. There was no opportunity to shoot at anything."

When the *Crevalle* dove for her attack she was dead ahead of the first ship in the center column of ships which, according to Captain Walker, looked like a cruiser; a good target to take on first. Thus, when the range to the warship was fourteen thousand yards "Battle Stations, Torpedo Attack" was called away. But there was no sense of urgency since the closing rate on a wildly zigging bunch of ships making only eleven knots was only about a thousand yards every three minutes making for a long, drawn-out approach.

The mood in the conning tower was upbeat. Good things were about to happen. Although the patrol so far had been long and depressing with no successes after great hopes had been raised, now with the torpedoes operating reliably, perhaps all of the *Crevalle*'s torpedoes would be fired and she'd go home with a goodly bag of ships.

George, the assistant approach officer, was buzzing around the conning tower making tactical suggestions in a friendly low-pitch, confidential manner to everyone in the conning tower. Below, Walt Mazzone stood by as battle diving officer and didn't have to suffer from this change in George's attitude—one that exuded such friendliness towards all that it was downright sickening.

When a 5,500 yard range to the nearest ship was obtained by the ST radar in number one scope, the captain complained that he'd lost sight of the ships. Heavy rainfall had drawn a curtain over them. The only hope then of getting off torpedoes was to lock the listening sound head on the noise of the heaviest approaching screws. There was a sound-bearing dial over the chart desk that indicated the bearing on which the sound head was oriented, while a loudspeaker beside the sound dial broadcast the noises being picked up by the sound head. A 360° sweep of the sound head moreover showed where the heavy propeller beats of convoy ships were located. The bearings of the escorts' light screws were also discernible.

One pair of light, high-speed screw sounds grew rapidly in intensity and their bearing moved swiftly to the right. This indicated that an escort was passing the *Crevalle* close aboard. The captain swung the scope to the bearing of the escort's screws and vaguely saw through the heavy downpour a Japanese fleet destroyer. One of their first string. It was passing about one hundred yards off the stern, according to the captain's estimate. The periscope's radar scope unfortunately was a blanket of white light making the radar return from the destroyer impossible to distinguish. The range was also too short for a stern tube shot, although all fish in both rooms were ready in their tubes.

A target with very heavy propeller beats was spotted by the captain. He could barely see it but identified it as a tanker. The stadimeter range taken through the periscope read 2,200 yards. The tanker was definitely closing the *Crevalle*'s position. But a check-swing of the scope revealed two freighters close to the *Crevalle* with one of them about to run over the top of the *Crevalle*'s stern. The captain watched the threatening maru closely and had standard speed rung up to pull the stern clear. But he'd wasted too much time worrying about clearing the freighter. As he started to swing the scope back to the tanker, a four goal-post cargo ship hove into sight with a small angle-on-the-bow. She was followed by another big cargo ship.

With the ST's scope blanketed by the surrounding rain, the captain was forced to guess at the ranges to the ships moving by. He couldn't take the time for individual stadimeter readings. Moreover, the captain's guesses as to range all seemed bad. The bearing rates—evident on each ship on which the captain steadied the scope, were much higher than they should have been for the ranges he estimated.

Unquestionably, the situation was too complex for the captain to do both the periscope job and at the same time try to make difficult tactical decisions. It was assumed that George as assistant approach officer would be doing the same job Captain Munson did in the earlier patrols. Yet George didn't have the years of submarine training that it took for this sort of capability and hence, was of little help.

"Let's go after the four-goal-post ship," I begged the captain.

"What's her bearing?" he asked, indicating that he'd lost track of what seemed like the only good target to shoot at.

"160° relative, Captain."

At this he ordered, "Left full rudder. We'll get her with the stern fish." Then he forgot that the *Crevalle* was still swinging rapidly to port when he took his next look at the big freighter.

"Steady on a course," I pleaded. The solution on the TDC was going all haywire.

"Steady as you go," the captain snapped to the quartermaster on the wheel. Then, "Here's the set-up." He called out, "Mark the bearing. The range is about nine hundred yards."

"The range is much closer," I cautioned.

But the captain ordered, "Fire all four torpedoes at the target."

The gyro angles being fed into the torpedoes aft were over 90° right when the first torpedo left the tubes and the final and fourth torpedo went out with a 122° right gyro angle.

All four torpedoes missed, their wakes passing far astern of the big ship. I heard a mumbled "Oh, shit."

While the four torpedoes aft were being fired, the soundman shouted over the loudspeaker that there were very loud screws close aboard.

The captain swung the scope to the bearing shown by the pointer on the sound head's direction dial. With an almost unintelligible shout, the captain excitedly said, "Get this set-up. It's an aircraft carrier with a forty degree port angle-on-the-bow. And use a range of one thousand yards." But this range was too optimistic. It was also noted that there was nothing quiet or coolly efficient about the *Crevalle*'s fire control team at this point in the attack. As the saying goes, "Everything had gone to hell in a basket."

Then the captain rotated the scope to see if the *Crevalle* was about to be run down by another ship. "Here's an escort passing to port.". . . "That's the stern of a big ship.". . . "Here's another destroyer. But he's closing us with a big angle-on-the-bow." The captain was getting diverted again from his main target, the carrier.

"Get back on the carrier. Get back on the carrier," I muttered.

As the captain swung the scope towards the carrier's bearing, he cried out with anguish, "Bring me up. Bring me up." And then down to Mazzone, and much louder, "Bring me up. You've ducked the periscope."

Mazzone called back up through the hatch, "I can't hold the boat up. I'm using four degrees up-angle but the boat's getting heavy aft."

Then an agitated voice over the loudspeaker tremulously reported, "The after room is flooding."

As I was picturing the carrier tearing off the *Crevalle*'s conning tower, the captain ordered Mazzone to flood negative and go deep. And disgustedly he snorted, "Break off the attack. That's it."

Next he called the after room: "Can you control the flooding? How bad is it?"

An apologetic voice answered, "A poppet valve jammed open on number nine tube, but we've got it closed and the flooding is stopped."

"Christ," the captain growled.

In a matter of seconds a depth charge crashed overhead. It was lucky that the *Crevalle* was taken deep so rapidly. Somebody's guardian angel was working real hard. An escort had undoubtedly sighted the periscope and charged in for the kill without anyone being aware of his attack.

The next fifty-seven depth charges that exploded close to the *Crevalle* were not a great worry and there was little "sweating-it-out" for the next hour. The *Crevalle* remained in good shape to resume the chase after the convoy. No glass or instruments were shattered.

At one point while the *Crevalle* was at deep submergence listening to the screws of attacking destroyers weaving patterns of depth charge runs over or near the *Crevalle*, the soundman reported, "I hold light, fast screws passing close aboard. It sounds like a submarine making 280 rpm."

A Japanese submarine making about seventeen knots would have just about that number of revolutions per minute on her screws. "There goes our Jap sub loaded with the German technology," I concluded.

By 1900 the *Crevalle* was free of searching destroyers and was surfaced to take another crack at the convoy. With three diesels bent on the screws, the *Crevalle* headed north once more to get ahead of the mass of ships that seemed unscathed.

When Captain Walker called Dumbo on voice radio to report that he'd failed to get any ships, he also asked, "How are we doing?"

"So far we've struck out," was Dumbo's pained reply.

Wolves? Whitaker's Wolves were more like a bunch of Lapdogs.

Dumbo then advised Patsy to start the *Crevalle* on another end-around up the port side of the convoy. Dumbo said he would stay on the surface and shadow the convoy from well astern of the ships. "I'll keep giving you the course and speed of the main body of ships," Whitaker emphasized.

The convoy was sufficiently fast and the *Crevalle* was so far behind it that it would take several hours to get to a position ahead of the convoy for a night surface attack. One of the escorting destroyers had done its job well by forcing the *Crevalle* to run deep until nightfall.

The waning moon was not due to rise until after 0200. Thus, the dense blackness all around the *Crevalle* for the next seven hours promised little interference from Japanese antisubmarine aircraft. The surface search radar had to be used at infrequent intervals only and then for momentary single sweeps.

For the next several hours the occasional radar sweeps indicated that the escorting destroyers on the port side of the convoy were using a clever and disturbing tactic. Their circular screen had been expanded so that the destroyers patrolled their stations at about six miles from the mass of ships they were protecting. The destroyers in the van were pinging away with their active sonars searching for submerged submarines that tried to sift their way into the formation of ships. On the other hand, the destroyers on the flanks of the convoy remained quiet and crept at the speed of the convoy, so as to ensure long sonar listening ranges against loud submarines making high speed on the surface. Thus, with the *Crevalle* making 17.5 knots on three engines, her noisy movement was being detected by a screening destroyer that would peel off from the formation and head to intercept the *Crevalle*. This forced Captain Walker to slow the *Crevalle* so that her screws were no longer detectable at long range. Then the destroyer would start pinging to find the *Crevalle*. After about five minutes of futile searching, the destroyer would turn around and return at high speed to his station in the circular screen.

So much time was wasted avoiding the screening destroyers on the port side of the convoy that hope for a night attack slowly faded. Captain Walker, when he climbed down into the conning tower from the bridge, moved wearily as he studied the red-lit radar plot. With a sagged face, narrowed eyes and with a slow shaking of his head from side to side, he regarded the *Crevalle*'s position pessimistically.

Yet earlier in the night he had scrambled up and down the ladder with much vigor and his voice had been eager and high-pitched. The imminence of battle had pepped him up. But the frequent delays eventually sapped his normally ebullient vitality.

Then, about 0100 on July 26, Dumbo called to say, "There's a large hole in the convoy's screen and I'm heading on in at high speed for a surface attack. Here's for luck!"

How Whitaker's *Flasher* had moved ahead of the *Crevalle* up the port flank of the convoy was a mystery. But hopefully, at that moment, the *Flasher*'s attack could change the whole complexion of the situation. Discreet radar sweeps shortly showed the *Flasher* going east through the circular screen of destroyers then moving northward to get to the bow of the convoy before heading directly towards the port column of ships for a discharge of her remaining six torpedoes.

At 0214, two explosions were heard from the direction of the convoy, out to the east. Then there was a much heavier explosion from the same general direction. This was spectacularly followed by a massive sheet of flame that rose skyward from a torpedoed tanker in the center column of ships.

At this point Captain Walker called me to the bridge to see the fireworks. The sky was so brightly lit by the erupting flames that the ships in the port column were easily seen in dark silhouette against the raging oil fires on the damaged tanker. One of the big ships in the port column was well down by the stern. Moreover, the *Flasher* was startlingly visible and looked like a tiny, gray mouse in the center of a large number of ferocious black cats. She was scurrying north to go back through the screen just astern of the lead destroyer. But suddenly every ship in the convoy started wildly blowing whistles as gunfire erupted on all of the ships. Big guns boomed, red tracer shells criss-crossed the skies and some of the tracers were directed at the *Flasher*. So not unexpectedly, she suddenly dove, like a mouse disappearing into a hole in the floor. In short order, a few sporadic depth charge explosions were heard that indicated a nuisance antisubmarine counterattack to ensure that the *Flasher* went deep and stayed there until the convoy was well clear of the area.

The captain chuckled quietly and began humming a tune as he studied the scene of destruction through his binoculars. He was delighted that Whitaker had gotten in his licks. More to the point, he should have been concerned with the *Crevalle*'s precarious position, because the *Crevalle* had started in for an attack and was passing through the destroyer screen on the port side of the convoy. The bright fires rising from the burning tanker's deck at that instant made the *Crevalle* more visible to the destroyers than the *Flasher* had been. Yet all of the escort interest was focused on the disappearing *Flasher* and the sinking ships.

Unfortunately, as a result of the *Flasher*'s attack, the convoy had zigged to the east leaving the *Crevalle* astern of the convoy and "out in left field."

At 0405, shortly before dawn, distant explosions were heard coming from the eastern side of the convoy. Then the muffled booms of big guns drifted across the waters while red streaks from small caliber tracer shells rose from the horizon like Fourth of July skyrockets. The *Angler* was finally helping the wolfpack strategy.

A sliver of waning moon had risen, but the cloud cover allowed only a faint amount of light to filter through and make ships distinguishable. The *Crevalle* remained relatively invisible in the light from a rising moon. Only her bow wake seemed enhanced in its whiteness. Thus she remained unseen by the destroyers of the protective screen.

Then, there was good news from Jim Blind, the radar officer. "All the ships have come to a dead stop."

The information on the convoy galvanized the very exhausted fire control team into renewed optimism and alertness. Getting overly tired, it was feared, would dull Captain Walker's capability to calcu-

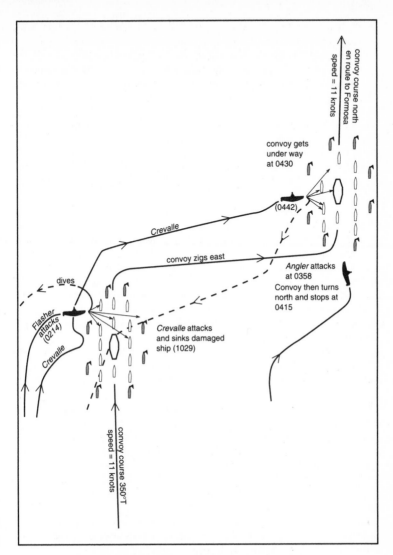

Figure 7.2 Wolfpack action, July 26, 1944

late the risks involved, just as the Dragon's skipper Pete Ferrall had seemingly neglected to recognize the dangers involved in his attacks on Christmas day of '42. And like the Dragon's experience, the officers would also tend to get sloppy in their performance of their battle duties. But being pooped out and mentally dulled had a good side to it. It pushed fear far into the back of a man's mind, with risk to one's life scarcely thought about. The great bravery shown by men in many battles could be explained by their utter weariness.

It was reassuring to hear the bright firmness in George's voice as he called out bearings on the escorts in sight. Dick Bowe, the battle officer of the deck, could also be heard cheerfully laughing about the way the situation was developing. Even the captain showed an unusual amount of vigor as he scrambled down into the conning tower to check Jim's radar plot to ascertain where he could best get at the ships in the port column.

Then, Jim observed that the convoy was once again underway but had zigged to the north, making the *Crevalle*'s attack on the surface a piece of cake.

At 0422, with only ten minutes remaining until the first light of dawn, the captain put all four engines on the line and rang up flank speed. The *Crevalle* then raced through the screen and at the port column of ships. The captain's last words as he left the conning tower and climbed to the bridge were, "We're not going to have enough time to bore in and get the carrier. We'll just have to settle for the freighters close at hand."

The tubes forward and aft were made ready with six feet running depth set on each torpedo. It still wasn't certain that the depth problem of the torpedoes had been corrected.

When the radar range to the lead ship of the near column was 2,200 yards the captain ordered "commence firing the forward tubes." George had been instructed to lay his TBT on the two lead ships so as to get two hits in the first, put the third torpedo between the two ships in the hope of getting a stray hit in a ship in the second column à la the *Flasher*, and then ensure two hits in the second ship—while saving the sixth torpedo for a threatening escort.

With five torpedoes launched the captain ordered hard right rudder and swung the *Crevalle* around for stern tube shots.

Just before the first of the stern torpedoes was launched, George reported seeing three flashing hits, two in the first ship and one in the second.

George aimed the stern torpedoes so that two would hit in the second ship and two in its following ship. These were very big cargo ships and there wasn't enough time to get piggish and try to get single hits in a couple more ships. The range was 2,900 yards when the stern torpedoes were fired but the set-up on the TDC looked excellent. Soon, two more explosions were clearly heard in the conning tower that coincided with the time of run for the after torpedoes.

On the bridge it was reported that a huge column of smoke had risen from the second ship and that the lead ship had taken a large up-angle and was about to sink. This ship was later identified as the

Aki Maru of 11,409 tons. The second ship, identified as the *Amigasan Maru* of 7,600 tons, had fires break out all along her main deck. Then with a big explosion, she seemed to disintegrate and disappeared from view. Meanwhile, gunfire had erupted on many ships. An escort swung a bright searchlight over the waters trying to pick up the fleeing *Crevalle*. The captain, without slowing had headed her south, trying to escape on the surface so rapidly that the convoy protectors could not catch up. The inside of the conning tower resonated with the big bangs of large caliber gunfire. That was par for the course but hard on the ears.

Then George spotted a huge splash close to the *Crevalle*. That did it. It convinced the captain that the *Crevalle* was in the sights of one of the ships. So he lost interest in trying to make a clean getaway and dove the *Crevalle*. Dick reported after he'd dropped into the conning tower that a last look had showed the lead ship with only its bow out of water. Then at 0447 there was a heavy explosion that swished water through the *Crevalle*'s superstructure, indicating that the shock wave produced by the exploding ship was so great that its force extended over a mile in the direction of the *Crevalle*. The ship had blown up as it sank.

The *Crevalle* by that time had sped down through isothermal water to 350 feet, where a thermal layer was discovered that produced a six-degree change in water temperature in the next one hundred feet of depth. That was what the captain felt would hide the *Crevalle* from the pursuing destroyers as it prevented both their active and passive search sonars from holding contact on a submarine hiding within such a cold layer. The captain also ordered the *Crevalle* headed at five knots towards the scene of where the *Flasher* had attacked the convoy. He felt that there might be a ship in that location that still needed to be sunk by one of Whitaker's Wolves. And, so sure was the captain of the *Crevalle*'s immunity, because of the density of the thermal layer in which the *Crevalle* coasted, that he announced he was going to his cabin for about two hours of sleep. "Wake me when your dead-reckoning track shows the *Crevalle* to be about seven miles from where the *Flasher* hit the big tanker."

As soon as the captain left the conning tower the men were secured from their battle stations, even though a destroyer had peeled off from the convoy and was following the *Crevalle* as though he divined her intent to return to the scene of the first crime. The destroyer pinged away, conducting an active sonar search. At frequent intervals the destroyer would stop to listen carefully for any noise that the sub he was chasing might make. It was like a hunter in a forest steadily calling out to get an answering cry from a nearby hunter. But failing to hear a reply, he would stop to pick up the faintest noise that might pin-point a threat to his safety.

At 0700 the captain was called back to the conning tower and the *Crevalle* was brought up to periscope depth. All noise from the pursuing destroyer had disappeared. A quick look, however, showed a Fubuki-type destroyer lying dead in the water at about two thousand yards range. The crew was called back to their battle stations and all tubes forward were made ready to fire. Though the *Crevalle* was at dead quiet and the captain showing only a foot of scope, the Fubuki cranked up his engines and headed for the *Crevalle* at full speed while pinging in the short-scale attack mode. Back down to four hundred feet went the *Crevalle* and no depth charge explosions followed her down.

For the next hour and a half the *Crevalle* edged towards the position where the *Flasher*'s tanker had burned up. Reports by the soundman indicated that there were now two destroyers circling out ahead of the *Crevalle* at a considerable distance. So at 0850 the captain eased the *Crevalle* up to periscope depth once more. With only six inches of scope showing he determined that the two destroyers were patrolling clockwise around a large stopped ship that was about twelve thousand yards distant. He studied the big freighter which looked brand new and didn't show any signs of being damaged. "Perhaps it had engine trouble and might start up in a moment," he guessed. Then rapidly, he decided his tactics to get four torpedoes into this valuable target that was being so closely guarded by the best of the Japanese ASW warships. "We'll go back down to four hundred feet, head for the target at five knots for about an hour, and then if we can pick a hole between the two circling destroyers, we'll pop up fast and fire at the ship as soon as I get a bearing. Then we'll go back deep and under the target so the destroyers will be picked off our back by the sinking ship. Hopefully, it won't sink on the *Crevalle*." It was a really nice plan. And down the *Crevalle* went to four hundred feet to start the approach.

After an hour of numb, no-talk waiting with the *Crevalle* churning in towards the freighter, the soundman reported that he held a single set of screws off the *Crevalle*'s port beam. She was then on her way through the circle being patrolled by the two destroyers. So the captain brought the *Crevalle* up smartly to periscope depth. He pushed the scope out of the water, got a range to the target ship with the periscope radar of "two thousand yards," and marked the bearing with, "I'm on the center of the target." At this, and with a good fire control solution, four torpedoes were fired, spread along three quarters of the estimated target length.

All of the torpedoes were heard to hit. The captain observed the first torpedo striking the center of the maru and said that a large sheet of billowing flames covered her bridge. The second threw a vast cloud of debris into the air. And then a bomb hit close to the

Crevalle's periscope. The captain had failed to look into the air for aircraft. "Down express" the captain shouted. The attack had progressed far too easily.

When the bomb blast shook the conning tower it knocked the ship's movie camera off the number one periscope where the quartermaster was about to record the sinking of the big freighter. It landed on Jim Blind's feet making him cry out as though mortally wounded. "You lucky devil," Dick Bowe smirked. "That will earn you a Purple Heart."

On the way to deep submergence the sonar's loudspeaker broadcast the wrenching, screeching and wailing of a ship being torn apart. Some of the sounds also came from overhead as the *Crevalle* ducked under the sinking ship. At the same time there were fourteen depth charge explosions well astern of the *Crevalle*. The attacking destroyer was not risking ploughing through the ship's wreckage. But out on the other side of the disintegrating ship, the *Crevalle* took a string of twelve more depth charges that were close but shallower than the *Crevalle*, which was quietly cruising at four hundred feet.

The captain decided that the ship sunk was the 8,800-ton *Aobasan Maru*.

All afternoon there were sporadic depth charge attacks by the two destroyers that refused to give up and rejoin their convoy. Initially, the charges exploded overhead, apparently with a one-hundred-meter depth setting. But successive attacks were increasingly far astern of the escaping *Crevalle*. And when one of the destroyers speeded up and his sonar could be dimly heard yelping on short scale, the string of ten charges he laid produced explosions that were several miles astern of the *Crevalle*. It was guessed that the sub had been leaking oil and it was on this trail that the destroyers had made their attacks.

After dark, the destroyers abandoned the chase. Their screw noises faded out. I was asleep on my feet after thirty-seven hours of no-sleep, tension-packed, but satisfying submarine action.

When back on the surface, Captain Walker called Dumbo on voice radio and gave him the results of the *Crevalle*'s attacks on the convoy. When he "Rogered" Patsy's message, Captain Whitaker sounded genuinely pleased at the results.

Whitaker then told of his night attack eighteen hours earlier. He said that the *Flasher* was headed home and that Captain Walker should take command of what was left of the wolfpack and "get some more ships." A wolfpack of two submarines?

Whitaker's follow-up explanation of his attack at 0211 of the twenty-sixth indicated that he'd seen two hits in the first ship he fired at and one hit in the second and that a stray torpedo had gone through the port column of ships and hit a tanker that burned up and sank. He felt certain that he'd sunk a big freighter, and the tanker that lit up the skies so brightly. And that he'd possibly damaged a second very large cargo ship. His voice shook as he recalled how the *Flasher* tried to escape on the surface but then the gunfire had gotten so close that he was forced to dive.

An hour after Whitaker's voice transmission, Frank Hess of the *Angler* came on the air and reported that his attack at 0401 of the twenty-sixth had netted him only one hit although he shot ten of his torpedoes. He added that a half hour later he'd heard several distant explosions and then his soundman had reported hearing the noises of ships breaking up. The *Crevalle*'s targets going down? He also mentioned that at 1029 he heard four explosions far to the west of the *Angler*. This checked with the *Crevalle*'s attack on the stopped freighter.

Before midnight a most welcome message was decoded that told of Alan Banister in the *Sawfish* sinking the Japanese submarine I-29, the one carrying the German equipment. *Sawfish* was part of a wolf-pack with *Tilefish* and *Rock* that was back-stopping Whitaker's Wolves if the Jap sub slipped through Whitaker's three-sub formation. The loss of this sub in Bashi Channel was crippling to the Japanese war effort and was possibly the most important contribution made by a U.S. submarine in the Pacific War.

On July 28 (my birthday), Captain Walker directed the *Angler* to form a scouting line with the *Crevalle* and move quietly, without any quack-quacking on voice radio, towards Cape Bolinao. And this paid off.

At 0905, Mazzone, the OOD, spotted through the periscope the tops of merchant ships heading north towards the *Crevalle*. Within a few minutes an eight-ship convoy with four escorts hove into view. The lead escort was a Chidori. And that was bad news from our past experience with this type of ASW warship.

The captain selected as the best target, a large maru with cage masts and a canopy of steel latticework that ran up over the bridge then aft over the stack and from there down to a break in the well deck. The captain guessed that the ship's cage-like mantle was some sort of protection from objects falling out of the sky. But what? His description checked exactly with the picture of the 8,800-ton *Hakubasan Maru* shown in the Japanese Merchant Ships book. Her gray paint-job also indicated she was a naval auxiliary, an important ship.

The convoy was making only seven knots with its course taking the group of ships close to Piedra Point Light on Cape Bolinao. Thus the *Crevalle*'s submerged approach on the convoy's starboard bow seemed perfect, until a periscope look showed all of the ships zigging directly towards the *Crevalle* with the Chidori showing a large broad bow wake and charging at the *Crevalle*'s scope. The captain muttered, "This guy looks like a mad pit-bull with a helluva big bone in his teeth." So the firing of torpedoes was a bit frantic.

The *Hakubasan Maru* showed a zero angle-on-the-bow as the captain ordered, "Commence fire." He said that there was a big ship which fit the description of the *Aden Maru* that was astern and just off the port side of the *Hakubasan Maru*. And that a half degree spread on the torpedoes should favor the port side of the target ship so that one or two torpedoes might miss the *Hakubasan Maru* and go on to hit the *Aden Maru*. What optimism.

On the Chidori rushed, and down sped the *Crevalle* to 450 feet while six torpedoes raced at the naval auxiliary. On the way deep there were two convincing torpedo explosions properly timed for hits in the *Hakubasan Maru*. With her bow torn off she would nose under shortly. Soon there were four, very close bone-rattling depth charges from the Chidori that shook the *Crevalle* violently, throwing men against equipment and starting jet-spraying leaks through hull packing glands. All rooms were called over the sound-powered telephone to report their damage. But none had anything serious that couldn't be fixed by the men in the room.

The bathythermograph had shown an isotherm—no change in temperature of the water—all the way down to 450 feet and the captain was reminded that, if the Japanese were using a 150-meter depth setting on their charges, the *Crevalle* was at the wrong depth. So the captain eased the *Crevalle* down to five hundred feet with ultra quiet conditions set. Then when there were eleven close explosions followed by eight more very close ones, he ordered, "550 feet." That was 138 feet deeper than the *Crevalle*'s test depth. But there were no looks of grave concern on anyone in the conning tower. No one even bent his head and cocked his ears to listen for the creaks or groans that would indicate that the hull was being over-stressed by the great pressure of the sea at that depth.

At 550 feet and dead quiet, and with the gyros and lighting motor generator secured, the Chidori still hung onto his submarine contact. This was a birthday party? Back and forth the Chidori directed his sound gear, pinging first to one side of the *Crevalle* then the other and periodically laying more depth charges close overhead. Finally, the captain got tired of using large turns to throw off the aim of the Chidori. So he just put the *Crevalle* on a steady course at two knots and said, "To hell with it." Anything above "dead slow" and the *Crevalle* was rattling like a Model T Ford.

The conning tower had become a shambles of pieces of glass, chunks of insulation corking, and on the deck a pile of soggy papers dumped off the chart desk.

Mazzone reported from his diving station that the *Crevalle* was getting heavier and heavier from water leaking into the boat and that he would have to come up to four hundred feet in order to control her if dead slow was continued. The expansion of the hull at the shallower depth would lighten the *Crevalle* somewhat, and add an hour or so of dead-slow running at ultra quiet. Then, wonder of wonders, the pinging slowly died out so that by 1630 the captain felt it was safe to start up the ventilation blowers and the lighting generator and head the *Crevalle* south. She was headed home.

Miraculously, all of the *Crevalle*'s equipment seemed to be working OK.

After dark, she was surfaced and on three engines with the fourth on battery charge, she hurried towards the Sulu Sea and Lombok Pass. At the first opportunity Captain Walker called the *Angler* and told her skipper that "you are now the commander of a single-sub wolf pack" and "good luck." Then he turned to me and said, "Now Ruhe . . . break out all that liquor you have stashed away and we'll celebrate." So I passed the word over the loud speaker system that the crew could "splice the main brace" (à la Hank Munson) and that, "The liquor will be in the mess hall, courtesy of Rocky Langfeldt and his pals." Then I told Dick Bowe and George to go to the mess hall and be sociable but to make sure nobody imbibed too much of the stuff. Shortly, as expected, Langfeldt ran to me with tears in his eyes and begged that I not give his liquor away. But I kept a stony-faced blank expression. After hearing some moaning pleas, I smilingly said, "Langfeldt, you'll earn a lot of bucks with the crew from this generous gesture of yours." Then I turned away.

We weren't home yet. After dawn I was out on the *Crevalle*'s main deck looking for the source of the many rattles that were heard when she was running fast submerged. Much of the decking and iron framing had been torn loose by the shock of many close depth charges. However, using a couple of men, the topside damage was temporarily repaired by tieing down everything that was loose with white line.

The trip back to Fremantle was without event. When the *Crevalle* raced through Laparan Pass there were no spying small craft. The same was true for transiting Sibutu Passage and Makassar Strait. Only at Lombok Strait was there potential action. But a Chidori that the captain spotted several miles off, was easily avoided.

On August 6, the *Crevalle* moored beside a fuel barge in Exmouth Gulf and topped off with fuel oil, then in three days she was near Fremantle Harbor. Enroute, the *Crevalle*'s radar picked up interference that seemed to be coming from U.S. submarines on their way north to patrol areas. But unlike Munson, Captain Walker gave the submarines a wide berth and didn't feel compelled to advise the other skippers about how to conduct their patrols to get a good bag of ships.

The three days also gave me a good chance to summarize lessons from this successful patrol.

As to the efficiency of wolfpacks, it would appear that enemy anti-submarine warfare efforts to pin down and destroy one U.S. submarine gave the other submarines in a wolfpack a better chance to exploit weaknesses in the enemy's protective screen. So the wolfpack was a big plus when attacking a Japanese convoy. On the other hand, a single submarine encountering the same convoy would more likely be frustrated in its attack by the level of efficiency shown by enemy ASW escorts. Perhaps some of the efficiency exhibited by our specific convoy's escorts was due to their understanding of what our subs were up to by their DFing and monitoring of "Whitaker's Wolves" plain-language voice transmissions. Fewer, shorter and more secure communications were certainly indicated. It wasn't evident that the quack-quack of our submarines had created confusion and dumb decisions on the part of the convoy commanders. Moreover, there was plenty of time in most cases for encryption and decryption of wolfpack messages. Again, being a Silent Service made sense.

In fact, it was the continuous submarine attacks on the convoy by the three submarines, over a twenty-four-hour period that caused radical changes in convoy course and a slowdown in the convoy's advance. This allowed Whitaker's Wolves to regain attack positions after being pinned down by ASW warships and falling far astern of the convoy. Importantly, persistent attacks when ships are within striking distance, nets additional sinkings. An eleven-knot convoy was speedy enough to cause our submarines long delays in regaining an attack position. A fourteen-knot convoy would probably make only a single attack possible by each submarine. Thus, for higher speed convoys, a three-sub pack might not be appropriate. Against a high speed twenty-knot fleet of warships, many subs would have to be staggered along the fleet's path in order to achieve a few significant sinkings.

The newly installed bathythermograph proved invaluable on this patrol. The increased efficiency of Japanese ASW ships, described in the material that was read at the start of this patrol, was evident in their sonar searches and their precision of depth charge drops. Only the protection of a thermal layer offered the *Crevalle* a good degree of safety from lethal depth charges. But although the ASW ships frequently placed their depth charges well, the great inefficiency of this weapon rarely gave satisfactory results. One depth charge in a hundred might create serious submarine damage. What the Japanese seemed to need were ship-launched acoustic homing torpedoes, like the Germans were using in the Atlantic and the technology for which was probably carried in the I-29 that was sunk by the *Sawfish* on its way to Japan.

If ever I doubted that a guardian angel had been assigned to hover over my shoulder at all times, this patrol convinced me that being a Christian was the best insurance one could have for getting back home at the end of the war.

Significantly, the *Crevalle's* torpedoes functioned well. Finally. Eleven devastating hits out of twenty-three torpedoes fired had bottomed over thirty-four-thousand tons of Japanese shipping. It was a great boost to the U.S. war effort. Whitaker's additional six ships sunk, including a cruiser, made his Wolves about the most productive of all wolfpacks. One marked failure of the *Crevalle's* fire control team was its lack of capability to fire torpedoes when the periscope and its radar were blanketed by a dense sheet of rain. Using only sound bearings (which were available) for a firing solution was possible and should have been trained for.

By mid-morning of August 9, the *Crevalle* was tied up in Fremantle Harbor. The welcoming party on the dock consisted of the admiral, a few of the refit crew who used this as an excuse to loaf for a few minutes, and Miles Refo with three of his sailors from the *Jack*. The sailors were menacingly carrying baseball bats. Refo's intent was clear. He wanted his portable, electric sump pump back and no stalling. So after Admiral Christie went below to talk to the captain, I didn't beat around the bush. Friendly like, I yelled over to Miles that I'd have his pump brought topside and we'd be delighted to deliver it back to the *Jack*. "It was only borrowed for this tough patrol, " I apologetically told Refo.

Miles acted very friendly but insisted that his men would carry it back to the *Jack* by themselves. He wasn't going to let it get out of his sight. So I gave in easily. He didn't trust a *Crevalle* man?

Later, when back at Lucknow, Miles and I joked about the theft of his sump pump, while I shared some of my ration of twenty-four quarts of Bulimba beer with him. The *Jack*, under Art Krapf, had just sunk four ships so Miles was in a good mood and let bygones be bygones. There was lots to drink about.

The *Crevalle* had steamed 11,727 miles in fifty days and had used 132,000 gallons of fuel oil. Although severely depth-charged, the portable sump pump had never been put to use, probably because it was there ready to be used. And there were no serious discrepancies that would delay the *Crevalle* from getting back to sea in three weeks.

The admiral's words of wisdom appended to the *Crevalle's* war patrol report were:

"It is felt that the effectiveness of wolfpacks in areas of concentrated shipping increase in geometric proportion to the number of submarines utilized."

The admiral also cited the *Crevalle* as "a sturdy ship with a stout-hearted crew," in his comments on the *Crevalle*'s fourth war patrol. And that was true. But was "concentrated shipping" still possible?

A footnote to this patrol was supplied by Bing Gillette of the *Lapon* who was at Lucknow on my arrival there. He said that the *Lapon* along with the *Raton* were stationed to intercept the Jap sub I-29, the one carrying the German technology, and that by some sort of confusion the *Lapon* was submerged and saw a submarine rushing past on the surface. The *Lapon*'s skipper, certain that it was the I-29 buzzing by on schedule, let go two torpedoes and then checked fire—unsure that the submarine was Japanese. *Raton* people reported feeling and hearing a dull thud that they thought was a dud torpedo hitting their targeted sub. But Gillette reassured me that both of the torpedoes the *Lapon* fired had missed.

8

Disaster

The crew's return to the *Crevalle* on Wednesday, August 23, 1944, a week before her planned departure for a fifth war patrol, brought everyone back to the reality of war. During rest leave the war was kept well in the background. But then, while the crew was readying the *Crevalle* for sea, they began to focus on their capability to fight once more.

There were several very sobering dispatches that were part of a mass of message traffic that needed reading. One told of the submarine *Flier* being blown up by a mine in Nasubata Channel near Balabac—the same channel that the *Crevalle* had safely traversed five times during her last three patrols. Perhaps her success in avoiding the mines, planted on either side of the channel, made the transits of succeeding submarines a bit less careful in their navigation. Only the people on the bridge of the *Flier* got off as she sank. The skipper, Jack Crowley, and fourteen of the crew swam north toward an island but only eight made it. There they were found by Filipino guerrillas. The *Redfin* then picked them up on August 30 and brought them back to Fremantle. Crowley, while with the guerrillas, reported that he'd heard from friendly natives that Manny Kimmel's *Robalo* had also hit a mine earlier in the month, and that there were supposedly some survivors from that sinking who were now prisoners of war.

Aside from getting caught up on messages and correspondence, the first day back on the *Crevalle* was merely an excuse to recuperate from the ship's party the night before at the Cabarita Restaurant in Perth.

The *Crevalle*'s party was unlike earlier S-boat parties that were marked by rowdy conduct and much drinking. The *Crevalle*'s crew were well behaved and sober throughout the night. Significantly, the

266

crew consisted of mainly young, well-educated reserves who would quit the Navy as soon as the war was over. Finally, the captain had suggested a gang-sing. He lead the singing with the Cabarita band doing the accompanying.

By contrast, a party for the officers of the four boats that were in port and that was held at Molinari's Restaurant outside of Perth got pretty well out of hand by closing time. The party became very noisy when one of the execs led a series of insulting cheers for the skippers assembled. The one that got the most laughs and that made the most noise went: "*Steelhead, Hammerhead, Hardhead* (the names of the boats represented at the party), and Walker." Then the Aussie girls had to add their favorite train yell for Captain Walker: "W...A...L...K...E...R, W..A..L..K..E..R.., W.A.L.K.E.R, Walker, Walker, Walker." Then with Captain Walker very pleased at the recognition being given him, the girls added: "THE STINKER!" and giggled uncontrollably—deflating their "choir director."

This started much throwing of food. First the skippers lobbed some rolls at the exuberant girls. They promptly pelted the skippers with their rolls, using cricket-bowling deliveries. Then, handfuls of food were tossed until Captain Walker called a halt to the food throwing.

But things got worse when a very rough table game was suggested that the girls immediately took to. It was a Naval Academy game used to enliven messhall meals and a means for hazing the plebes.

The girls at the word "Go" dove under the table and changed sides as quickly as possible—fighting their way past girls coming from the other direction. There was much squealing and screaming coming from under the table after "Go" had been shouted. The Aussie girls were certainly enthusiastic games-players. Then the girls were directed to do it once more, "but this time you've got to drag your chair along with you as you exchange places." This made the game go totally to pot. The table was upset, food fell to the floor, glassware was smashed and chairs were broken.

This caused old man Molinari, the owner of the restaurant, to rush in and scream at the top of his voice: "Out . . . Out . . . Out . . . All of you get out of here. Now! . . . Now! . . . Now! . . . All of you . . . Out! . . . Out! . . . Out!"

Before leaving, I grabbed the girl I had brought to the dinner around her legs and boosted her up to the white-washed ceiling so she could place an imprint of her red lips where it was readily seen. The rest of the officers thought this was a great idea and tried the same thing with their girls. But certain heavy girls caused a collapse of the pair, with much roaring laughter and affectionate hugging. It was a protest of Molinari's actions. Molinari, on the other hand, after we left began showing his guests at his restaurant the red lipstick signatures and bragged that they were made "by some of the leading young women of Perth." He should have reduced his bill for the evening. But as usual, all the officers chipped in to pay for the damage done and for the clean-up necessary.

On return to the *Crevalle*, early on Saturday morning, Jim Blind announced that he was marrying Mary Law of Perth that evening after the day's training exercises at sea. Mary was the daughter of "an industrialist and leader in public and social service," according to a Perth newspaper. Jim warned that Mary's father had shown little enthusiasm for his daughter marrying a U.S. naval officer, and that nothing had been planned for the "small, family-marriage affair." The captain reacted to this information by instructing Jim and Dick Bowe to stay in port and make "proper arrangements" for the wedding, with a "nice reception afterwards." The captain was stunned by Jim's announcement. He felt that giving his permission for Jim to marry was Navy protocol. And excluding the *Crevalle* officers from the marriage ceremony was intolerable. To the captain, it was "a *Crevalle* affair." Dick and the woman driver of the *Crevalle*'s official automobile in impromptu fashion did a fine job of making the affair click. Dick admitted later that he'd asked two of his classmates from the Naval Academy to the wedding and then suggested that he needed their ration of gin for the party he planned after the wedding.

When the *Crevalle* returned to port late Saturday afternoon, all of the *Crevalle*'s officers except George hurried from Fremantle to Perth for the 6:30 p.m. wedding in St. Mary's church.

The wedding proved hardly auspicious. The evening was murky and gloomy, the church was cold and clammy and only a few people were in attendance. The bride was in a pink street dress and wearing a floppy, pink hat. She was given away by her brother because her father didn't attend the wedding.

Dick reported that he couldn't find enough swords to do the crossed-swords bit as the bride and groom left the wedding. The submariners had left their dress swords at home in the States.

The reception at the home of Mary's sister was a much better affair. Loosened up with martinis and much good food, the party steadily improved. Lots of toasts were given, with Jim giving several very complimentary toasts to Mary's mother, Mary's family, and particularly to Mary herself. Jim, the *Crevalle*'s highly intelligent radar officer, was particularly smooth when oiled up a bit. Then the captain, in a grand gesture considering the *Crevalle* was about to leave on patrol, announced that he was giving Jim a week's leave for a honeymoon and would arrange to have Jim fly to Darwin and rejoin the *Crevalle* there. Mary accepted this with an unsmiling reserve, perhaps fearing that her submariner husband might not last out the war on a boat like the *Crevalle*.

The party then degenerated into a sing-session around the piano. When it got particularly loud, Mary's mother unceremoniously shooed all the guests out of her daughter's house. But not before Dick Bowe had put on a good show of popping popcorn in a frying pan, much to the amazement of the Aussies who'd never seen or eaten any popcorn.

On August 30th, the submarine rescue ship *Chanticleer* was used as the *Crevalle*'s target during her final day of training prior to going on patrol. Four fish were fired at *Chanticleer* and all were evaluated as hits. One of the torpedoes was an electric-driven Mk-18 torpedo that made only thirty-five knots. But its wakelessness made it a good weapon to fire at destroyers since they'd never know they were being shot at until they were hit.

After return to port, the *Crevalle* was loaded with eight Mk-18's, with only six more Mk-14's available and they were distributed three to each torpedo room. That was all the torpedoes that were available in Fremantle. Another ten torpedoes were to be loaded at Darwin. The shortage of torpedoes had become critical. Like Captain Walker's salvoes of six torpedoes against a single ship on several occasions, the skippers of the U.S. subs were still too ingrained with lessons of duds, erratics and prematures to risk only one or two torpedoes on a valuable target.

At a presentation of awards on the day before departure, the squadron commander, Captain Eliot Bryant, pinned a Navy Cross on Captain Walker for his successes during the *Crevalle*'s third patrol. At the same time, George and I received Silver Stars for actions on the *Crevalle*'s second patrol. The citation for my Silver Star used the words "for gallantry in action." When I looked up gallantry in the dictionary, I was amused to find that archaically it meant "conspicuous bravery and gay indifference to danger." Did the "gay indifference" suggest that singing "Nelly Kelly" during an attack rated a fine decoration?

Departure time for the *Crevalle*'s fifth war patrol was set for 1345 on September 1, 1944. It was one year from the day she'd left the States and headed for the war in the Pacific. In the year just completed her skippers had won a Navy Cross on each patrol and the crew had been awarded the Submarine Combat Pin with three stars for the *Crevalle*'s four successful patrols. The pin meant that on each patrol, one or more Japanese ships had been sunk.

The morale of the crew was high and the word had quietly been passed that the Operation Order had the *Crevalle* making a swing up through the Philippines and then on to Pearl where she'd do voyage repairs before proceeding back to Mare Island for an overhaul.

The *Crevalle* was a badly battered boat that needed a rest and rejuvenation. Still, like the *Rasher* under Hank Munson, which on her way back for an overhaul ran into a large convoy of Japanese ships, it was hoped the *Crevalle* would have the same sort of luck. A few more important ship sinkings and she'd be a shoo-in for a Presidential Unit Citation.

With a few senior officers assembled on the dock for the send-off, Captain Walker stepped aboard, a little late. All lines were then thrown free, and the *Crevalle* was backed clear of the pier. The captain was, as usual, involved in the one-last-drink business.

All of the *Crevalle*'s men who were being left behind lined the dock and cheered her departure. Though they knew the *Crevalle* was headed back to the United States for an overhaul at the end of the patrol, they had found the Australians so continuously hospitable and its girls so attractive and friendly that they wanted to stick around a bit longer.

For the first three days going north, the usual daily training dives and emergency drills including hand-diving the boat were conducted, and the trip to Darwin became quite boring. However, because opening the ballast tank vents by hand was becoming increasingly difficult due to the vent levers getting stiffer and stiffer to move, there was much strength-club activity with muscles being strengthened so the levers could be mule-hauled open. In fact, the tougher it got to keep the *Crevalle* operating smoothly, the stronger most of the crew became.

Then there was a fire in the forward torpedo room. It caused a great deal of thick, black, choking smoke and it drove all of the men in the forward room aft, without anyone determining what the source of the fire was. When fire-fighting masks were donned by the damage-control team, some of the firefighters were able to enter the forward room and determine that the smoke had been caused by a burned-up coil in the sound gear. Cutting off electric power to the forward room and spraying the coil with a fire extinguisher was all it took.

But the captain was suddenly furious about all the mistakes and wrong procedures that he claimed to have observed as the crew put the fire out. Consequently, he called me to his cabin and said that we'd hold several fire drills a day until "things were straightened out." Then he growled, "You waited too long to take action. We could have had a really serious emergency, Ruhe."

I took over the dive prior to the fire emergency and was first aware of there being a fire up forward when smoke began pouring into the control room. The *Crevalle* was surfaced immediately, all ventilation-duct flappers were closed, and doors were put on the latch as the fire fighting team was called away. Things had gone smoothly but the fire caused the captain to get moody and withdrawn from the lively bull sessions of the wardroom, where he told particularly interesting stories about the submariners on the Asiatic Station before the war.

There was one annoyance as the weather got hotter and hotter as the *Crevalle* moved towards the equator. The air-conditioning system became erratic and then finally broke down two days after leaving Fremantle. The broken part in the system was ordered by radio from the supply officer in Perth who would have it flown to Darwin for pickup on the *Crevalle's* arrival there. The damaged part seemed to have suffered shock damage rather than the usual wear and tear.

On September 7, the *Crevalle* met the *Stingray* outside of the swept channel leading down to Darwin. The *Stingray* had the Darwin pilot aboard so the *Crevalle* followed in her wake about five hundred yards astern.

On entering the large bay that formed the harbor of Darwin, it was evident that there were at least five more sunken ships with their masts jutting above the water than when the *Crevalle* had left Darwin about three months ago. Also some of the houses along the seaward side of the bluff beyond the pier were charred with fire damage and showed gaping holes where shrapnel from bomb blasts had ripped into the sides of the houses. This sort of destruction was surprising since the British RAF pilots who'd helped win the Battle of Britain had guaranteed that their Spitfires would easily handle the Japanese Zeroes that provided air cover for the bombing raids against Darwin.

Jim Blind was waiting on the pier as the *Crevalle* was tied up on the outboard side of the submarine rescue ship, *Coucal*. Jim had a sly, I-ate-a-mouse smile on his face and waved the air-conditioning part tantalizingly towards the *Crevalle* crewmen who were topside. Jim's honeymoon was over. The captain confirmed this as he waved a welcome towards Jim, followed by a gesture that said, "Now come back aboard and get your radars squared away." Then, the captain headed for the airfield for some "recreation" with the RAF Spitfire pilots.

After observing that the *Crevalle* was hooked up to a fueling line in order to top off her fuel tanks, I checked on the delivery of ten Mk-14 torpedoes to give us a full load of fish.

Then a softball game was arranged between the *Crevalle* and the *Nautilus*. Comdr. Dave Byerly, *Coucal's* skipper, donated fifty quarts of beer for the game and fifty more quarts for the *Crevalle's* crew while ashore. Quarts? It was evident that the ballgame would go to pot and it would take a fifteen-run last inning to win such a beer blast.

After the torpedoes were loaded from a barge, I promised Commander Whitford, who was in charge of the port of Darwin, that the *Crevalle* would pass through the harbor net before midnight.

But Captain Walker didn't get back to the *Crevalle* until after midnight. He had with him, ten drunk RAF fliers who "had to see the captain's boat." So it was another half hour before the *Crevalle* was underway and headed north, and the net gang had to be rousted out of bed to get the harbor net reopened.

All day of the eighth, the *Crevalle* plowed across rough seas to clear the eastern side of the island of Timor. Twice she was forced to dive when planes closed to six miles. Then just before midnight a closing radar contact proved to be the submarine *Narwhal*, returning from the Philippines. A sister ship of the *Nautilus*, she had the same kind of twin, six-inch deck guns. Importantly, she'd actually sunk a freighter with her big guns. But her usual jobs involved picking up refugees, resupplying guerrilla troops and landing commandos.

On the ninth there was no air activity. Evidently the pounding of air bases on Celebes Island by the planes out of Darwin was having its effect. The *Crevalle* rode the surface during the day as she passed through the Banda Sea and headed for Makassar Strait. This was the pathway to the west side of the Philippines where the *Crevalle* was to join two other submarines and for a short time conduct wolf-pack operations with them.

On September 10th, the *Crevalle* moved slowly towards Selat Salajar passage, north of Kabia Island and close to the southern coast of Celebes. She was killing time so as to go through Salajar passage in total darkness.

However, as the *Crevalle* was clearing the narrow, restricted pass in moonless blackness, the radarman began tracking two small contacts. They were probably patrol craft and were not visible when the range to them had fallen to under four thousand yards. The *Crevalle* was kept well clear of the contacts, giving them a wide berth. This produced no thrill whatsoever, despite the possibility that the contacts might have been high-speed patrol boats armed with torpedoes and machine guns.

Then at dawn on the eleventh after a trim dive had been made, the trouble started!

Because of the proximity of Makassar City and the high probability of morning air patrols from the airfields there, the *Crevalle* was surfaced very rapidly. Using high speed on the motors, and a ten-degree up-angle, deviated from normal procedure. But getting a quick look all around by the first man on the bridge seemed important. If a surface or air threat was spotted close aboard, the *Crevalle*'s high speed could get her back under in a matter of seconds. It was a riskier way to surface a boat, but it made good sense when operating close to a land background from which an aircraft might suddenly appear.

The radar sweeps prior to surfacing had shown no contacts and a final periscope look using the large-barrel periscope with its four times magnification confirmed this.

The "All clear . . . Surface" order was then relayed to the diving station in the control room and "full speed" was rung up by the helmsman in the conning tower.

The diving officer, Dick Bowe, first called out "twenty-five feet" as the *Crevalle* passed that depth, shooting to the surface. Then, "nineteen feet."

Through the scope I watched the bow break the surface and toss the seas off the forward part of the boat. At that moment, the quartermaster, on verifying that the upper hatch was well out of water by checking the depth gauge, hammered the dogs on the hatch loose. As the hatch sprang open and only drippings of water were coming through the opening, Bill Fritchen, the gunnersmate, nimbly scrambled to the bridge from his position at the top of the ladder. Jim Blind, the officer of the deck followed close behind. But just as the third man going to the bridge, a lookout, started moving upward, a torrent of water poured through the upper hatch. The solid mass of water entering the boat washed both he and another lookout below him on the ladder, down through the lower hatch and into the control room.

At the first sign of the vast amount of water pouring into the conning tower I shouted, "Blow all ballast." I knew something had gone dreadfully wrong.

When I swung the scope to dead ahead, the bow had disappeared below the seas and a sharp down-angle had taken over the boat. The *Crevalle*, making high speed, was inadvertently diving!

The quartermaster immediately groped for the lanyard on the upper hatch in the midst of the flow of water. He hoped to pull the hatch off its catch and get it shut. But he was swept down into the control room as well. This left only the helmsman and myself still in the conning tower, while the two men on the bridge remained unaccounted for.

The *Crevalle* was going to the bottom unless one of the hatches could be closed in the conning tower. A glance at the depth gauge just before the lights went out showed the *Crevalle* passing eighty-five feet and going deep rapidly.

Quickly flipping on the emergency battle lanterns, their thin, yellow light showed the conning tower rapidly filling with sea water. The cold seas that had invaded the normally warm conning tower caused me to feel a trembling chill through my body. And it wasn't from fear. There was no time for that to develop.

Dimly, I could see the helmsman pinned to the forward bulkhead by the sharp down-angle on the boat. His arm was up in the torrent of water groping for the hatch lanyard to pull the upper hatch off its latch.

I was holding onto the barrel of the periscope to prevent my lunging forward into the wall of water pouring downward. The water around me was knee deep and rising. It seemed imperative to get the upper hatch shut.

But how about closing the lower hatch? It didn't occur to me that if the hatch was closed, both of us above it would be drowned.

Obviously the men in the control room had been unable to pull that hatch off its latch and get it closed. The water dumping into the control room defeated their best efforts.

By ducking under the water, I could see that the newly installed floor matting had been sucked into the lower hatch and was restricting the flow of water to the room below. The matting was too thick and large to be drawn through the hatch; hence it clogged the flow of water sufficiently so that the level of water in the conning tower was rising rapidly. Shortly, the helmsman and I would be completely submerged and fighting for air.

I tugged and tugged, but futilely, at the thickly cushioned matting.

When I straightened up to get a lung full of air the water had risen above my neck. The battle lanterns which were now below the surface of the water produced a pale light—like the underwater lights in a swimming pool—sufficient to read the depth gauge. It showed 130 feet and the movement of its hand towards a greater depth was slowing perceptibly. I watched the gauge like I would a menacing poisonous snake.

The deck underfoot, still sloping down, had begun to vibrate heavily from great motor power being applied to the screws. The *Crevalle* was backing with maximum power.

Up to that moment I had had no chance to think about anything except getting the hatches shut. But now momentarily I clearly remembered the story told to me by Comdr. Tony Miers, the skipper of the British submarine *Torbay*, who'd operated in the Mediterranean in 1941, and who'd been at Lucknow during the *Crevalle*'s rest leave to tell about the successful tactics he'd used to earn him the Victoria Cross. The story was about how a pillow that he used on his chair on the bridge of the *Torbay* had been washed into the locking device on the *Torbay*'s upper hatch while an emergency dive was being made to evade a bombing attack. Though Miers said that he had scrambled to the control room and shut the lower hatch from below before the conning tower with an open hatch was totally flooded, the extra ten tons of water added to his boat's weight had made it a touch-and-go thing as the *Torbay* sank precipitously. "The rating on the dive, however, handled it nicely," Miers had concluded.

My thought at that moment was that there was a lot more than ten tons of water in the *Crevalle* to worry about, and that instead of my whole life flashing before my eyes in the next few seconds, as I might have expected, all I could visualize was Tony Miers' damned pillow, jammed in his sub's upper hatch.

Then it occurred to me that this was a helluva dirty trick being played on my Carol and our two kids. I felt like a sky diver whose parachute wouldn't open, making death certain in the next few seconds.

My ears had become searingly painful from the great pressure being built up in the top of the conning tower.

Another try at pulling the floor matting out of the lower hatch was attempted. Ducking under the water, I groped for a handhold on the matting.

But just then the upper hatch slammed shut with a loud bang and the water noise stopped. God had closed the hatch!

The depth gauge showed 150 feet and was moving slowly deeper while the inclinometer indicated that the boat had a forty-two-degree down-angle. Above the silence in the conning tower, the noise of the ballast tanks being blown could be heard.

The hand on the depth gauge finally stopped at 190 feet then started moving back towards shallower readings. However, the large down-angle remained as the *Crevalle*, stern first, shot upwards towards the surface. The *Crevalle* was backing "emergency."

As the depth gauge passed nineteen feet, the *Crevalle*'s sharp angle began to disappear until she finally squatted down flat on the ocean. With that, I shoved the upper hatch open and peered topside to look for signs of Fritchen and Jim Blind. But the bridge was quiet and empty, like an abandoned jail cell.

When on the bridge, a quick check showed Jim's motionless head about twenty yards off the starboard bow while Fritchen was straight ahead but further off and waving his arms vigorously. My first reaction was to shout, "All stop."

A glance forward showed the *Crevalle*'s main deck awash which meant that she was barely afloat, despite the ballast tanks having been blown. Then, noting that the stern motion was still rapid, I yelled, "All ahead standard." Alarmingly, the *Crevalle* was getting more distant from Fritchen and Jim Blind.

The captain who followed me to the bridge sized up the situation and took over. He instructed me to go below "and get Mazzone up here on the double to rescue the men in the water." So I slid down the ladder to the control room as though I was going down a fire-pole.

Mazzone was close at hand and rapidly responded to my "Get up to the bridge fast, Walt. It's a matter of life or death."

The bow planesman, Bob Yeager, was wearing the headset of a functioning sound-powered telephone. All other interior communications had been flooded out. Thus, Yeager had relayed my "All stop" to the maneuvering room and just as easily sent my "All ahead standard" back to the watch on the motor controllers. Soon there was the throb of ahead power being applied to the screws.

Dick Bowe, at the diving station, seemed dazed. Drenched with water he appeared to be in a state of shock. He muttered something about the stern planes jamming on hard dive and said he suspected that the main ballast tank vents were open when the tanks were being blown. That meant that the high pressure air entering the tanks would have gone right out through the vents, doing little to stop the *Crevalle's* descent to the bottom, which was 1,200 feet down.

Chief Howard, who operated the diving manifold, was shaking noticeably and looked highly disturbed by the chain of events. He stammered that he couldn't remember whether the vents were open or closed when the *Crevalle's* tanks were being blown. He hadn't heard my shout of "Blow all ballast" and it was Mr. Bowe, he said, who ordered the tanks blown.

Ballast tank vents were normally kept open during a surfacing where enemy aircraft attack was likely. This was routine, since a bomb exploded under the *Crevalle* with closed vents could put a lot of gas into the tanks giving the boat excessive buoyancy—forcing the boat to lie helplessly on the surface and unable to dive.

The stern planesman, a veteran of all of the *Crevalle's* patrols and noted for his calm performance under all sorts of pressures created by enemy actions, admitted that when he heard the upper hatch being opened he began rigging his stern planes to the neutral position for surface running. Then he noted that although he had taken off the tilting power, the planes continued to move toward a "hard dive" position and against the stops. There, they jammed and couldn't be moved except by hand operation. But he was unable to haul the stern planes back to neutral since the water pouring down the hatch nearly drowned him while the slant of the boat had him hanging to the tilting wheel so he wouldn't slide to the front of the control room.

It was the *Crevalle's* high speed on surfacing, with hard dive on the stern planes that had forced her back under.

At any rate, there were several inches of water over the control room deck and the pump room below was full of water. Thus the *Crevalle* had more than forty tons of excess water that would make her go down like a rock if any attempt was made at this moment to dive her. The situation was worse than having a dead albatross around one's neck. Since all electric equipment was flooded out in the conning tower, control room and pump room, the *Crevalle* would have to stay on the surface until the water was removed manually. Until then the enemy planes that were expected overhead had to be engaged with the twenty-millimeter guns. So I told George to collect his gun crews and get them to the bridge as rapidly as possible to hold off aircraft until the water was bailed out by hand.

With the helmsman steering manually in the conning tower and wearing a sound-powered telephone headset, all maneuvering orders from the bridge were efficiently carried out as the captain headed the *Crevalle* back towards the men in the water. He conned the boat to pick up the nearest man, Jim Blind. But then he complained that he'd lost sight of Jim's head and asked Mazzone, who was down on the main deck to do the lifesaving job, for Jim's location. Mazzone coached the captain to the spot where Jim had been last seen but there was no sign of him struggling underwater to get back up for another breath of air. Unbelievably, Jim had admitted earlier that he'd never learned how to swim. Evidently, Sub School's hurry-up, wartime curriculum no longer included underwater escape work. That would have revealed Jim's fatal shortcoming.

In short order, the captain maneuvered the boat close to Fritchen, who was thrashing around trying to stay afloat. Mazzone then dove in and swam to Fritchen to offer help, but Mazzone was waved off and together they swam to the *Crevalle*'s side where Mazzone pulled the exhausted Fritchen up to the main deck.

The captain feared that Fritchen had been injured as the boat sank precipitously out from under him. But Fritchen, between long gasps for breath, indicated that he'd had an easy time getting free of the sinking *Crevalle*. He first scrambled up to the lookout platform, then kept climbing higher and higher up the ladder on the shears and finally stepped off into the water as the shears went completely under. "First thing, I got rid of my binoculars and my shoes and then I just waited, treading water. I knew the *Crevalle* would be back up soon and I'd be picked up." He had a good "what-me-worry?" attitude. He was cheerful and seemed little affected by his hazardous experience.

With Fritchen taken care of, the captain kept the *Crevalle* circling the spot where Jim's head had disappeared, and this was continued for the next five hours. But no trace of Jim was ever found.

Extra lookouts arrived on the bridge as well as both twenty-millimeter gun crews. George was the officer of the deck and would be a real tiger for fighting off enemy aircraft. He would undoubtedly take over one of the guns to get himself "a Jap." George was directed to stay on the bridge until enough water was removed from the pump room to allow the *Crevalle* to dive. It could be many hours, since a check on the high pressure air banks showed them to be virtually empty. The frantic blowing of the main ballast tanks had been continued far too long, with much of the air being wasted by being blown through open vents.

The *Crevalle* was in a tough spot without any air in the high pressure air flasks and, as it turned out, the low pressure air blower was flooded out and useless, as were the trim and drain pumps for pumping water overboard. Again, the *Crevalle* was dishearteningly without a portable sump pump for such an emergency.

How the *Crevalle* had gotten into this helpless fix was easy to reconstruct. But how she was going to dive again with no existing way of blowing or pumping her tanks to get back up, was an urgent problem. George came up with the solution: "Let's hook our Mk-14 torpedoes into the high pressure air topping-off line and bleed their three thousand-pound air into the high pressure air banks. We should be able to get enough air into the banks to get us home." With sixteen Mk-14's aboard it seemed that one problem was solved. The next was to get the excess water out of the boat. And so a bucket brigade was formed from the pump room and up the ladder to the bridge.

When Ronnie Loveland, arrived on the bridge to help George with the air defense, the captain went below to assess the situation.

He found all the equipment in the conning tower inoperative, including the radar. The radio room in the after part of the control room had been flooded, so all radio equipment was soaked with salt water and was unusable. There was no way to call for help. In the control room all electric power was shorted out. This forced the bow and stern planes and the steering gear to be hand operated. The periscope hoisting motors were flooded out, with the scopes in a down-position. The gyro compasses were inoperative but we still had the old, compensated armored tank compass to get home with, as was done on the third patrol.

Most worrisome was the considerable amount of water that had flowed into the forward battery room before the door to the control room was shut. If much of the sea water had seeped into the battery well there'd be chlorine gas to contend with and that would seriously impair all efforts to get the *Crevalle* back into shape. In addition, the freshwater tanks in the battery well had broken loose because of the heavy down angle and been smashed open against the forward bulkhead. Feeling the shock from the tanks hitting the bulkhead, those in the wardroom thought that the *Crevalle* had hit the bottom. Getting the water out of the battery well was critical, so the electricians were busy passing up buckets of water to men in the passageway who then passed the buckets to the control room where they were handed to the bucket brigade.

Mazzone also mentioned to me, when he joined the line that was passing the buckets of water upward, that he'd been in the wardroom when the water flowed by in the passageway. It washed a lookout up against the torpedo room door, where he injured his legs. The watertight door had then been closed and "Water was over the glass eye port in the control room door when I tried to get aft. I thought that this was 'it,' and started praying."

The mystery was, who had given the order to back emergency? Dick Bowe didn't know, so I called the maneuvering room and the men back there didn't know. At this, Bob Yeager, the bow planesman during the inadvertent dive, sheepishly said: "When the *Crevalle* started down out of control no one said anything on the sound-powered phones. So I asked, 'Is any officer on this line?' When there only silence I decided the *Crevalle* was in extremis so I said, 'All back emergency.' I looked around to get Mr. Bowe's approval but Mr. Bowe and Chief Howard were piled up against the forward bulkhead and were underwater, and the depth gauge was already at 130 feet with its hand moving deeper rapidly." Yeager was very apologetic for having taken this preemptive action. But my broad, approving, atta-boy smile reassured him that he'd done something commendable.

Crewmen crowded the control room, eager to take a place in the bucket brigade line. They wanted something to do to get their mind off the terrifying moments they'd just been through. Only a few of the crew had been engrossed in fighting the flow of water, getting doors and ventilation ducts tightly closed, or securing objects like torpedoes that could be catapulted forward because of the large down-angle. They were the lucky ones. Those, however, who knew that, as Mazzone expressed it, "everything was going to hell in a basket" and could only stand helplessly doing nothing, were in a distraught state of shock. Their faces looked strained and haggard.

As men in the bucket line dropped out due to exhaustion, they were immediately replaced by those who had to lose themselves in fatiguing work. The pace of swinging the buckets upwards to the next man was frantic. The wear and tear on a man's arms produced a painful weariness. I lasted only half an hour before I had to drop out of the line. But most of the strength club stuck it out longer. Notably, Mazzone who was halfway up the ladder, hanging by one arm and lifting buckets of water with the other, stayed in his position for almost two hours. Occasionally, buckets on the way up to the bridge hit projections and were dumped on the men blow, dousing them and keeping them cool.

After five hours of bailing at a feverish pace, the water in the pump room was low enough for the captain to decide that diving the *Crevalle* had become practical.

Since no enemy aircraft had appeared, the twenty-millimeter gun crews were ordered below and preparations were made to very gently dive the boat by hand. Trimming of the boat would be accomplished by using small amounts of high pressure air to push water slowly between the trim tanks.

Finally, with all stations for diving reporting "manned" over the sound-powered phones, the word "Dive" was passed to all rooms. The men on the motor controllers then produced a dead slow speed, and the musclemen on the balky main ballast tank vents wrestled them open.

The *Crevalle* sank ever so gradually and sank on an even keel. She had learned her lesson the hard way. More than ever, I thought of the *Crevalle* as an amiable woman who was controlling our fate.

Once deep at two hundred feet, work was focused on restoring electric power. In the pump room the water had been lowered to a level where the trim pump could be flushed with freshwater, ridding the sea water's salt from the motor's windings. When the trim pump motor was well rinsed and indicating a good conductivity, electric power was delivered by cables run from the motor generator set in the forward torpedo room. Lined up with the pump room drain, the trim pump pumped the bilge water for about a half an hour and then the motor burned up.

During the bailing effort, I heard that the second lookout, who was washed off the ladder to the bridge, had hit the control room deck so hard that he'd fractured his coccyx. A check on his condition showed him to be loudly groaning with pain and being tended by Chief Osborne in the crew's bunkroom. Doc Osborne had given him a shot of morphine to put him asleep.

Surprisingly, there were no other serious injuries reported, even though, when the *Crevalle* took her big down-angle many of the crew lost their footing and fell forward into the morass of equipment that cluttered each compartment.

Staying submerged during the day was no problem since there had been no flooding into the after battery compartment. The bank of batteries there were functioning normally, supplying sufficient electricity to meet all demands. But to surface safely required a raised periscope. The radars were inoperable so there was no other way of knowing if an enemy ship was close at hand. Work was therefore focused on making the flooded hoist motors work. Though they were thoroughly washed with freshwater they still wouldn't operate. The same was true for all other equipment in the pump room. None could be fired-up and turned over.

Disgusted with the lack of progress, George who was in charge of much of the repair work, ordered the auxiliary men to jack number one periscope up to a raised position. This was painstakingly accomplished by clamping a wrench on the lock nut at the end of the armature of the motor and giving it an eighth of a turn before a new wrench grip was required. The tightness of the arrangements of equipment in the pump room allowed only this much latitude in jacking over the hoist motor's shaft. Thus it took thousands of straining and grunting wrench movements with two days of nut turning to get the scope to a fully raised position.

Meanwhile, surfacing was done blind and after dark. The *Crevalle* fortunately surfaced into an empty sea and in time for me to get some questionable star sights using a scarcely discernible horizon. The fix generated seemed good enough to get the *Crevalle* started back through Selat Salajar passage, headed for Darwin.

Three engines were bent on the screws and the fourth was put on battery charge. Charging the forward batteries was a questionable process since the grounds on the batteries added up to almost 220 volts, almost as much as the batteries should normally deliver. Yet they were actually functioning.

At seventeen knots and with extra lookouts on the bridge, the *Crevalle* sped eastward to get to a diving position by dawn with deeper water and less constricting reefs. The dry and chilly air being sucked down through the conning tower hatch, cooled the boat to the relief of the men who were dead tired and trying to get some rest. Without air conditioning, the temperature inside the boat had soared to over one hundred degrees. Despite the improved conditions below, many of the men who weren't busy with recovery work, walked slowly up and down through the boat looking like zombies. They couldn't sleep and they looked drained of all vitality. Their faces were drawn and their eyes stared vacantly. They still hadn't recovered from the frightening moments.

One small ship was passed during the night. It was clearly visible in the dim light from a sliver of moon, and was carefully evaded at considerable range. But the *Crevalle*'s light gray paint-job made her invisible at almost any range.

On diving at first light, the *Crevalle* was eased down to two hundred feet with the diving functions carried out by hand. Making 2-1/2 knots, her course was set to go safely past the underwater reefs shown on the chart of the area. Her course was also designed to have the *Crevalle* surface a few miles south of a small volcanic island whose cone rose steeply from the seas. Batu Ata Island was an excellent landmark.

Four work parties were formed with the entire crew involved for six-hour shifts of cleanup and repair. A few men like Pitts the radioman, Chief Biehl the radarman, and George, never stopped working. They would finally doze off alongside the piece of equipment they were working on, then snap back awake and continue to try to lick the problem of getting it working. It was for them most disheartening. But they kept at it.

Throughout the daylight hours, a close check was kept on what the sonarman was hearing on the barely operable JP listening gear. If the *Crevalle*, running blind, was headed for a submerged reef, it was expected that the sonarman would at least pick up the noise of the seas swishing around the coral outcroppings. That would provide enough information for changing the course so as not to plow into a rock-hard reef. The Coast Pilot for the Banda Sea area indicated that there was a one-knot easterly set. This, I felt, was properly accounted for during the day's submerged running. But, feeling that the tank compass was sufficiently reliable to steer by, a course was set to take the *Crevalle* safely past Batu Ata Island.

Just after dusk with the number one periscope still not in its fully raised position and useless, the soundman reported, "All's quiet on the JT." He followed this with, "There are no reef noises, Sir." It seemed safe to surface blind. The vents were closed by hand and a small amount of high pressure air was bled into the main ballast tanks as the *Crevalle* eased directly to the surface from her two hundred foot running depth.

The depth gauge in the conning tower was functioning satisfactorily. So when it read nineteen feet, the captain had the upper hatch opened and was first to get to the bridge. I followed. As navigator, my first concern was the location of Batu Ata. So I eagerly scanned the seas ahead of the *Crevalle* to spot this distinctive landmark. There was nothing as far as I could see. No volcanic island rising out of the seas. "Where the hell is the island?" I shouted back at the captain who was on the after part of the bridge.

"Look behind you, Ruhe" he snapped with a distinct sneer in his voice.

What I saw dead astern made me blink and catch my breath. I felt ill. There was Batu Ata about a mile directly behind the *Crevalle*. The island's bulk subtended about twenty degrees across the *Crevalle*'s stern and her steep sides suggested that the sub should have run hard aground as she approached the island.

But the *Crevalle* was on the eastward side of the island, going away from it, not headed for it. Seemingly, the *Crevalle* had gone straight through a subterranean tunnel in the base of the volcano and come out the other side unscathed. It was thoroughly baffling.

The only possible explanation was that the *Crevalle* had come close to Batu Ata many minutes before surfacing and then been caught in a strong current that swept around the island and pushed the sub safely clear beyond the island.

"How did you do it, Ruhe?" The nasty way the captain said that, implied that Ruhe-the-great-navigator had really blown it. "A few more like this," he snarled, "and we'll have used up all of our nine lives."

At least the island provided an excellent departure point for the night surface running on three engines.

The captain was in a bad mood, but was still showing a slight sense of humor.

None of the salted gear had been brought back into operation. Chief Pitts had promised to get the radio transmitter operating by the time the *Crevalle* was surfaced. That was real *Crevalle* optimism because he couldn't get enough power for it to oscillate over 600 cycles and that wasn't a high enough frequency to send a message to Darwin. Pitts had discovered that a speed relay in the forward room motor generator didn't function properly. So his power source was unreliable. A product of depth charge damage? At the same time, Chief Biehl wasn't giving up hope of getting a radar back in commission. Yet there was no sign that he'd be able to fire one up before getting to port. Without a surface search radar, the *Crevalle* might get plugged by a U.S. submarine coming north to go on patrol. Two of our boats were due in Darwin a day after the *Crevalle* had left and would have departed on patrol a day or so ago.

Another day was spent in submerged running at two hundred feet. By 1600, the periscope had finally been jacked to a fully raised position and would stay up until arrival in Darwin. On the plus side, it had now become feasible to run on the surface through Wetar Passage east of Timor since, if driven under by an aircraft, occasional looks at periscope depth could keep the *Crevalle* free of land obstructions. Thus a day would be saved in getting back to port, where some semblance of safe operability could be restored.

The effect on the crew of the oppressively high damp heat in the boat along with the exhaustion and the frustration was downright destructive. When it was found that equipment that had been broken down, after back-breaking work to be repaired, when reassembled still didn't work, some of the men grew listless with debilitating weariness. The *Crevalle*'s men remained in a black, fatalistic and pessimistic mood. And after their recent brush with death their imaginations were running riot. They foresaw that, as their unidentified submarine closed Darwin, they'd be bombed and shelled and mistakenly sunk by the Australian defense forces.

The men's nerves were raw. There were frequent angry outbursts of cursing at each other. They flared up to relieve the continual tension generated by the uncertainty of surmounting the odds against "making it."

Walt Mazzone, normally a placid rock of a man, had fallen into a foul mood and would angrily snarl at an enlisted man who came to him with a dumb request. And even worse, he raised hell with the captain for needling "to get things working." The captain, on the other hand, had gotten overly talkative, and pooh-poohed every suggestion made by any of the officers for improving the *Crevalle*'s chance of survival during the trip to Darwin. But then, grudgingly, he'd go along with the suggestion. The captain's attitude seemed to be one of "you got me into this mess. Now get me out of it."

Shortly after daylight, the *Crevalle*, while still on the surface, entered the pass between Wetar and Romang Islands. Soon, several planes were sighted heading south towards Darwin. Ours or theirs? It didn't matter. The risk of being spotted was high, so down the *Crevalle* went, still in hand operation.

By 1800, Chief Pitts had the radio transmitter operating but only at low frequency. He tried broadcasting a distress signal on 450 kcs, the ship's S.O.S. frequency. But before anyone answered, the transmitter went dead and Pitts started all over again with his repair work.

Just after a brilliant sunrise on the fifteenth of September, a gray-painted sub with the familiar silhouette of an Electric Boat Company fleet submarine, headed for the *Crevalle*. Certain that the approaching submarine was friendly, Captain Walker closed the other boat to hailing distance. She was Larry Edge's *Bonefish*.

After much shouting back and forth, it was determined that headquarters back in Perth had been trying to raise the *Crevalle* by radio for the past four days, but without success. And that Larry Edge would send a message to Darwin alerting the people there that the *Crevalle* would be off the outer sea buoy of the swept channel at noon, and Radio Darwin would inform the staff in Perth that the *Crevalle* was unable to answer their messages because her transmitter was flooded out.

It was likely that the staff, when it didn't get an answer from the *Crevalle* had assumed that she was lost. But after only four days of dead silence from the *Crevalle*, they still wouldn't have taken any action to declare her "Overdue and presumed lost."

All of the crew were breathing easier as the *Crevalle* raced towards Darwin. There was even some laughter at expressed fears that there was still a chance of being mistakenly bombed before arriving in port. "U.S." was painted in large white letters on the main deck both fore and aft and two big American flags were tied down on the deck. The recognition signal flares were broken out, the proper two colors were selected for September 15 and the bridge watch was rehearsed as to when to light them off.

Deplorably, before getting to the outer buoy, the recognition flares were pulled when first one then another plane insisted upon flying directly at the *Crevalle*. Both flew over with bomb-bay doors open and kept on going towards Darwin. It was very scary. The planes appeared to be on their way home from a bombing mission.

Before entering the swept channel, the signal station on the promontory northeast of Darwin was raised and identification signals were properly exchanged.

The *Crevalle* was in the clear and on her last leg.

Then, the entrance buoys couldn't be spotted. I suspected that the *Crevalle* wasn't steering a very accurate course with her crude, armored-tank compass. Luckily, off to starboard was the Australian minesweeper *Mercedes*. She was sweeping for mines which, it was believed, had been laid by a Japanese submarine sighted in the vicinity the previous day.

The enemy sub might easily have been submerged in the *Crevalle*'s path with a good opportunity to torpedo her. Another of the *Crevalle*'s lives used up?

The skipper of the *Mercedes* coached Captain Walker as to how to get the *Crevalle* to the center of the swept channel and then proceed south to the entrance boom. From there on in, "We'd be taken care of."

After a half hour wait at the entrance boom, a tug and pilot arrived to lead the *Crevalle* into the harbor and alongside the *Coucal*.

Commander Byerly, the *Coucal*'s skipper, was amazed and much pleased to see the *Crevalle* back safe and sound. "Hey," he joyfully shouted to Captain Walker, "you guys are supposed to be lost." He acted mystified about any message from *Bonefish* telling of *Crevalle*'s arrival, and it wasn't until several hours later that he received a message from Perth saying that the *Crevalle* was due at the sea buoy at 1200 and to escort her into port.

The captain, of course, dashed off to see his RAF pals and to drown his sorrows with a few drinks.

Commander Byerly put all of his crew on the job of getting the *Crevalle* sufficiently repaired so she could travel safely back to Perth. Then he had an IC motor generator installed in the forward room and delivered a small five-amp radio transmitter to Pitts with which Pitts would have to make do until the *Crevalle*'s transmitter was totally overhauled. And he gave a *portable sump pump* to Mazzone. Had we had that pump earlier, it would have taken no more than three hours to get all of the water out of the pump room. Byerly apologized for not being able to do anything about the *Crevalle*'s crapped-out air-conditioning system.

Late in the afternoon, Commander Byerly took me aside to explain that the *Crevalle*'s crew looked haggard and in very bad shape. He felt that I might not have recognized the severe impact that the *Crevalle*'s casualty had had on the crew. He strongly recommended that the *Crevalle* lay over for a few days until the men were better recovered from their ordeal.

When the captain returned to the boat at about midnight, I briefed him on the poor progress of the work being done and told him of Commander Byerly's concerns relative to our crew and his recommendation that they needed more rest and stabilization.

The captain was in no mood for this gloomy report. He merely muttered, "We'll get underway at 1800 tomorrow and go home." As he headed for his bunk he added, "We've made it OK so far. So the rest of the trip should be easy." He made that sound final.

The Crevalle did get underway on schedule and cleared the swept channel shortly before dark. The magnetic tank compass was still being used, but the helmsman now had an electrically energized rudder angle indicator to aid in his steering. Before, he was coached by phone as to the angle put on the rudder when he rotated the steering wheel.

Before the Crevalle had rounded Charles Point heading south, a message was received from Darwin telling the Crevalle to return to the entrance to Darwin to rendezvous with the Coucal who would escort the Crevalle to Fremantle. Commander Byerly was showing his great concern for the men of the Crevalle, evidently believing that the boat couldn't make it home on her own and needed his help.

Escorted by the Coucal, there was little worry about being bombed by U.S. aircraft, and following the Coucal meant that the tank compass didn't have to be relied on. Still, on the eighteenth, the Coucal led the Crevalle towards a dangerous reef, indicating that her navigation was no better than mine. By continuing to take star sights and checking the Crevalle's position by good fixes, I was able to recommend a course-change to keep the Crevalle clear of another disaster. One more of the Crevalle's lives used up?

With the state of tension and nervous strain, the two worst enemies of submariners, markedly reduced in the minds of the crew, I felt sufficiently relaxed to reflect on how lucky I had been to be fully occupied in trying to stay alive during the Crevalle's disaster. No psychological scar had left its imprint on my normal temperament. Thus, unlike most of the crew, including Mazzone and the captain, I had not felt unreasonably irritable and short of temper after the incident.

I suppose it should have been expected that the last patrol before going home would be the most dangerous one. Comdr. Tony Miers, the British submariner, had warned me of this, citing his own close calls on his final and eleventh patrol. He also noted that Britain's number one submarine ace, Lt. Comdr. M.D. Wanklyn in Upholder, after sinking six warships and fifteen merchantmen, had been lost without a trace on his twenty-fifth and final patrol. Might the Upholder have suffered an operational accident like the Crevalle's? I also recalled Sam Dealey in Harder and Mush Morton in Wahoo, the finest of U.S. aces, had been lost on their last patrols before going home.

Perhaps the Crevalle's war up to the fifth patrol had been too easy on her crew. The men were always well fed; the submarine was usually comfortable; there were no afflictions; the men had the feeling of being successful warriors, and they were seemingly light-hearted and highly optimistic about their future. Had they been too easygoing for their own good?

On these uncomplicated final nights of this aborted patrol, I would go topside to get some relief from the oppressive heat below and to escape from my nagging self-doubts about my response during the *Crevalle*'s disastrous dive. On perceiving the bow going under, should I have immediately ordered, "All back emergency"? And might a more clear-headed attempt to get one of the hatches closed saved Jim Blind and reduced the excessive flooding into the boat?

On the bridge, I was exhilarated by the cool "down under" spring breeze and marvelled at the brilliance of the stars in the thin, clean atmosphere of the southern latitudes. The stars in the heavens resembled a magnificent chandelier of sparkling diamonds that swayed with the rolling of the boat. Moreover, there were glorious and thrilling moments, picking out the three bright stars in the belt of Orion the hunter, gazing at the giant star Canopus, locating Sirius the dog star, and spotting the Southern Cross just above the horizon. It was a rejuvenation, a delivery from adversity's dark, somber clouds of reproach to an optimistic feeling of having a favorable destiny under God's star-studded heavens.

On the nineteenth, the *Coucal* turned her escort duty over to the Australian cruiser *Adelaide* and returned to Darwin. The *Adelaide* was heading back to Fremantle after many days of operations in the Indian Ocean and seemed to be in a terrific hurry to get to port by the twenty-second. Her wardroom officers wanted to attend a cocktail party a few hours after tieing up in Fremantle.

The *Crevalle* would have been content with an arrival early on the morning of September 23rd, before people went to work. There was a general feeling that she should sneak in, in disgrace for her ill-fated patrol.

However, the cocktail party took priority and the *Crevalle* was pushed to the limit of her surface speed by the thirsty, party-loving crowd of Australian officers on the *Adelaide*. The seas were running high, causing mountains of water to pour over the *Crevalle*'s bridge with every heavy pitch into the head seas. On the bridge, it was a chilly, soaking, and unpleasant experience. The watch, wearing oil skins, were all tied down at their stations so as not to be swept overboard by a wave which crashed down on the bridge as it swept over the *Crevalle*. Despite the beating being taken by the men topside, the skipper of the *Adelaide* kept calling for more speed. It was easy for the cruiser's skipper to recommend a faster pace when he was sitting in an enclosed, dry bridge, with his ship receiving little pounding from the waves. He certainly didn't appreciate what submarine life was like, particularly in heavy seas. Surface ship people never understood the submariner's problems. But perhaps that was a good thing. The surface ship antisubmarine effort always seemed less than very intelligent.

On the twentieth, the *Adelaide* reported a sizeable radar contact that disappeared when closed within four miles. Since two Nazi subs were reported to be operating off the west coast of Australia, it was probable that the *Adelaide* had flushed a U-boat. A wide berth was thus given to the spot where radar contact had been lost.

At dawn on the twenty-second, the *Adelaide* broke free of the *Crevalle* and hurried on to Fremantle, making at least twenty-five knots. The Aussies seemed overly eager to be rid of the crippled *Crevalle*, who might delay their getting to the all-important cocktail party. I had thought that Australian warships always carried a good supply of hard liquor aboard which was doled out sparingly throughout a cruise. But perhaps the Australian Navy suffered from the wartime liquor rationing, unlike the U.S. submarine force which was generously supplied with booze while in port.

The *Crevalle* pulled into Fremantle Harbor at 1300, right at the end of the workers' lunch break. This might have swelled the size of the welcoming party on the dock. It was the biggest mob that the *Crevalle* had enjoyed as a boat returning from patrol and it was the most cheering, clapping gang of people that I'd seen assembled for any submarine's return. It made me sheepish to actually be welcomed back. It was gratifying to realize that the *Crevalle* was a well-liked boat and that her crew had such an endearing affinity with the Australians.

A good-sized band blared "Bless 'Em All," "Anchors Aweigh," and "Waltzing Matilda" above the hub-bub of shouted remarks. "You guys sure used up all of your nine lives," could be emphatically heard, loud and clear. I had the thought that "Waltzing Matilda" had practically become a second national anthem for the Yank submariners.

At the work conference convened after the *Crevalle*'s arrival, it was decided to keep the *Crevalle*'s men aboard, with no leave for anyone. The "voyage repairs" were to be split between the *Crevalle*'s crew and the tender's team of workers. The "no leave" created much griping, particularly amongst the men who had visualized one last fling with their Aussie sweethearts. Actually, towards the end of the repairs, the men were allowed to go on liberty. So the *Crevalle* eventually left Australia with a happy crew.

Delivering the bad news to Mary Blind was such a distressing and dreaded task that the captain asked me to accompany him to her home. Our emotional mission proved even more disturbing than could have been guessed. Mary was wan and terribly depressed. She listened thoughtfully to Frank's explanation of how Jim met his death. But she seemed to have a trace of suspicion in her eyes that would indicate she didn't quite believe what she was being told. Perhaps, watching her closely, I was too ready to believe that her eyes also held a slightly accusing look. It made me feel guilty that I hadn't gotten the upper hatch quickly closed, from down in the conning tower. Moreover, I recognized that for every tragedy in the boats, the skipper was always felt to be at fault, and usually the exec as well. That was taken for granted by those concerned with a disaster involving men or machinery.

Mary didn't ask any questions to clarify the captain's story. She asked, however, that we talk to her parents, who she said, "want to know all about Jim's death." They proved to be attentive, troubled listeners who were more difficult to talk to than Mary. But they seemed satisfied on hearing that Jim had died heroically—a consequence of his submarine war.

A Board of Investigation into the *Crevalle*'s accident was convened by Commander Seventh Fleet on the recommendation of Admiral Christie. The admiral also said that the *Crevalle*, when her voyage repairs were completed satisfactorily, would proceed directly back to Mare Island for overhaul.

The Board consisted of Captain Eliot Bryant with Commander Lent and Commander Zoellers as board members and with Ray Dubois of the *Flasher* as the recorder. Just before I was to tell my story to this Board, Admiral Christie, in an aside to me, whispered, "We just want to make sure that this sort of thing won't happen to another one of our boats. So feel free to tell what you yourself think happened." I felt a bit insulted by this but respectfully answered that I was pretty much disconnected from the chain of events and wasn't actually sure that anyone was at fault. It was still a mystery to me how the upper hatch had managed to get closed.

The Board seemingly didn't want to hang any individual for what had happened. So they decided that the stern planes' movement to hard dive could have been caused by a materiel failure and that most of the high pressure air could have been blown out through the flood holes in the ballast tanks because the *Crevalle* was at such a sharp down-angle. They also felt that backing emergency had saved the boat, and wondered who had given the backing order. Yeager, the bow planesman, when he testified, explained that he'd often heard that when everything was going wrong, the screws should be backed emergency. So when he failed to hear anyone giving the order over the sound-powered phones, he'd gone ahead and said, "All back emergency." And that action was not questioned by the Board that said that the conduct of the *Crevalle*'s crew proved exemplary throughout this incident.

The most important finding of the Board, as precisely recorded here, proved to be:

"There is strong evidence to support the belief that Lieutenant Blind sacrificed his life by staying at the conning tower hatch until he had unlatched it thus allowing it to close with the flow of water, and thereby enabling his shipmates within the boat to bring her back to the surface."

For this courageous action, Jim Blind was later awarded a Navy Cross, posthumously.

The *Crevalle* sailed from Fremantle on October 18, 1944, headed for Mare Island, California, and a major overhaul. While passing through Bass Strait, south of Melbourne, Australia, an American Liberty ship with an Armed Guard aboard, not knowing about recognition signals, opened fire on the *Crevalle* with a five-inch gun. But the shells fell short and the *Crevalle* proceeded on her way, avoiding the friendly(?) ship. Near Makin Island, the *Crevalle* encountered a Japanese merchant ship. But the big gun observed on her main deck made it impractical to sink the cargo ship with gunfire.

On arrival in the States, I was detached from the *Crevalle* and ordered to take command of the *Sturgeon*—the old war-weary boat that was famous for the message sent by her skipper on the sinking of his first ship in February, 1942: "Sturgeon no longer a virgin." Moreover, "Virgin Sturgeon" became an always used gang song at every submarine song session.

At the end of the *Sturgeon*'s overhaul in December, 1944 she proved so unreliable in her tests that instead of going to the far Pacific for more war patrols, she was transferred to New London, Connecticut, to serve as a school boat until the end of the war.

For me the submarine war had ended at the close of 1944.

In the first part of 1945 and until the war in the Atlantic ended in May, there was German U-boat activity off the end of Long Island where the school boats operated. The *Sturgeon* was kept continuously on the alert for a possible attack by a patrolling German submarine. But nothing materialized. Twice, however, the *Sturgeon*'s soundman picked up the noises of a submerged and unidentified submarine. Apparently, the U-boat, in both cases heard the *Sturgeon* close by, so it went ultra-quiet and was no longer locatable. Also, the school boat operating areas were swept for submarine laid mines, but evidently the Germans had stopped that type of offensive in the waning years of the Atlantic War.

There was no local celebration at the end of the war with the Germans on May 4, 1945. We submariners in the Atlantic scarcely noticed the difference the cessation of the European war made in operating procedures. And there was seemingly no weight lifted from anyone's shoulders.

When peace with Japan was publicized on August 15, 1945, I joined the spontaneous and happy demonstration of thousands of people marching up and down the main street of Allentown, Pennsylvania. Carrying my two-year-old daughter on my shoulders while dragging my reluctant three-year-old son along (my wife declining to join us), I was tolerantly amused at all the friendly, hysterical hugging, and noisy congratulating of each other for bringing the war to a close, and cheering for anyone in uniform. Fortunately, I wore a Hawaiian beach shirt and wasn't identified as one who was expected to be madly celebrating this historical moment. Too many of my close submarine friends had been lost in the Pacific War for me to be feeling any sense of elation.

Epilogue

The *Crevalle's* skipper, Comdr. Francis D. Walker, Jr., was relieved of his command by Comdr. Everett Steinmetz in December, 1944. Walker was then ordered to command the *Odax* and put her in commission, but too late to return to the war.

The *Crevalle* made two more war patrols and her skipper earned a Navy Cross on both her sixth and seventh run. The *Crevalle* penetrated a Japanese minefield on her seventh patrol to sink three ships in the Sea of Japan. She returned through the same minefield and arrived back at her base, little the worse for the wear and tear.

George Morin, Walt Mazzone, and Dick Bowe remained aboard the *Crevalle* until the end of the war. George became the executive officer of the *Crevalle* for her last two runs. He stayed in submarines in peacetime and much later had command of a nuclear submarine. Mazzone went to pharmacy school after the war, and while in the Navy's Underseas Medical Research Program he made a free ascent from 319 feet depth without the use of a breathing apparatus. A world record. Dick Bowe lost a leg in an automobile accident in 1946 and retired from the Navy to become a businessman in Baltimore, Maryland.

Capt. Henry G. Munson completed nine war patrols as skipper, setting a record for the most U.S. patrols in command. In 1960, as Oceanographer of the Navy, he initiated a deep sea oceanography program that was of great importance in the operations of U.S. strategic and attack nuclear submarines during the Cold War.

On return to the United States, the S-37 was retired from service. Dome Reynolds held a series of diesel engineering jobs for the remainder of the war. Tex Lander had command of *Ronquil* on her last three patrols. Bobby Byrnes had command of the S-35 on her eighth and final patrol. Billy Gibson ended the war in a fleet boat. Tom Baskett won two Navy Crosses as CO of the *Tautog* and the *Tench*.

The *Seadragon* was retired from combat in late 1944. On her final run, the eleventh, she sank three ships winning a Navy Cross for her skipper, Jim Ashley. Rollo Miller had seven runs on the *Redfin*, and was in command of her for her last two war patrols. In early July, 1945, *Redfin* was assigned to making mine location probes along the coast of Honshu, Japan, to make possible the bombarding of Japanese coastal cities. Franz Hoskins, one of the very few Navy

Reserve officers to have command of a submarine, had the *Trutta* on her second run. On June 24, he shelled the island of Hirado Shima in Tsushima Strait as a diversionary tactic to make the Japanese think that the big submarine raid into the Sea of Japan would be through Tsushima Strait. Luther Johnson ended the war on a newly commissioned fleet boat. Bob Yeager, the heroic planesman, remained on the *Crevalle* until the end of the war.

GLOSSARY OF TERMS

Abeam	Other ship 90° from own sub
All hands	All members of the crew
ALNAV	All Navy message
Amps	Amperes—a unit of electric current
ASW	Antisubmarine Warfare
Auxiliaryman	Man who maintains auxiliary equipment
Banjo	Device to solve torpedo firing problem
Beam	Extreme width of ship
Bilging	Making others look bad/flunking
Bone in his teeth	Warship showing a large bow wake
Broach	Sub inadvertently coming out of the water
Broadside to	Showing the beam to another ship
Brow	Portable ramp between sub and pier
Brown bag	Paper bag for carrying things ashore to friends
Cigarette deck	Deck aft of bridge
CO	commanding officer
Cobber	Australian man
Combing/Coaming	A raised frame around hatches to keep out the water
ComSubRon 5	Commander Submarine Squadrons
Conn	Steer the boat
Conning tower	An armored tower from which steering or firing is directed
Crash dive	An emergency rapid dive
Crew	The men who man a boat
Digger	Australian soldier
Dogged down	Fastened with dogs

Dogging it	Loafing
Dogs	Holding-down lugs
Fathom	Six feet
Field Day	Clean-up day
Fish	Torpedoes
Fried	Punished
Greenhorn	Newcomer aboard sub
Head	Toilet
Header	Top of diesel engine
Helm	Steering wheel
Isothermal	Same temperature
Is-Was	Celluloid device to help solve the torpedo firing problem
Juice	Electricity/amperes
Laying to	Stopped in the water
Mate	Pal/close friend
Mess	Eating compartment
Normal approach course	90° to the target's track
Over the hill	Disappeared over the horizon
OOD	Officer of the Deck
Pigboat	Sub that is like a pigsty
Pooped out	Tired out
Port	The side of a ship or sub that is on the left of someone aboard facing the bow
Pulled the plug	Opened the vents and submerged
Quartermaster	Enlisted man who keeps ship's log and is well qualified in bridge routine
Rate/rating	Job description
Relief crew	Crew of men who go aboard sub during rest leave
Rigged/rigged out	Set up, arranged/contrivance put in operation
Roger	Received

Sacked out	Sleeping in bunk
Screws	Propellers
SD radar	An air search radar
Shears	Structure above the bridge
Sheila	Australian girl/woman
Single up	Reduce holding lines to a single one
Skivvies	Underwear
Sluffing off	Doping off/making errors
Snorkel	Telescopic intake pipe to provide air to diesel engines
Stadimeter	Device for measuring range
Starboard	The side of a ship or sub that is on the right of someone aboard facing the bow
Star man	Grade point average of over 3.6 in school
Station bill	Listing of crew's drill stations
To mast	A sort of court to award punishment or commendations
Tender	Ship that supports subs
Track	Determine course of target
Wardroom	Officers' dining area
XAV	A seaplane tender

Index

299

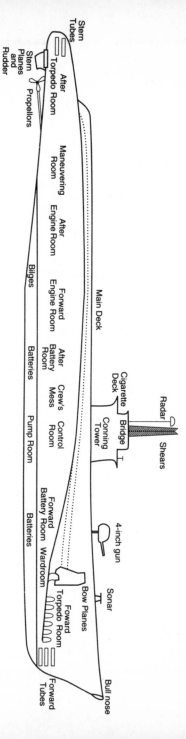

A Fleet Boat

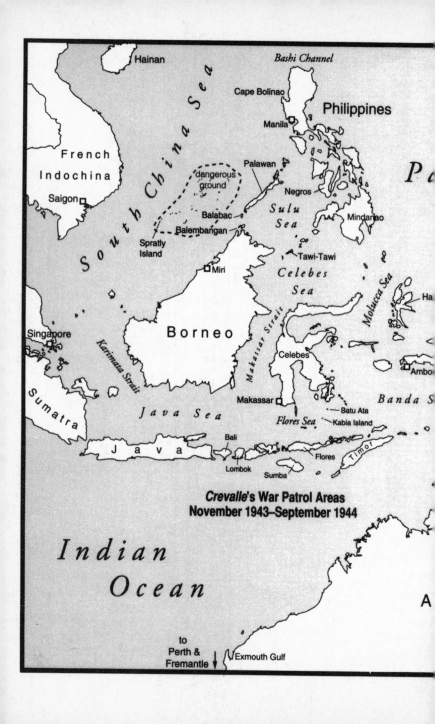

Crevalle's War Patrol Areas
November 1943–September 1944

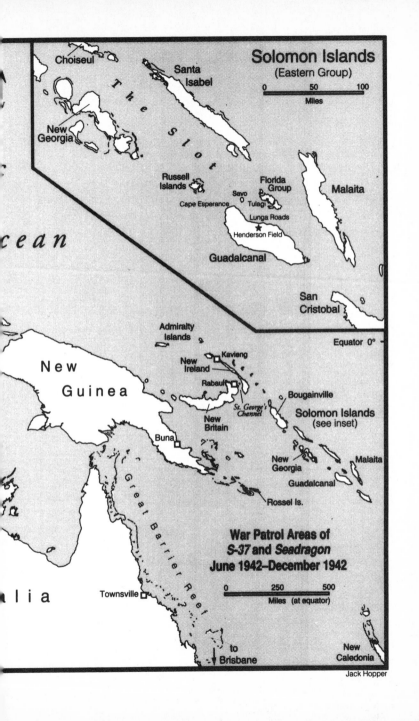

Solomon Islands
(Eastern Group)

Choiseul

Santa
Isabel

The Slot

New
Georgia

Russell
Islands

Savo

Florida
Group

Malaita

Cape Esperance

Tulagi

Lunga Roads

★

Henderson Field

Guadalcanal

San
Cristobal

0   50   100
Miles

ocean

Admiralty
Islands

Equator 0°

New
Ireland

Kavieng

New
Guinea

Rabaul

Bougainville

St. George's
Channel

New
Britain

Solomon Islands
(see inset)

Buna

New
Georgia

Malaita

Guadalcanal

Rossel Is.

War Patrol Areas of
S-37 **and** ***Seadragon***
June 1942–December 1942

Great Barrier Reef

Townsville

alia

0   250   500
Miles   (at equator)

to
Brisbane

New
Caledonia

Jack Hopper